THE
BUILDING
PLAN BOOK

COMPLETE PLANS FOR
21 AFFORDABLE HOMES

Affectionately dedicated to my son, Ray,
whose efforts to have me adhere to a strict time
budget are well appreciated.

THE
BUILDING PLAN BOOK

COMPLETE PLANS FOR 21 AFFORDABLE HOMES

ERNIE BRYANT

TAB BOOKS Inc.
Blue Ridge Summit, PA 17214

FIRST EDITION
FIRST PRINTING

Copyright © 1986 by TAB BOOKS Inc.
Printed in the United States of America

Library of Congress Cataloging in Publication Data

Bryant, Ernie.
The building plan book.

1. Small houses—United States—Designs and plans.
I. Title.
NA7205.B74   1986   728.3′7′0222   86-5880
ISBN 0-8306-0814-1
ISBN 0-8306-2714-6 (pbk.)

Contents

Acknowledgments

John Hartley, Architect, Eastford, Connecticut.
As a successful architect, John Hartley contributed greatly to this book. His professional advice, suggestions, and contribution to this publication are deeply appreciated.

Portland Willamette Company, Portland, Oregon.
Manufacturer of fireplace accessories. The article entitled *Fireplace Planning* is printed in this book with Portland Willamette's permission.

Chartpak, 1 River Road, Leeds, Massachusetts.
Certain graphics, which are depicted on elevations and perspectives within the pages of this book, are the courtesy of Chartpak.

Andrew Quigley, Pomfret, Connecticut.
Andrew Quigley graciously granted me an interview and gave me a complete tour of his owner-built house. The article entitled *The Owner-Built Experience* is a result of the information gathered through his assistance.

John Hinchman, Pomfret, Connecticut.
Chairman of the Pomfret Planning Commission.

Preface

The 1980 Census revealed that, for the first time in America's history, Americans were moving to, and settling in, nonurban areas. The rural landscape is gradually giving way to more dwellings; suburban areas are becoming more densely populated. The demand for housing in these areas is being met by a variety of housing types, including apartments and condominiums, but the choice of most Americans of all economic strata remains the single-family, detached home. In many areas, demand exceeds supply. In many cases, a new house is the best solution. A bewildering array of books and magazines tantalize the prospective home builder with ideas usually in the form of undimensioned floor plans and a strategically taken perspective rendering. Only by mailing for plans, often at considerable cost, can these houses be more carefully scrutinized.

In *The Building Plan Book: Complete Plans for 21 Affordable Homes*, Ernie Bryant has created a useful resource for the owner, builder, or, as is increasingly popular, the owner/builder. Spurning the log homes, envelope houses, Trombé walls, and the other fads and fashions of the popular press, Mr. Bryant has designed a variety of house types, sizes, and styles to appeal to a broad cross section of the American public. His dimensioned plans, elevations, and sections, plus his structural and electrical plans, provide most of the information that an individual working with the local building official can use to build a house—the necessity that is in danger of becoming a luxury.

John B. Hartley AIA
Architect

Symbols and Abbreviations

Following, in no particular order, are symbols and abbreviations that are found on various plans throughout this book.

' = foot
" = inches
$^o/_c$ = on center
Ⓓ = diameter
CLG. HT. = ceiling height
P.C. = poured concrete
COL. = column
R.O. = rough opening
CLO. = closet
LIN. = linen
LAUN. = laundry
REF. = refrigerator
FTG. = footing
D.H. = double-hung

D.H.P.W. = double-hung picture window
BSMT. = basement
CSMT. = casement
S.C. = solid core
H.C. = hollow core
SLDG. = sliding
SYM. = symbol
QTY. = quantity
S.R. = Sheetrock, a trademark for plasterboard
O.H.DR. = overhead door
MAN. = manufacturer
WIN. = window
T/W = to the weather
CONT. = continuous
VENT. = ventilation
2-2 × 4 = two 2 × 4 wood-framing members.
2/16 = two wood framing members 16 feet long.

Introduction

The idea of owning and living in their own house is a dream that remains undiminished for Americans. It is interesting to note that four factors relating to this dream are changing: the American household has shrunk in size; the typical household needs less space; couples elect to have smaller homes; and more people live alone. Therefore, there is a demand for smaller houses.

As an architectural draftsman, I enjoy browsing through the many plan books that occupy a shelf or two at my local magazine store. These plan books (actually, they're magazines) consist mainly of a number of floor plans of various houses accompanied by a perspective of the house. If the reader desires a full set of building plans of a particular house, all he has to do is to fill out the coupon at the back of the magazine and send it in with a specified amount of money.

Now, I have nothing against those plan books. I think they're great! However, as I leafed through the pages of various plan books, I noticed that most of those house plans had multinumbered bedrooms and usually two bathrooms, and were usually pictured as elegant homes with a high price tag.

It was then that I figured there were others who wanted to build a house but couldn't afford a high-priced mansion. Financing must be a problem for many people. Although many people would like to build, they find it hard to acquire the required down payment or for some reason are unable to obtain financing from other sources.

So I said to myself, "Self, why doesn't somebody publish a plan book of smaller, affordable houses?" Now, I'm doing just that. However, this plan book is not just a magazine with floor plans and perspectives of numerous houses. This is the ultimate plan book!

As a free-lance architectural draftsman, people who are planning to build usually engage my services to provide a complete set of working drawings from which their house could be built. My fee is an added expense for them.

The Building Plan Book does not contain just a perspective and floor plans of various houses like the "plan book" magazines do. This book features complete working drawings for houses of varying types and sizes. It contains complete building plans; hence, the title: *The Building Plan Book: Complete Plans for 21 Affordable Homes.*

For the cost of the book, you will have complete working drawings for 21 different houses. Some of the plans in this book might not meet your desires, but if your dream house is within these pages, you will have a set of complete building plans for just the price of this publication.

A complete set of working drawings includes the following:

☐ Perspective—an architectural rendering showing what the house would look like when viewed at an angle.

☐ Floor Plans—a layout of the rooms including exterior and interior dimensions, door and window location, and direction of floor joists.

☐ Foundation Plan—a drawing showing the thickness of the foundation wall and footing, location of lally columns, and chimney/fireplace footing.

☐ Cross Section or Staff Section—cutaway view of the

house showing how it is constructed.

- ☐ Front Elevation—view of the front of house.
- ☐ Right Elevation—view of the right side of house.
- ☐ Rear Elevation—view of the rear of house.
- ☐ Left Elevation—view of the left side of house.
- ☐ Electrical Layout—floor plan showing where switches, outlets, etc. are to be located.
- ☐ Framing Plans—working drawings showing where wood members are to be placed.
- ☐ Materials List—list of materials needed to construct the shell of the structure.

In addition, there is a standard detail sheet depicting various aspects of house construction. Certain plans will have an enhancement sheet, which is not a part of the building plans, but whose only purpose is to show you what the house would look like if changes or modifications were made.

If you are a single person seeking a home of your own, you might enjoy looking at the efficiency dwellings this book has to offer. If you are a young couple just embarking on a new career with plans for starting a family, or an elderly couple whose family has grown and are seeking a smaller home, you would also find this book useful.

In addition to efficiency dwellings, this book also contains plans for ranches, raised ranches, capes, two-story houses, a split-level, and a duplex. These houses are of varying sizes for families of varying sizes.

If you are skilled in one of the building trades, you will be able to construct the house from the plans provided. Even if your house will be contractor-built, by using the enclosed plans you could save a lot of money by avoiding drafting fees.

If you are just toying with the idea of building in the future, this book will be very helpful, educational, and informative.

Feel free to make cosmetic changes as you see fit. You might prefer horizontal siding instead of the vertical siding that your favorite house depicts on the elevation. You might even have a preference for double-hung windows instead of casement windows. However, do not make structural changes without consulting with a competent builder, contractor, or architect.

As an architectural draftsman, I am qualified to design residential structures. In addition to being

designed for comfort and convenience, the houses in this book have also been designed for safety.

If the house plans call for a 2 x 8 ridge, there is a reason. If the plans call for a 3-2 x 10 beam in the basement, there's also a reason. Certain wood members in house construction are standard and/or have been designed and calculated to withstand specific loads.

If you prefer a different type of window than what the plans call for, inform your builder of your preference before construction on your house begins. Care must be taken to ensure that each window and door has a header large enough to support the weight of the load it must carry. Therefore, it is essential that someone (builder, architect, draftsman) with a knowledge and understanding of house construction be informed of your desires to change window styles and sizes.

All the plans in this book with a full basement have an exterior basement entry/exit. As a fire precaution, it is wise to have another basement entry/exit, in addition to the interior stairway.

The plans within this book have been designed with a fairly level grade. However, all building lots do not have a level grade, and your lot could be one of them. Therefore, it might be necessary, convenient, or more desirable to have a basement entry of a different type than the one depicted in the plans. However, the foundation for the basement entry should conform to the manufacturer's specifications.

You won't be needing the interior basement stairway if you decide to have a basementless house. In such a case, the area occupied by the stairway could be used to house your water heater and heating plant, washer, and dryer.

The houses in this book that have no fireplace have a chimney to receive the furnace flue. The chimney will not be needed if you have electric heat.

There are many options concerning a fireplace. Perhaps you'd like to add another flue for a metal fireplace in the living room. Maybe you'd like a cast-iron wood stove in the kitchen. If you have a masonry fireplace, perhaps you'd prefer cut stone instead of brick. How about a raised hearth instead of a floor-level one? A metal fireplace might be more preferable to you in place of one of masonry.

It is wise to discuss your fireplace and chimney needs and desires with your mason in the house planning stages.

All the houses within the pages of this book, consist of perspectives, floor plans, a foundation plan, a cross section or staff section, elevations, framing plans, and electrical layouts.

Section I
Efficiency Dwellings

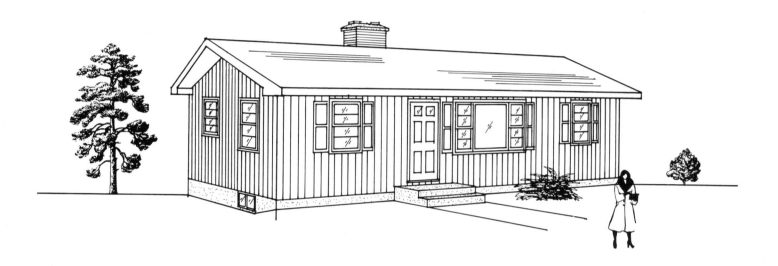

SLIM-RAY

DESIGNED & DRAWN BY E. BRYANT

16' X 38'

With 608 square feet of living space, the Slim-Ray, with its vertical siding and flying gable roof, is an ideal efficiency dwelling for the single person or couple.

The centrally located living room has a large picture window on the front wall and a fireplace accented by two double-hung windows on the rear wall. In addition to a U-shaped kitchen, this cozy house has a dining area, bedroom, and bath.

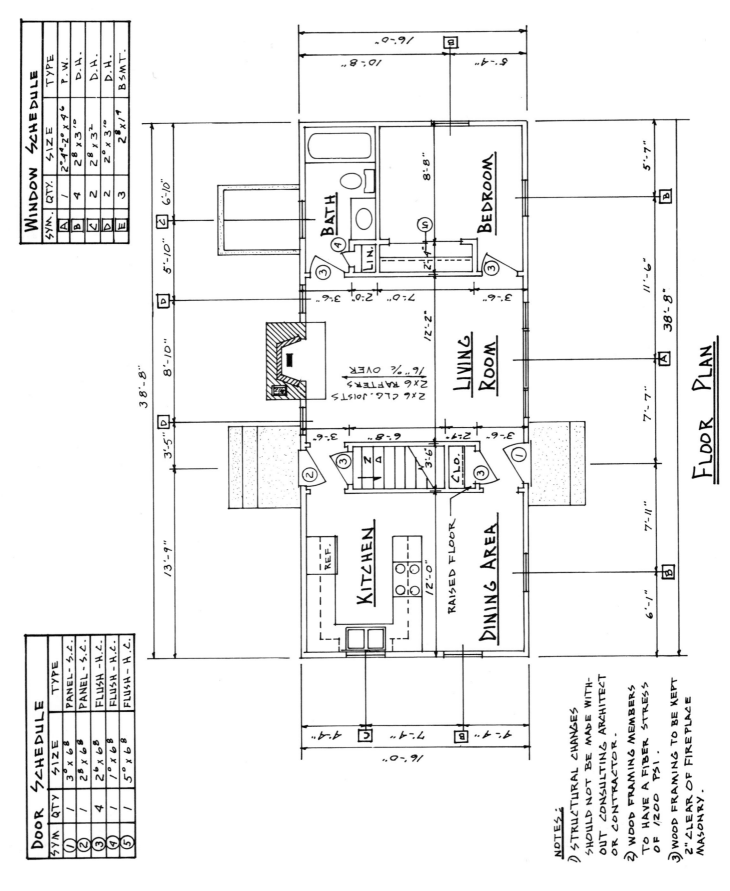

WINDOW SCHEDULE

SYM.	QTY.	SIZE	TYPE
A	1	2'-4"-2'-0"x9'6	P.W.
B	4	2'8"x3'-0"	D.H.
C	2	2'8"x3'2	D.H.
D	2	2'-0"x3'-0"	D.H.
E	3	2'8"x1'4	BSMT.

DOOR SCHEDULE

SYM	QTY	SIZE	TYPE
1	1	3'-0"x6'-8	PANEL-S.C.
2	1	2'-8"x6'-8	PANEL-S.C.
3	4	2'-6"x6'-8	FLUSH-H.C.
4	1	1'-0"x6'-8	FLUSH-H.C.
5	1	5'-0"x6'-8	FLUSH-H.C.

BATH

BEDROOM

LIN.

2x6 CLG. JOISTS
2x6 RAFTERS
16 1/2" OVER

LIVING ROOM

KITCHEN

REF.

RAISED FLOOR

DINING AREA

FLOOR PLAN

NOTES:

1) STRUCTURAL CHANGES SHOULD NOT BE MADE WITHOUT CONSULTING ARCHITECT OR CONTRACTOR.

2) WOOD FRAMING MEMBERS TO HAVE A FIBER STRESS OF 1200 PSI.

3) WOOD FRAMING TO BE KEPT 2" CLEAR OF FIREPLACE MASONRY.

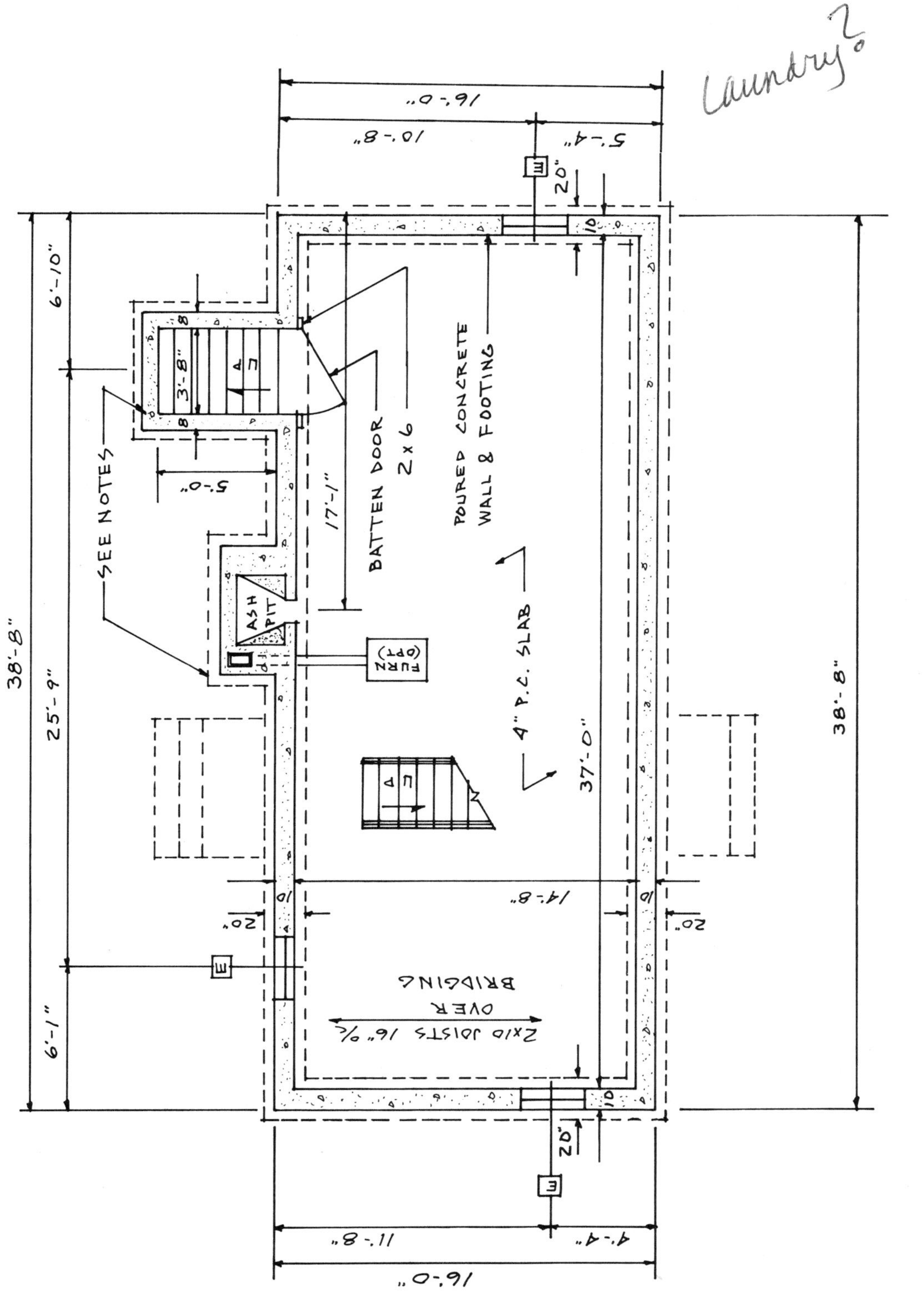

Laundry?

16'-0"

10'-8"

5'-4"

2'0"

10

6'-0"

8

8

3'-8"

5'-0"

8

38'-8"

25'-9"

SEE NOTES

BATTEN DOOR 2x6

17'-1"

POURED CONCRETE WALL & FOOTING

ASH PIT

FURN (OPT)

4" P.C. SLAB

37'-0"

14'-8"

2'0"

10

10

2'0"

6'-1"

E

BRIDGING

OVER

2x10 JOISTS 16" O/C

9'-6"

38'-8"

2'0"

E

11'-8"

4'-4"

16'-0"

NOTES:

1) FIREPLACE FOOTING TO BE 12" THICK; EXTEND 6".

2) BASEMENT ENTRY FOUNDATION TO CONFORM TO MANU-FACTURER SPECIFICATION.

FOUNDATION PLAN

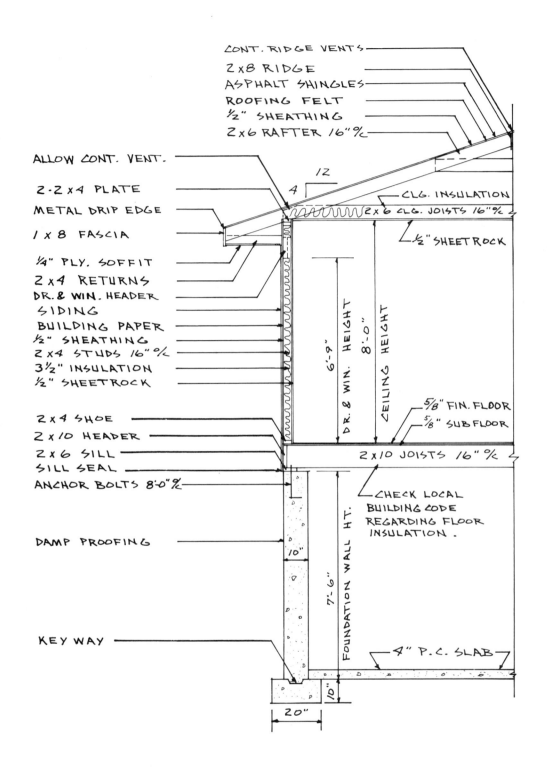

CONT. RIDGE VENTS
2 x 8 RIDGE
ASPHALT SHINGLES
ROOFING FELT
½" SHEATHING
2 x 6 RAFTER 16" ℀

ALLOW CONT. VENT.
2 - 2 x 4 PLATE
METAL DRIP EDGE
1 x 8 FASCIA
¼" PLY. SOFFIT
2 x 4 RETURNS
DR. & WIN. HEADER
SIDING
BUILDING PAPER
½" SHEATHING
2 x 4 STUDS 16" ℀
3½" INSULATION
½" SHEETROCK

2 x 4 SHOE
2 x 10 HEADER
2 x 6 SILL
SILL SEAL
ANCHOR BOLTS 8'-0" ℀

DAMP PROOFING

KEY WAY

12
4

CLG. INSULATION
2 x 6 CLG. JOISTS 16" ℀
½" SHEETROCK

6'-9"   DR. & WIN. HEIGHT
8'-0"   CEILING HEIGHT

5/8" FIN. FLOOR
5/8" SUBFLOOR
2 x 10 JOISTS 16" ℀

CHECK LOCAL
BUILDING CODE
REGARDING FLOOR
INSULATION.

10"

7'-6"   FOUNDATION WALL HT.

4" P.C. SLAB

10"

20"

STAFF SECTION

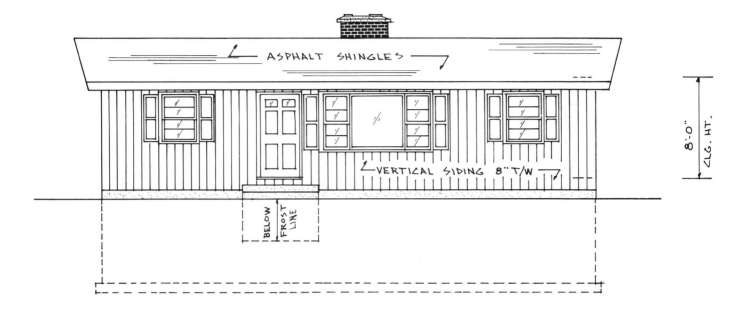

FRONT ELEVATION

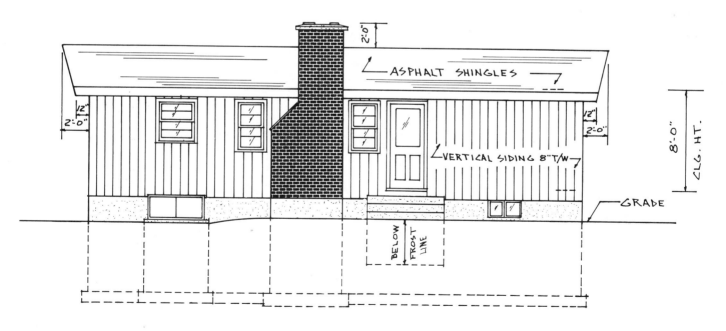

REAR ELEVATION

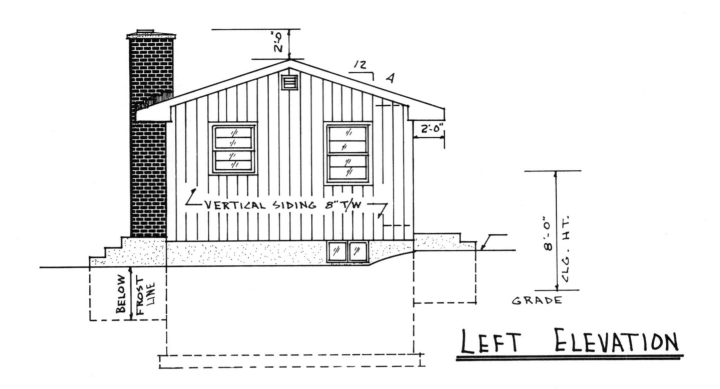

2'-9"

12

4

2'-0"

VERTICAL SIDING 8" T/W

BELOW FROST LINE

8'-0" CLG. HT.

GRADE

LEFT ELEVATION

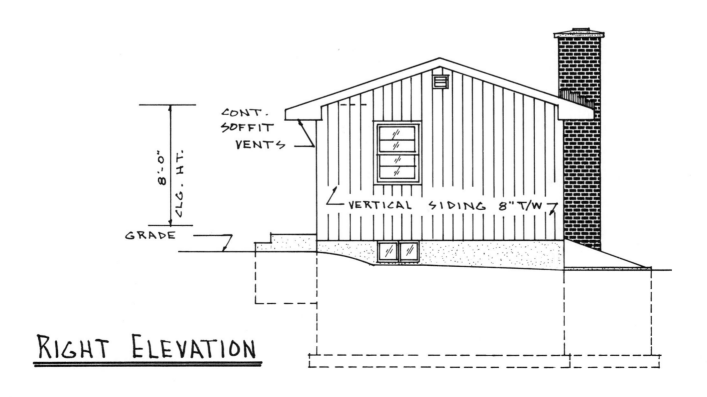

CONT. SOFFIT VENTS

8'-0" CLG. HT.

GRADE

VERTICAL SIDING 8" T/W

RIGHT ELEVATION

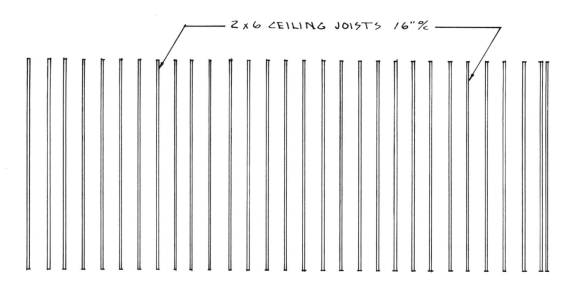

2×6 CEILING JOISTS 16"%

CEILING FRAMING PLAN

NOTES:
1) WOOD FRAMING TO BE KEPT 2" CLEAR OF FIREPLACE MASONRY.
2) DOUBLE JOISTS UNDER PARALLEL PARTITIONS.

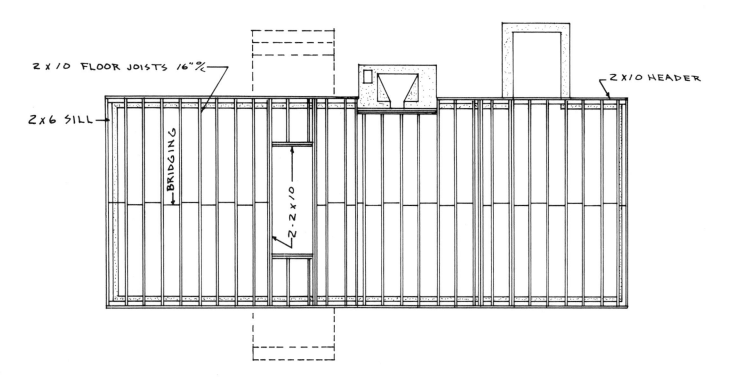

2×10 FLOOR JOISTS 16"%

2×6 SILL

BRIDGING

2-2×10

2×10 HEADER

FLOOR FRAMING PLAN

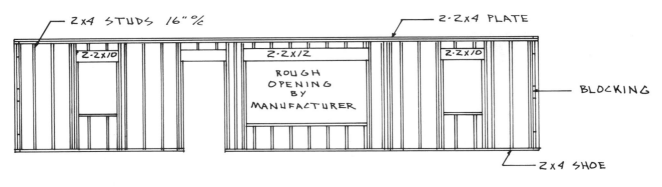

2x4 STUDS 16" ⁰⁄c   2·2x4 PLATE

2·2x10   2·2x12

ROUGH
OPENING
BY
MANUFACTURER

2·2x10

BLOCKING

2x4 SHOE

FRONT FRAMING PLAN

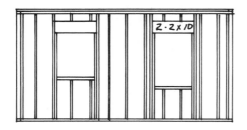

2·2x10

LEFT FRAMING PLAN

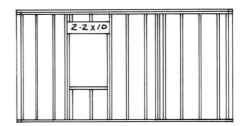

2·2x10

RIGHT FRAMING PLAN

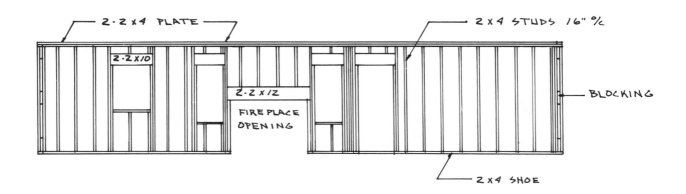

2·2x4 PLATE   2x4 STUDS 16" ⁰⁄c

2·2x10

2·2x12

FIRE PLACE
OPENING

BLOCKING

2x4 SHOE

REAR FRAMING PLAN

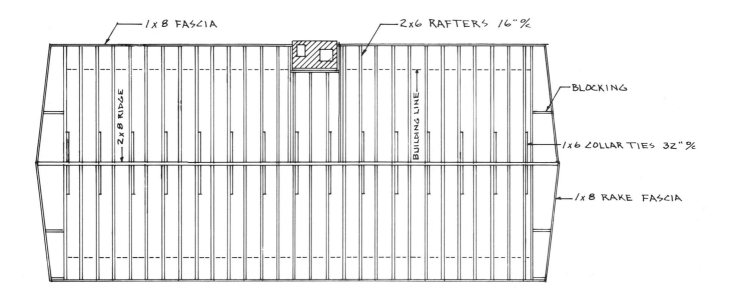

1 x 8 FASCIA

2x6 RAFTERS 16" %

2 x 8 RIDGE

BUILDING LINE

BLOCKING

1x6 COLLAR TIES 32" %

1x 8 RAKE FASCIA

ROOF FRAMING PLAN

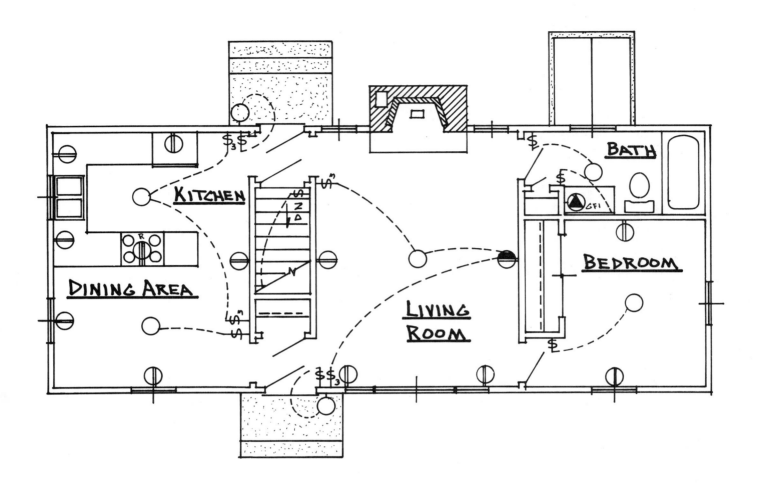

ELECTRICAL LAYOUT

ELECTRICAL SYMBOLS	
SYM.	ITEM
$	SINGLE-POLE SWITCH
$₃	THREE-WAY SWITCH
⊖	DUPLEX OUTLET
⊜	SPLIT-WIRED OUTLET
⊖R	RANGE OUTLET
▲GFI	GROUND FAULT INTERRUPTER
◯	LIGHTING OUTLET
▭	FLUORESCENT LIGHTING

MATERIAL LIST

FLOOR SYSTEM

2 × 10 Joists	35/16
2 × 10 Header	2/16 - 2/14 - 1/12
2 × 6 Sill	2/16 - 2/14 - 1/12
Sill Seal	110 Lineal Feet
Anchor Bolts	14
1/2" × 4' × 8' Plywood	19 Sheets

WALL SYSTEM

2 × 4 Shoe	2/16 - 2/14 - 1/12
2-2 × 4 Plate	4/16 - 4/14 - 2/12
2 × 4 Studs	106/8 - 4/10 - 1/12
(2 × 10) Door Headers	1/14
Window Headers	
(2 × 10)	3/12 - 1/10
(2 × 12)	2/10
Fireplace Header	
(2 × 12)	2/6
1/2" × 4' × 8' Sheathing	24 Sheets
3 1/2" Insulation	9 Rolls
Siding	779 Square Feet

INTERIOR

2 × 4 Studs	81/8
Door Headers	
(2 × 6	4/6 - 1/4
1/2" × 4' × 8' Sheetrock	53 Sheets

1 × 12 Shelving	2/8 - 1/3
Closet Pole	9 1/2 Lineal Feet
Baseboard	182 Lineal Feet
Ceiling Moulding	245 Lineal Feet

BASEMENT STAIRS

2 × 12 Stringers	2/14
2 × 10 Treads	3/12
Handrail	2/12

ROOFING SYSTEM

2 × 8 Ridge	2/14 - 1/16
2 × 6 Rafters	63/12
1 × 6 Colar Ties	15/6
1/4" × 24" Soffit	82 Lineal Feet
1 × 8 Fascia	82 Lineal Feet
1/4" × 12" Rake Fascia	
1 × 8 Rake Fascia	44 Lineal Feet
Roofing Felt	3 Rolls
1/2" × 4' × 8' Plywood	28 Sheets
Asphalt Shingles	27 Bundles

CEILING SYSTEM

2 × 6 Ceiling Joists	30/16
R-19 Insulation	13 Rolls

AUDREE

DESIGNED & DRAWN BY E. BRYANT

18' X 30'

With only 440 square feet of floor space, the Audree is an ideal dwelling for the single person or couple.

A fireplace, flanked by two double-hung windows, dominates the rear wall of the living room. Cafe doors give access to the I-shaped kitchen, which consists of a washer and dryer. A bedroom with closet space and a full bath complete the floor plan of this efficiency dwelling.

A cathedral ceiling is made possible through the utilization of scissor trusses in the roof system. Added floor space is obtained by a 1-foot cantilever in the front and back of the structure.

NOTES:

1) STRUCTURAL CHANGES
SHOULD NOT BE MADE WITH-
OUT CONSULTING ARCHITECT/
CONTRACTOR.

2) WOOD FRAMING MEMBERS
TO HAVE A FIBER STRESS
OF 1200 PSI.

DOOR SCHEDULE			
SYM	QTY	SIZE	TYPE
1	1	$3^0 \times 6^8$	PANEL-S.C.
2	2	$2^6 \times 6^8$	FLUSH-H.C.
3	1	$2^8 \times 6^8$	PANEL-S.C.
4	1	$1^6 \times 6^8$	FLUSH-H.C.
5	2	$2^6 \times 6^8$	CAFE DR.
6	1	$5^0 \times 6^8$	BIFOLD
7	1	$5^0 \times 6^8$	FLUSH-H.C.

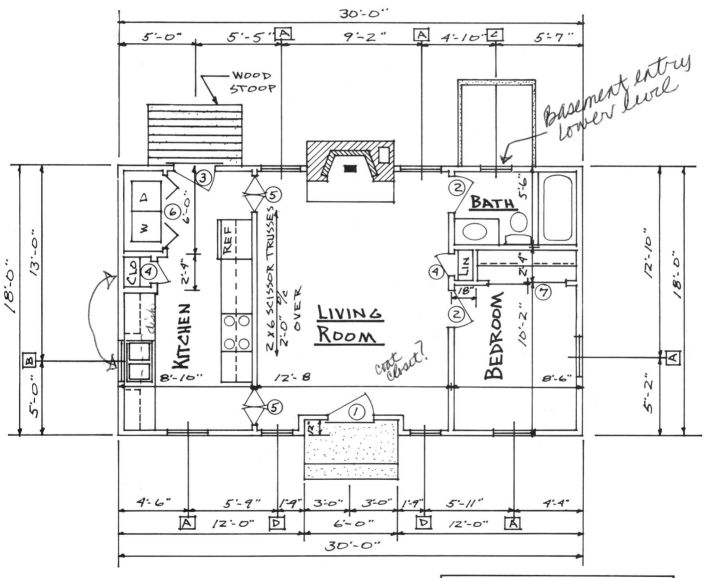

FLOOR PLAN

WINDOW SCHEDULE			
SYM	QTY	SIZE	TYPE
A	5	$2^8 \times 4^2$	DH
B	1	$2^8 \times 3^2$	DH
C	1	$2^0 \times 3^2$	DH
D	2	$2^0 \times 4^2$	DH

NOTES:
1) WOOD FRAMING TO BE KEPT 2" CLEAR OF FIREPLACE MASONRY.

2) CRAWL SPACE ENTRY FOUNDATION TO CONFORM TO MANUFACTURER SPECIFICATIONS.

3) DOUBLE JOISTS UNDER PARALLEL PARTITIONS.

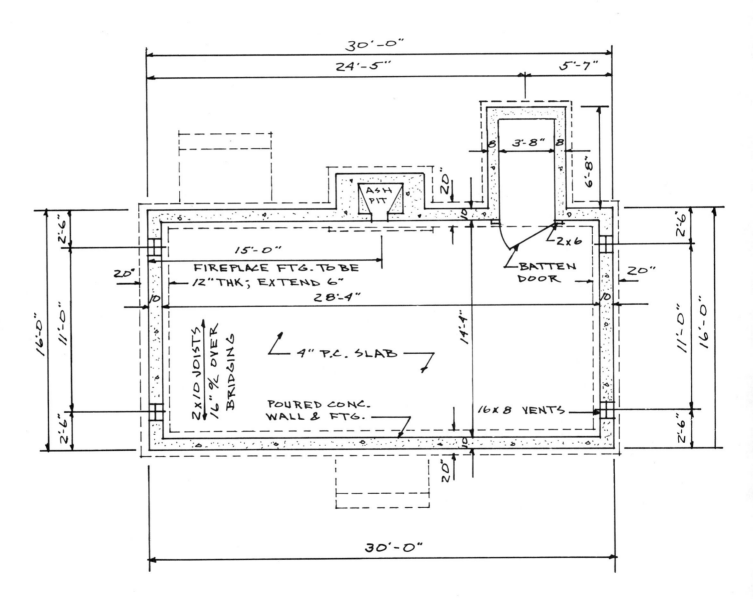

FOUNDATION PLAN

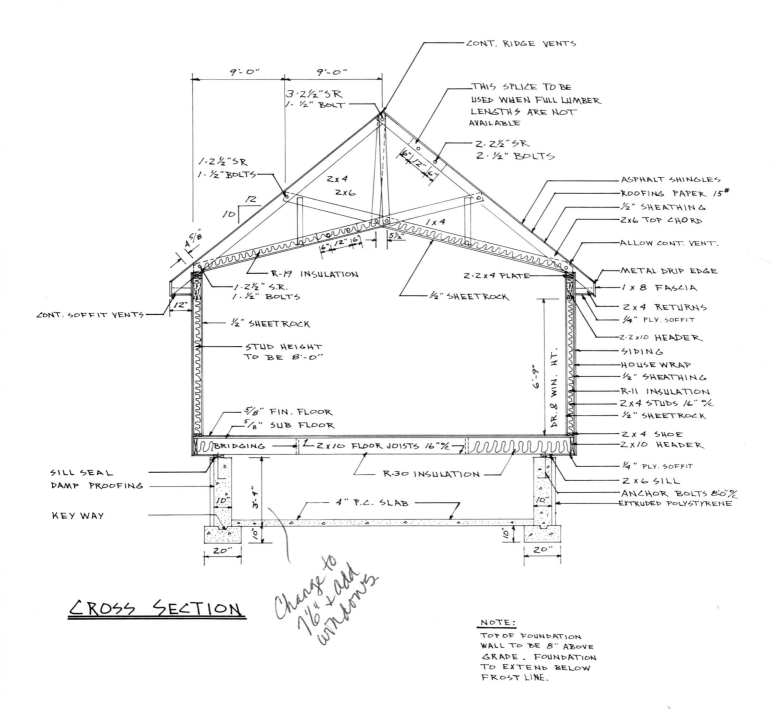

CONT. RIDGE VENTS

THIS SPLICE TO BE
USED WHEN FULL LUMBER
LENGTHS ARE NOT
AVAILABLE

9'-0"   9'-0"

3·2½"SR
1· ½" BOLT

2· 2½"SR
2· ½" BOLTS

1·2½"SR
1· ½"BOLTS

ASPHALT SHINGLES
ROOFING PAPER 15#
½" SHEATHING
2x6 TOP CHORD

2x4
2x6

12
10

1 x 4

ALLOW CONT. VENT.

5/8

5½"

R-19 INSULATION

2·2x4 PLATE

1·2½" S.R.
1· ½" BOLTS

½" SHEETROCK

METAL DRIP EDGE

1 x 8 FASCIA

2 x 4 RETURNS

¼" PLY. SOFFIT

2·2x10 HEADER

SIDING

HOUSE WRAP

½" SHEATHING

R-11 INSULATION

2x4 STUDS 16" °/c

½" SHEETROCK

CONT. SOFFIT VENTS

12"

½" SHEETROCK

STUD HEIGHT
TO BE 8'-0"

6'-9"

DR. & WIN. HT.

5/8" FIN. FLOOR
5/8" SUB FLOOR

2 x 4 SHOE
2x10 HEADER

BRIDGING

2x10 FLOOR JOISTS 16"°/c

¼" PLY. SOFFIT

SILL SEAL
DAMP PROOFING

R-30 INSULATION

2 x 6 SILL

ANCHOR BOLTS 8'0"°/c
EXTRUDED POLYSTYRENE

KEY WAY

3'-4"

4" P.C. SLAB

10"

10"

20"

20"

Change to 16" + add windows

CROSS SECTION

NOTE:
TOP OF FOUNDATION
WALL TO BE 8" ABOVE
GRADE. FOUNDATION
TO EXTEND BELOW
FROST LINE.

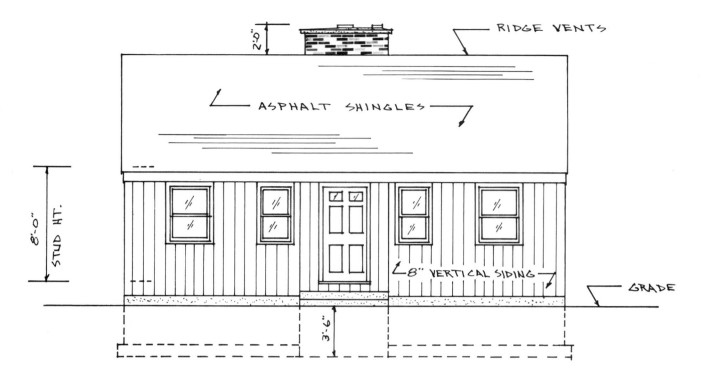

2'-0"

RIDGE VENTS

ASPHALT SHINGLES

8'-0" STUD HT.

8" VERTICAL SIDING

GRADE

3'-6"

FRONT ELEVATION

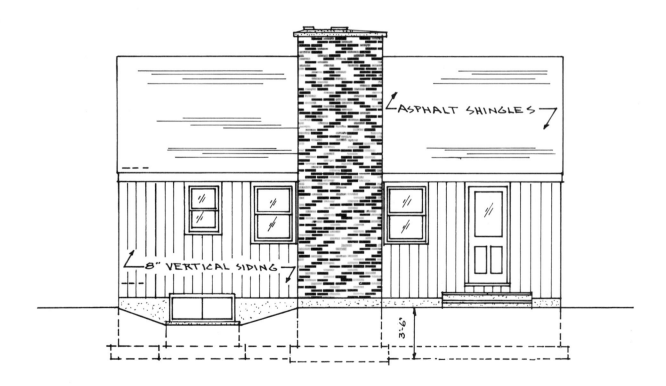

ASPHALT SHINGLES

8" VERTICAL SIDING

3'-6"

REAR ELEVATION

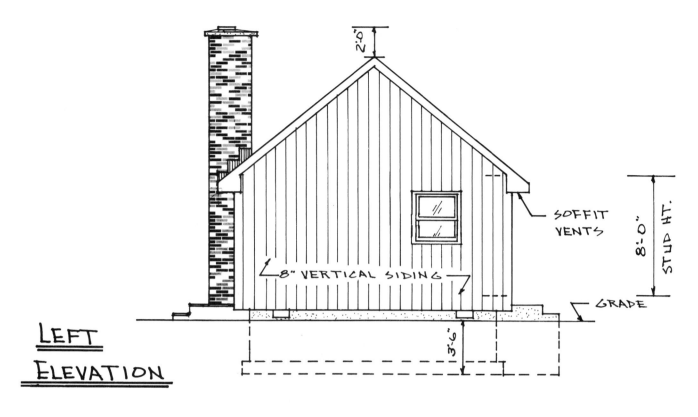

2'-0"

SOFFIT
VENTS

8'-0"
STUD HT.

8" VERTICAL SIDING

GRADE

3'-6"

LEFT
ELEVATION

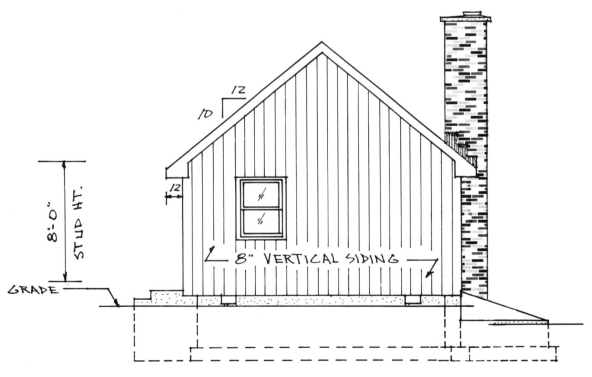

12
10

12

8'-0"
STUD HT.

GRADE

8" VERTICAL SIDING

RIGHT
ELEVATION

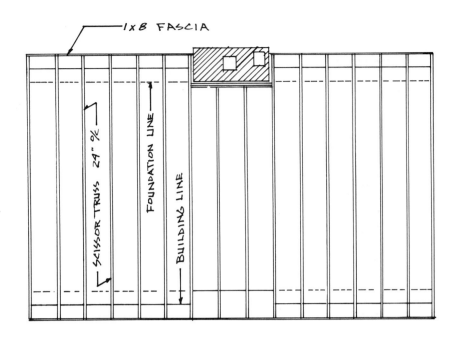

1×8 FASCIA

SCISSOR TRUSS 24" %

FOUNDATION LINE

BUILDING LINE

ROOF FRAMING PLAN

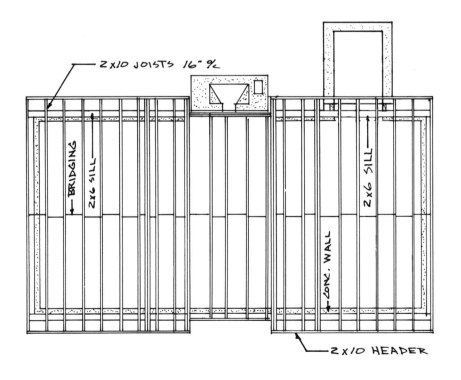

2×10 JOISTS 16" %

BRIDGING

2×6 SILL

CONC. WALL

2×6 SILL

2×10 HEADER

FLOOR FRAMING PLAN

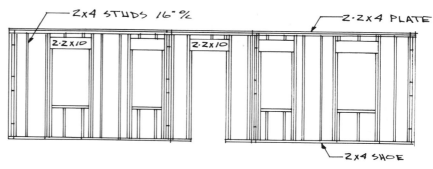

FRONT FRAMING PLAN

REAR FRAMING PLAN

RIGHT FRAMING PLAN

ROUGH
OPENING
BY
MANUFACTURER

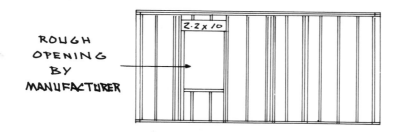

LEFT FRAMING PLAN

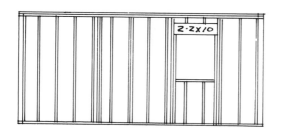

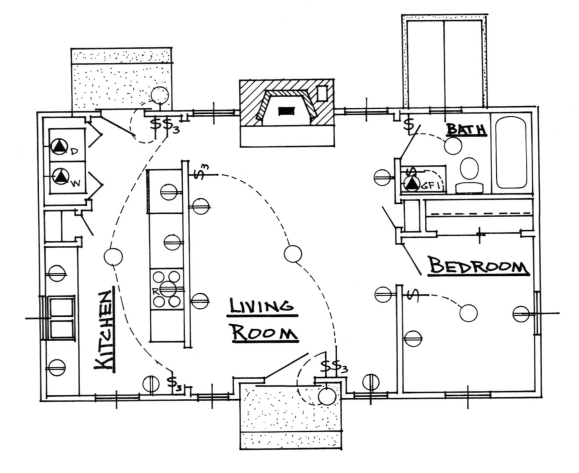

ELECTRICAL LAYOUT

SYM	ITEM
$	SINGLE-POLE SWITCH
$_3	THREE-WAY SWITCH
⊖	DUPLEX OUTLET
⊖R	RANGE OUTLET
◢W	WASHER OUTLET
◢D	DRYER OUTLET
◢GFI	GROUND FAULT INTERRUPTER
○	LIGHTING OUTLET
▭	FLUORESCENT LIGHTING

ELECTRICAL LAYOUT

MATERIAL LIST

FLOOR SYSTEM

2 × 10 Joists	23/18 - 4/16
2 × 10 Header	4/12 - 2/18
2 × 6 Sill	2/14 - 4/16
Sill Seal	92 Lineal Feet
Anchor Bolts	12
1/2″ × 4′ × 8′ Plywood	17 Sheets
Bridging	23 Pairs
R-30 Insulation	528 Square Feet
Cantilever Soffit	54 Lineal Feet

WALL SYSTEM

2 × 4 Shoe	2/14 - 2/16 - 2/18
2-2 × 4 Plate	4/14 - 4/16 - 4/18
2 × 4 Studs	113/8
Door Headers (2 × 10)	1/12
Window Headers (2 × 10)	4/12
1/2″ × 4′ × 8′ Sheathing	24 Sheets
R-11 3 1/2″ Insulation	9 Rolls
Siding	746 Square Feet
Air Infiltration Housewrap	746 Square Feet

CEILING SYSTEM

R-19 Insulation	8 Rolls

ROOFING SYSTEM

1″ × 8″ Fascia	54 Lineal Feet
1″ × 8″ Rake Fascia	52 Lineal Feet
Roofing Felt	2 Rolls
1/2″ × 4′ × 8′ Plywood	25 Sheets
Asphalt Shingles	24 Bundles
Scissor Trusses	14
Partial Scissor Trusses	2
1/4 × 12 Soffit	60 Lineal Feet

INTERIOR

2 × 4 Studs	72/8
Door Headers (2 × 8)	4/6 - 2/4 - 2/12
1/2″ × 4′ × 8′ Sheetrock	64 Sheets
1″ × 12″ Shelving	2/8
Closet Pole	1/6
Baseboard	199 Lineal Feet
Ceiling Moulding	229 Lineal Feet

JESSCA

DESIGNED & DRAWN BY E. BRYANT

Encompassing 896 square feet, the Jessca is a two-story efficiency dwelling designed with the single person and couple in mind.

The fireplace on the left wall of the living and dining area is accented by double-hung windows on each side. The front wall of this room is enhanced by a double-hung picture window, while the rear wall has a triple mullion.

The efficiency kitchen is located adjacent to the stairs, which give access to the second floor. Located on the upper level is a spacious bedroom with twin closets and a full-bath.

DOOR SCHEDULE

SYM.	NO.	SIZE	TYPE
1	1	$3^0 \times 6^8$	PANEL
2	1	$2^8 \times 6^8$	
3	4	$2^6 \times 6^8$	FLUSH-H.C.
4	1	$1^0 \times 6^8$	FLUSH-H.C.
5	2	$5^0 \times 6^8$	FLUSH-H.C.
6	1	$2^6 \times 6^8$	BI-FOLD

WINDOW SCHEDULE

SYM.	NO.	SIZE	TYPE
A	1	$2^0 - 4^2 - 2^0 \times 4^2$	P.W.
B	1	$8^0 \times 3^{10}$	TRIPLE MULL.
C	10	$2^8 \times 3^{10}$	DH
D	3	$2^8 \times 1^4$	BASEMENT

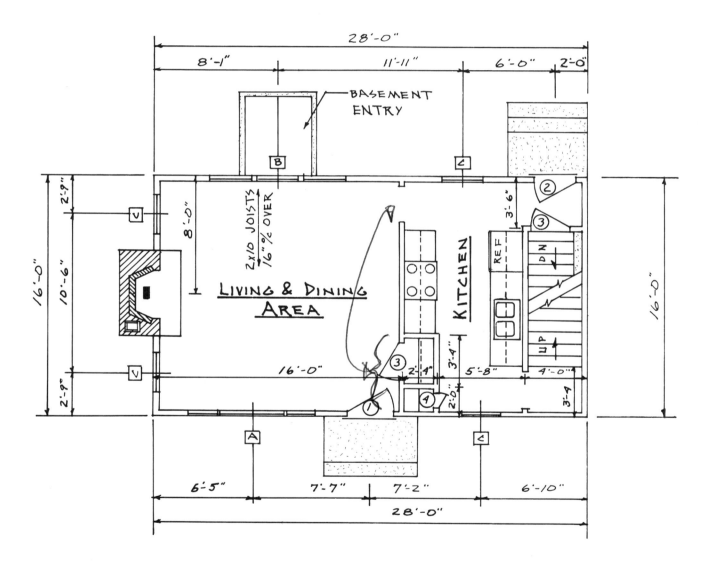

FIRST FLOOR PLAN

NOTES:

1) STRUCTURAL CHANGES SHOULD NOT BE MADE WITHOUT CONSULTING ARCHITECT OR CONTRACTOR.

2) WOOD FRAMING TO BE KEPT 2" CLEAR OF FIREPLACE.

3) WOOD FRAMING MEMBERS TO HAVE A FIBER STRESS OF 1200 PSI.

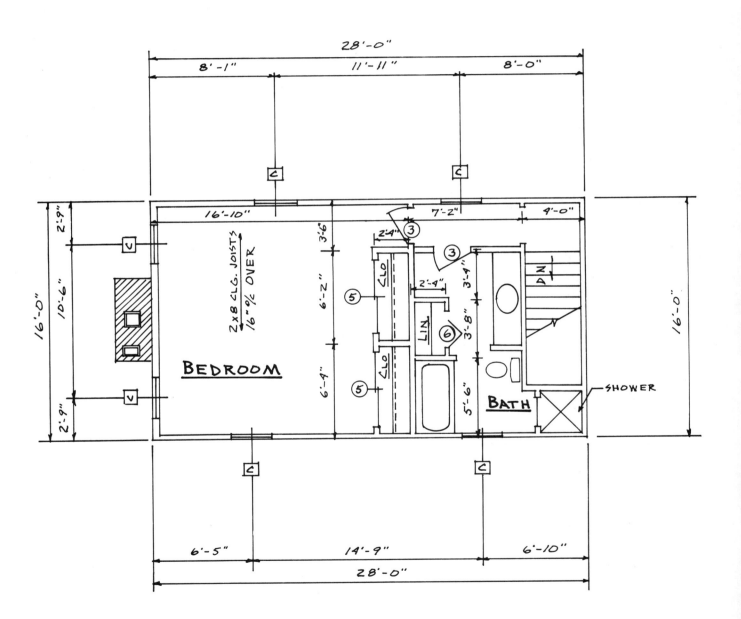

SECOND FLOOR PLAN

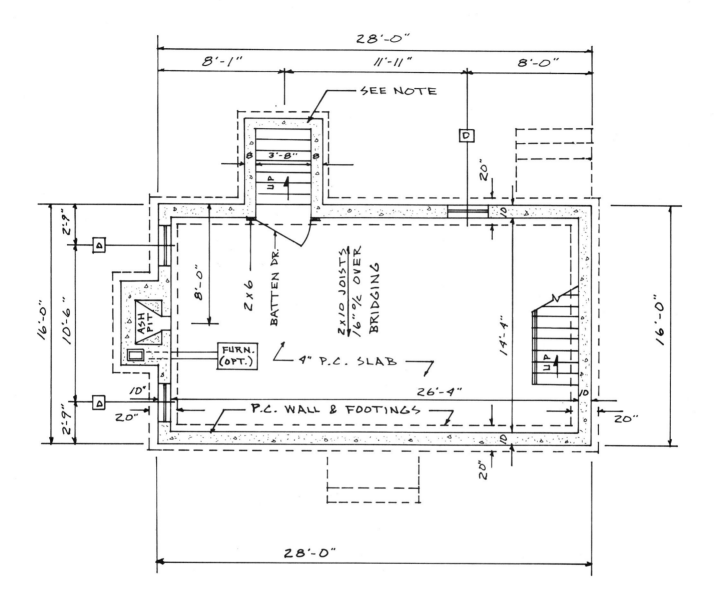

FOUNDATION PLAN

NOTE:
BASEMENT ENTRY FOUNDATION
TO CONFORM TO MANUFAC-
TURER SPECIFICATIONS.

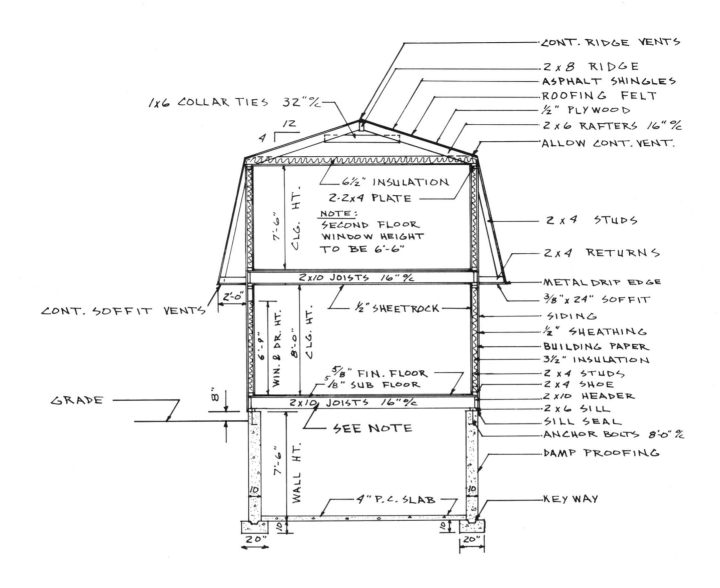

1x6 COLLAR TIES 32"%

CONT. RIDGE VENTS
2x8 RIDGE
ASPHALT SHINGLES
ROOFING FELT
½" PLYWOOD
2x6 RAFTERS 16"%
ALLOW CONT. VENT.

12
4

6½" INSULATION
2-2x4 PLATE

NOTE:
SECOND FLOOR
WINDOW HEIGHT
TO BE 6'-6"

7'-6" CLG. HT.

2x4 STUDS

2x4 RETURNS

2x10 JOISTS 16"%

METAL DRIP EDGE
3/8" x 24" SOFFIT

CONT. SOFFIT VENTS

2'-0"

½" SHEETROCK

SIDING
½" SHEATHING
BUILDING PAPER
3½" INSULATION
2x4 STUDS
2x4 SHOE
2x10 HEADER
2x6 SILL
SILL SEAL
ANCHOR BOLTS 8'0"%

6'-9" WIN. 2 DR. HT.   8'-0" CLG. HT.

5/8" FIN. FLOOR
5/8" SUB FLOOR

2x10 JOISTS 16"%

SEE NOTE

GRADE

8"

7'-6" WALL HT.

DAMP PROOFING

10

10

KEY WAY

4" P.C. SLAB

10

10

20"

20"

CROSS SECTION

NOTE:
CHECK LOCAL BUILDING
CODES REGARDING
FLOOR INSULATION.

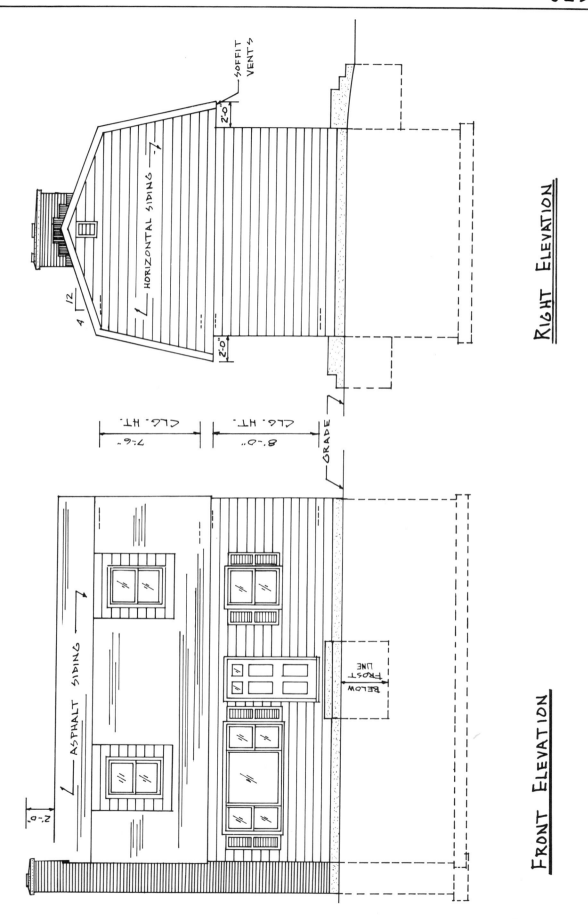

SOFFIT VENTS

2'-0"

HORIZONTAL SIDING

12
4

2'-0"

RIGHT ELEVATION

CLG. HT.
7'-6"

CLG. HT.
8'-0"

GRADE

ASPHALT SIDING

2'-0"

BELOW FROST LINE

FRONT ELEVATION

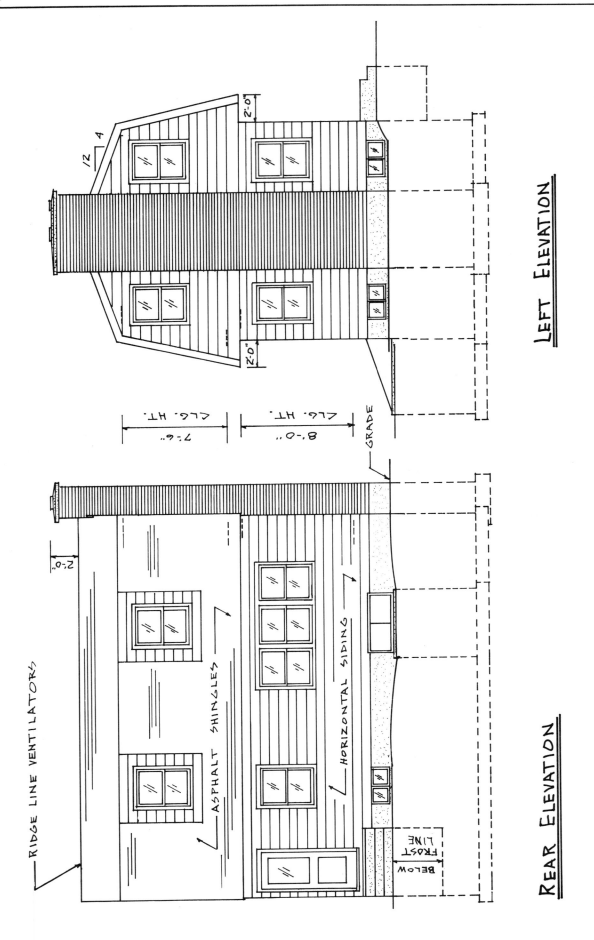

LEFT ELEVATION

REAR ELEVATION

NOTE:
DOUBLE JOISTS UNDER
PARALLEL PARTITIONS.

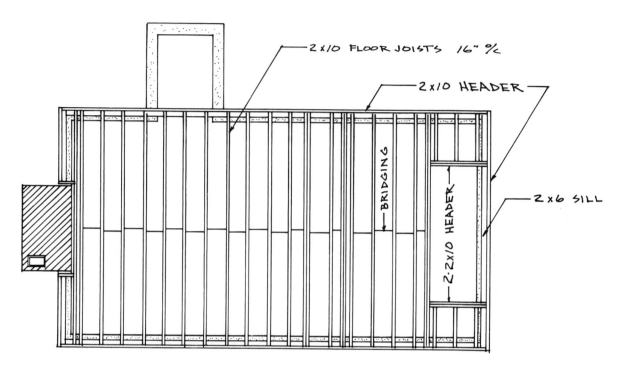

FIRST FLOOR FRAMING PLAN

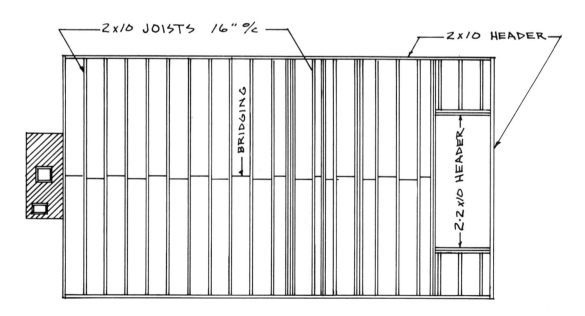

SECOND FLOOR FRAMING PLAN

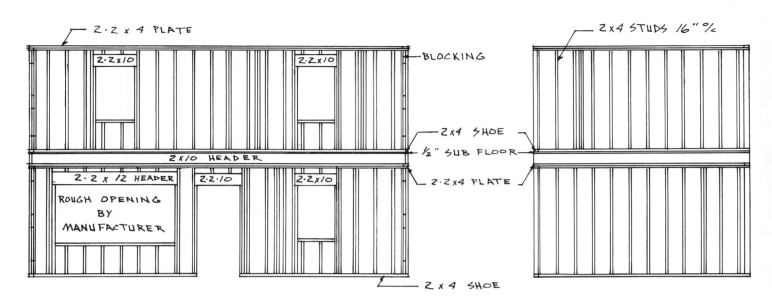

FRONT FRAMING PLAN

RIGHT FRAMING PLAN

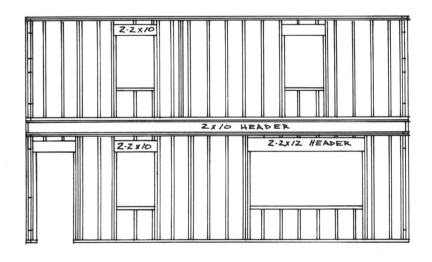

REAR FRAMING PLAN

LEFT FRAMING PLAN

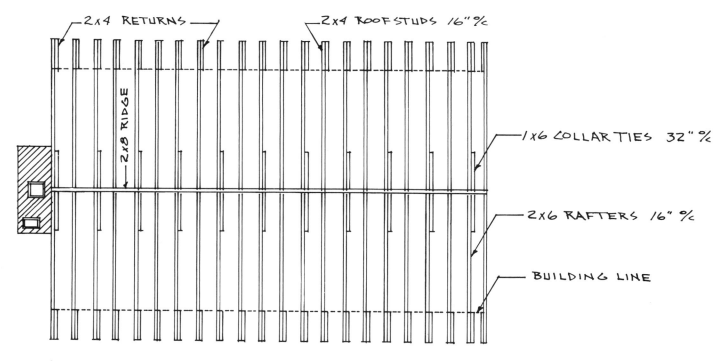

2x4 RETURNS — 2x4 ROOF STUDS 16" ⁰⁄c

2x8 RIDGE

1x6 COLLAR TIES 32" ⁰⁄c

2x6 RAFTERS 16" ⁰⁄c

BUILDING LINE

ROOF FRAMING PLAN

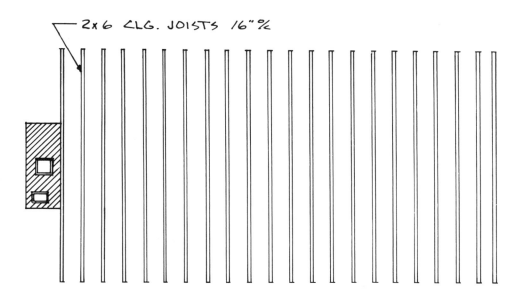

2x6 CLG. JOISTS 16" ⁰⁄c

CEILING FRAMING PLAN

ELECTRICAL SYMBOLS	
$	SINGLE-POLE SWITCH
$₃	THREE-WAY SWITCH
$₄	FOUR-WAY SWITCH
⊖	DUPLEX CONVENIENCE OUTLET
⊜	RANGE OUTLET
○	LIGHTING OUTLET
▬	FLUORESCENT LIGHTING
▲GFI	GROUND FAULT INTERRUPTER

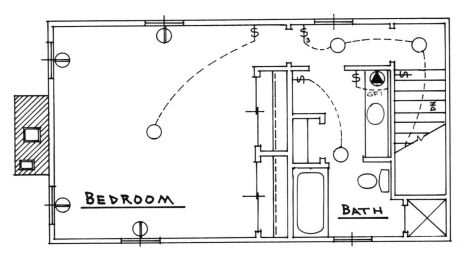

SECOND FLOOR
ELECTRICAL LAYOUT

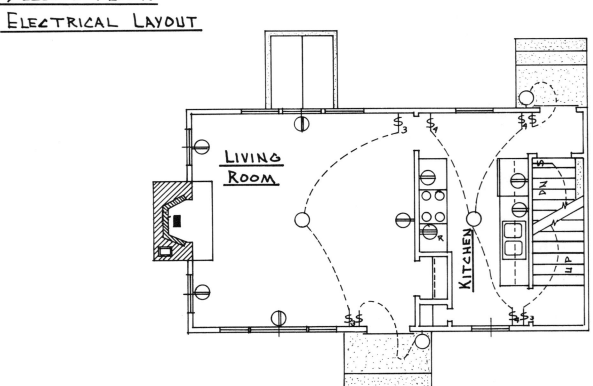

FIRST FLOOR
ELECTRICAL LAYOUT

MATERIAL LIST

FLOOR SYSTEM

2 × 10 Joists	55/16
2 × 10 Header	4/16 - 8/14
2 × 6 Sill	2/16 - 4/14
Sill Seal	85 Lineal Feet
Anchor Bolts	10
1/2" × 4' × 8' Plywood	26 Sheets
Bridging	36 Pairs

WALL SYSTEM

2 × 4 Shoe	2/16 - 4/14
2-2 × 4 Plate	4/16 - 8/14
2 × 4 Studs	173/8 - 2/10
Door Headers (2 × 10)	4/4
Window Headers	
2 × 12	4/10
2 × 10	20/4
1/2" × 4' × 8' Sheathing	43 Sheets
3 1/2" Insulation	16 Rolls
Siding	944 Square Feet
Fireplace Headers (2 × 12)	2/6
Air Infiltration Housewrap	944 Square Feet

CEILING SYSTEM

2 × 6 Ceiling Joists	22/16
6 1/2" Insulation	10 Rolls

ROOF SYSTEM

2 × 8 Ridge	2/14
2 × 6 Rafters	44/10
1 × 6 Collar Ties	11/6
1/4" × 24" Soffit	7/8
1 × 8 Rake Fascia	72 Lineal Feet
Roofing Felt	3 Rolls
1/2" × 4' × 8' Plywood	31 Sheets
Asphalt Shingles	31 Bundles
2 × 4 Gambrel Roof Studs	44/10
2 × 4 Gambrel Roof Returns	6/8

INTERIOR

2 × 4 Studs	159/8
2 × 6 Door Headers	3/12 - 2/10
1/2" × 4' × 8' Sheetrock	86 Sheets
1" × 12" Shelving	3/6 - 4/4
Closet Pole	2/6 - 1/4
Baseboard	321 Lineal Feet
Ceiling Moulding	388 Lineal Feet
2 × 12 Stair Stringers	2/14
Stair Risers	3/12 - 1/4
Stair Treads	3/12

BASEMENT STAIRS

Stringers (2 × 12)	2/14
Treads (2 × 10)	3/12
Handrail	1/14

IMPERIAL

DRAWN & DESIGNED BY E. BRYANT

28 x 32

Consisting of 704 square feet, the Imperial is an L-shaped efficiency dwelling.

After entering the house through the front entrance, you will find yourself in a full-sized living room with a fireplace that dominates the left wall. Adjacent to the living room is an I-shaped kitchen with appliances that have been conveniently placed.

The good-sized bedroom has ample window area, which provides good cross-ventilation. A full bath and ample closet space complete the floor plan of this efficiency dwelling.

The basement provides room for additional storage or a work area. The exterior of the structure boasts a roof-covered porch and 8-inch horizontal siding.

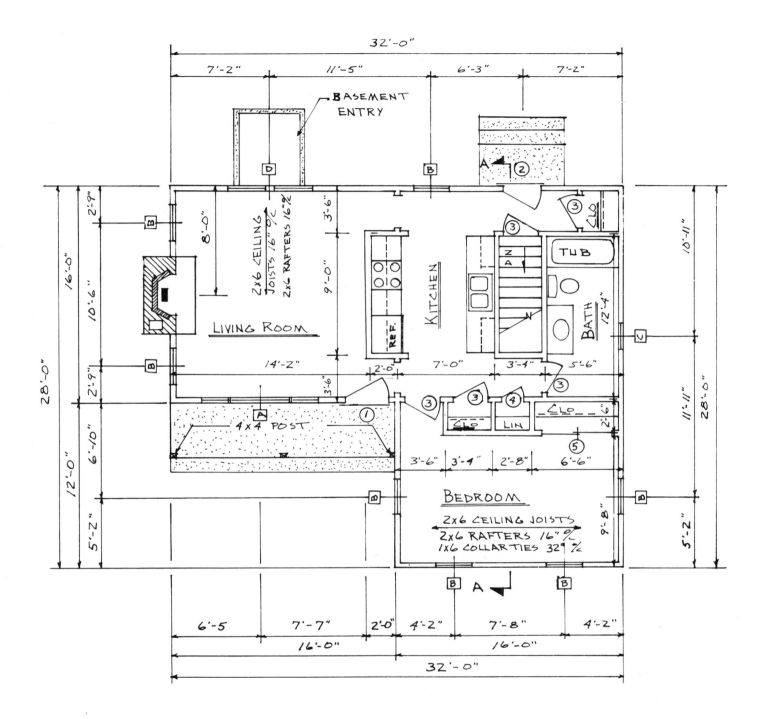

BASEMENT ENTRY

32'-0"

7'-2"   11'-5"   6'-3"   7'-2"

D   B   A ②

2'-9"   B

16'-0"   10'-6"   8'-0"   2x6 CEILING JOISTS 16" O/C   3'-6"   ③

28'-0"   2x6 RAFTERS 16" O/C   ③

9'-0"   Z A

TUB   10'-11"

LIVING ROOM   KITCHEN   BATH 12'-4"   C   28'-0"

2'-9"   B   14'-2"   7'-0"   3'-4"   5'-6"

2'-0"   3'-6"   ③   11'-11"

12'-0"   6'-10"   A 4x4 POST   ①   ③   ③   ④   CLO   2'-6"

CLO   LIN   ⑤

3'-6"   3'-1"   2'-8"   6'-6"

B   B   9'-8"   B

BEDROOM

2x6 CEILING JOISTS
2x6 RAFTERS 16" O/C
1x6 COLLAR TIES 32" O/C

5'-2"   5'-2"

B   A   B

6'-5   7'-7"   2'-0"   4'-2"   7'-8"   4'-2"

16'-0"   16'-0"

32'-0"

Floor Plan

IMPERIAL

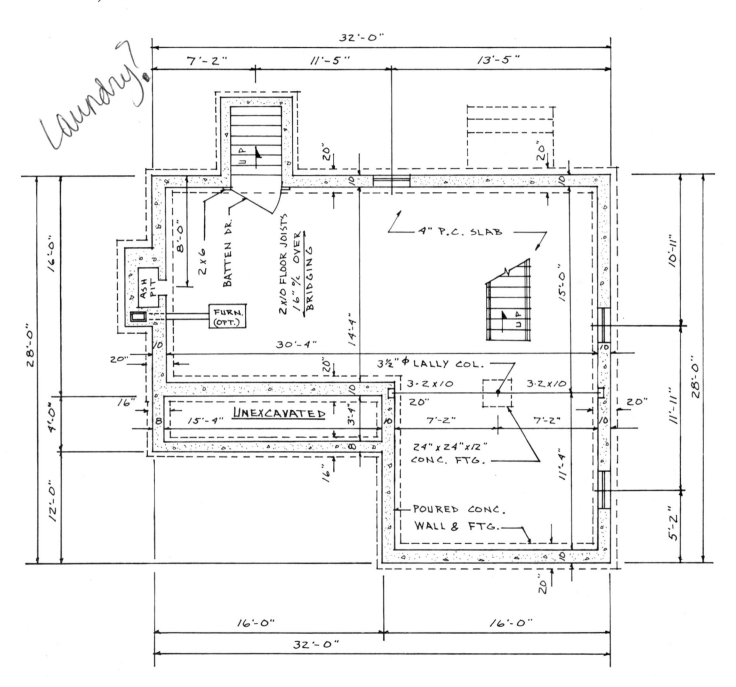

FOUNDATION PLAN

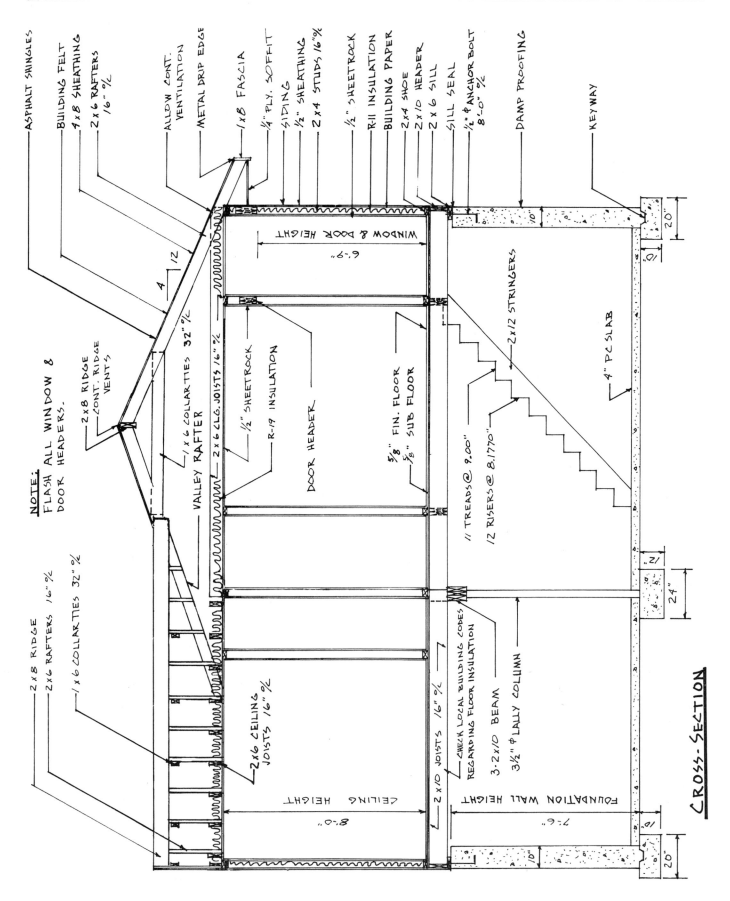

CROSS-SECTION

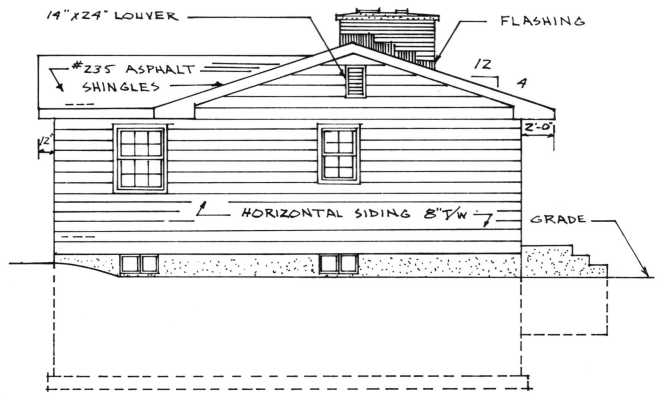

14"x24" LOUVER

FLASHING

#235 ASPHALT
SHINGLES

12
4

1/2"

2'-0"

HORIZONTAL SIDING 8" T/W

GRADE

RIGHT ELEVATION

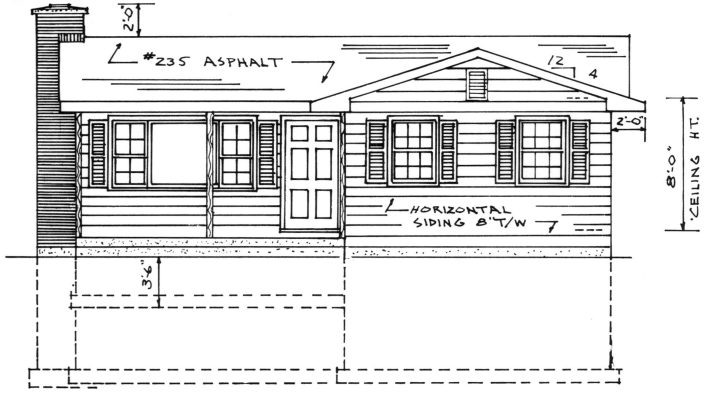

2'-0"

#235 ASPHALT

12
4

2'-0"

8'-0" CEILING HT.

HORIZONTAL
SIDING 8" T/W

3'-6"

FRONT ELEVATION

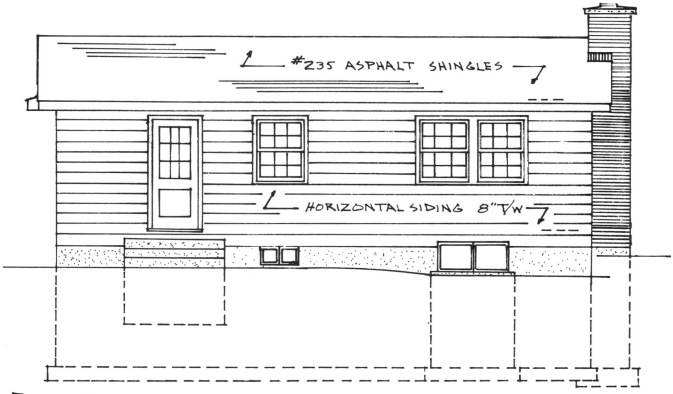

#235 ASPHALT SHINGLES

HORIZONTAL SIDING 8" T/W

REAR ELEVATION

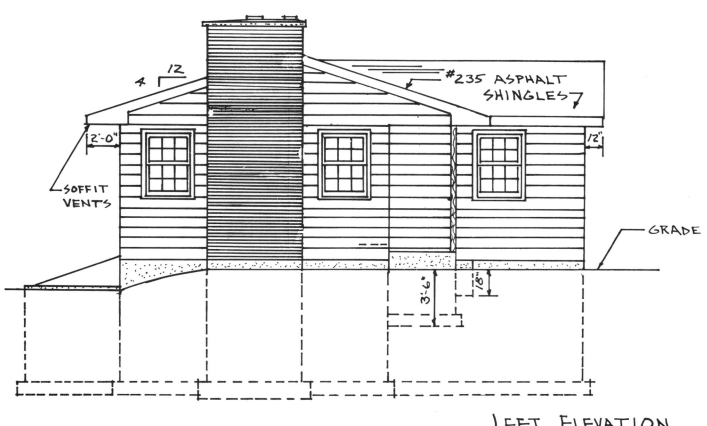

4 12

#235 ASPHALT SHINGLES

2'-0"

12"

SOFFIT VENTS

GRADE

3'-6"

18"

LEFT ELEVATION

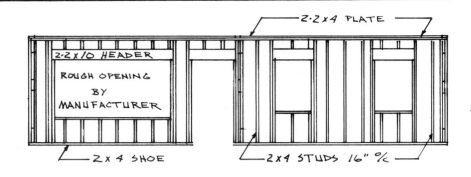

FRONT FRAMING PLAN

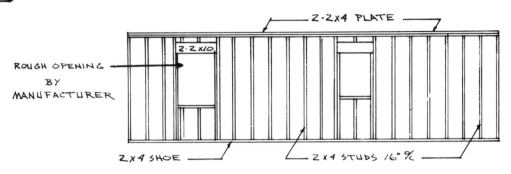

RIGHT FRAMING PLAN

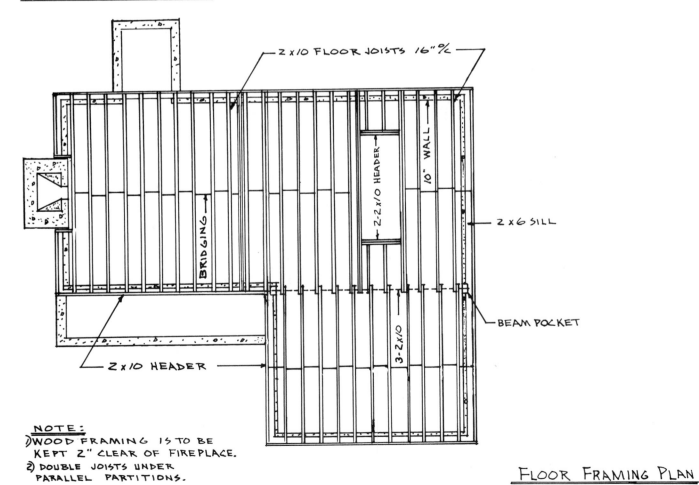

NOTE:
1) WOOD FRAMING IS TO BE
   KEPT 2" CLEAR OF FIREPLACE.
2) DOUBLE JOISTS UNDER
   PARALLEL PARTITIONS.

FLOOR FRAMING PLAN

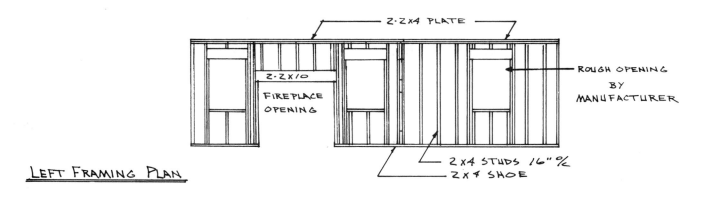

LEFT FRAMING PLAN

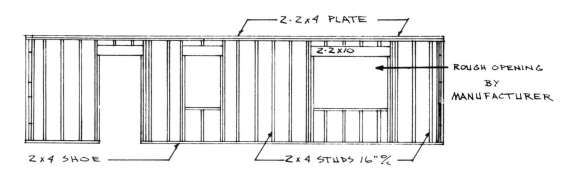

REAR FRAMING PLAN

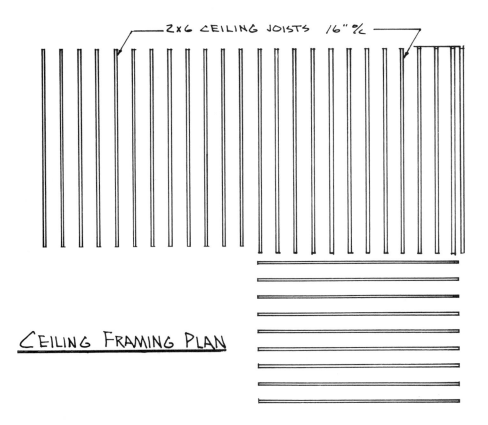

CEILING FRAMING PLAN

DOOR	SCHEDULE		
SYM.	NO.	SIZE	TYPE
①	1	$3^6 \times 6^8$	6 PANEL
②	1	$2^8 \times 6^8$	9 LIGHTS
③	5	$2^6 \times 6^8$	FLUSH - H.C.
④	1	$1^6 \times 6^8$	FLUSH - H.C.
⑤	1	$5^0 \times 6^8$	SLIDING - H.C.

WINDOW	SCHEDULE		
SYM.	NO.	SIZE	TYPE
A	1	$2^0 - 4^4 - 2^0 \times 4^2$	D.H. P.W.
B	7	$2^8 \times 3^{10}$	D.H.
C	1	$2^0 \times 3^2$	D.H.
D	1	$5^4 \times 3^{10}$	D.H. MULL.
E	3	$1^2 \times 2^4$	BSMT. WIN.

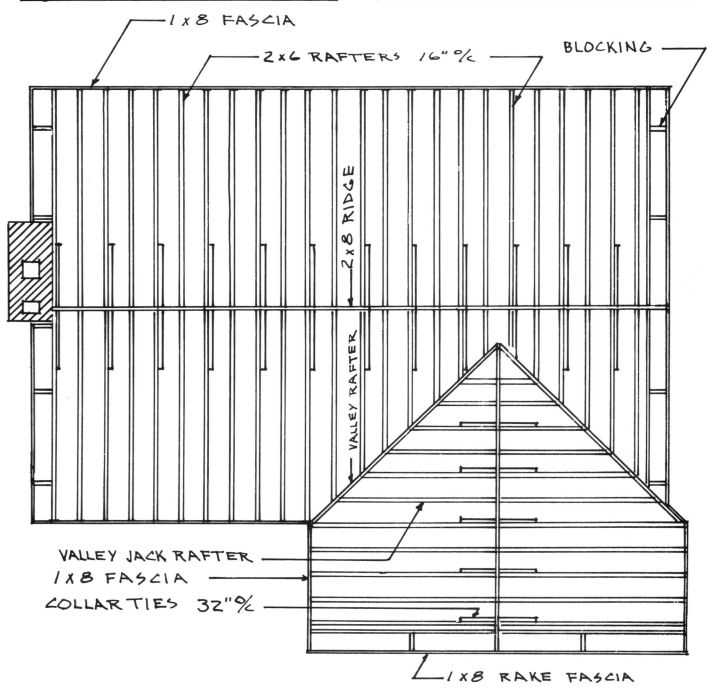

ROOF FRAMING PLAN

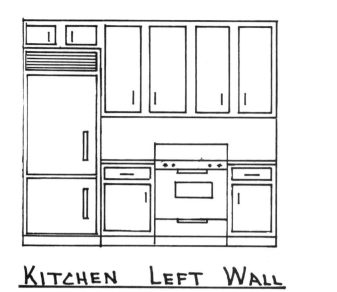

KITCHEN LEFT WALL

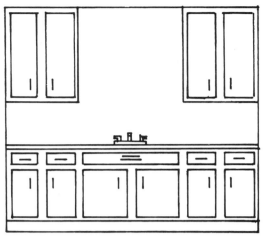

KITCHEN RIGHT WALL

LIVING ROOM PERSPECTIVE

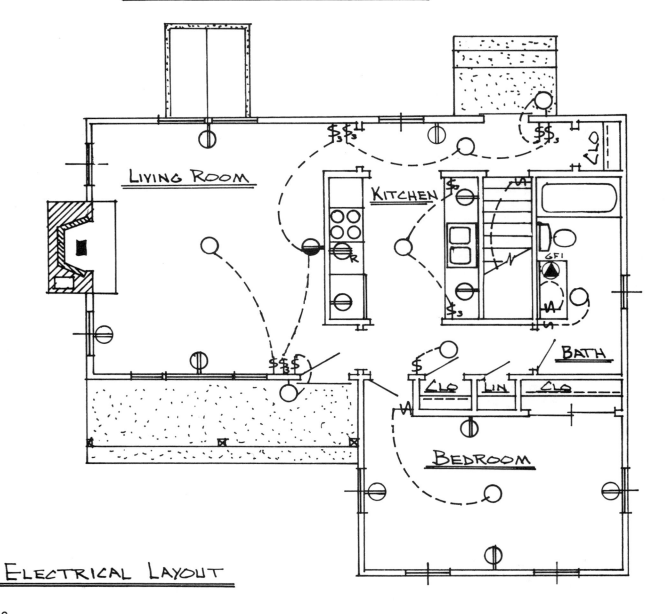

ELECTRICAL SYMBOLS

◯	LIGHTING OUTLET
─◯	WALL LIGHTING OUTLET
▭	FLUORESCENT LIGHTING
═⊖	DUPLEX OUTLET
═⬤	SPLIT-WIRED OUTLET
═⊖R	RANGE OUTLET
$	SINGLE-POLE SWITCH
$₃	THREE-WAY SWITCH
─◯GFI	GROUND FAULT INTERRUPTER

LIVING ROOM

KITCHEN

BATH

BEDROOM

ELECTRICAL LAYOUT

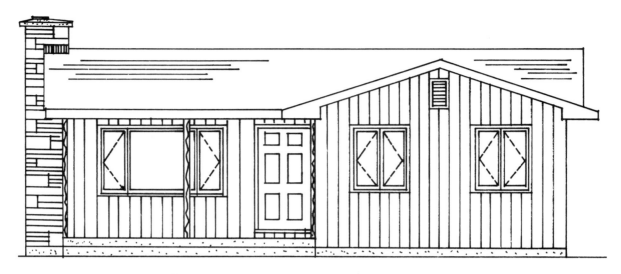

THIS IS 'WHAT THE IMPERIAL WOULD LOOK LIKE IF...'
PAGE. IT IS NOT PART OF THE BUILDING PLANS. ITS
ONLY PURPOSE IS TO SHOW YOU 'WHAT THE IMPERIAL
WOULD LOOK LIKE IF' MODIFICATIONS, ENHANCEMENTS
AND SUBSTITUTIONS WERE MADE.

FOR EXAMPLE, LET US ASSUME THAT YOU ARE
THRILLED WITH THE FLOOR PLAN OF THE IMPERIAL, BUT
YOU'RE NOT OVERLY EXCITED ABOUT THE EXTERIOR.

IF THAT'S THE SITUATION, YOU CAN GIVE THE HOUSE
A NEW LOOK WITH NO MAJOR STRUCTURAL CHANGES.

BY SUBSTITUTING VERTICAL SIDING, CASEMENT WINDOWS,
CUT STONE ON THE FIREPLACE AND ELIMINATING SHUTTERS,
THE FRONT ELEVATION OF THE IMPERIAL WOULD LOOK LIKE
THE ABOVE.

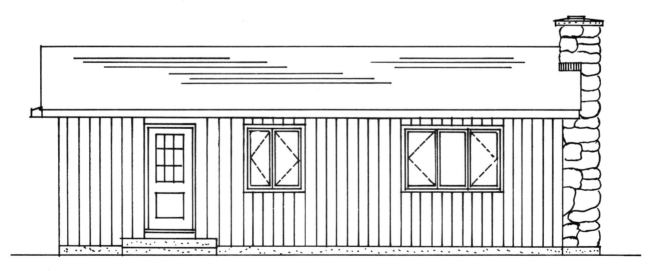

IF YOU PLAN TO HAVE A BASEMENTLESS HOUSE, YOU
WON'T BE NEEDING THE BASEMENT ENTRY... OR THE
BASEMENT WINDOWS. THE LACK OF THESE ITEMS WILL
AFFECT YOUR GRADE LEVEL.

MAYBE YOU'D PREFER A FIELD-STONE FIREPLACE.

MATERIAL LIST

FLOOR SYSTEM

2 × 10 Joists	26/16 - 11/12
2 × 10 Header	5/16 - 1/12 - 2/14
2 × 6 Sill	5/16 - 1/12 - 2/14
Sill Seal	120 Lineal Feet
Anchor Bolts	19
1/2″ × 4′ × 8′ Ply.	22 Sheets
Bridging	32 Pairs
3 1/2″ ⌀Lally Cols.	1/8
3-2 × 10 Beam	3/16

WALL SYSTEM

2 × 4 Shoe	5/16 - 1/12 - 2/14
2-2 × 4 Plate	10/16 - 2/12 - 4/14
2 × 4 Studs	117/8
Door Headers (2 × 10)	4/4
Window Headers (2 × 10)	2/10 - 16/4 - 2/6
Fireplace Header (2 × 10)	2/8
1/2″ × 4′ × 8′ Sheathing	34 Sheets
Building Paper	3 Rolls
3 1/2″ Insulation	11 Rolls
Siding	1071 Square Feet
4 × 4 Posts	3/8

CEILING SYSTEM

2 × 6 Ceiling Joists	31/16
2 × 6 Header	5/16 - 1/12 - 2/14
6 1/2″ Insulation	15 Rolls

ROOF SYSTEM

2 × 8 Ridge	2/12 - 1/10 - 1/18
2 × 6 Rafters	48/12
2 × 6 Valley Rafters	2/14
2 × 6 Valley Jack Rafters	5/12
1 × 6 Collar Ties	12/7 - 5/6
1/4″ × 24″ Soffit	65 Lineal Feet
1″ × 8″ Fascia	65 Lineal Feet
1/4″ × 12″ Rake Soffit	66 Lineal Feet
1″ × 8″ Rake Fascia	66 Lineal Feet
Roofing Felt	2 Rolls
1/2″ × 4′ × 8′ Ply.	20 Sheets
Asphalt Shingles	30 Bundles
Metal Drip Edge	8/10

INTERIOR

2 × 4 Studs	92/8
2 × 6 Door Headers	14/4 - 2/6
1/2″ × 4′ × 8′ Sheetrock	60 Sheets
1″ × 12″ Shelving	1/6 - 2/8
Closet Pole	1/6 - 1/3
Baseboard	232 Lineal Feet
Ceiling Moulding	258 Lineal Feet

BASEMENT STAIRS

2 × 12 Stringers	2/14
2 × 10 Treads	3/12
Handrail	2/12

BENJIM

DESIGNED & DRAWN BY E. BRYANT

By placing the front of the Benjim in a southerly direction, full advantage can be taken of the sun's rays. In addition to the fact that the bedroom will receive the morning sun, the living room will also benefit from the sun in the morning, as well as in the afternoon and evening.

By keeping the dwelling narrow, the use of lally columns and beams have been minimized. In spite of its size, the Benjim has full-sized rooms....a spacious kitchen, a roomy bedroom, and a good-sized living room. In addition to a centrally located bath, ample closet/storage space is abundant throughout the structure.

If you desire, the chimney can be enlarged to accommodate another flue, which could be used for a metal fireplace unit in the living room.

NOTES:
1. CHANGES IN BASIC CONSTRUCTION SHOULD NOT BE MADE WITHOUT CONSULTING CONTRACTOR.
2. FRAMING MEMBERS MUST BE KEPT 2" AWAY FROM CHIMNEY MASONRY.

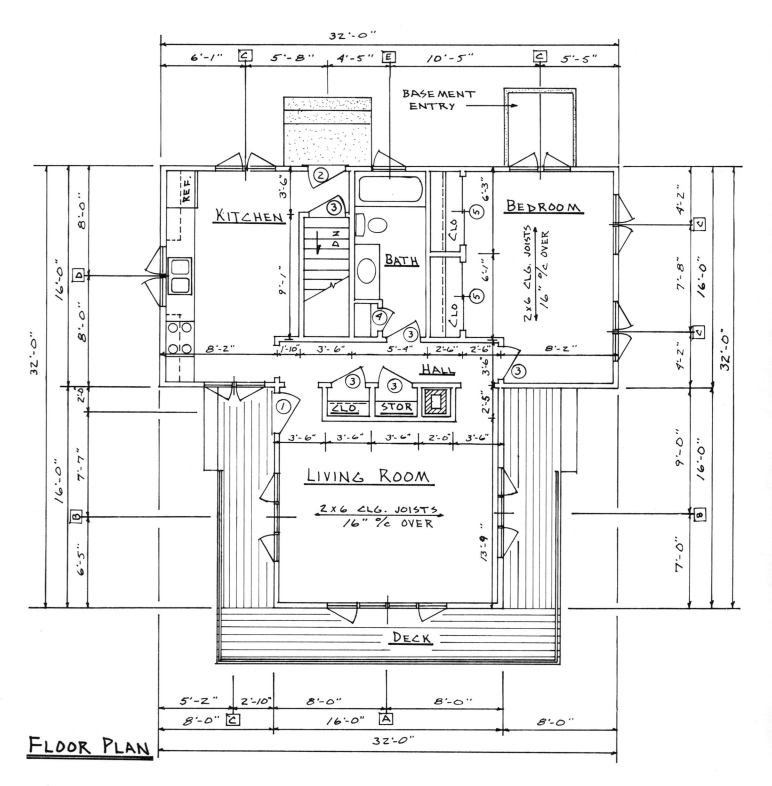

FLOOR PLAN

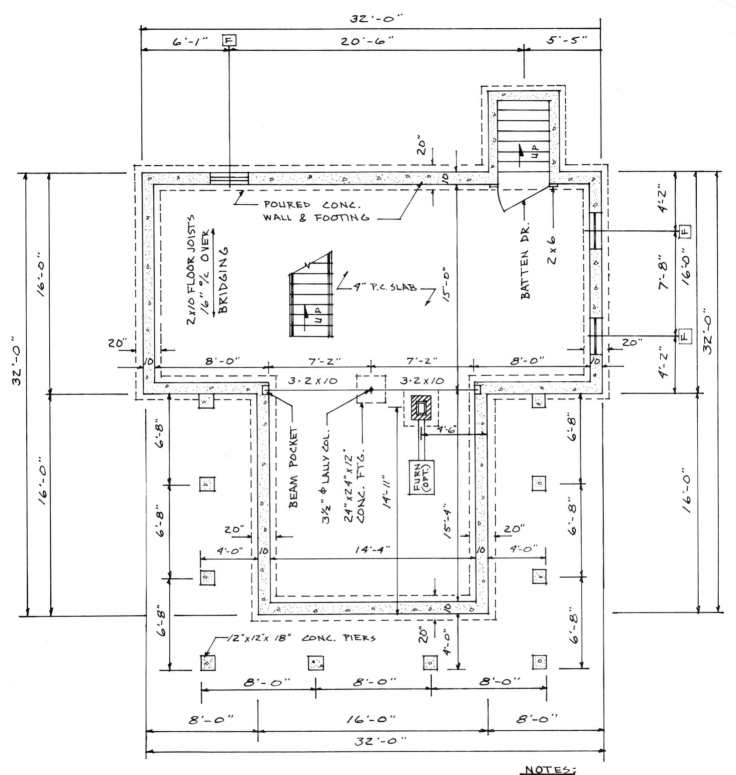

FOUNDATION PLAN

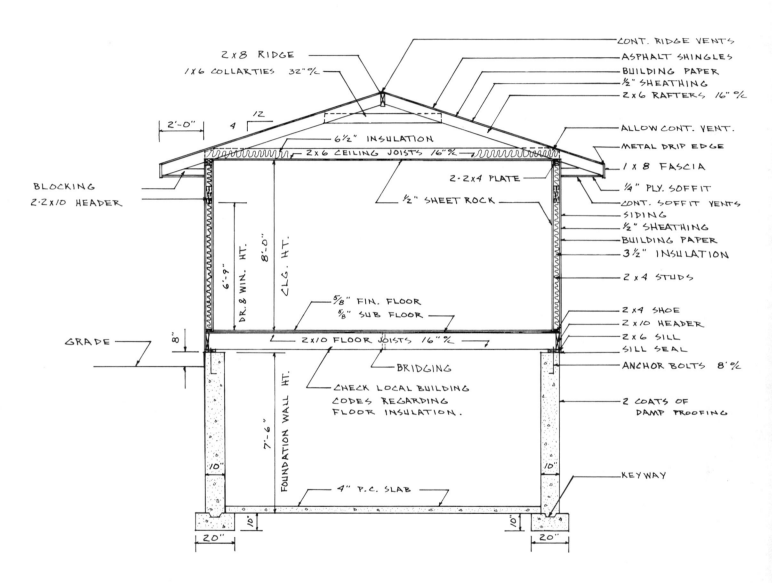

2 x 8 RIDGE

1 x 6 COLLARTIES 32" ⁰⁄ᴄ

CONT. RIDGE VENTS
ASPHALT SHINGLES
BUILDING PAPER
½" SHEATHING
2 x 6 RAFTERS 16" ⁰⁄ᴄ

2'-0"

4 12

6½" INSULATION

2 x 6 CEILING JOISTS 16" ⁰⁄ᴄ

ALLOW CONT. VENT.
METAL DRIP EDGE
1 x 8 FASCIA
¼" PLY. SOFFIT

2-2x4 PLATE

CONT. SOFFIT VENTS
SIDING
½" SHEATHING
BUILDING PAPER
3½" INSULATION

BLOCKING
2-2x10 HEADER

½" SHEET ROCK

2 x 4 STUDS

8'-0" CLG. HT.

6'-9" DR. & WIN. HT.

⅝" FIN. FLOOR
⅝" SUB FLOOR

2 x 4 SHOE
2 x 10 HEADER
2 x 6 SILL
SILL SEAL
ANCHOR BOLTS 8' ⁰⁄ᴄ

GRADE

8"

2 x 10 FLOOR JOISTS 16" ⁰⁄ᴄ

BRIDGING

CHECK LOCAL BUILDING
CODES REGARDING
FLOOR INSULATION.

2 COATS OF
DAMP PROOFING

7-6" FOUNDATION WALL HT.

10"

4" P.C. SLAB

10"

KEYWAY

10"

10"

20"

20"

CROSS SECTION

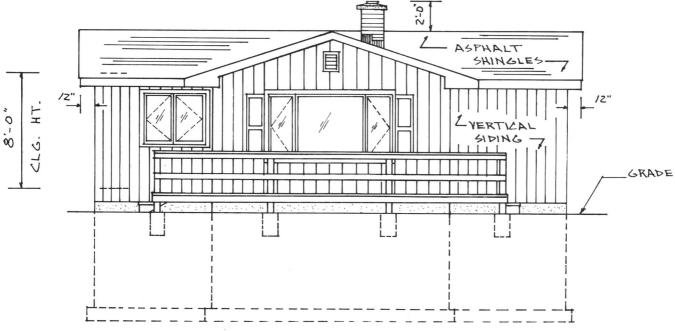

NOTE:
FLASH ALL WINDOWS
& DOOR HEADERS

ASPHALT
SHINGLES

VERTICAL
SIDING

GRADE

8'-0" CLG. HT.

12"

12"

2'-0"

FRONT ELEVATION

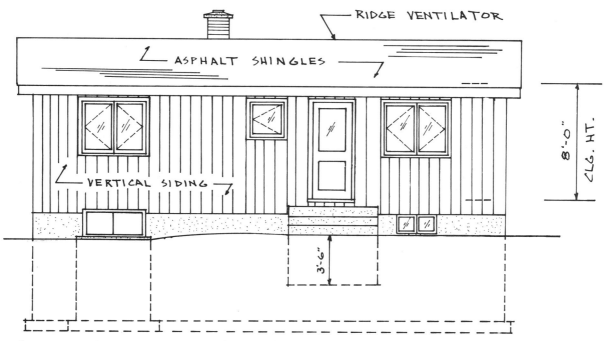

RIDGE VENTILATOR

ASPHALT SHINGLES

VERTICAL SIDING

8'-0" CLG. HT.

3'-6"

REAR ELEVATION

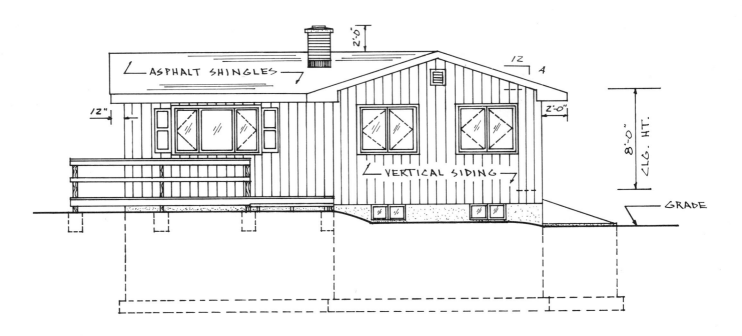

RIGHT ELEVATION

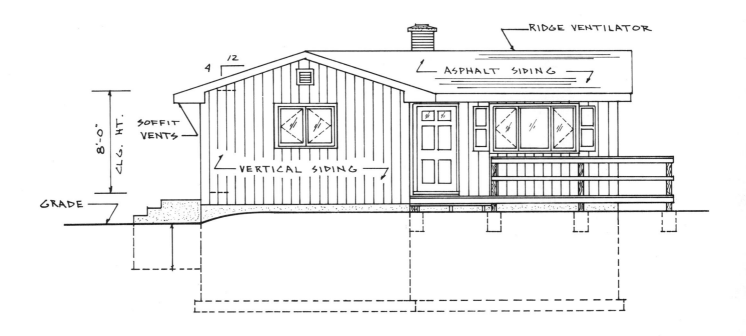

LEFT ELEVATION

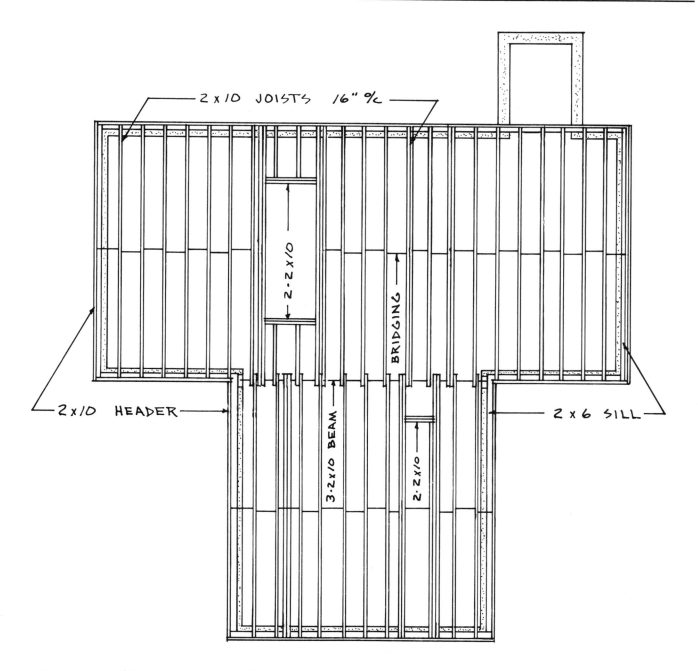

2 x 10 JOISTS 16" %

2 - 2 x 10

BRIDGING

2 x 10 HEADER

3 - 2 x 10 BEAM

2 - 2 x 10

2 x 6 SILL

FLOOR FRAMING PLAN

NOTE:
DOUBLE JOISTS UNDER
PARALLEL PARTITIONS.

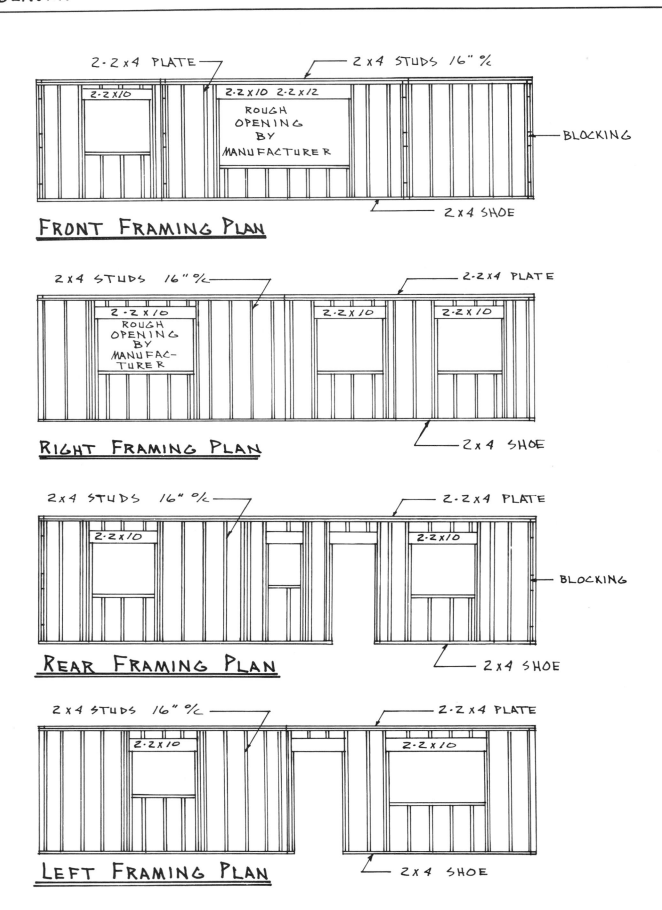

2·2x4 PLATE — — 2x4 STUDS 16" ℅

2·2x10

2·2x10 2·2x12
ROUGH
OPENING
BY
MANUFACTURER

BLOCKING

2x4 SHOE

FRONT FRAMING PLAN

2x4 STUDS 16" ℅ — — 2·2x4 PLATE

2·2x10
ROUGH
OPENING
BY
MANUFAC-
TURER

2·2x10

2·2x10

2x4 SHOE

RIGHT FRAMING PLAN

2x4 STUDS 16" ℅ — — 2·2x4 PLATE

2·2x10

2·2x10

BLOCKING

2x4 SHOE

REAR FRAMING PLAN

2x4 STUDS 16" ℅ — — 2·2x4 PLATE

2·2x10

2·2x10

2x4 SHOE

LEFT FRAMING PLAN

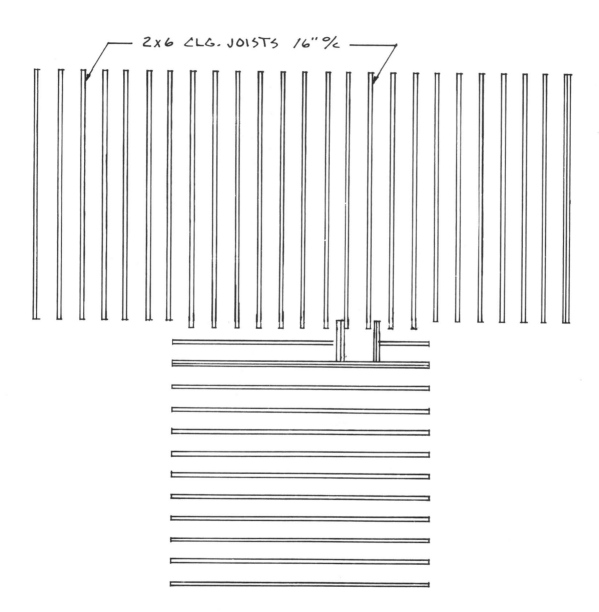

2x6 CLG. JOISTS 16" º/c

CEILING FRAMING PLAN

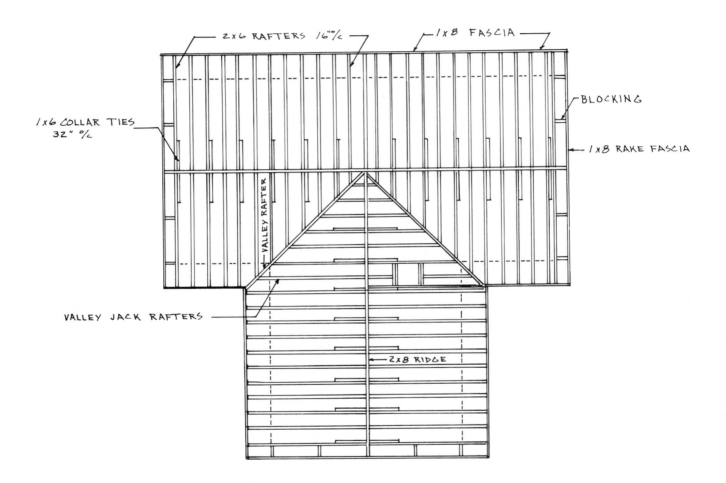

2x6 RAFTERS 16"°/c   1x8 FASCIA

BLOCKING

1x6 COLLAR TIES
32" °/c

VALLEY RAFTER

1x8 RAKE FASCIA

VALLEY JACK RAFTERS

2x8 RIDGE

ROOF FRAMING PLAN

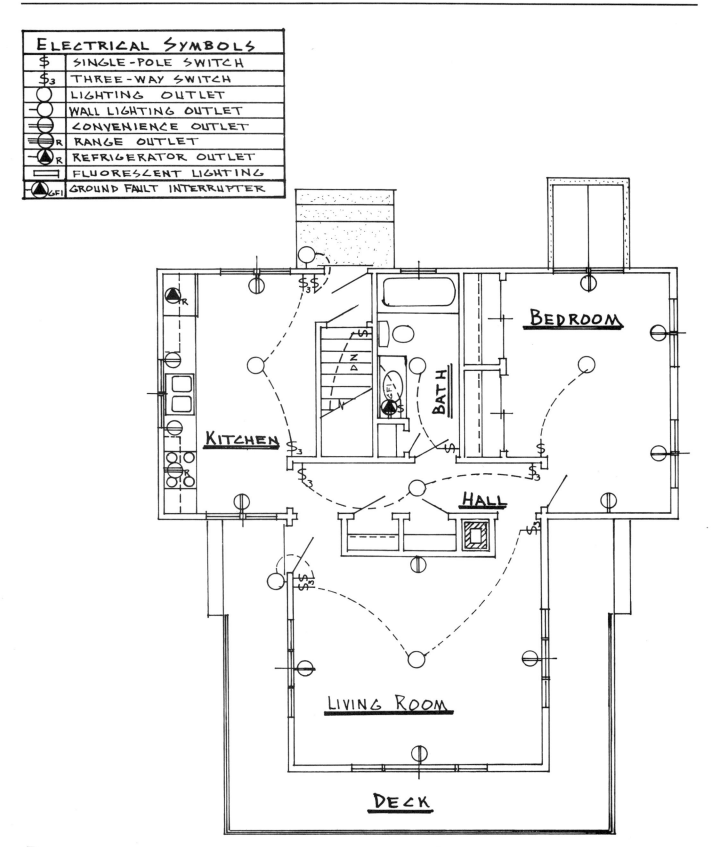

ELECTRICAL SYMBOLS

$	SINGLE-POLE SWITCH
$₃	THREE-WAY SWITCH
LIGHTING OUTLET
WALL LIGHTING OUTLET
CONVENIENCE OUTLET
RANGE OUTLET
REFRIGERATOR OUTLET
FLUORESCENT LIGHTING
GROUND FAULT INTERRUPTER

BEDROOM

BATH

KITCHEN

HALL

LIVING ROOM

DECK

ELECTRICAL LAYOUT

Door Schedule

SYM.	NO.	SIZE	TYPE
①	1	$3^0 \times 6^8$	PANEL-SOLID
②	1	$2^8 \times 6^8$	PANEL
③	5	$2^6 \times 6^8$	FLUSH-H.C.
④	1	$1^6 \times 6^8$	FLUSH-H.C.
⑤	2	$5^0 \times 6^8$	SLIDING-H.C.

Window Schedule

SYM.	NO.	SIZE	TYPE
A	1	$8^4 \times 4^7$	CSMT.
B	2	$6^4 \times 3^7$	CSMT.
C	5	$4^4 \times 3^7$	CSMT.
D	1	$4^4 \times 3^1$	CSMT.
E	1	$2^4 \times 3^1$	CSMT.
F	3	$2^8 \times 1^3$	BSMT. WIN.

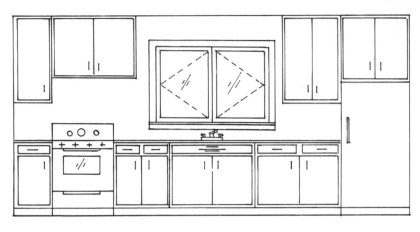

KITCHEN ELEVATION

STAIR DETAIL

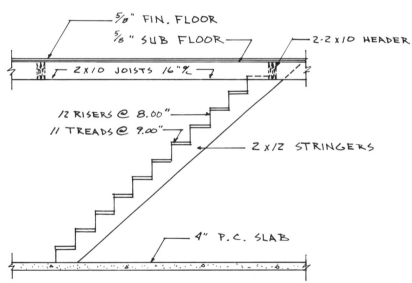

- $\frac{5}{8}$" FIN. FLOOR
- $\frac{5}{8}$" SUB FLOOR
- 2-2x10 HEADER
- 2x10 JOISTS 16"⁰⁄ᴄ
- 12 RISERS @ 8.00"
- 11 TREADS @ 9.00"
- 2x12 STRINGERS
- 4" P.C. SLAB

DECK DETAIL

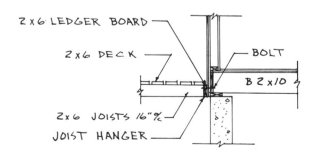

- 2x6 LEDGER BOARD
- 2x6 DECK
- BOLT
- B 2x10
- 2x6 JOISTS 16"⁰⁄ᴄ
- JOIST HANGER

THIS IS IT! THE 'WHAT
THE BENJIM WOULD
LOOK LIKE IF' PAGE.

BY ELIMINATING THE
CHIMNEY AND SHUTTERS
AND BY SUBSTITUTING
HORIZONTAL SIDING,
THE BENJIM WOULD LOOK
LIKE THIS.

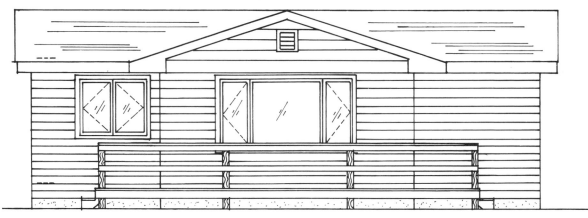

OR, IF YOU PREFER,
YOU COULD SUBSTITUTE
DOUBLE-HUNG WINDOWS,
ELIMINATE THE DECK
AND THE CHIMNEY....

... ADD A COUPLE OF
BASEMENT WINDOWS,
AND YOU WOULD HAVE
THE BENJIM LOOKING
LIKE THIS.

MATERIAL LIST

FLOOR SYSTEM

2 × 10 Joists	44/16 - 1/12
2 × 10 Header	7/16 - 2/8
2 × 6 Sill	7/16 - 2/8
Sill Seal	128 Lineal Feet
Anchor Bolts	16
1/2″ × 4′ × 8′ Ply	23 Sheets
Bridging	34 Pairs
3 1/2″ ⌀ Lally Col.	1/8
3-2 × 10 Beam	3/16

WALL SYSTEM

2 × 4 Shoe	7/16 - 2/8
2-2 × 4 Plate	14/16 - 4/8
2 × 4 Studs	129/8 - 3/12
Door Headers (2 × 10)	2/8
Win. Headers (2 × 12)	2/10
Win. Headers (2 × 10)	5/10 - 6/8
1/2″ × 4′ × 8′ Sheathing	29 Sheets
Building Paper	3 Rolls
3 1/2″ Insulation	11 Rolls
Siding	892 Square Feet

INTERIOR

2 × 4 Studs	66/8
Door Headers (2 × 6)	14/4
Door Headers (2 × 8)	4/6
1/2″ × 4′ × 8′ Sheetrock	33 Sheets
1″ × 12″ Shelving	4/6
Closet Pole	2/6 - 1/4

Baseboard	190 Lineal Feet
Ceiling Moulding	200 Lineal Feet

BASEMENT STAIRS

Treads (2 × 10)	3/12
Stringers (2 × 12)	2/14
Handrail	2/12

CEILING SYSTEM

Ceiling Joists (2 × 6)	37/16
Header (2 × 6)	7/16 - 2/8
6 1/2″ Insulation	744 Square Feet - 16 Rolls

ROOF SYSTEM

2 × 8 Ridge	2/12 - 1/10 - 1/14
2 × 6 Rafters	59/12
2 × 6 Valley Rafters	2/16
2 × 6 Valley Jack Rafters	4/12 - 6/14 - 3/10
1 × 6 Collar Ties	20/6
1/4″ × 24″ Soffit	84 Lineal Feet
1 × 8 Fascia	84 Lineal Feet
1/4″ × 12 Rake Soffit	63 Lineal Feet
1 × 8 Rake Fascia	63 Lineal Feet.
Roofing Felt	3 Rolls
1/2″ × 4′ × 8′ Ply.	29 Sheets
Asphalt Shingles	30 Bundles
Metal Drip Edge	9/10

DECK

2 × 6 Flooring	224 Square Feet
4 × 4 Posts	10/4
2 × 4 Railings	4/12 - 4/14
2 × 6 Cap	2/12 - 2/14
2 × 6 Joist Hangers	43

Article I

Preconstruction Phase

If you are planning to build a house, you probably assume that there are governing bodies which have rules and regulations pertaining to house size limits, lot size, health, and environment in regard to residential dwellings.

You also probably wonder which agency you should contact, why you should contact it, and when. Let's assume that you're going to build one of the houses in this book on a piece of land you already own. What's your first step? Where do you go? Whom do you see?

It is advisable to take a trip to the town hall in the town in which you will build and talk to the town clerk. He will be able to refer you to the proper agencies and commissions with whom you will need to deal, including the planning commission, planning/zoning commission, inland/wetlands commission, health department, and the building inspector.

PLANNING COMMISSION

Before you build, you should contact the planning commission. This commission usually is composed of appointed or elected members whose goal is to protect the best interests of the town.

Talk to the members of the planning commission and explain what you plan to do, what you plan to build, and when you plan to build it. They will usually offer guidance and suggestions concerning the needed size of the building lot for the desired size and placement of the house.

Although the rules of the planning commission are governed by the state, there are few instances when the planning commission will not approve residential construction.

PLANNING/ZONING COMMISSION

If you live in an area that has zoning, you will not have to contact the planning commission; instead, you will have to contact the planning/zoning commission. This agency has more power to enforce its rules and regulations than the planning commission does.

For example, if you plan to operate a business out of your home after it is built, you should check with the zoning commission first. The area in which you are building might not be zoned for home business.

INLANDS/WETLANDS COMMISSION

In the event that wetlands exist on your property, you will be referred to the inlands/wetlands commission. The members of this commission will instruct you to build a certain distance from the wetlands. They will also stipulate that your septic system be located a safe distance from the wetlands.

HEALTH DEPARTMENT

Before you build that dream house of yours, you will need to have a percolation test done. This test is also known as a perk test or seepage test.

The health department must get involved in matters pertaining to septic systems and the like. After you inform the department of health that you are building a house and wish to install a septic system, the department will send you an Application for Service, which you are to fill out and return.

Some of the questions to be answered on the application are:

- Is any part of the property a designated wetland?
- Do any easements exist on the property?
- Is the property within 1/8 mile of a sewer line?
- Is a sewer line proposed?
- What is the type of structure (residential, commercial, farm, church, industrial, etc.)?

After you answer these questions and state whether the soil test is to be for a new sewage disposal, repair of an existing disposal system, or a proposed subdivision (fees will vary), return the application with the required fee and a plot plan of the property.

At an agreed-upon time, a representative of the department of health will perform the perk test on your property. You are expected to have a backhoe and a backhoe operator there during this time.

An 8-foot hole is dug with the backhoe, in which the representative will make smaller perk holes. Water is placed in these perk holes, and the rate of water seepage is recorded to determine the suitability of the soil for a rate system.

If the rate of water seepage is too slow or too fast, approval will not be granted. In which case, you will need an engineered system. Such a system must be designed by a registered engineer.

After the septic system has been installed, a representative from the department of health will inspect it before it is covered.

The department of health also stipulates the distances from the septic system to the house, the septic system to the well, and the amount of property needed for the septic system.

Where a well is required for new construction, a water analysis and a Well Permit and Well Completion Report, which is obtained from the driller, must be in the hands of the department of health before an Occupancy Report can be obtained from the building official.

BUILDING INSPECTOR

After you have contacted the planning commission, the inlands/wetlands commission, and the department of health to determine the particulars of building on your property, you should approach the local building inspector with a set of plans of your proposed house. It is his job to make sure that construction in his area meets all code requirements. He should have had experience in one of the building trades.

If you obtained building plans which were drawn in another state, they should be made to conform to the code requirements of the state and town where you plan to build.

It is the building inspector's responsibility to make on-site inspections at various times during construction. It is his job to:

- Inspect the footing before the foundation wall is poured.
- Inspect the plumbing before the concrete floor is poured, in cases where plumbing is located beneath a concrete floor.
- Inspect electrical service.
- Inspect rough plumbing and electrical wiring.
- Conduct a final inspection, after which a Certificate of Occupancy is issued.

Section II

Ranch-Style Homes

ERNRAY

DESIGNED & DRAWN BY E. BRYANT

The Ernray is a 26-foot-×-42-foot ranch-style house with 1092 square feet of living space.

The walls consist of 2-×-6 studs spaced every 24 inches. The increased stud size allows for increased wall insulation.

The roof consists of pre-engineered trusses, also spaced every 24 inches, which make it possible to increase the thickness of insulation in the attic. The use of insulation in the floor system, which consists of 2-×-10 joists spaced every 24 inches, is another energy-saving option.

The exterior of the dwelling has shuttered double-hung windows on the front and horizontal siding throughout.

A fireplace dominates the right interior wall of the living room, while a double-hung picture window occupies the front wall.

An I-shaped kitchen and a dining room are accessible from the living room. Three bedrooms with plenty of closet space complete the floor plan of this one-story residential dwelling.

NOTES:
1) STRUCTURAL CHANGES SHOULD NOT BE MADE WITHOUT CONSULTING ARCHITECT/CONTRACTOR.

2) WOOD FRAMING MEM-BERS TO HAVE A FIBER STRESS OF 1200 PSI.

3) WOOD FRAMING TO BE KEPT 2" CLEAR OF FIREPLACE MASONRY.

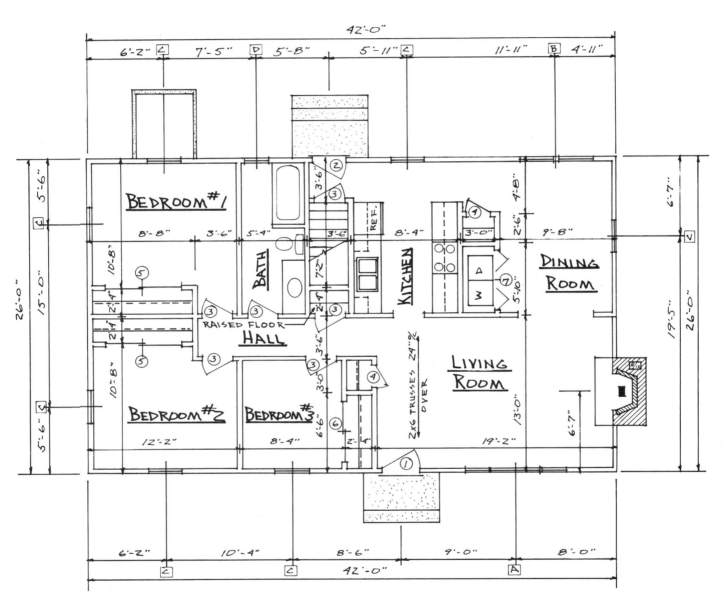

FLOOR PLAN

NOTES:
1) FIREPLACE FOOTING TO BE 12" THICK; EXTEND 6".

2) BASEMENT ENTRY FOUNDATION TO CONFORM TO MANUFACTURER SPECIFICATIONS.

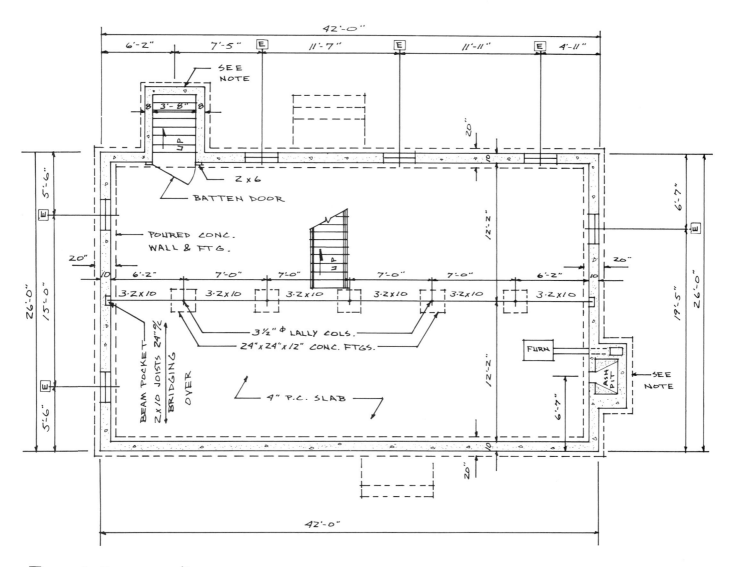

FOUNDATION PLAN

DOOR SCHEDULE			
SYM	QTY	SIZE	TYPE
1	1	$3^0 \times 6^8$	PANEL-S.C.
2	1	$2^8 \times 6^8$	PANEL-S.C
3	6	$2^6 \times 6^8$	FLUSH-H.C.
4	2	$2^0 \times 6^8$	FLUSH-H.C.
5	2	$6^0 \times 6^8$	SLDG.-H.C.
6	1	$5^0 \times 6^8$	SLDG.-H.C.
7	1	$5^0 \times 6^8$	BI-FOLD

WINDOW SCHEDULE			
SYM	QTY	SIZE	TYPE
A	1	$2^{04} 2^0 \times 4^2$	D.H.P.W.
B	1	$2 \cdot 2^8 \times 3^{10}$	D.H. MULL.
C	7	$2^8 \times 3^{10}$	D.H.
D	1	$2^0 \times 3^2$	D.H.
E	6	$2^8 \times 1^4$	BSMT.

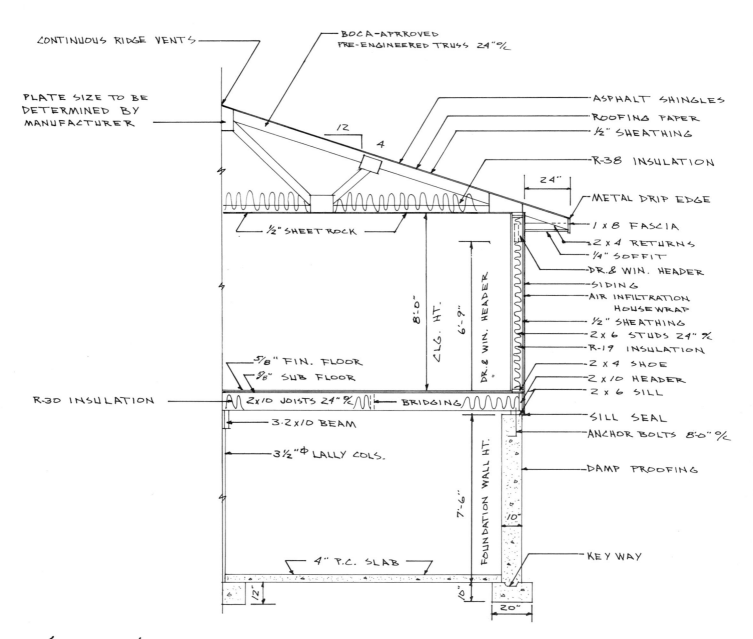

STAFF SECTION

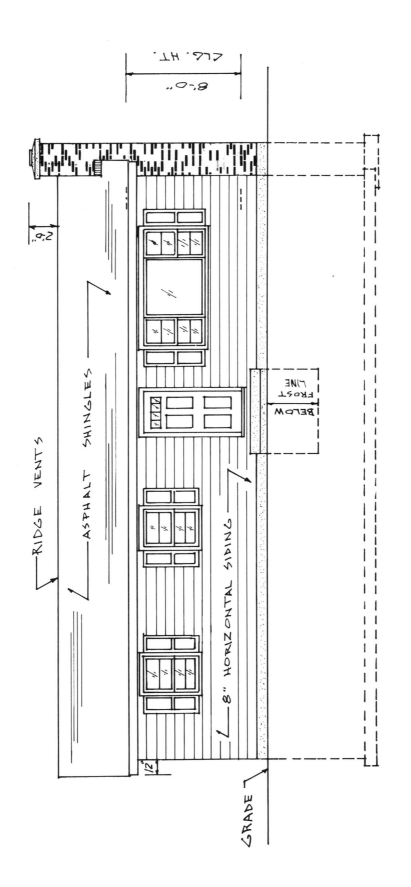

FRONT ELEVATION

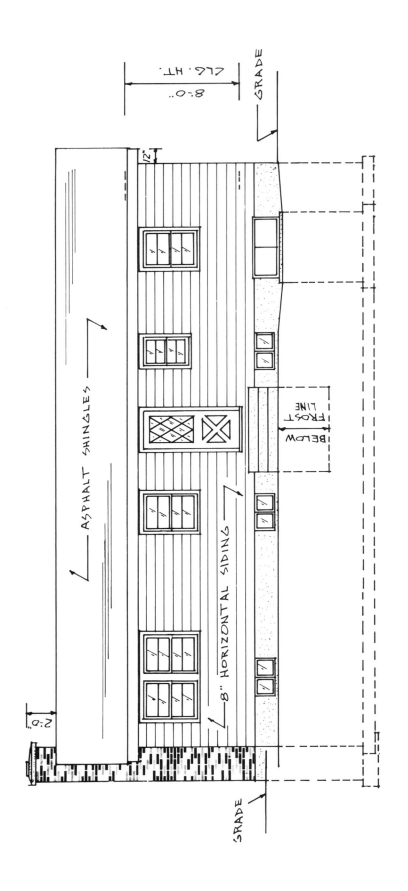

REAR ELEVATION

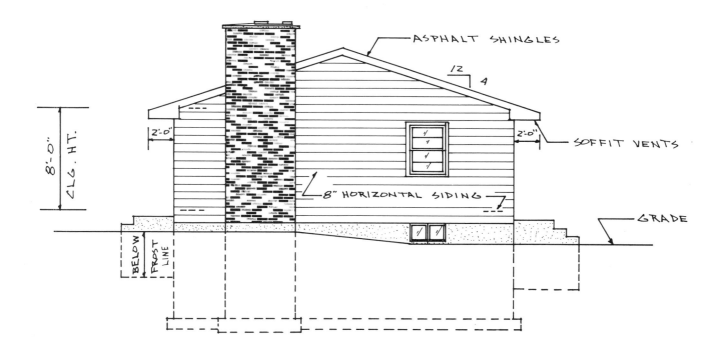

ASPHALT SHINGLES

12
4

2'-0"

SOFFIT VENTS

8'-0" CLG. HT.

2'-0"

8" HORIZONTAL SIDING

GRADE

BELOW FROST LINE

RIGHT ELEVATION

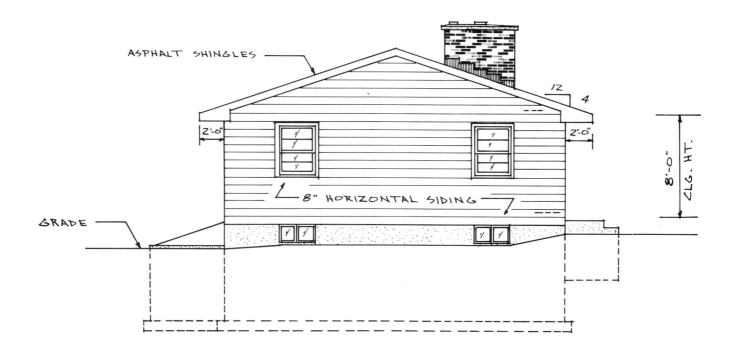

ASPHALT SHINGLES

12
4

2'-0"

2'-0"

8'-0" CLG. HT.

8" HORIZONTAL SIDING

GRADE

LEFT ELEVATION

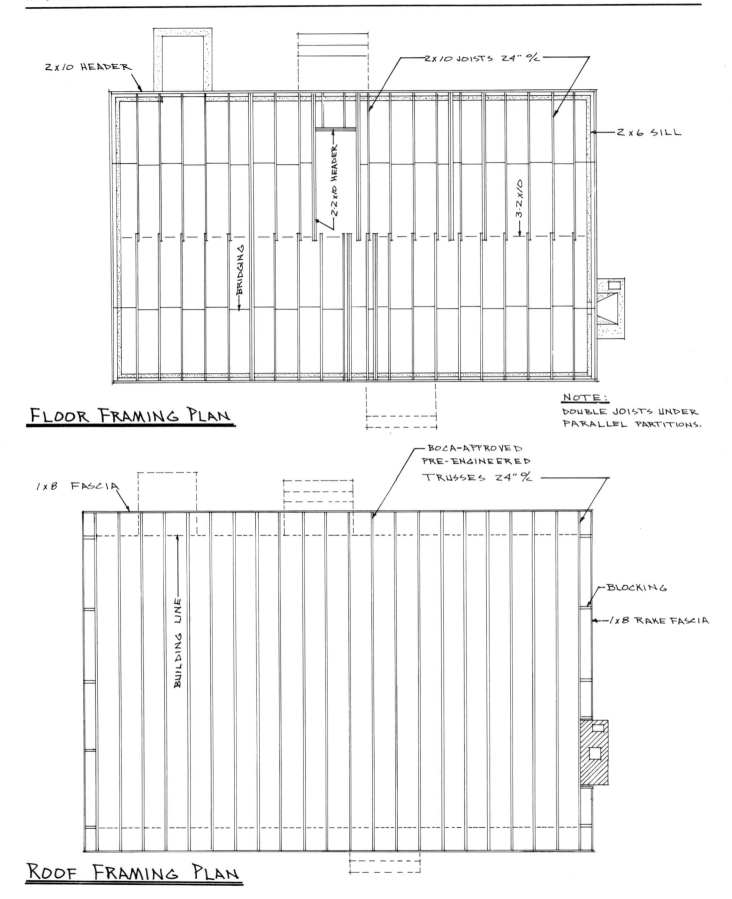

FLOOR FRAMING PLAN

2x10 HEADER

2x10 JOISTS 24" %

2x6 SILL

2-2x10 HEADER

BRIDGING

3-2x10

NOTE:
DOUBLE JOISTS UNDER
PARALLEL PARTITIONS.

ROOF FRAMING PLAN

1x8 FASCIA

BOCA-APPROVED
PRE-ENGINEERED
TRUSSES 24" %

BUILDING LINE

BLOCKING

1x8 RAKE FASCIA

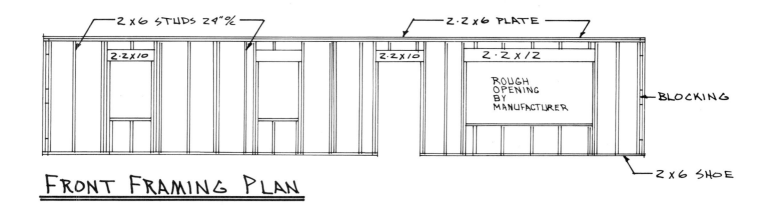

2 X 6 STUDS 24" ⁰⁄꜀   2·2 X 6 PLATE

2·2 X 10   2·2 X 10   2·2 X 12

ROUGH
OPENING
BY
MANUFACTURER

BLOCKING

2 X 6 SHOE

FRONT FRAMING PLAN

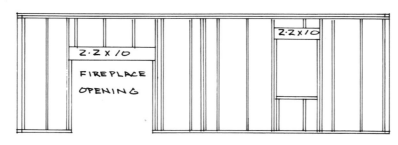

2·2 X 10   2·2 X 10

FIREPLACE
OPENING

RIGHT FRAMING PLAN

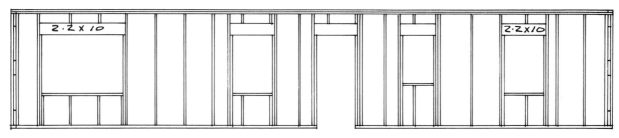

2·2 X 10   2·2 X 10

REAR FRAMING PLAN

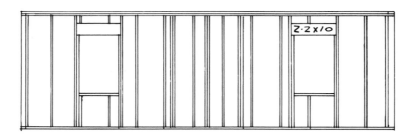

2·2 X 10

LEFT FRAMING PLAN

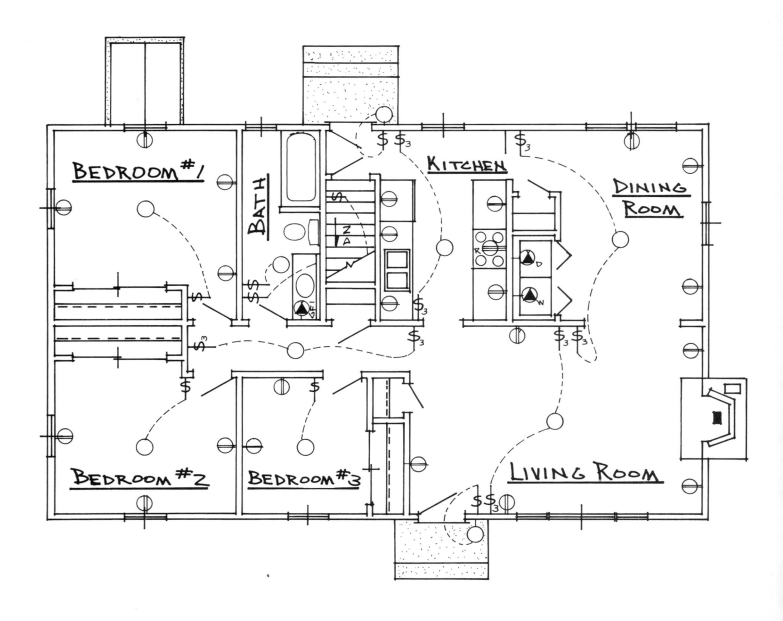

ELECTRICAL LAYOUT

ELECTRICAL SYMBOLS	
SYM	ITEM
$	SINGLE-POLE SWITCH
$₃	THREE-WAY SWITCH
⊖	DUPLEX OUTLET
⊖ᵣ	RANGE OUTLET
△ᵥ	WASHER OUTLET
△ᴅ	DRYER OUTLET
△ᴳᶠᴵ	GROUND FAULT INTERRUPTER
◯	LIGHTING OUTLET
▭	FLUORESCENT LIGHTING

MATERIAL LIST

FLOOR SYSTEM

2 × 10 Joists----------------------52/14
2 × 10 Header--------------------2/12 - 8/14
2 × 6 Sill----------------------------2/12 - 8/14
Sill Seal-----------------------------136 Lineal Feet
Anchor Bolts-----------------------16
1/2" × 4' × 8' Plywood------33 Sheets
Bridging-----------------------------43 Pairs
3 1/2" ⌀ Lally Columns---------5/8
3-2 × 10 Beam--------------------9/14
Insulation----------------------------1016 Square Feet

WALL SYSTEM

2 × 6 Shoe-----------------------2/12 - 8/14
2-2 × 6 Plate--------------------4/12 - 16/14
2 × 6 Studs-----------------------119/8 - 1/10
2 × 10 Door Headers----------1/14
Window Headers (2 × 10)----4/14 - 1/12 (2×12) 2/10
1/2" × 4' × 8' Sheathing----32 Sheets
R-19 Insulation--------------------12 Rolls
Siding---------------------------------1010 Square Feet
Fireplace Header (2 × 10)---1/12
Air Infiltration Housewrap------1010 Square Feet

CEILING SYSTEM

R-38 Insulation----------------------1040 Square Feet

ROOF SYSTEM

1/4" × 24" Soffit----------------------11/8
1 × 8 Fascia----------------------------11/8
1/4" × 12" Rake Soffit----------58 Lineal Feet
1 × 8" Rake Fascia---------------58 Lineal Feet
Roofing Felt--------------------------2 Rolls
1/2" × 4' × 8' Plywood---------19 Sheets
Asphalt Shingles---------------------20 Bundles
BOCA Approved
Pre-engineered Trusses----------22

INTERIOR

2 × 4 Studs----------------------------176/8
Door Headers (2-2 × 6)----------5/12 - 1/10 - 4/8 - 1/6
1/2" × 4' × 8' Sheetrock------94 Sheets
1" × 12" Shelving----------------6/8
Closet Pole----------------------------3/8 - 1/4
Baseboard----------------------------342 Lineal Feet
Ceiling Moulding---------------------451 Lineal Feet

BASEMENT STAIRS

2 × 12 Stringers--------------------2/14
2 × 10 Treads----------------------3/12
Handrail-------------------------------2/12

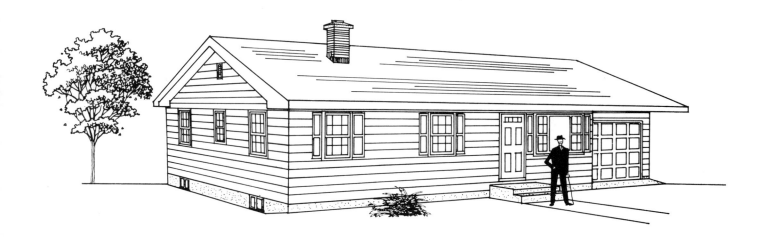

DESIGNED & DRAWN BY E. BRYANT

The Garen is a one-story ranch-style with an attached one-car garage. Excluding the garage, this residential dwelling has 1149 square feet of living space.

The floor plan of the Garen is a well-planned layout of convenience. The centrally located kitchen, which has been designed for convenience, is adjacent to the dining area and accessible through a cafe door.

A ceiling beam separates the dining area from the living area. Interior access to the garage is also made from the dining area.

For the growing family, this structure also features three bedrooms, each with ample closet space, a full bath, and a washer and dryer.

Double-hung windows and horizontal siding accent the exterior of this ranch-style house.

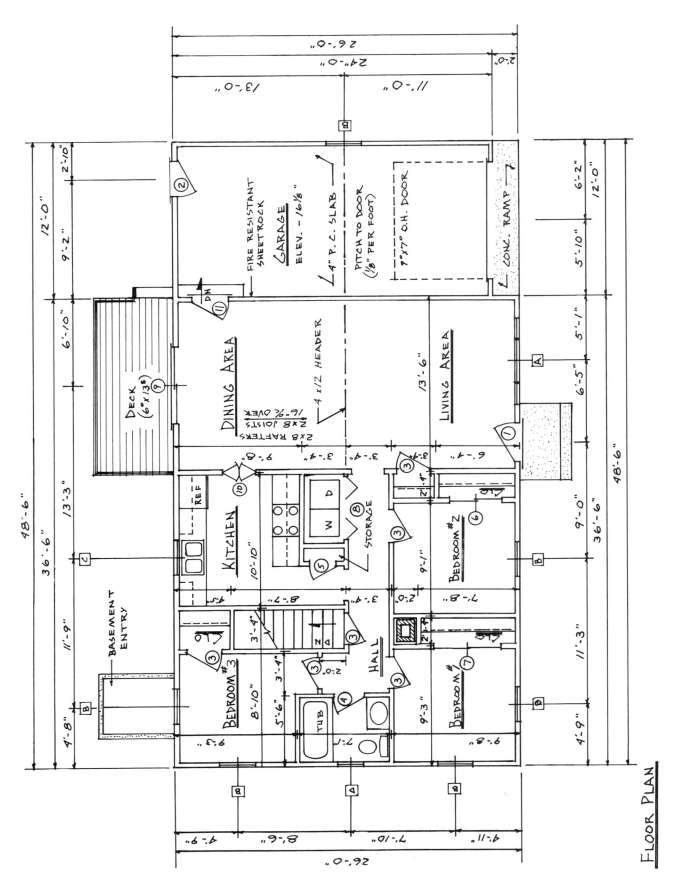

FLOOR PLAN

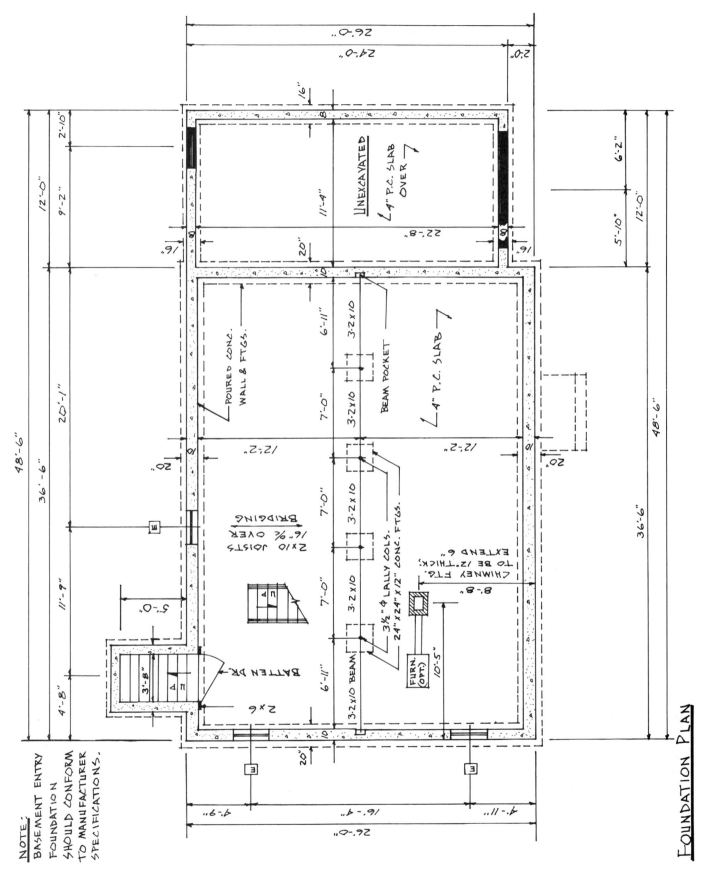

NOTE:
BASEMENT ENTRY
FOUNDATION
SHOULD CONFORM
TO MANUFACTURER
SPECIFICATIONS.

FOUNDATION PLAN

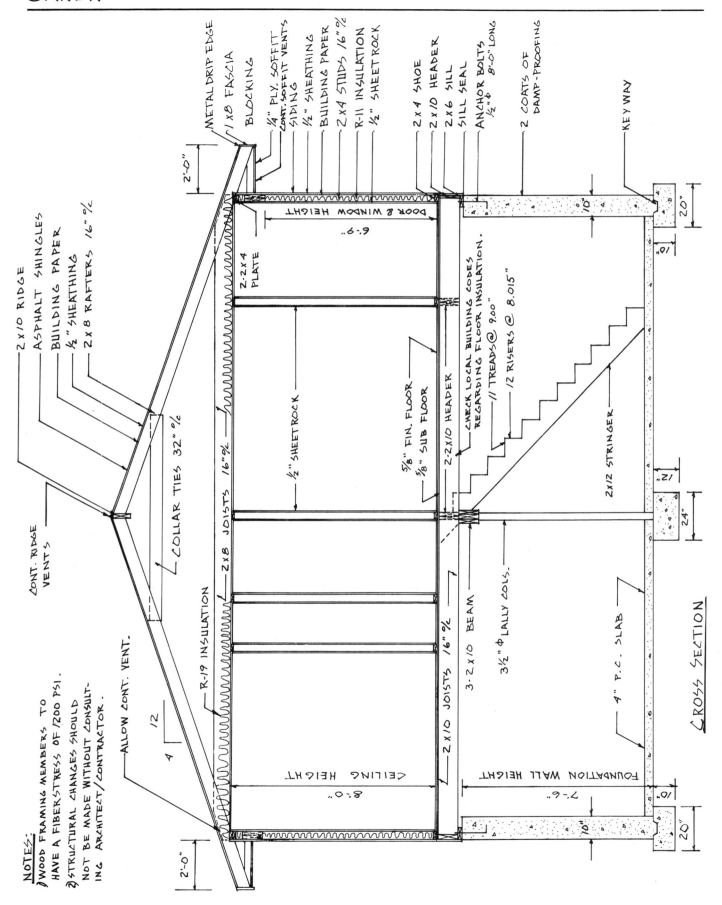

NOTES:
1) WOOD FRAMING MEMBERS TO HAVE A FIBER-STRESS OF 1200 PSI.
2) STRUCTURAL CHANGES SHOULD NOT BE MADE WITHOUT CONSULTING ARCHITECT/CONTRACTOR.

CROSS SECTION

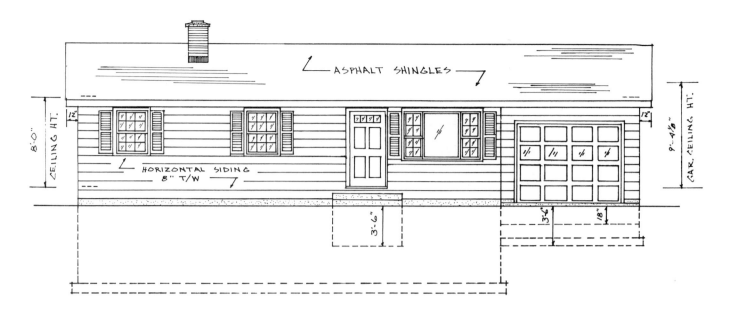

ASPHALT SHINGLES

HORIZONTAL SIDING
8" T/W

8'-0" CEILING HT.

9'-4⅛" GAR. CEILING HT.

12"

3'-6"

3'-6"

18"

FRONT ELEVATION

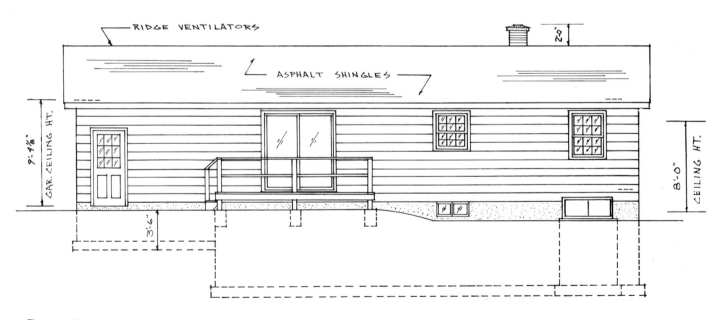

RIDGE VENTILATORS

ASPHALT SHINGLES

2'-0"

9'-4⅛" GAR. CEILING HT.

8'-0" CEILING HT.

3'-6"

REAR ELEVATION

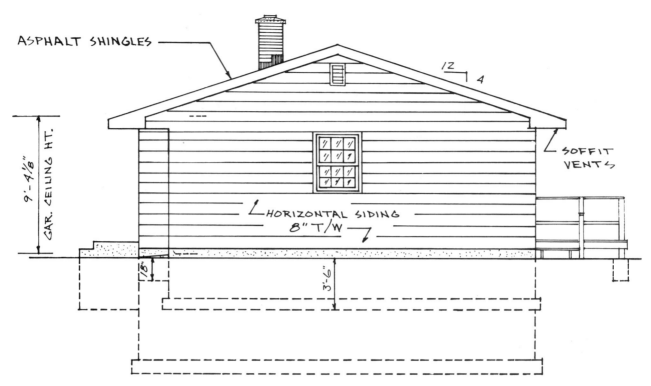

ASPHALT SHINGLES

12 ⌐ 4

SOFFIT VENTS

9'-4⅛" GAR. CEILING HT.

HORIZONTAL SIDING
8" T/W

18"

3'-6"

RIGHT ELEVATION

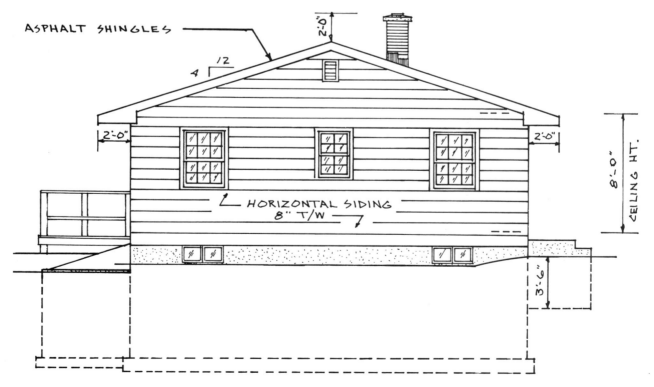

ASPHALT SHINGLES

2'-0"

4 ⌐ 12

2'-0"

2'-0"

8'-0" CEILING HT.

HORIZONTAL SIDING
8" T/W

3'-6"

LEFT ELEVATION

84

NOTES:
1) DOUBLE JOISTS UNDER PARALLEL PARTITIONS.
2) JOISTS SHOULD OVERLAP

A MINIMUM OF 4".

3) WOOD FRAMING TO BE KEPT 2" CLEAR OF CHIMNEY MASONRY.

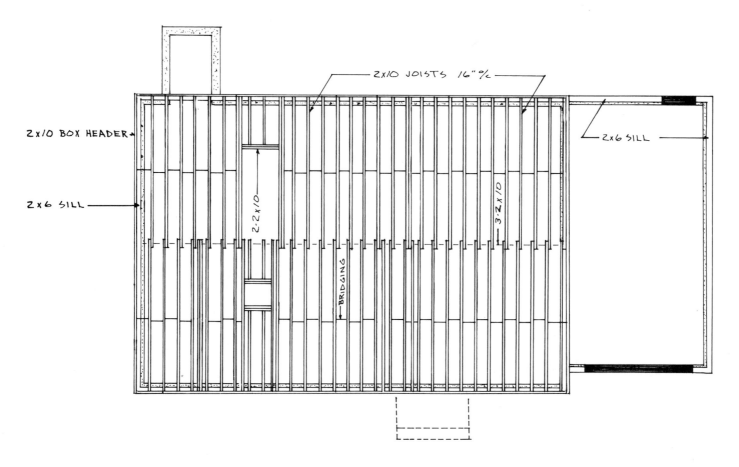

2x10 JOISTS 16" %

2x6 SILL

2x10 BOX HEADER

2x6 SILL

2-2x10

3-2x10

BRIDGING

FLOOR FRAMING PLAN

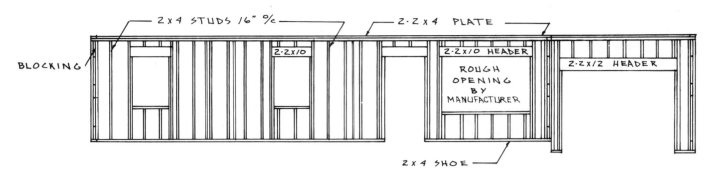

FRONT FRAMING PLAN

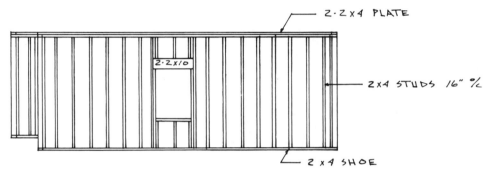

RIGHT FRAMING PLAN

REAR FRAMING PLAN

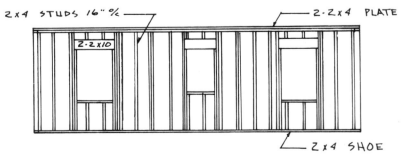

LEFT FRAMING PLAN

WINDOW SCHEDULE

SYM.	NO.	SIZE	TYPE
A	1	1^8-3^4-1^8 x 4^2	PW
B	6	2^8 x 3^{10}	DH
C	1	2^8 x 3^2	DH
D	1	2^0 x 3^2	DH
E	3	2^8 x 1^4	BSMT.

DOOR SCHEDULE

SYM.	NO.	SIZE	TYPE
1	1	3^6 x 6^8	PANEL
2	1	2^8 x 6^8	PANEL
3	6	2^6 x 6^8	FLUSH
4	1	2^4 x 6^8	FLUSH
5	1	2^0 x 6^8	FLUSH
6	1	4^0 x 6^8	SLIDING (FL.)
7	1	5^0 x 6^8	BI-FOLD
8	1	5^0 x 6^8	SLIDING
9	1	6^0 x 6^8	SLIDING
10	1	2^6 x 3^8	CAFE
11	1	2^8 x 6^8	FIRE DR.

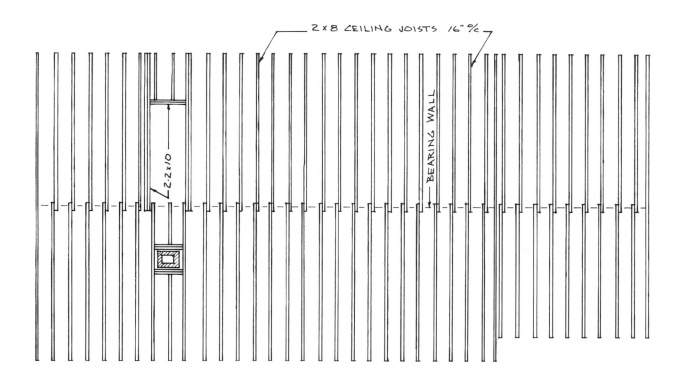

2 X 8 CEILING JOISTS 16" %c

BEARING WALL

2-2 X 10

CEILING FRAMING PLAN

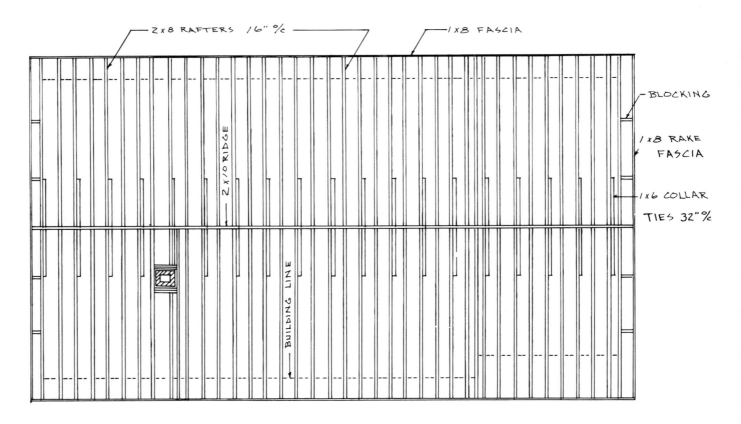

2x8 RAFTERS 16" %c   1x8 FASCIA

BLOCKING

1x8 RAKE FASCIA

1x6 COLLAR TIES 32" %c

2x10 RIDGE

BUILDING LINE

ROOF FRAMING PLAN

ELECTRICAL SYMBOLS

⊖	DUPLEX OUTLET
⊖	DUPLEX OUTLET - SPLIT WIRED
⊖R	RANGE OUTLET
▲D	DRYER OUTLET
▲W	WASHER OUTLET
▲GFI	GROUND FAULT INTERRUPTER

ELECTRICAL SYMBOLS

$	SINGLE POLE SWITCH
$₃	THREE-WAY SWITCH
$₄	FOUR-WAY SWITCH
◯	LIGHTING OUTLET
⊣◯	WALL LIGHT OUTLET
▭	FLUORESCENT LIGHT

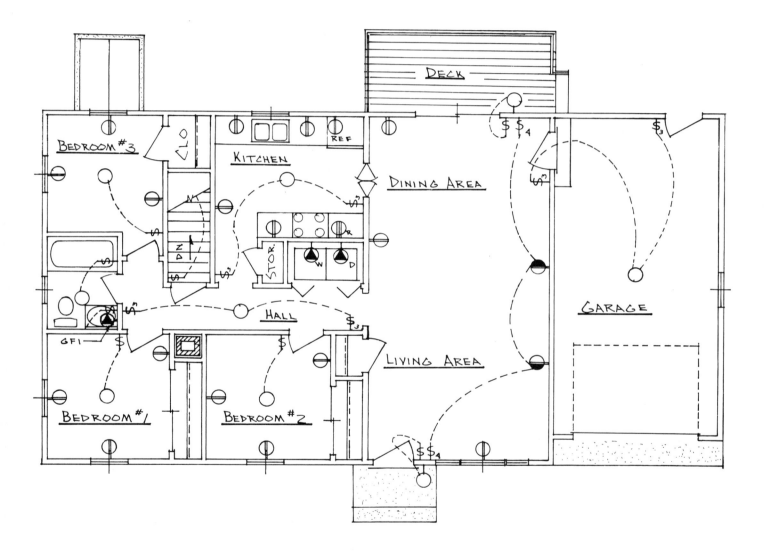

ELECTRICAL LAYOUT

MATERIAL LIST

FLOOR SYSTEM

2 × 10 Joists	69/14
2 × 10 Header	3/14 - 5/12
2 × 6 Sill	149 Lineal Feet 3/14 - 5/12
Sill Seal	149 Lineal Feet
Anchor Bolts	20
1/2" × 4' × 8' Plywood	31 Sheets
Bridging	53 Pairs
3 1/2" Ø Lally Columns	4/8
3-2 × 10 Beam	3/14 - 6/12

WALL SYSTEM

2 × 4 Shoe	3/14 - 5/12
2-2 × 4 Plate	6/14 - 10/12
2 × 4 Studs	99/8
Door Headers	
2 × 12	2/10
2 × 10	4/4 - 2/8
Window Headers (2 × 10)	16/4 - 2/8
1/2" × 4' × 8' Sheathing	31 Sheets
3 1/2" Insulation	11 Rolls
Siding	972 Square Feet
Air Infiltration Housewrap	972 Square Feet

GARAGE

2 × 6 Sill	3/12 - 1/6
2 × 4 Shoe	3/12 - 1/6
2 × 4 Studs	40/10
2 × 8 Header	3/12 - 1/6
Fireproof Sheetrock	(4 × 10) 9 Sheets
Ceiling Joists	(2 × 8) 9/14 - 9/12

CEILING SYSTEM

2 × 8 Ceiling Joists	57/14
6 1/2" Insulation	20 Rolls

ROOF SYSTEM

2 × 8 Ridge	2/14 - 2/12
2 × 6 Rafters	80/16
1 × 6 Collar Ties	19
3/8" × 24" Soffit	88 Lineal Feet
1" × 8" Fascia	88 Lineal Feet
3/8" × 12" Rake Soffit	64 Lineal Feet
1" × 8" Rake Fascia	64 Lineal Feet
Roofing Felt	4 Rolls
1/2" × 4' × 8' Plywood	51 Sheets
Asphalt Shingles	50 Bundles
3/8" × 36" Soffit	13 Lineal Feet
Metal Drip Edge	11/10

INTERIOR

2 × 4 Studs	145/8
Door Headers	
(2-2 × 6)	20/4 - 6/6
1/2" × 4' × 8' Sheetrock	94 Sheets
1" × 12" Shelving	1/8 - 1/6 - 1/4 - 1/6
Closet Pole	1/8 - 1/6 - 1/3
Baseboard	199 Lineal Feet
Ceiling Moulding	199 Lineal Feet
Header (4" × 12' × 26')	3/14 - 3/12

BASEMENT STAIRS

2 × 12 Stringers	2/14
Treads (2 × 10)	3/12
Handrail	2/12

DECKS

Flooring	84 Square Feet
4 × 4 Posts	3/6
Railings (2 × 4)	40 Lineal Feet
Cap (2 × 6)	20 Lineal Feet

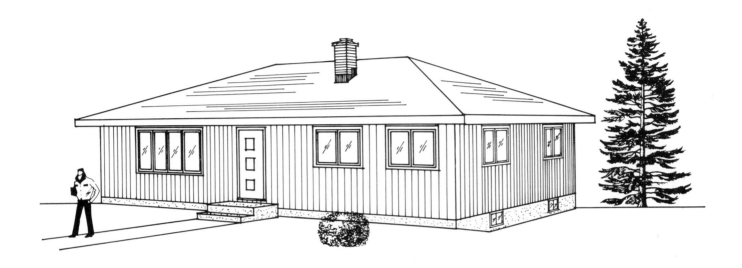

BARRETINA

DESIGNED & DRAWN BY E. BRYANT

The Barretina is a one-story house with a hip roof. Vertical siding and casement windows enhance the exterior of this residential structure.

The large living room is separated from the dining room by a six-foot arch. A patio door gives access from the dining room to an outside deck.

A U-shaped kitchen is located between the dining room and the washer and dryer. Situated near the full-bath are two bedrooms with ample closet space.

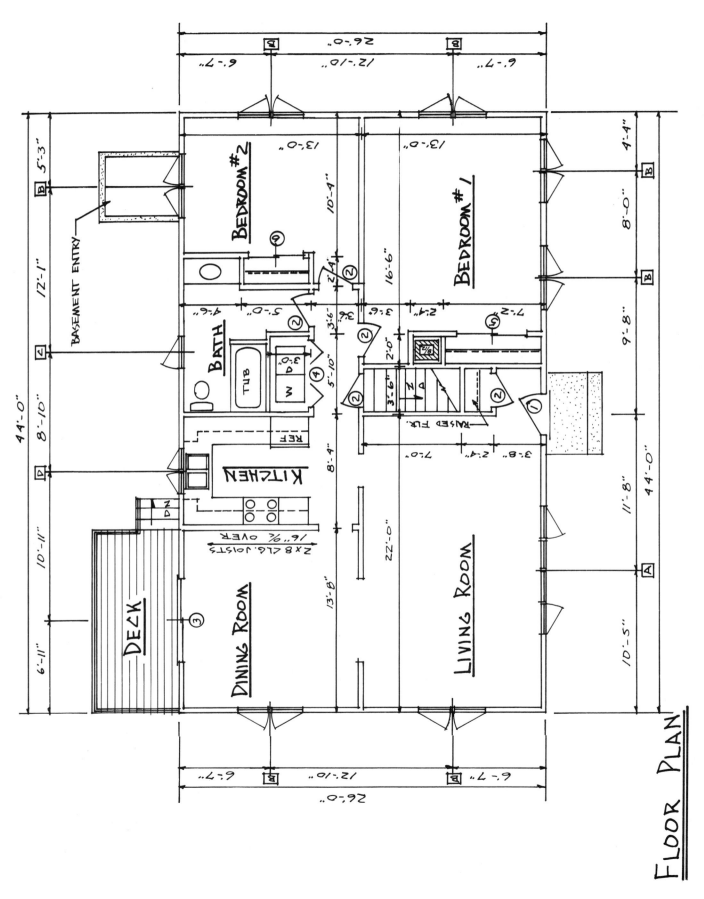

FLOOR PLAN

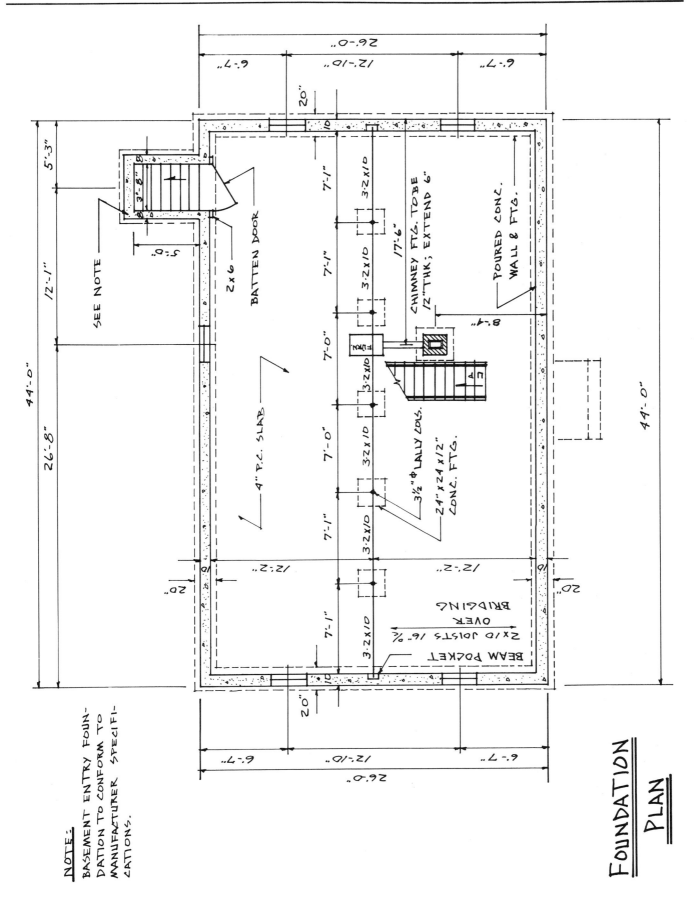

NOTE:
BASEMENT ENTRY FOUNDATION TO CONFORM TO MANUFACTURER SPECIFICATIONS.

SEE NOTE

2x6

BATTEN DOOR

4" P.C. SLAB

3-2x10

3-2x10

3-2x10

3-2x10

3-2x10

3-2x10

3-2x10

CHIMNEY FTG. TO BE 12" THK; EXTEND 6"

POURED CONC. WALL & FTG.

3½"Ø LALLY COLS.

24"x24x12" CONC. FTG.

BEAM POCKET

2x10 JOISTS 16" O/C OVER BRIDGING

5'-3"

12'-1"

26'-8"

44'-0"

3'-8"

5'-0"

26'-0"

6'-7"

12'-10"

6'-7"

20"

10

7'-1"

7'-1"

7'-0"

7'-0"

7'-1"

7'-1"

17'-6"

8'-4"

44'-0"

20"

10

12'-2"

12'-2"

16

20"

26'-0"

6'-7"

12'-10"

6'-7"

20"

10

FOUNDATION
PLAN

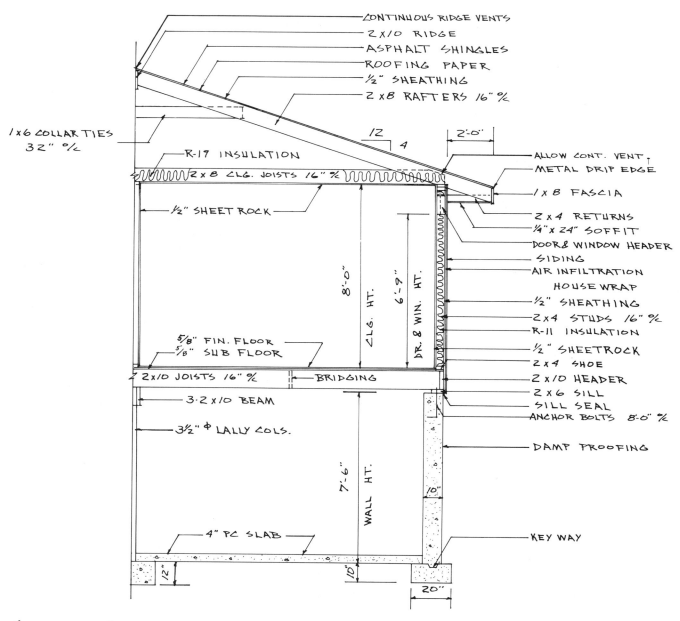

STAFF SECTION

NOTES:

1) STRUCTURAL CHANGES SHOULD NOT BE MADE WITH-OUT CONSULTING ARCHITECT/CONTRACTOR.

2) WOOD FRAMING MEMBERS TO HAVE A FIBER STRESS OF 1200 PSI.

3) CHECK LOCAL BUILDING CODE REGARDING FLOOR INSULATION.

DOOR SCHEDULE

SYM	QTY	SIZE	TYPE
①	1	$3^0 \times 6^8$	PANEL- S.C.
②	5	$2^6 \times 6^8$	FLUSH- H.C.
③	1	$6^0 \times 6^8$	PATIO DR.
④	1	$5^0 \times 6^8$	BI-FOLD
⑤	1	$5^0 \times 6^8$	FLUSH- H.C.
⑥	1	$4^0 \times 6^8$	FLUSH- H.C.

WINDOW SCHEDULE

SYM	QTY	SIZE	TYPE
A	1	$9^4 \times 4^6$	CSMT.
B	7	$4^8 \times 3^4$	CSMT.
C	1	$2^4 \times 3^4$	CSMT.
D	1	$3^4 \times 3^0$	CSMT.
E	1	$2^8 \times 1^4$	BSMT

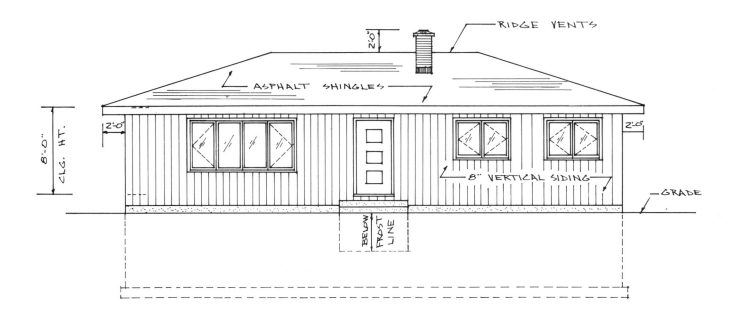

RIDGE VENTS

ASPHALT SHINGLES

2'-0"

8'-0" CLG. HT.

2'-0"

2'-0"

8" VERTICAL SIDING

GRADE

BELOW FROST LINE

Front Elevation

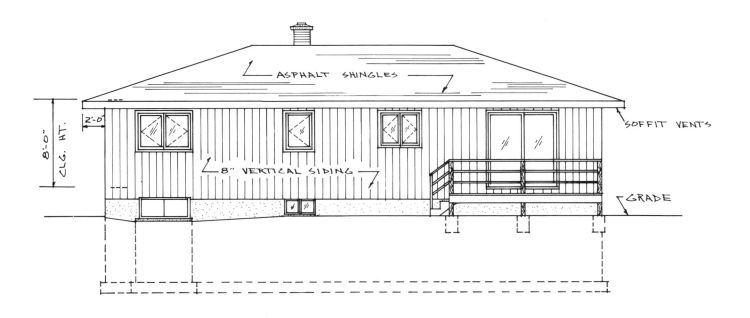

ASPHALT SHINGLES

SOFFIT VENTS

8'-0" CLG. HT.

2'-0"

8" VERTICAL SIDING

GRADE

Rear Elevation

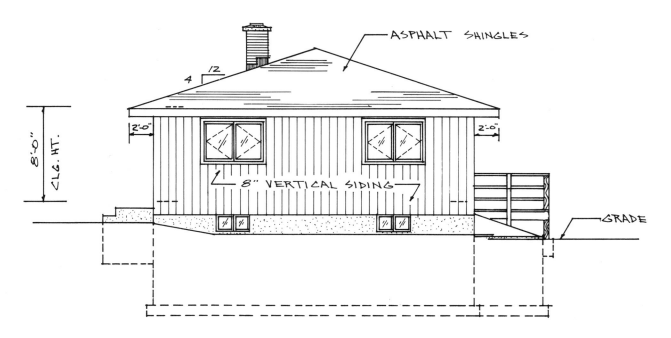

RIGHT ELEVATION

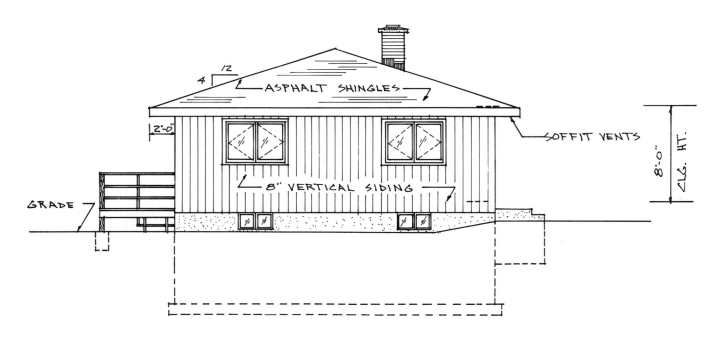

LEFT ELEVATION

NOTES:
1) DOUBLE JOISTS UNDER PARALLEL PARTITIONS.

2) WOOD FRAMING

TO BE KEPT 2" CLEAR OF CHIMNEY MASONRY.

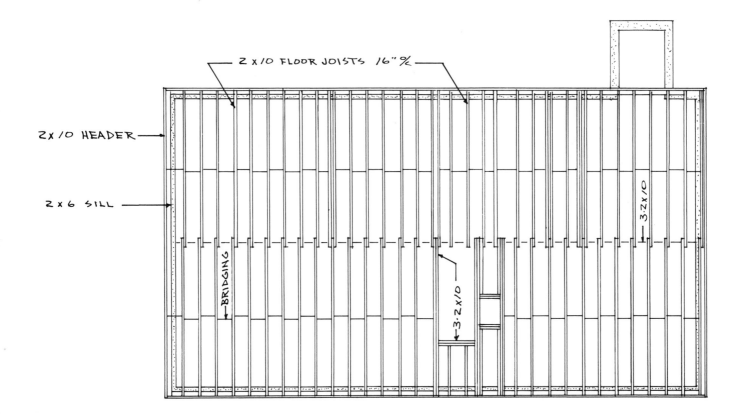

2 X 10 FLOOR JOISTS 16" ⁰∕ᶜ

2X 10 HEADER

2 X 6 SILL

BRIDGING

3·2X/0

3·2X/0

FLOOR FRAMING PLAN

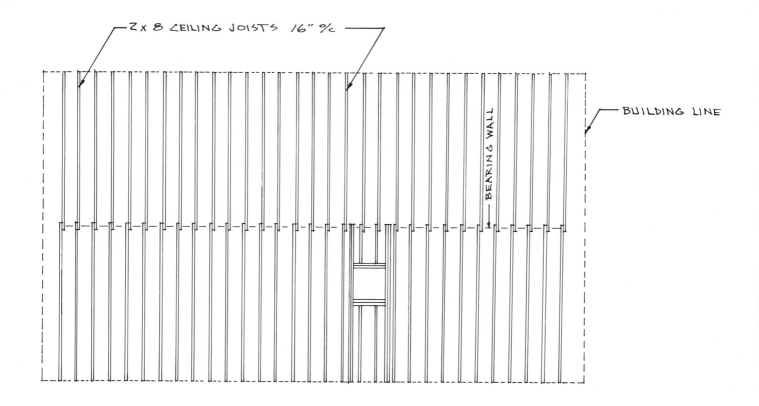

2 x 8 CEILING JOISTS 16" %

BEARING WALL

BUILDING LINE

CEILING FRAMING PLAN

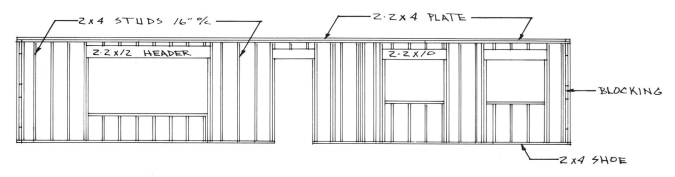

FRONT FRAMING PLAN

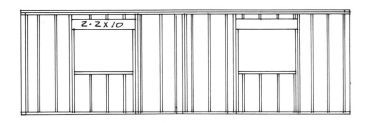

LEFT FRAMING PLAN

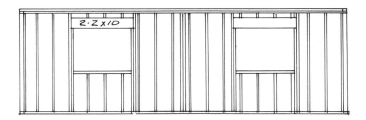

RIGHT FRAMING PLAN

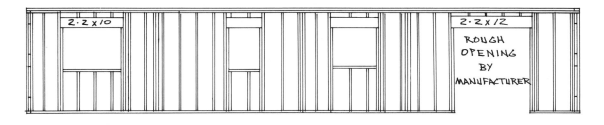

REAR FRAMING PLAN

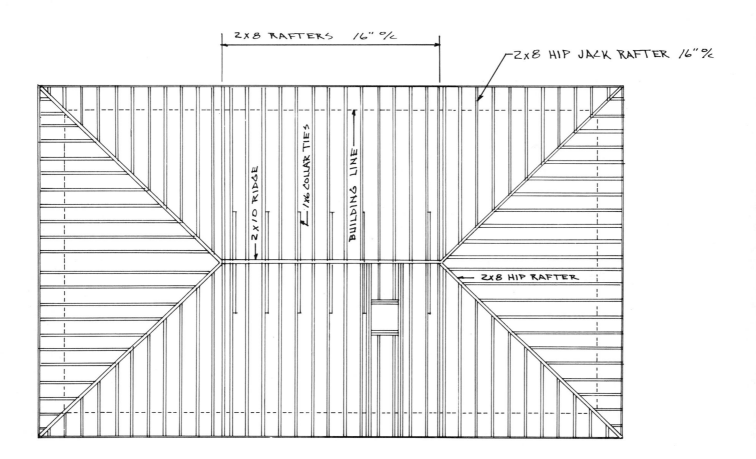

2X8 RAFTERS   16" %c

2x8 HIP JACK RAFTER 16" %c

2X10 RIDGE

1X6 COLLAR TIES

BUILDING LINE

2X8 HIP RAFTER

ROOF FRAMING PLAN

ELECTRICAL SYMBOLS

SYM	ITEM
$	SINGLE-POLE SWITCH
$₃	THREE-WAY SWITCH
	DUPLEX OUTLET
R	RANGE OUTLET
	SPLIT-WIRED OUTLET
GFI	GROUND FAULT INTERRUPTER
W	WASHER OUTLET
D	DRYER OUTLET
	LIGHTING OUTLET
	FLUORESCENT LIGHTING

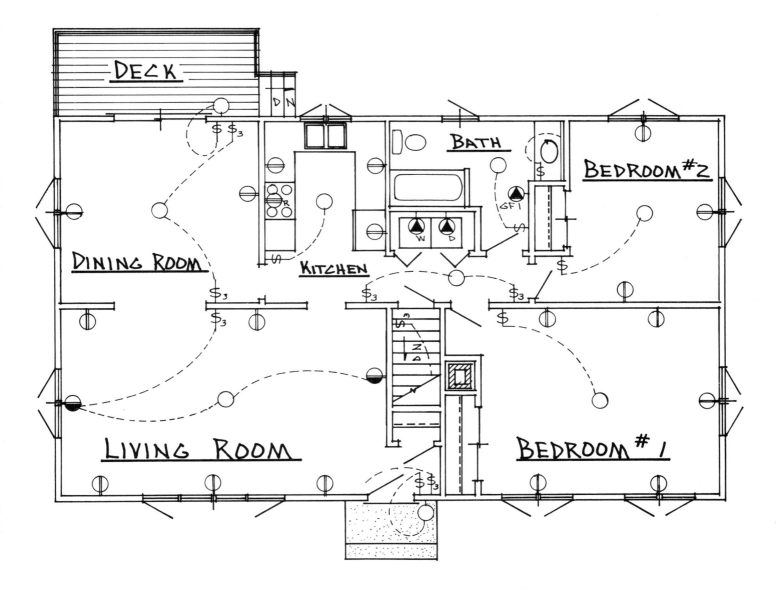

ELECTRICAL LAYOUT

MATERIAL LIST

FLOOR SYSTEM
2 × 10 Joists	72/14
2 × 10 Header	2/16 - 6/14 - 2/12
2 × 6 Sill	2/16 - 6/14 - 2/12
Sill Seal	140 Lineal Feet
Anchor Bolts	17
1/2" × 4' × 8' Plywood	35 Sheets
Bridging	60 Pairs
3 1/2" ⌀ Lally Columns	5/8
3-2 × 10 Beam	5/14—4/16

WALL SYSTEM
2 × 4 Shoe	2/16 - 6/14 - 2/12
2-2 × 4 Plate	4/16 - 12/14 - 4/12
2 × 4 Studs	137/8 - 7/10
Door Headers	
2 × 12	1/14
2 × 10	1/8
Window Headers	
2 × 12	2/10
2 × 10	7/10 - 1/8 - 1/6
1/2" × 4' × 8' Sheathing	30 Sheets
R-11 Insulation	11 Rolls
Siding	946 Square Feet
Air Infiltration Housewrap	946 Square Feet

CEILING SYSTEM
2 × 8 Ceiling Joists	64/14 - 3/10
R-19 Insulation	24 Rolls

ROOF SYSTEM
2 × 10 Ridge	1/18
2 × 8 Rafters	34/16 - 1/10
2 × 8 Hip Rafters	8/12
2 × 8 Hip Jack Rafters	20/14 - 4/12 - 26/10 - 7/8
1 × 6 Collar Ties	6/10
1/4" × 24" Soffit	20/8
1 × 8 Fascia	156 Lineal Feet
#15 Roofing Felt	3 Rolls
1/2" × 4' × 8' Plywood	32 Sheets
Asphalt Shingles	34 Bundles

INTERIOR
2 × 4 Studs	153/8
2 × 8 Door Headers	7/6 - 1/14 - 2/12 - 1/10
1/2" × 4' × 8' Sheetrock	94 Sheets
1" × 12" Shelving	2/8
Closet Pole	2/8
Baseboard	193 Lineal Feet
Ceiling Moulding	277 Lineal Feet

BASEMENT STAIRS
2 × 12 Stringers	2/14
2 × 10 Treads	3/12
Handrail	2/14

DECK
Flooring	84 Square Feet
4 × 4 Posts	3/6
Railings	75 Lineal Feet

ARLIN

DESIGNED & DRAWN BY E. BRYANT

The Arlin is a one-story ranch-style house with an attached one-car garage. It has 960 square feet of living area, excluding the garage.

Brick veneer enhances the front of the dwelling, while horizontal siding is displayed throughout the rest of the structure.

The dining area, which is readily accessible to the kitchen and living room, has access to a spacious deck.

A washer and dryer are located in the midst of three bedrooms, which have ample closet space. The design of the full bath and the location of the kitchen sink allow for back-to-back plumbing.

The brick veneer, the shuttered double-hung windows, and the distinctive garage doors add a sense of individuality to this residential dwelling.

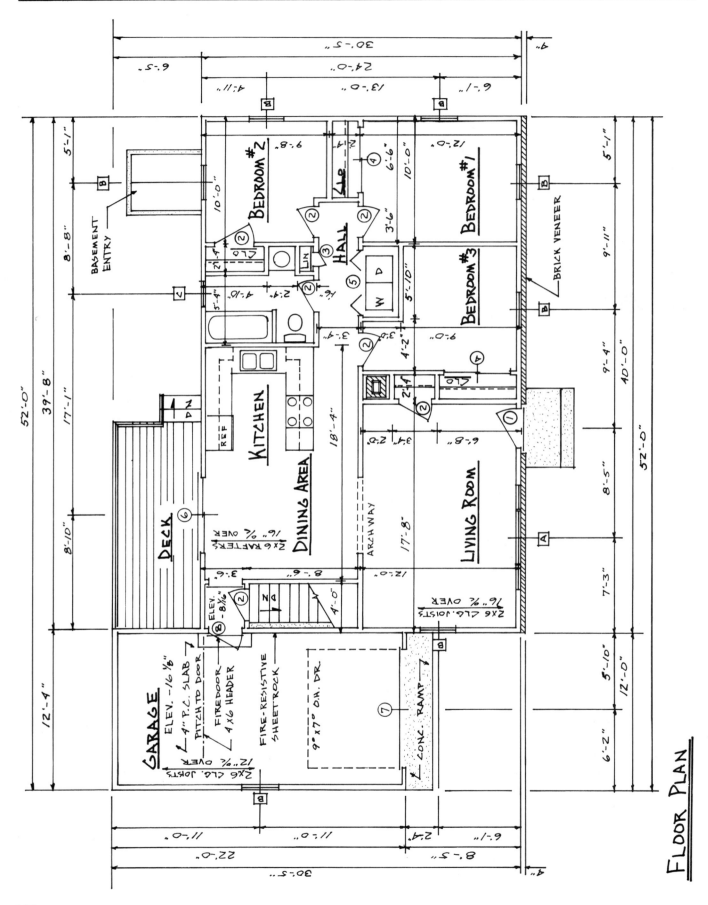

FLOOR PLAN

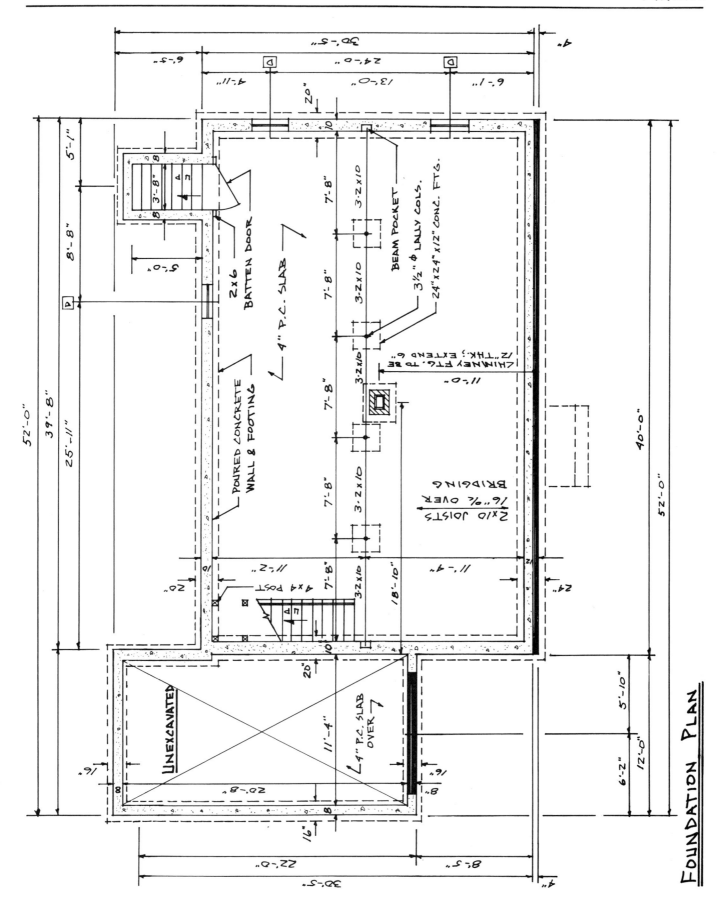

FOUNDATION PLAN

UNEXCAVATED

POURED CONCRETE WALL & FOOTING

2x6 BATTEN DOOR

4" P.C. SLAB

BEAM POCKET

3½" Ø LALLY COLS.

24"x24"x12" CONC. FTG.

CHIMNEY FTG. TO BE 12" THK., EXTEND 6"

2x10 JOISTS 16"%, OVER BRIDGING

4x4 POST

4" P.C. SLAB OVER

3-2x10

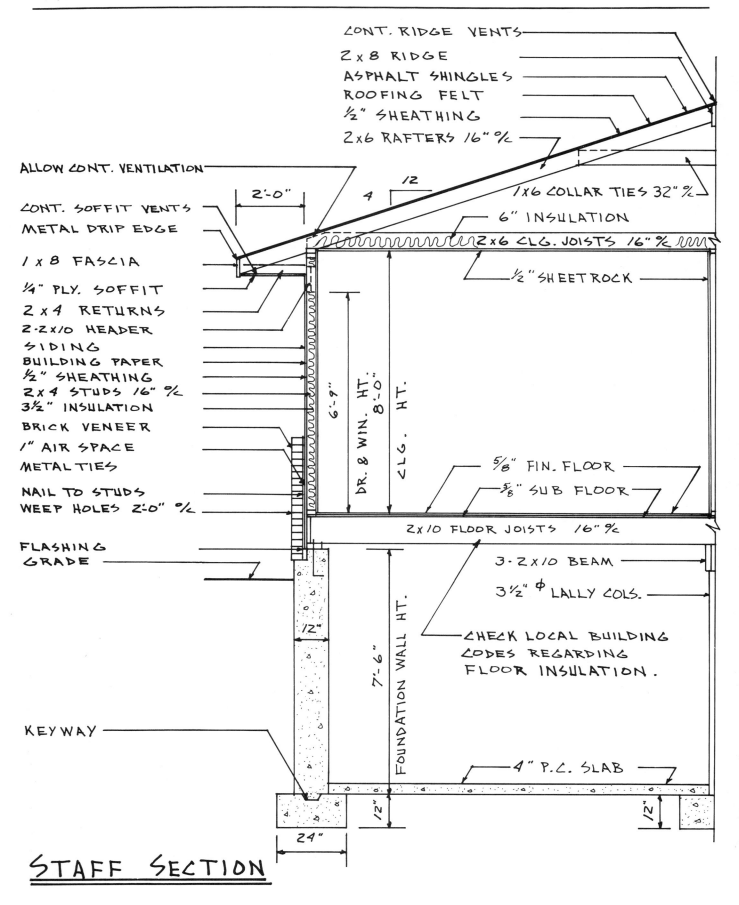

CONT. RIDGE VENTS
2 x 8 RIDGE
ASPHALT SHINGLES
ROOFING FELT
½" SHEATHING
2 x 6 RAFTERS 16" O/C

ALLOW CONT. VENTILATION

1 x 6 COLLAR TIES 32" O/C

6" INSULATION

2 x 6 CLG. JOISTS 16" O/C

CONT. SOFFIT VENTS
METAL DRIP EDGE

1 x 8 FASCIA

¼" PLY. SOFFIT
2 x 4 RETURNS
2 - 2 x 10 HEADER
SIDING
BUILDING PAPER
½" SHEATHING
2 x 4 STUDS 16" O/C
3½" INSULATION
BRICK VENEER
1" AIR SPACE
METAL TIES

NAIL TO STUDS
WEEP HOLES 2'-0" O/C

FLASHING
GRADE

KEYWAY

½" SHEETROCK

DR. & WIN. HT. 6'-9"

CLG. HT. 8'-0"

⅝" FIN. FLOOR
⅝" SUB FLOOR

2 x 10 FLOOR JOISTS 16" O/C

3 - 2 x 10 BEAM

3½" ∅ LALLY COLS.

CHECK LOCAL BUILDING
CODES REGARDING
FLOOR INSULATION.

FOUNDATION WALL HT. 7'-6"

12"

4" P.C. SLAB

12"

12"

24"

2'-0"

4   12

STAFF SECTION

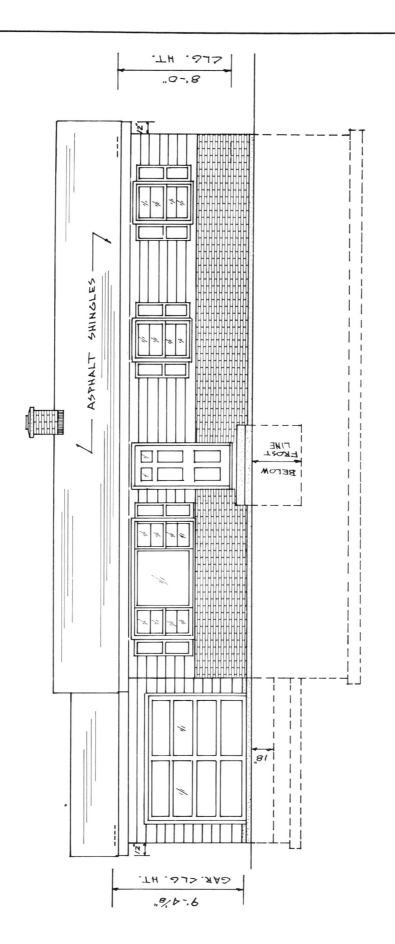

FRONT ELEVATION

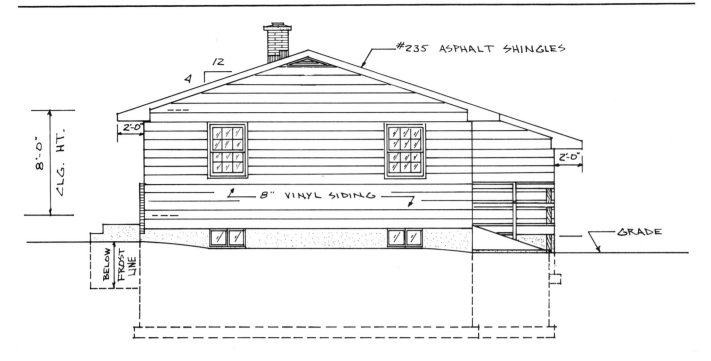

RIGHT ELEVATION

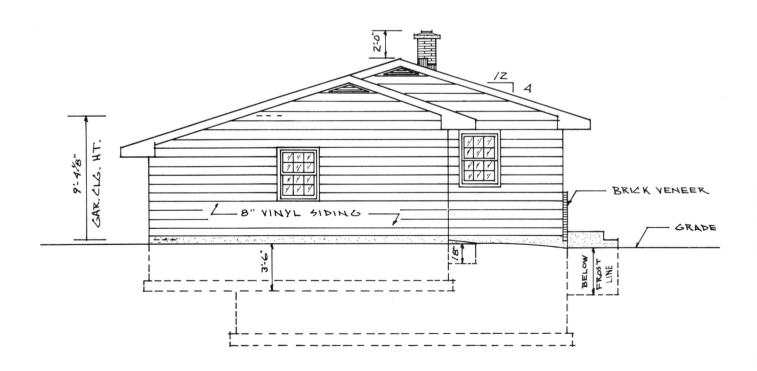

LEFT ELEVATION

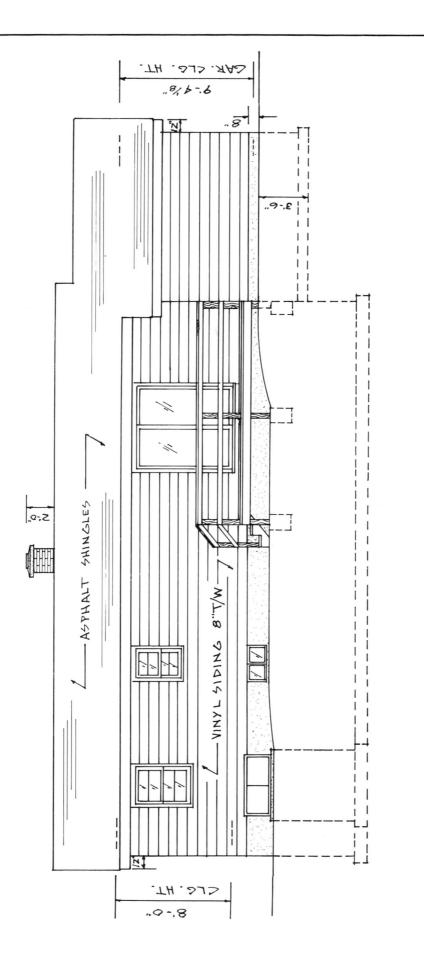

REAR ELEVATION

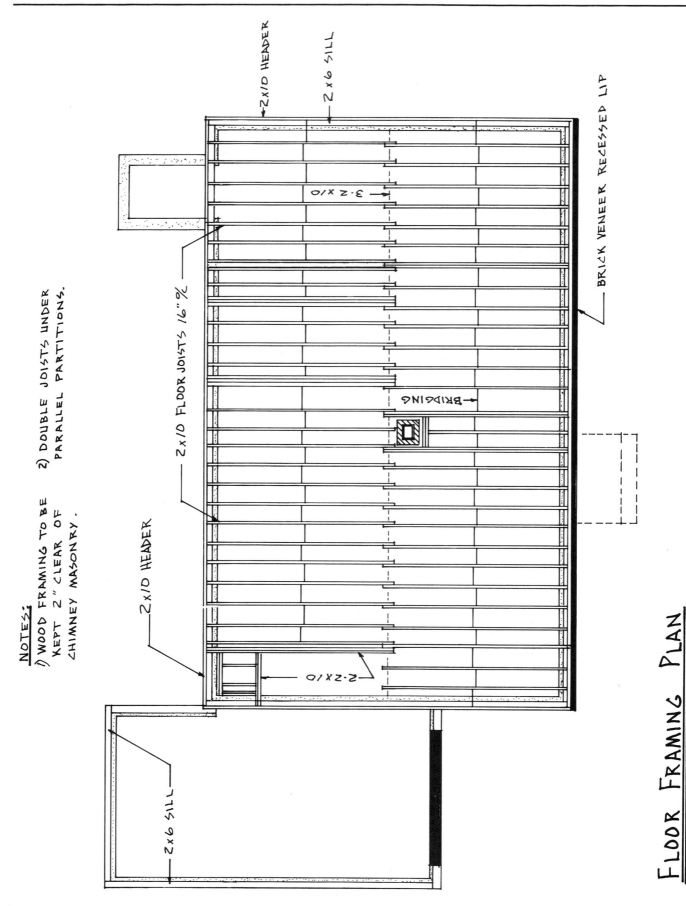

NOTES;
1) WOOD FRAMING TO BE KEPT 2" CLEAR OF CHIMNEY MASONRY.
2) DOUBLE JOISTS UNDER PARALLEL PARTITIONS.

2x10 HEADER

2x6 SILL

2x10 HEADER

2x6 SILL

BRICK VENEER RECESSED LIP

2x10 FLOOR JOISTS 16" %

3-2x10

BRIDGING

2-2x10

FLOOR FRAMING PLAN

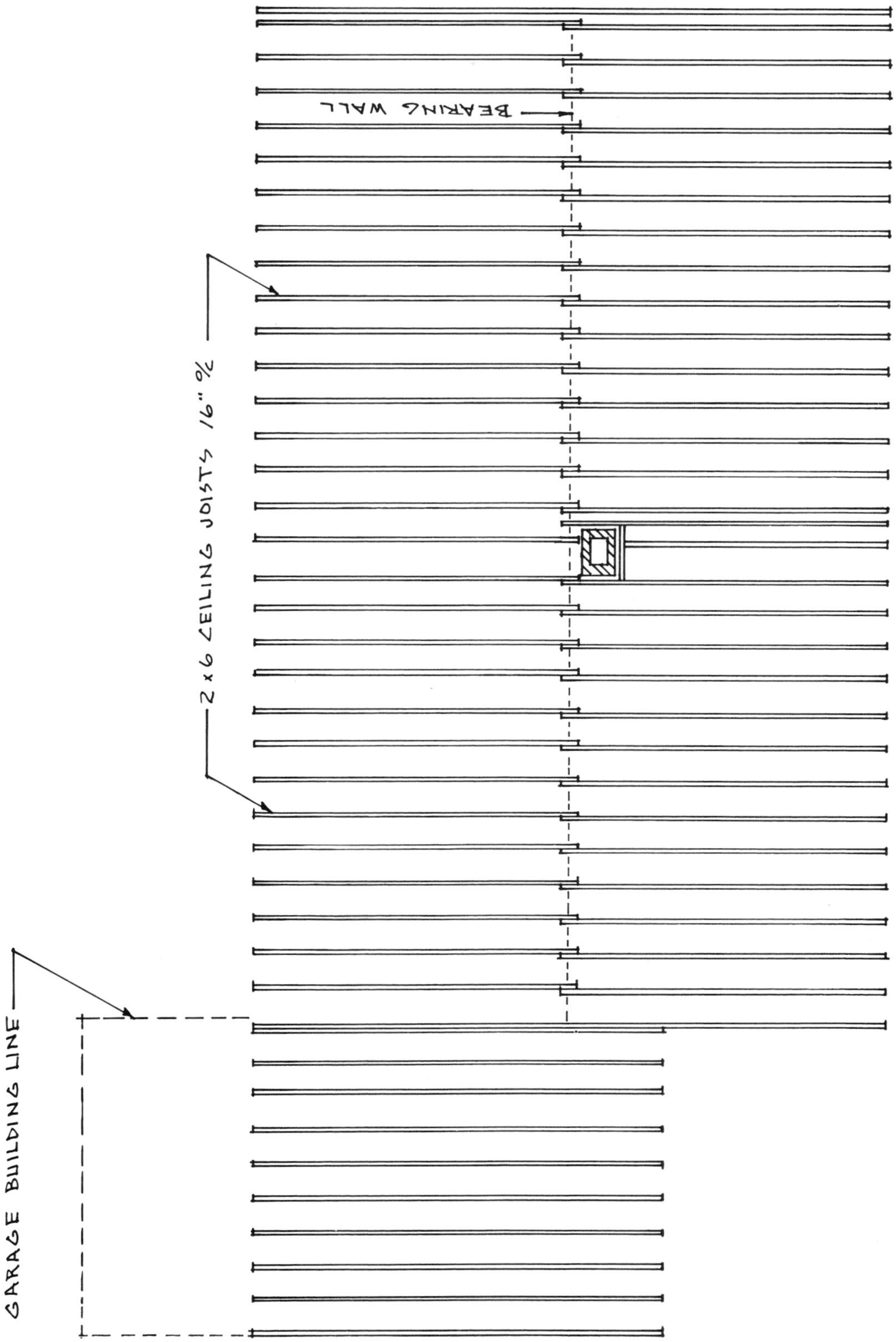

BEARING WALL →

2×6 CEILING JOISTS 16" ⁰⁄ₒ

GARAGE BUILDING LINE

CEILING FRAMING PLAN

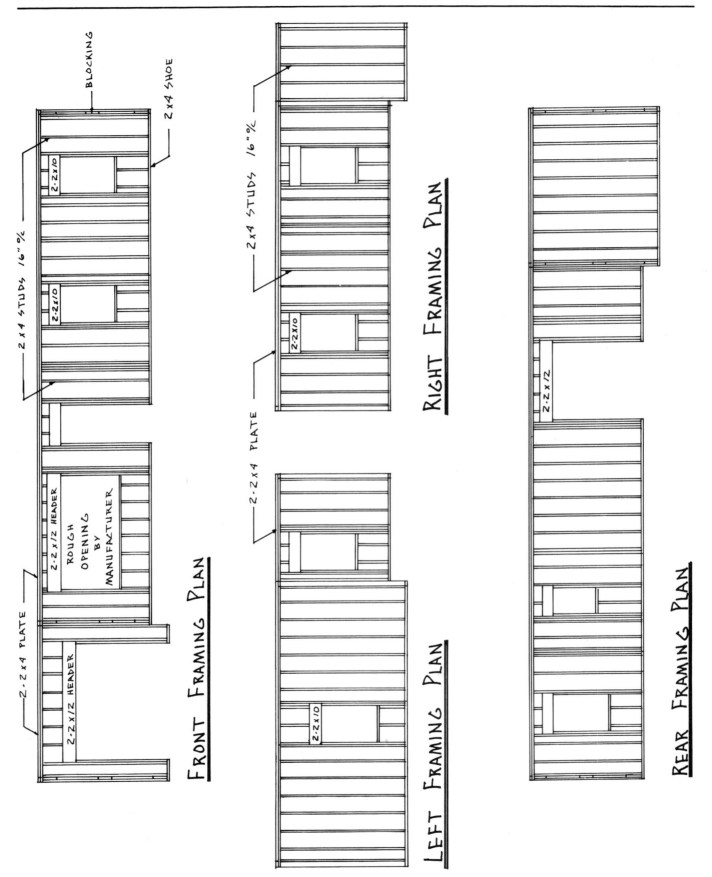

FRONT FRAMING PLAN

RIGHT FRAMING PLAN

LEFT FRAMING PLAN

REAR FRAMING PLAN

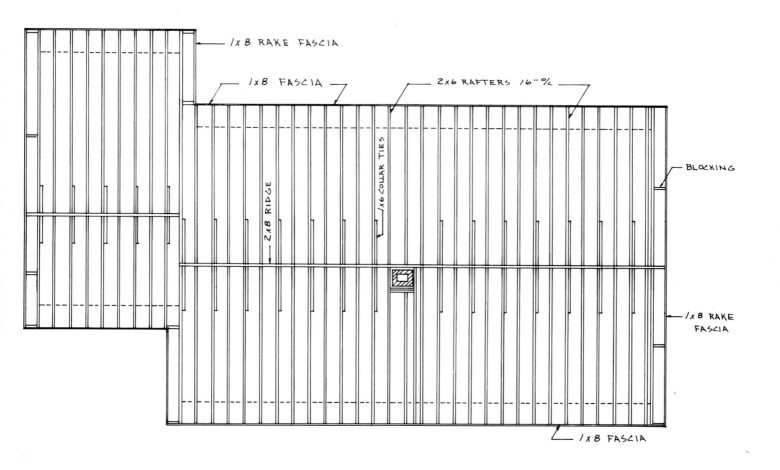

1 x 8 RAKE FASCIA

1 x 8 FASCIA

2 x 6 RAFTERS 16" %

BLOCKING

2 x 8 RIDGE

1 x 6 COLLAR TIES

1 x 8 RAKE FASCIA

1 x 8 FASCIA

ROOF FRAMING PLAN

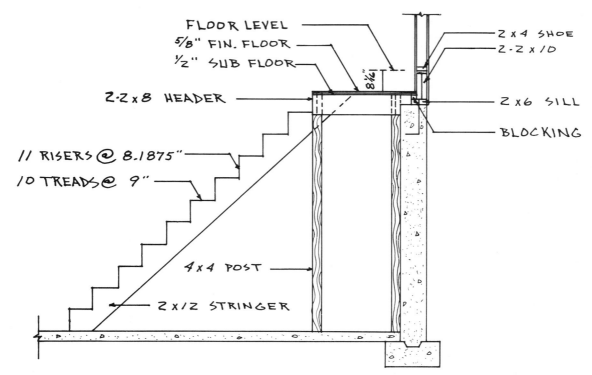

FLOOR LEVEL
5/8" FIN. FLOOR
1/2" SUB FLOOR
2-2 x 8 HEADER
11 RISERS @ 8.1875"
10 TREADS @ 9"
4 x 4 POST
2 x 12 STRINGER
8 1/16"
2 x 4 SHOE
2-2 x 10
2 x 6 SILL
BLOCKING

STAIR DETAIL

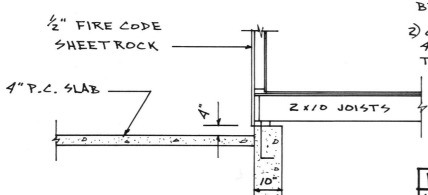

1/2" FIRE CODE SHEETROCK
4" P.C. SLAB
4"
2 x 10 JOISTS
10"

GARAGE/HOUSE FLOOR DETAIL

NOTES:

1) STAIRWAY LANDING TO BE 8 1/16" BELOW FLOOR LEVEL OF HOUSE.

2) GARAGE FLOOR SLAB TO BE 4" BELOW THE TOP OF FOUNDATION WALL.

DOOR SCHEDULE			
SYM.	QTY	SIZE	TYPE
1	1	$3^0 x 6^8$	PANEL-S.C.
2	7	$2^6 x 6^8$	FLUSH-H.C.
3	1	$1^0 x 6^8$	FLUSH-H.C.
4	2	$5^0 x 6^8$	SLDG.-H.C.
5	1	$5^0 x 6^8$	BI-FOLD
6	1	$6^0 x 6^8$	GL. PATIO DR.
7	1	$9^0 x 7^0$	GAR. O.H. DR.
8	1	$2^6 x 6^8$	FIRECODE DR.

WINDOW SCHEDULE			
SYM.	QTY.	SIZE	TYPE
A	1	$2^0 4^4 - 2^0 x 4^2$	P.W.
B	7	$2^8 x 3^{10}$	D.H.
C	1	$2^0 x 3^2$	D.H.
D	3	$2^8 x 1^4$	BSMT.

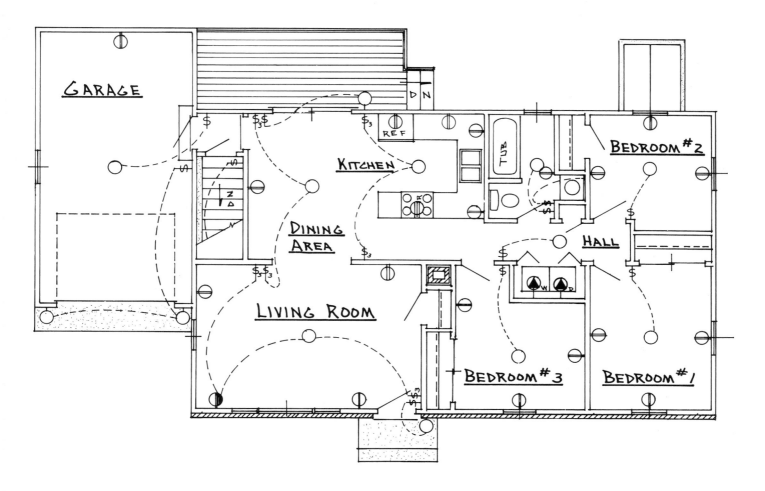

GARAGE

KITCHEN

REF

TUB

BEDROOM #2

HALL

DINING AREA

LIVING ROOM

BEDROOM #3

BEDROOM #1

ELECTRICAL LAYOUT

ELECTRICAL SYMBOLS	
SYM.	ITEM
$	SINGLE-POLE SWITCH
$₃	THREE-WAY SWITCH
⊖	DUPLEX OUTLET
⊖	SPLIT-WIRED OUTLET
⊖R	RANGE OUTLET
▲W	WASHER OUTLET
▲D	DRYER OUTLET
○	LIGHTING OUTLET
▭	FLUORESCENT LIGHTING

MATERIAL LIST

FLOOR SYSTEM
2 × 10 Joists------------------- 66/12
2 × 10 Header------------------ 6/12 - 4/14
2 × 6 Sill------------------------ 10/12 - 4/14
Sill Seal-------------------------- 173 Lineal Feet
Anchor Bolts-------------------- 22
1/2″ × 4′ × 8′ Plywood---- 29 Sheets
Bridging--------------------------- 55 Pairs
3 1/2″ Ø Lally Columns------- 4/8
3-2 × 10 Beam---------------- 6/14 - 3/12

CEILING SYSTEM
2 × 6 Ceiling Joists--------- 63/12 - 10/16
R-19 Insulation------------------ 19 Rolls

WALL SYSTEM
2 × 4 Shoe----------------------6/12 - 4/14
2-2 × 4 Plate------------------ 12/12 - 8/14
2 × 4 Studs-------------------- 135/8 - 44/10
Door Headers
    2 × 12----------------------2/8 - 2/10
    2-2 × 10----------------------2/14
Window Headers
    2-2 × 12 - 2/10--------------
    2-2 × 10----------------------4/14
1/2″ × 4′ × 8′ Sheathing-- 35 Sheets
R-11 3 1/2″ Insulation-------- 13 Rolls
Siding ----------------------------- 1112 Square Feet
    1/2 × 4 × 10
Firecode Sheetrock------------ 4 Sheets
Air Infiltration Housewrap--- 1112 Square Feet

ROOF SYSTEM
2 × 8 Ridge---------------------4/14
2 × 6 Rafters------------------62/16 - 9/10 - 10/18

1 × 6 Collar Ties------------14/8 - 5/6
1/2″ × 24″ Soffit-------------15/8
1 × 8 Fascia------------------6/14 - 2/12
1/4″ × 12″ Rake Soffit----9/8
1″ × 8″ Rake Fascia------1/10 - 3/16 - 1/18 - 1/8
Roofing Felt--------------------4 Rolls
1/2″ × 4′ × 8′ Plywood---49 Sheets
Asphalt Shingles-------------47 Bundles

INTERIOR
2 × 4 Studs----------------------163/8
Door Headers
    2 × 8------------------------- 2/12
    2 × 10----------------------6/6
Sheetrock------------------------68 Sheets
1″ × 12″ Shelving----------2/8 - 2/6
Closet Pole----------------------2/6 - 1/8
Baseboard ----------------------242 Lineal Feet
Ceiling Moulding--------------331 Lineal Feet

BASEMENT STAIRS
Stringers-------------------------(2 × 12) 2/14
Treads----------------------------(2 × 10) 3/12
Handrail--------------------------1/14

DECKS
Flooring (2 × 6)---------------112 Square Feet
Posts (4 × 4)-------------------3/6
2 × 4 Railings----------------44 Lineal Feet
2 × 6 Cap---------------------22 Lineal Feet
2 × 6 Joists-------------------13/8
2 × 6 Header-----------------2/16
2 × 10 Treads---------------1/16

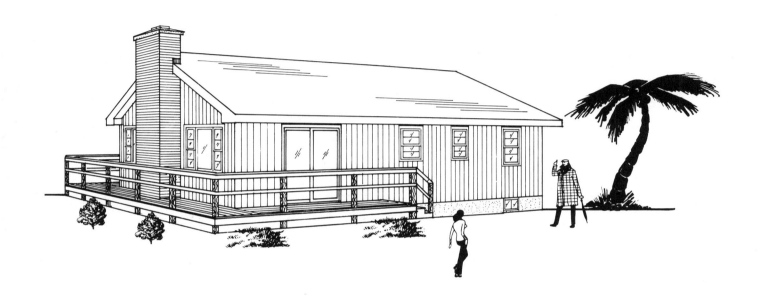

DESIGNED & DRAWN BY E. BRYANT

The Stevid is a one-story house with 1,040 square feet. The front of the living room is dominated by a centered fireplace and two double-hung picture windows.

Over the living room and dining area, a cathedral ceiling is made possible by the use of scissor trusses.

A six-foot patio door on each side of this spacious area gives access to a wrap-around deck.

Three bedrooms, a full bath, and a kitchen complete the floor plan of this residential dwelling.

The exterior consists of 8-inch vertical siding.

117

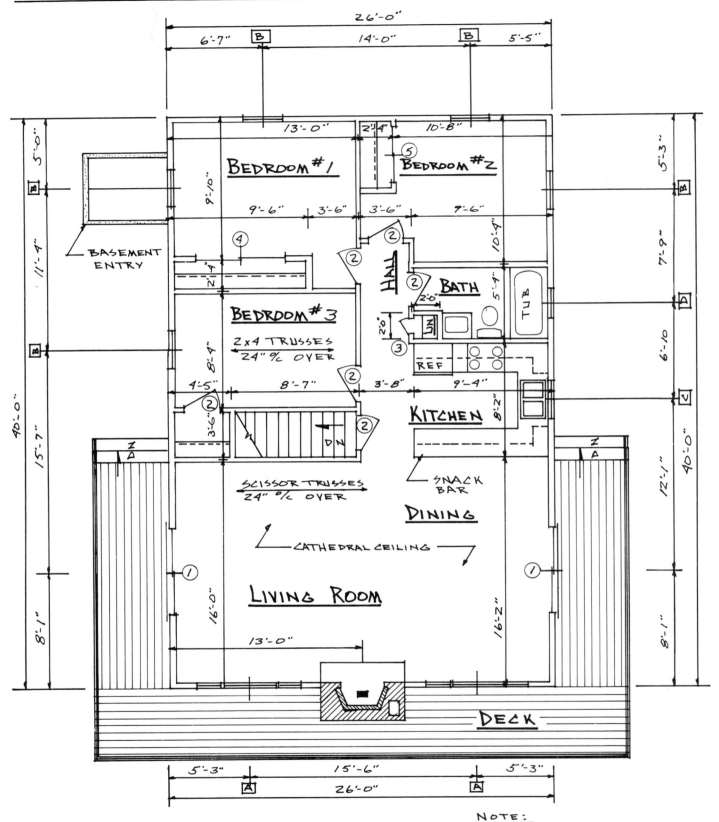

FLOOR PLAN

NOTE:
STRUCTURAL CHANGES SHOULD
NOT BE MADE WITHOUT CONSULT-
ING ARCHITECT / CONTRACTOR.

NOTE:
WOOD FRAMING TO BE KEPT 2"
CLEAR OF FIREPLACE MASONRY.
INSULATE WITH FIBERGLASS
BETWEEN MASONRY & WOOD.

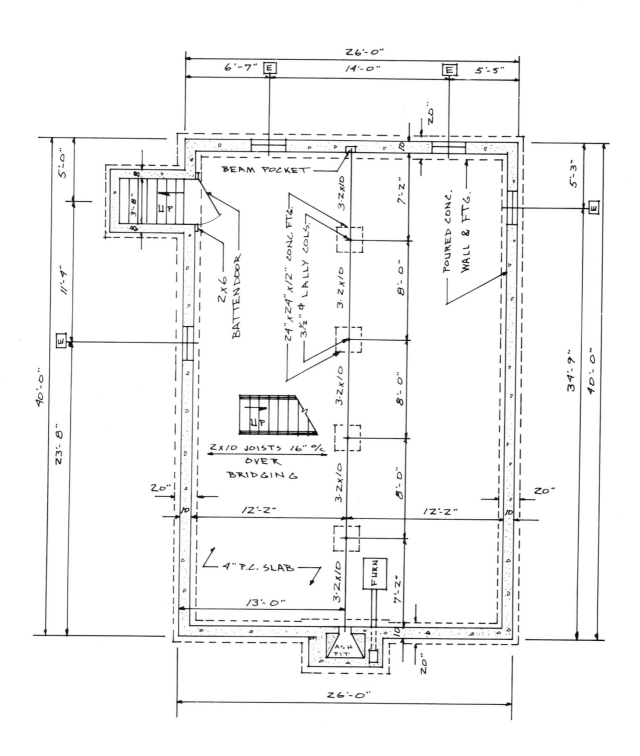

NOTE:
BASEMENT ENTRY FOUNDATION
TO CONFORM TO MANUFACTURER
SPECIFICATIONS.

NOTE:
FIREPLACE FTG. TO BE 12" THK;
EXTEND 6".

FOUNDATION PLAN

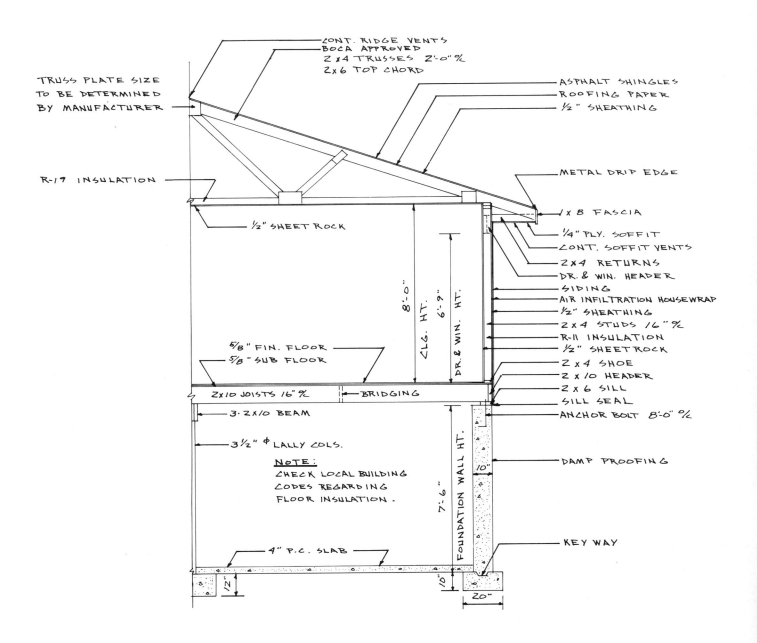

TRUSS PLATE SIZE
TO BE DETERMINED
BY MANUFACTURER

CONT. RIDGE VENTS
BOCA APPROVED
2x4 TRUSSES 2'-0" %
2x6 TOP CHORD

ASPHALT SHINGLES
ROOFING PAPER
1/2" SHEATHING

METAL DRIP EDGE

R-19 INSULATION

1x8 FASCIA
1/4" PLY. SOFFIT
CONT. SOFFIT VENTS
2x4 RETURNS
DR. & WIN. HEADER
SIDING
AIR INFILTRATION HOUSEWRAP
1/2" SHEATHING
2x4 STUDS 16" %
R-11 INSULATION
1/2" SHEETROCK
2x4 SHOE
2x10 HEADER
2x6 SILL
SILL SEAL
ANCHOR BOLT 8'-0" %

1/2" SHEET ROCK

8'-0"

CLG. HT.

6'-9"

DR. & WIN. HT.

5/8" FIN. FLOOR
5/8" SUB FLOOR

2x10 JOISTS 16" %

BRIDGING

3-2x10 BEAM

3 1/2" ⌀ LALLY COLS.

NOTE:
CHECK LOCAL BUILDING
CODES REGARDING
FLOOR INSULATION.

FOUNDATION WALL HT.

7'-6"

10"

DAMP PROOFING

4" P.C. SLAB

KEY WAY

12"

10"

20"

STAFF SECTION

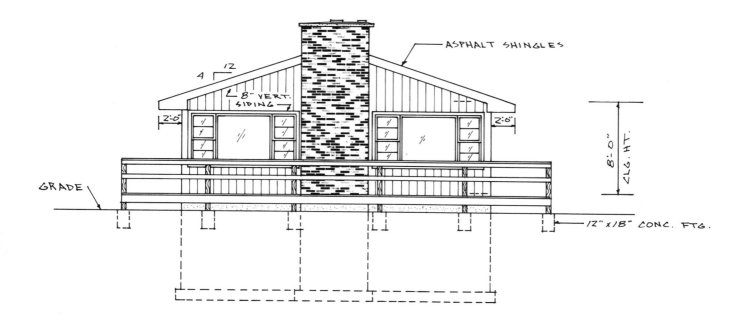

ASPHALT SHINGLES

4 | 12

8" VERT. SIDING

2'-0"

2'-0"

8'-0" CLG. HT.

GRADE

12" x 18" CONC. FTG.

FRONT ELEVATION

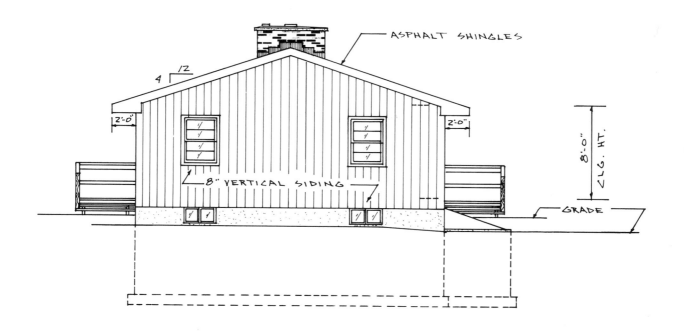

ASPHALT SHINGLES

4 | 12

2'-0"

2'-0"

8'-0" CLG. HT.

8" VERTICAL SIDING

GRADE

REAR ELEVATION

STEVID

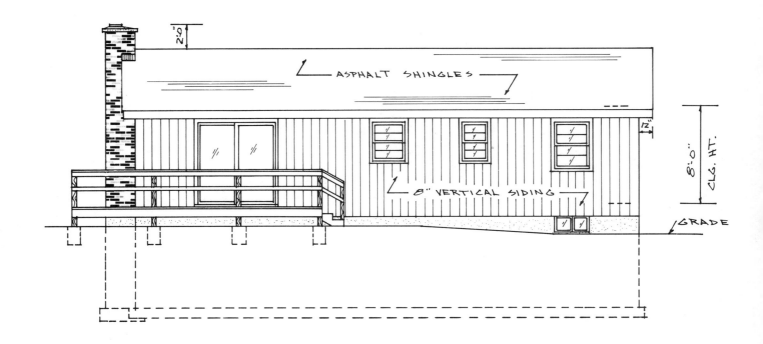

Right Elevation

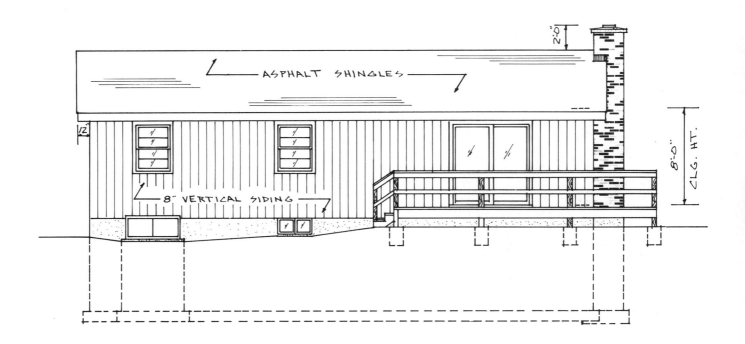

Left Elevation

122

NOTES:

1) WOOD FRAMING MEMBERS
TO HAVE A FIBER STRESS
OF 1200 PSI.

2) DOUBLE JOISTS UNDER
PARALLEL PARTITIONS.

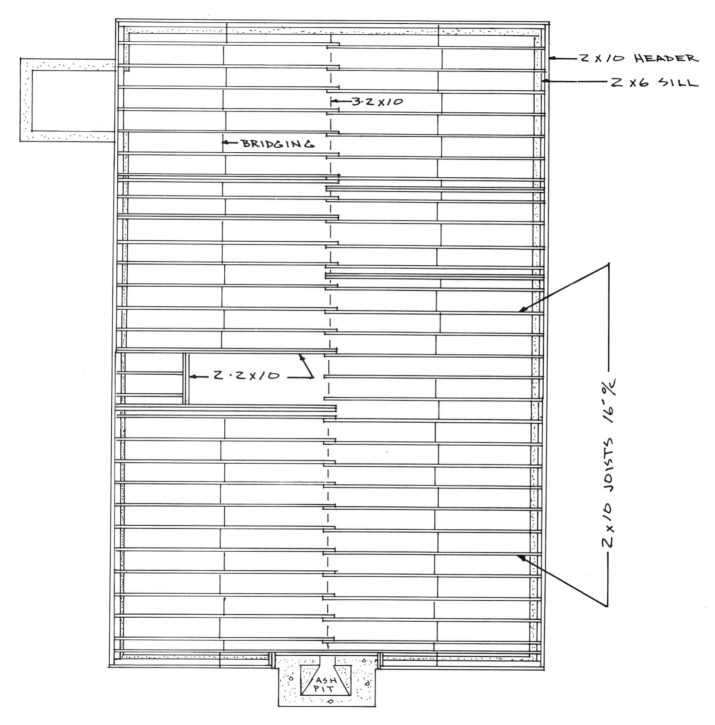

2 X 10 HEADER

2 X 6 SILL

3·2X10

BRIDGING

2·2X10

2X10 JOISTS 16"⅌

ASH PIT

FLOOR FRAMING PLAN

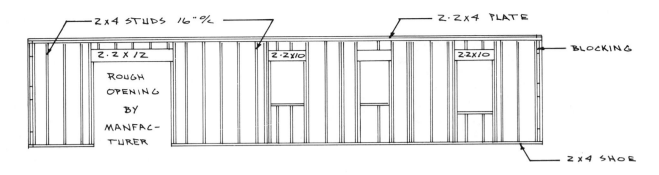

RIGHT FRAMING PLAN

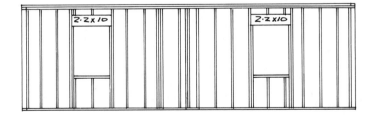

FRONT FRAMING PLAN

REAR FRAMING PLAN

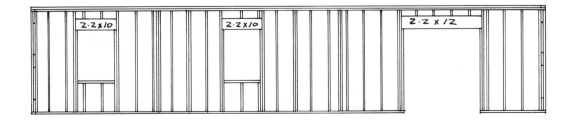

LEFT FRAMING PLAN

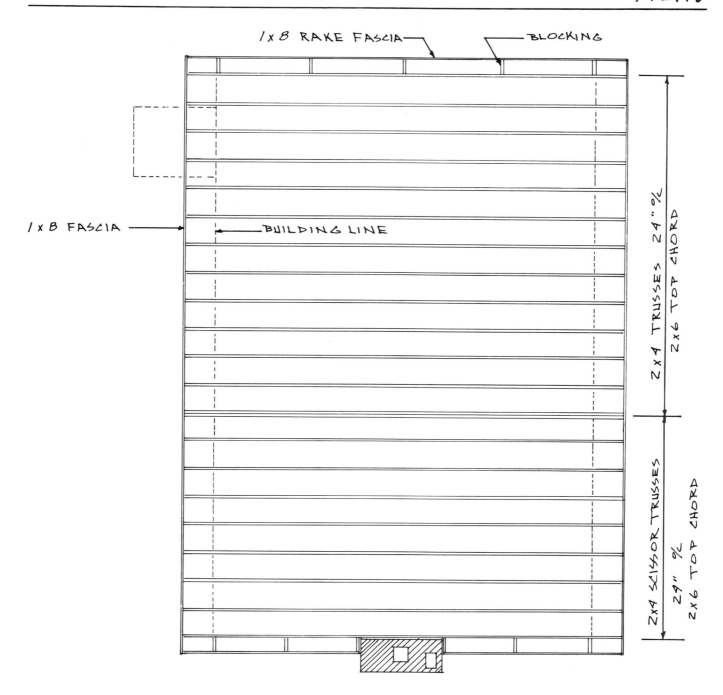

ROOF FRAMING PLAN

DOOR SCHEDULE			
SYM	QTY	SIZE	TYPE
①	2	6°x 6⁸	PATIO DR.
②	6	2⁶x 6⁸	FLUSH - H.C.
③	1	1°x 6⁸	FLUSH-H.C.
④	1	6°x 6⁸	SLDG.-H.C.
⑤	1	4°x 6⁸	SLDG.-H.C.

WINDOW SCHEDULE			
SYM	QTY	SIZE	TYPE
A	2	2°-4⁹-2°x4²	D.H.P.W.
B	5	2⁸x 3¹⁰	D.H.
C	1	2⁸x 3²	D.H.
D	1	2°x 3²	D.H.
E	4	2⁸x 1⁷	BSMT.

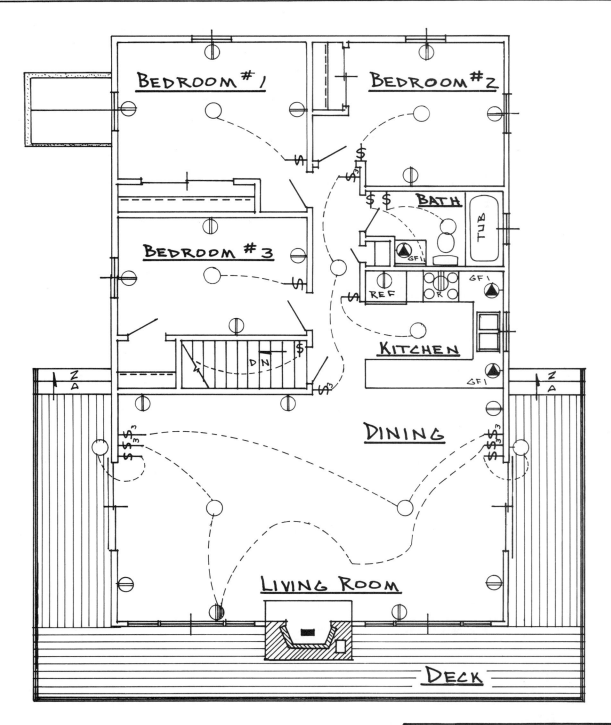

ELECTRICAL LAYOUT

ELECTRICAL SYMBOLS	
SYM	ITEM
$	SINGLE-POLE SWITCH
$₃	THREE-WAY SWITCH
⊖	DUPLEX OUTLET
⬤	SPLIT-WIRED OUTLET
⊖R	RANGE OUTLET
▲GFI	GROUND FAULT INTERRUPTER
◯	LIGHTING OUTLET
▭	FLUORESCENT LIGHTING

MATERIAL LIST

FLOOR SYSTEM
2 × 10 Joists---------------------------- 67/14
2 × 10 Header---------------------------- 6/14 - 4/12
2 × 6 Sill------------------------------- 6/14 - 4/12
Sill Seal------------------------------- 132 Lineal Feet
Anchor Bolts---------------------------- 16
1/2" × 4' × 8' Plywood------------- 33 Sheets
Bridging-------------------------------- 58 Pairs
3 1/2" ⌀ Lally Columns---------------- 4/8
3-2 × 10 Beam-------------------------- 6/14 - 3/12

CEILING SYSTEM
Insulation------------------------------ 1016 Square Feet

WALL SYSTEM
2 × 4 Shoe----------------------------- 6/14 - 4/12
2-2 × 4 Plate------------------------- 12/14 - 8/12
2 × 4 Studs--------------------------- 124/8 - 2/10
Door Headers 2-2 × 12-------------- 2/14
Window Headers
   (2-2 × 12)---------------------------- 4/10
   (2-2 × 10)---------------------------- 7/6
1/2" × 4' × 8' Sheathing----------- 28 Sheets
R-11 Insulation------------------------- 10 Rolls
Siding---------------------------------- 879 Square Feet
Air Infiltration Housewrap------------- 879 Square Feet
Fireplace Header (2-2 × 12)-------- 1/12

ROOF SYSTEM
1/4" × 24" Soffit--------------------- 80 Lineal Feet
1 × 8 Fascia--------------------------- 80 Lineal Feet
1/4" × 12" Rake Soffit-------------- 64 Lineal Feet
1 × 8 Rake Fascia--------------------- 64 Lineal Feet
Roofing Felt--------------------------- 4 Rolls
1/2" × 4' × 8' Plywood------------- 42 Sheets
Asphalt Shingles----------------------- 42 Bundles
2 × 4 Trusses------------------------- 13
Scissor Trusses----------------------- 9

INTERIOR
2 × 4 Studs--------------------------- 140/8
Door Headers (2-2 × 10)------------ 4/12 - 1/10
1/2" × 4' × 8' Sheetrock---------- 88 Sheets
1 × 12 Shelving----------------------- 1/10 - 2/8
Closet Pole---------------------------- 1/10 - 1/5
Baseboard------------------------------ 1376 Lineal Feet
Ceiling Moulding----------------------- 1390 Lineal Feet

BASEMENT STAIRS
2 × 12 Stringers---------------------- 2/14
2 × 10 Treads------------------------- 3/12
Handrail-------------------------------- 2/14

DECK
2 × 6 Flooring------------------------- 330 Square Feet
4 × 4 Posts---------------------------- 6/10
2 × 4 Railing-------------------------- 156 Lineal Feet
2 × 6 Cap------------------------------ 78 Lineal Feet

Article II

Financing

Home ownership is one of the best investments a family can make. In addition to being an investment in the future, it has the advantage of tax-deductible interest and property tax plus equity gain. The technology available today, coupled with a wide array of advanced building materials, enables the construction of homes that are beautiful to look at and comfortable to live in, while being durable and energy efficient.

Nowadays, varied finance packages are available to the home buyers. Several types are described here.

There are fixed-rate loans to help buyers who have fixed incomes. They involve fixed interest rates and equal monthly payments of principal and interest until the debt is paid. They offer stability and a long-term tax advantage. However, interest rates could be higher than other types of financing.

First-time buyers with increasing incomes can take advantage of a graduated payment mortgage. Its lower monthly payments will rise gradually over a number of years before leveling off for the duration of the term. Although this loan is easier to qualify for, the buyer's income must be able to keep pace with these scheduled payment increases.

Buy-downs can also be helpful in enabling lower-income families to acquire a home. Usually, a developer or third party would provide an interest subsidy, thereby lowering monthly payments. Such a financial package enables buyers with lower incomes to qualify. In addition, it offers a break from high payments during the earlier years.

If you are going to build a house, you should shop around for a financial plan that suits your needs. There are many mortgage plans available: assumable mortgage, balloon mortgage, flexible-rate mortgage, growing equity mortgage, land contract, renegotiable rate mortgage, rent with option, reverse annuity mortgage, shared appreciation mortgage, seller take-back, wraparound, zero rate, and low-rate mortgage.

Many of these plans are not typical traditional mortgages. However, even though they involve more risk for the buyer, they also feature lower interest rates, thereby allowing more buyers to qualify.

Government mortgages such as Farmers Home Administration (FmHA) have guidelines for maximum income. They are intended to benefit low- and moderate-income wage earners. To obtain a Farmers Home loan, the borrower must qualify under the income guidelines.

Veterans Administration (VA) loans are also available for veterans. This federal agency encourages private lending agencies to make liberal mortgages available to honorably discharged veterans or their widows.

To make mortgages more affordable for home buyers and a good investment for lenders, the Federal Housing Administration (FHA) issues mortgage loans made by FHA-approved lenders on houses that meet FHA standards.

Section III

1 1/2-Story Houses

LOULIAN

DESIGNED & DRAWN BY E.BRYANT

Consisting of 1,380 square feet of living space, the Loulian is a one and one-half-story residential house with double-hung windows and horizontal siding on the exterior.

This dwelling features an airlock, a roomy living room, and a good-sized kitchen with washer and dryer. Also on the main floor are two bedrooms, a full bath, and ample closets.

The upper floor consists of two bedrooms, a half bath with a roof window, and storage space.

NOTES:

1) BATH TO HAVE MECHANI-
CAL VENTILATION.

2) WOOD FRAMING TO BE
KEPT 2" CLEAR OF
CHIMNEY MASONRY.

3) STRUCTURAL CHANGES
SHOULD NOT BE MADE
WITHOUT CONSULTING
ARCHITECT/CONTRACTOR.

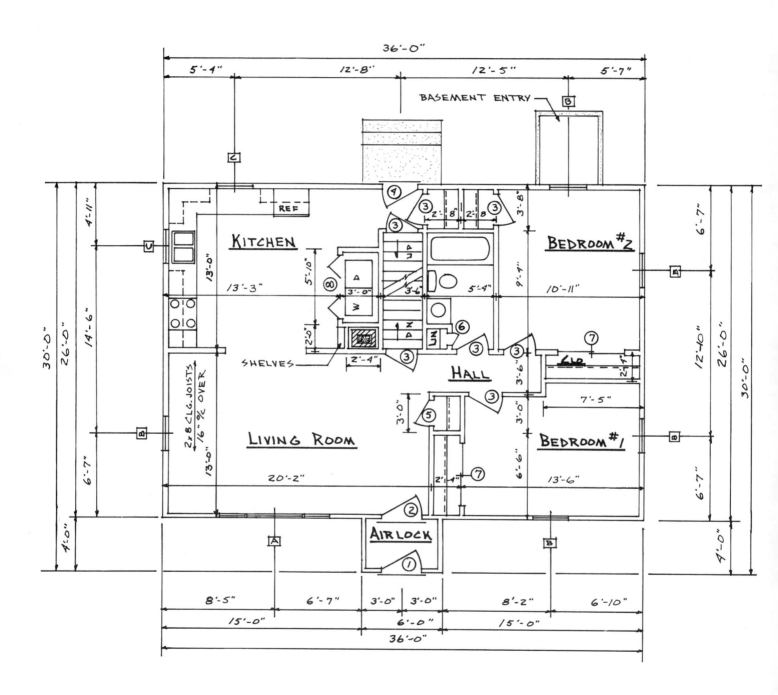

FIRST FLOOR PLAN

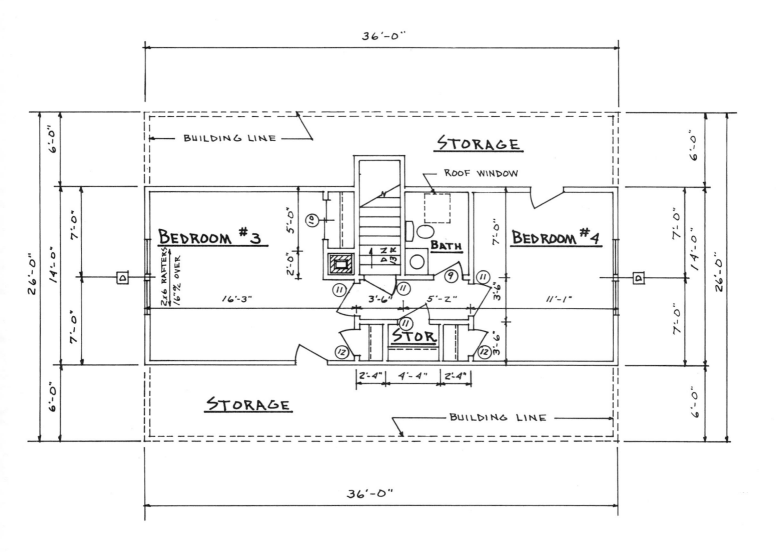

SECOND FLOOR PLAN

DOOR SCHEDULE			
SYM.	NO.	SIZE	TYPE
①	1	$3^0 \times 6^8$	PANEL-S.C.
②	1	$3^0 \times 6^8$	PANEL-S.C.
③	7	$2^6 \times 6^8$	FLUSH-H.C.
④	1	$2^8 \times 6^8$	PANEL
⑤	1	$2^0 \times 6^8$	FLUSH-H.C.
⑥	1	$1^0 \times 6^8$	FLUSH-H.C.
⑦	2	$5^0 \times 6^8$	SLIDER-H.C.
⑧	1	$5^0 \times 6^8$	BI-FOLD
⑨	1	$2^4 \times 6^6$	FLUSH-H.C.
⑩	1	$3^0 \times 6^6$	SLIDER-H.C.

DOOR SCHEDULE			
SYM.	NO.	SIZE	TYPE
⑪	4	$2^6 \times 6^6$	FLUSH-H.C.
⑫	2	$2^0 \times 6^6$	FLUSH-H.C.

WINDOW SCHEDULE			
SYM.	NO.	SIZE	TYPE
A	1	$2^0 4^{-2^0} \times 4^2$	DH PW
B	5	$2^8 \times 3^{10}$	DH
C	2	$2^8 \times 3^2$	DH
D	2	$5^8 \times 3^{10}$	DH MULL.
E	5	$2^8 \times 1^4$	BSMT.

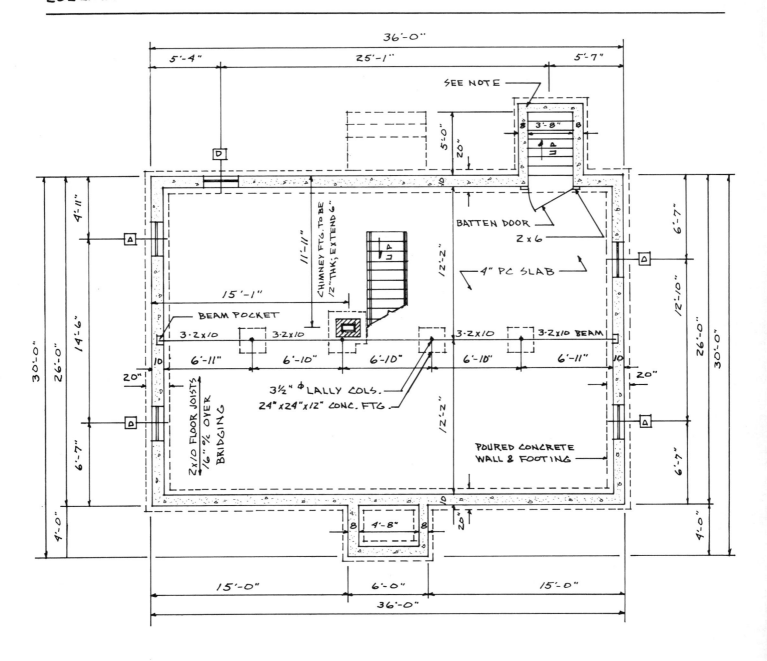

FOUNDATION PLAN

NOTE:
BASEMENT ENTRY
FOUNDATION TO CONFORM
TO MANUFACTURER
SPECIFICATIONS.

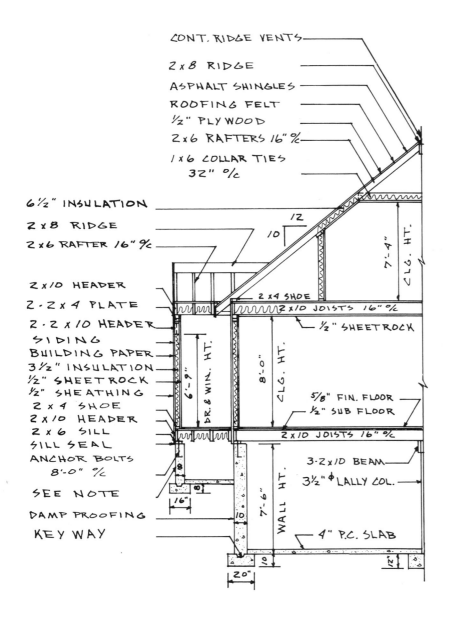

CONT. RIDGE VENTS
2 x 8 RIDGE
ASPHALT SHINGLES
ROOFING FELT
½" PLYWOOD
2 x 6 RAFTERS 16" %
1 x 6 COLLAR TIES
32" %

6½" INSULATION
2 x 8 RIDGE
2 x 6 RAFTER 16" %

2 x 10 HEADER
2 · 2 x 4 PLATE
2 · 2 x 10 HEADER
SIDING
BUILDING PAPER
3½" INSULATION
½" SHEETROCK
½" SHEATHING
2 x 4 SHOE
2 x 10 HEADER
2 x 6 SILL
SILL SEAL
ANCHOR BOLTS
8'-0" %

SEE NOTE

DAMP PROOFING
KEY WAY

CLG. HT.
7'-4"

12
10

2 x 4 SHOE
2 x 10 JOISTS 16" %
½" SHEETROCK

8'-0"
CLG. HT.

DR. & WIN. HT.
6'-9"

5/8" FIN. FLOOR
½" SUB FLOOR

2 x 10 JOISTS 16" %

WALL HT.
7'-6"

3 · 2 x 10 BEAM
3½" ø LALLY COL.

4" P.C. SLAB

16"
10
20"
12"

NOTES:
1) SECOND FLOOR WINDOW HEIGHT TO BE 6'-6"
2) COLLAR TIES TO BE 8'-8" LONG.
3) AIRLOCK FOUNDATION TO BE BELOW FROST LEVEL.
4) CHECK LOCAL BUILDING CODES REGARDING FLOOR INSULATION.

STAFF SECTION

SOFFIT DETAIL

2 x 4 SHOE
METAL DRIP EDGE
1 x 8 FASCIA
¼" PLY. SOFFIT
2 x 4 RETURNS
SIDING
½" SHEATHING

2 x 10 JOISTS 16" %
½" SHEETROCK

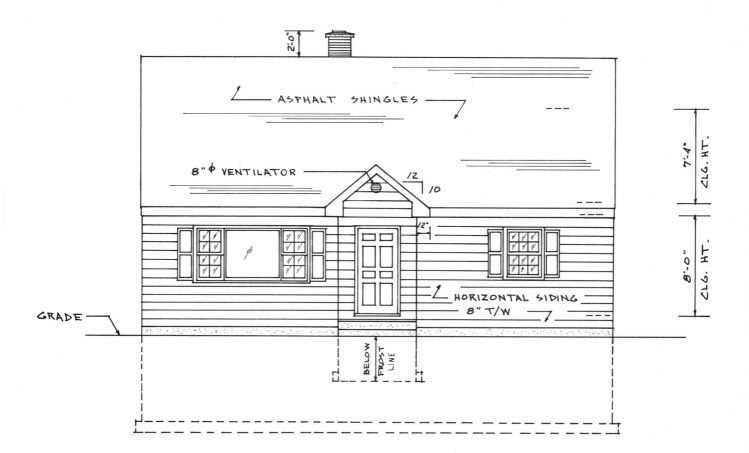

FRONT ELEVATION

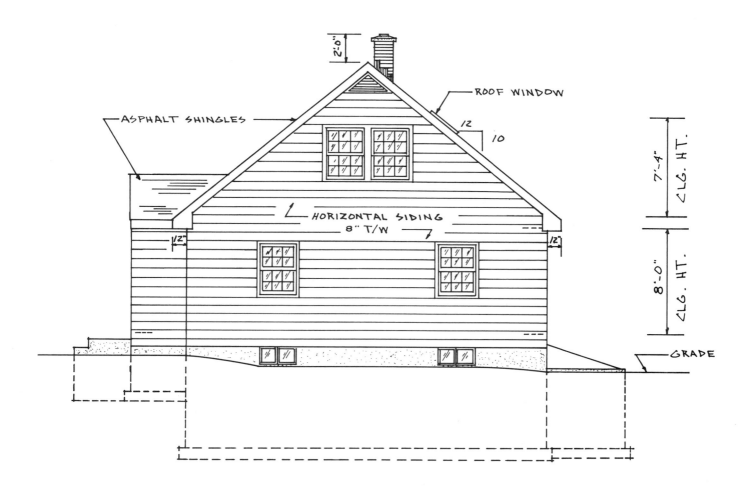

ASPHALT SHINGLES

ROOF WINDOW

12
10

2'-0"

HORIZONTAL SIDING
8" T/W

12"

12"

7'-4" CLG. HT.

8'-0" CLG. HT.

GRADE

RIGHT ELEVATION

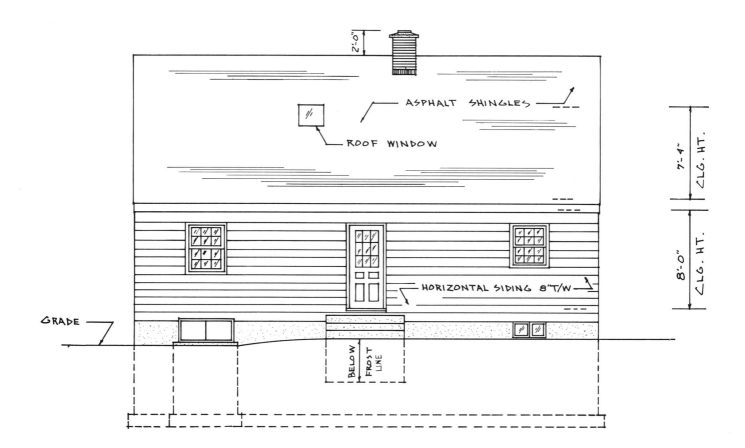

ASPHALT SHINGLES

ROOF WINDOW

HORIZONTAL SIDING 8"T/W

7'-4" CLG. HT.

8'-0" CLG. HT.

2'-0"

GRADE

BELOW FROST LINE

REAR ELEVATION

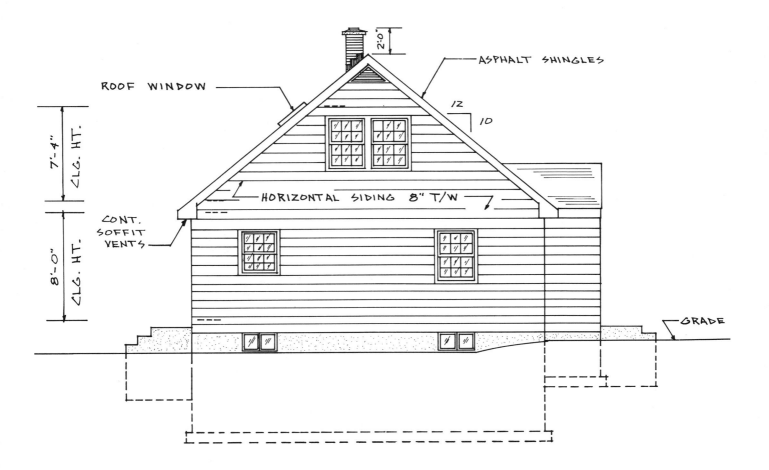

ROOF WINDOW

ASPHALT SHINGLES

12
10

HORIZONTAL SIDING 8" T/W

CONT. SOFFIT VENTS

7'-4" CLG. HT.

8'-0" CLG. HT.

2'-0"

GRADE

LEFT ELEVATION

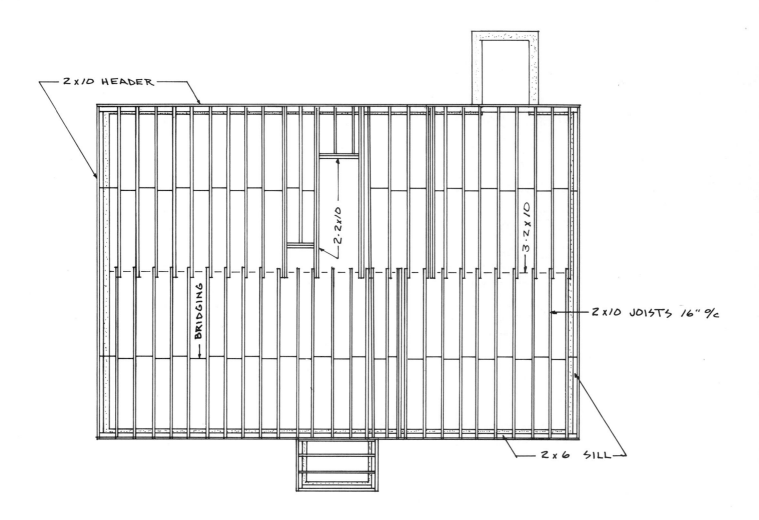

2x10 HEADER

2·2x10

3·2x10

BRIDGING

2x10 JOISTS 16" %c

2x6 SILL

FIRST FLOOR FRAMING PLAN

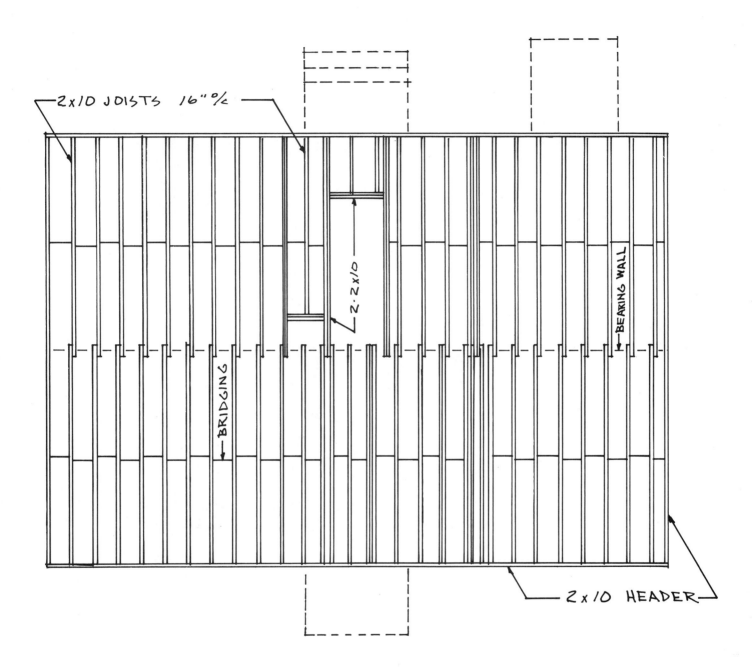

2x10 JOISTS 16" %

2·2x10

BRIDGING

BEARING WALL

2x10 HEADER

Second Floor Framing Plan

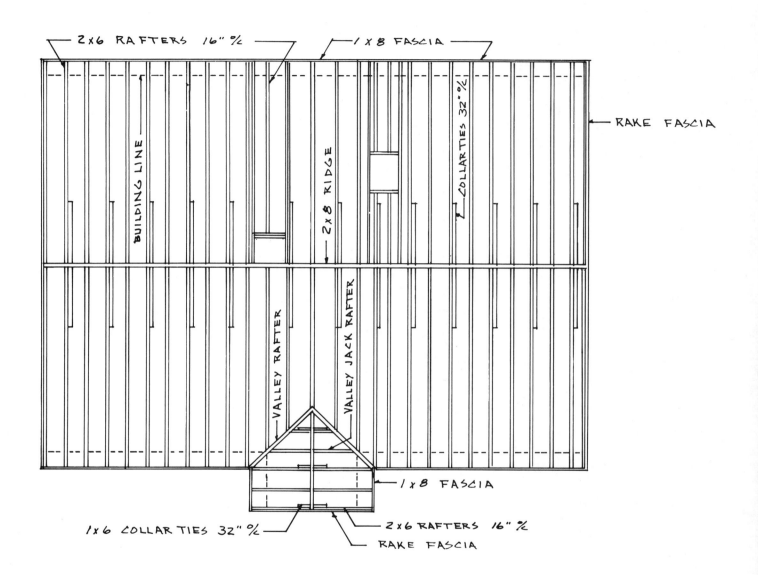

ROOF FRAMING PLAN

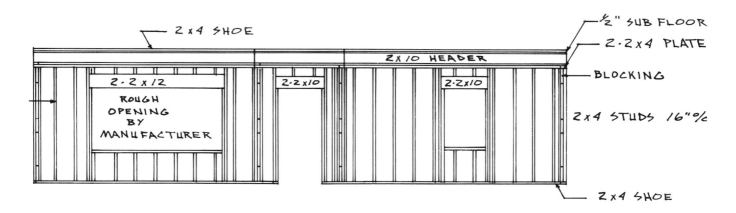

2 x 4 SHOE

½" SUB FLOOR

2·2x4 PLATE

2 x 10 HEADER

BLOCKING

2·2x12

ROUGH OPENING BY MANUFACTURER

2·2x10

2·2x10

2x4 STUDS 16"%

2x4 SHOE

FRONT FRAMING PLAN

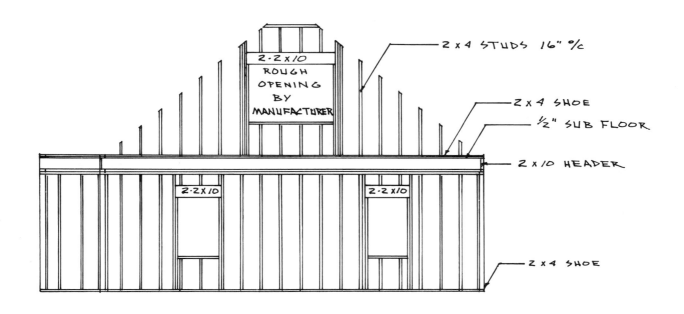

2x4 STUDS 16"%

2·2x10

ROUGH OPENING BY MANUFACTURER

2x4 SHOE

½" SUB FLOOR

2x10 HEADER

2·2x10

2·2x10

2x4 SHOE

RIGHT FRAMING PLAN

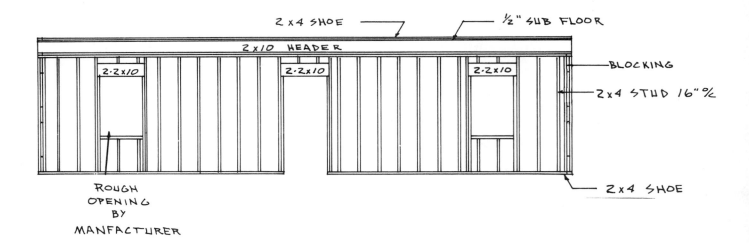

REAR FRAMING PLAN

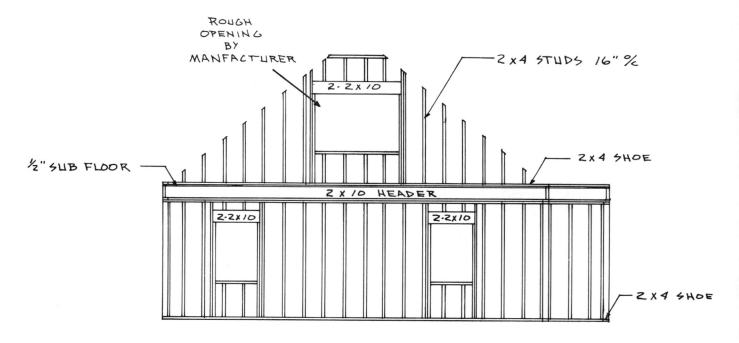

LEFT FRAMING PLAN

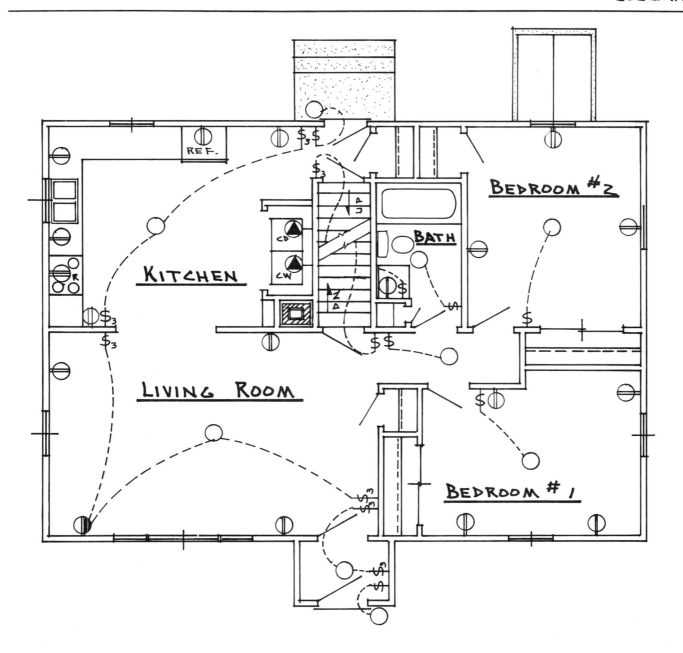

First Floor Electrical Plan

Electrical Symbols	
SYM.	ITEM
$	SINGLE-POLE SWITCH
$₃	THREE-WAY SWITCH
⊖	CONVENIENCE OUTLET
⊖	RANGE OUTLET
⊿	SPECIAL PURPOSE OUTLET
○	LIGHTING OUTLET
▭	FLUORESCENT LIGHTING
⊖	SPLIT-WIRED OUTLET

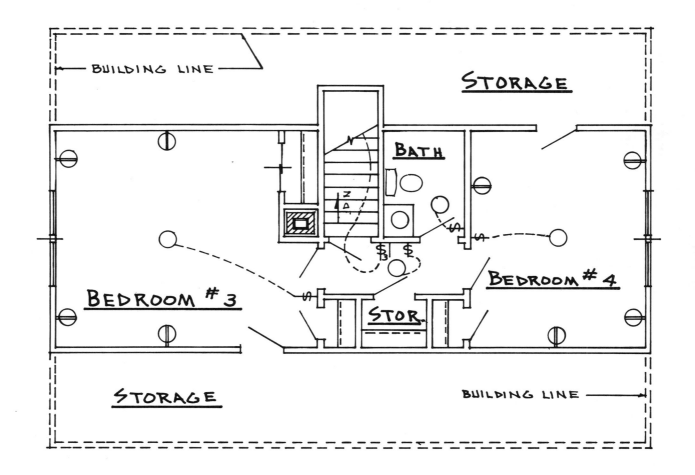

SECOND FLOOR ELECTRICAL PLAN

NOTE:
ELECTRICAL SYMBOLS
FOUND ON FIRST FLOOR
ELECTRICAL PLAN.

Alternative Floor Plan Suggestions
For The Loulian

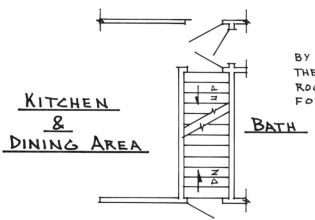

Kitchen & Dining Area

Bath

By eliminating the chimney and by placing the washer and dryer in the basement, more room would be available in the kitchen for a dining area.

Bedroom #2

Bath

Linen Closet

If a larger vanity is preferred in the first floor bath, the linen closet could be located in the hall.

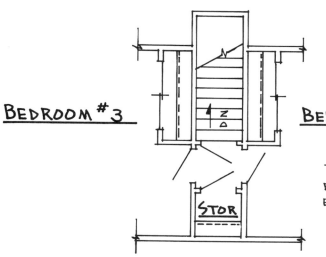

Bedroom #3

Bedroom #4

Stor

The second floor bath could be eliminated, if it is not desired, thereby enlarging both upper rooms.

MATERIAL LIST

FLOOR SYSTEM

2 × 10 Joist------------------------ 125/14
2 × 10 Header-------------------- 16/12 - 4/14
2 × 6 Sill---------------------------- 6/12 - 2/14
Sill Seal------------------------------ 124 Lineal Feet
Anchor Bolts------------------------ 15
1/2" × 4' × 8' Plywood------ 59 Sheets
Bridging------------------------------- 50 Pairs
3 1/2" ⏀ Lally Columns-------- 4/8
3-2 × 10 Beam-------------------- 4/12 - 2/14 - 1/8

CEILING SYSTEM

6 1/2 Insulation---------------------- 17 Rolls

WALL SYSTEM

2 × 4 Shoe--------------------------- 8/12 - 2/14
2-2 × 4 Plate---------------------- 16/12 - 4/14
2 × 4 Studs----------------------- 164/8 - 1/10
Door Headers (2 × 10)--------- 4/4
Window Headers
   2 × 10--------------------------- 4/6 - 14/4
   2 × 12--------------------------- 2/10
1/2" × 4' × 8' Sheathing---- 42 Sheets
3 1/2" Insulation------------------- 16 Rolls (1327 Sq. Ft.)
Siding---------------------------------- 1327 Square Feet
Air Infiltration Housewrap------ 1327 Square Feet

ROOF SYSTEM

2 × 8 Ridge----------------------- 3/12
2 × 6 Rafters-------------------- 56/20 - 6/4
2 × 6 Valley Rafters---------- 2/6
2 × 6 Valley Jack Rafters-- 3/4 - 3/16 - 2/18
1 × 6 Collar Ties---------------- 13/10
1/4" × 12" Soffit--------------- 10/8
1" × 8" Fascia------------------- 10/8
1" × 8" Rake Fascia---------- 5/10 - 4/8
Roofing Felt------------------------ 4 Rolls (1341 Square Feet)
1/2" × 4' × 8' Plywood----- 42 Sheets (1341 Square Feet)
Asphalt Shingles----------------- 41 Bundles

INTERIOR

2 × 4 Studs--------140/8 - 78/6 - 75/8
Door Headers (2 × 8)---------- 15/6
1/2" × 4' × 8' Sheetrock--- 107 Sheets
1" × 12" Shelving-------------- 7/8
Closet Pole------------------------- 4/8 - 1/4
Baseboard--------------------------- 533 Lineal Feet
Ceiling Moulding----------------- 623 Lineal Feet
Stair Stringers (2 × 2)-------- 2/14
Stair Risers----------------------- 3/12 - 1/4
Stair Treads----------------------- 3/12

BASEMENT STAIRS

Stringers (2 × 12)--------------- 2/14
Treads (2 × 10)------------------ 3/12
Handrail----------------------------- 2/14

KEVLENE

DESIGNED & DRAWN BY E. BRYANT

The Kevlene is a one and one-half-story house with a shed dormer on the rear of the structure. Excluding the garage, it has 1,474 square feet of living space.

The lower level consists of living room, dining room, kitchen, bath, and two bedrooms. The upper level has a bedroom, bath, guest room, and plenty of storage space. The guest room and bedroom each have two roof windows.

Double-hung windows and horizontal siding complement the exterior of this residential dwelling.

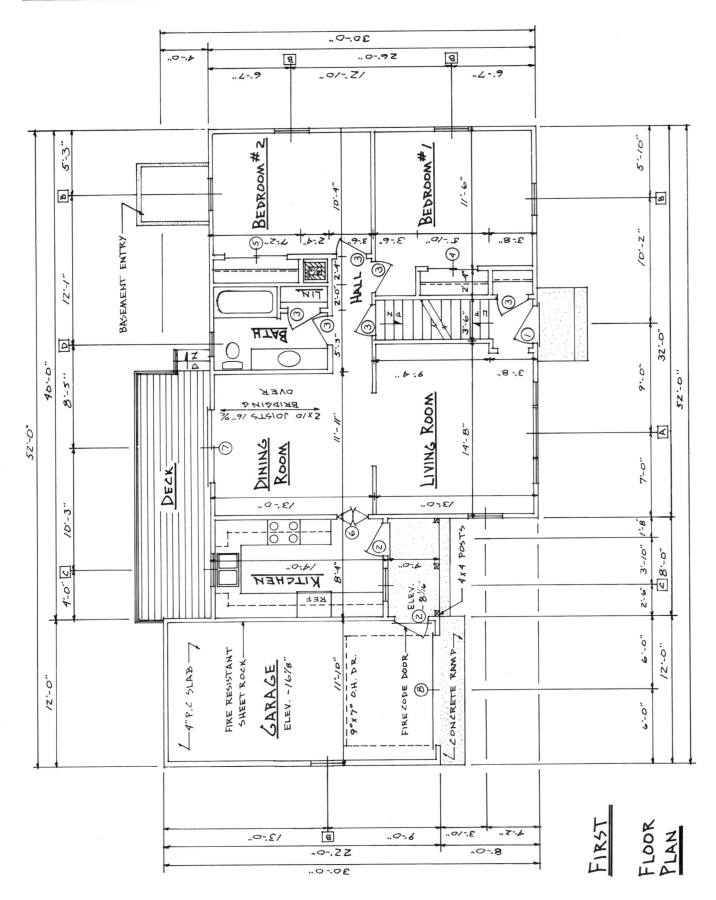

First

Floor
Plan

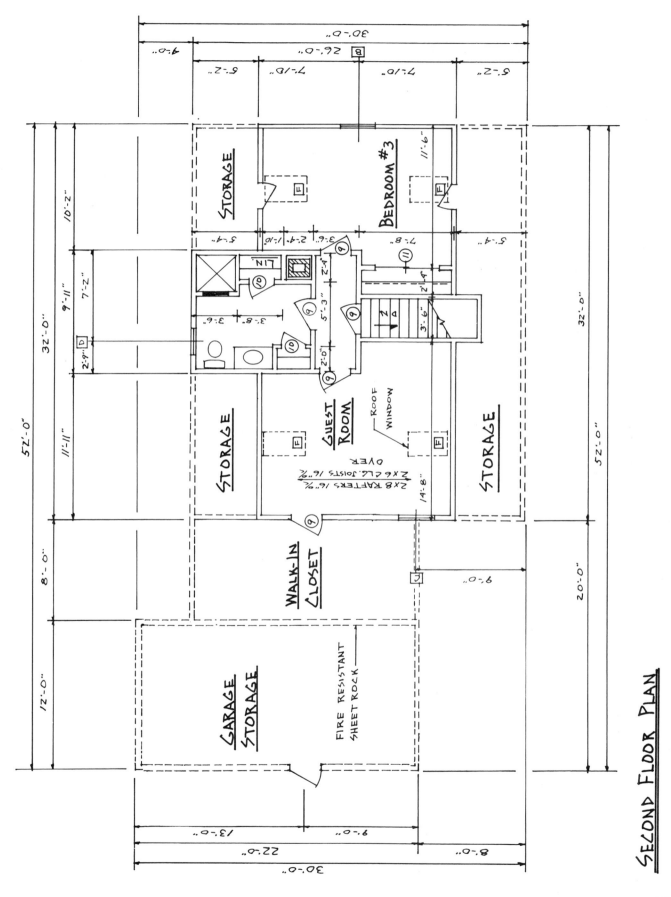

SECOND FLOOR PLAN

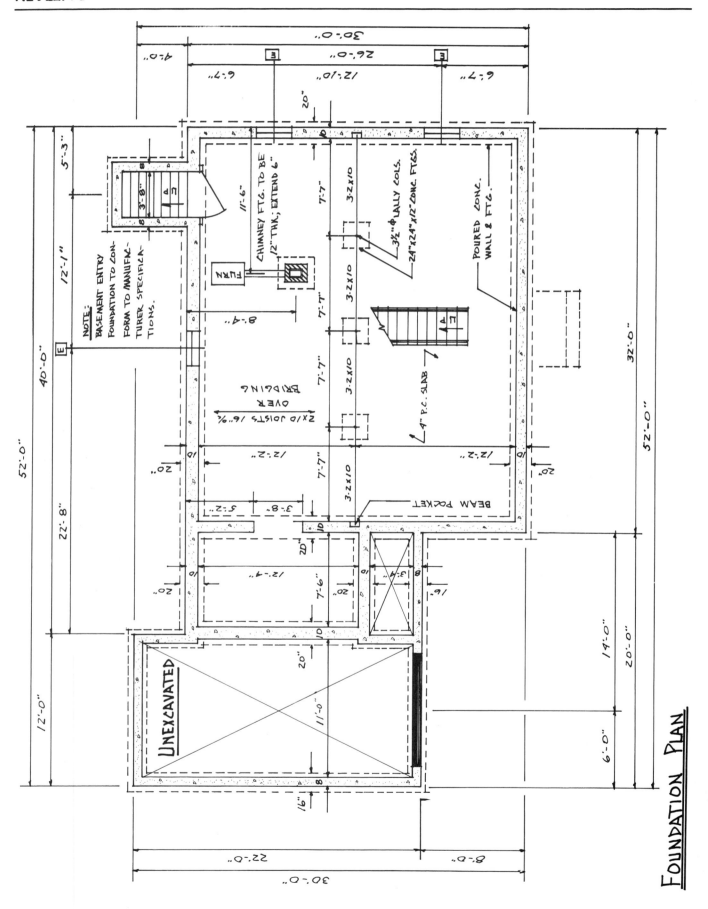

NOTE:
BASEMENT ENTRY FOUNDATION TO CONFORM TO MANUFACTURER SPECIFICATIONS.

CHIMNEY FTG. TO BE 12" THK.; EXTEND 6"

FURN

3½" Ø LALLY COLS.
24"X24"X12" CONC. FTGS.

POURED CONC. WALL & FTG.

BEAM POCKET

2X10 JOISTS 16"¾ OVER BRIDGING

4" P.C. SLAB

UNEXCAVATED

30'-0"
26'-0"
6'-7"
12'-10"
6'-7"
4'-0"
5'-3"
11'-6"
7'-7"
7'-7"
8'-4"
12'-1"
40'-0"
52'-0"
7'-7"
12'-2"
7'-7"
20"
3'-8"
22'-8"
5'-2"
12'-2"
20"
20"
12'-4"
7'-6"
20"
3'-4"
16"
11'-0"
12'-0"
16"
22'-0"
8'-0"
30'-0"
32'-0"
52'-0"
14'-0"
20'-0"
6'-0"
3'-8"
20"
20"
10
10

Foundation Plan

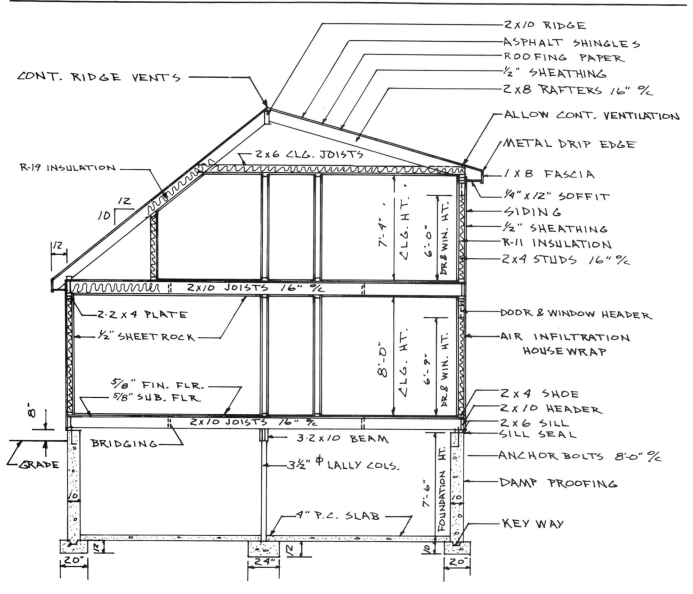

Labels on the cross section diagram:

- CONT. RIDGE VENTS
- R-19 INSULATION
- 2x6 CLG. JOISTS
- 2x10 RIDGE
- ASPHALT SHINGLES
- ROOFING PAPER
- ½" SHEATHING
- 2x8 RAFTERS 16" ⁰⁄c
- ALLOW CONT. VENTILATION
- METAL DRIP EDGE
- 1x8 FASCIA
- ¼"x12" SOFFIT
- SIDING
- ½" SHEATHING
- R-11 INSULATION
- 2x4 STUDS 16" ⁰⁄c
- 7'-4" CLG. HT.
- 6'-0" DR. & WIN. HT.
- 2x10 JOISTS 16" ⁰⁄c
- 2·2x4 PLATE
- ½" SHEET ROCK
- DOOR & WINDOW HEADER
- AIR INFILTRATION HOUSE WRAP
- 8'-0" CLG. HT.
- 6'-9" DR. & WIN. HT.
- 5/8" FIN. FLR.
- 5/8" SUB. FLR.
- 2x4 SHOE
- 2x10 HEADER
- 2x6 SILL
- SILL SEAL
- 8"
- BRIDGING
- 2x10 JOISTS 16" ⁰⁄c
- 3·2x10 BEAM
- GRADE
- 3½" ⌀ LALLY COLS.
- 7'-6" FOUNDATION HT.
- ANCHOR BOLTS 8'-0" ⁰⁄c
- DAMP PROOFING
- 4" P.C. SLAB
- KEY WAY
- 20"
- 24"
- 20"

CROSS SECTION

DOOR SCHEDULE

SYM	QTY	SIZE	TYPE
1	1	3⁰ x 6⁸	PANEL-S.C.
2	2	2⁸ x 6⁸	PANEL-S.C.
3	6	2⁶ x 6⁸	FLUSH-H.C.
4	1	4⁰ x 6⁸	SLDG.-FLUSH
5	1	5⁰ x 6⁸	SLDG.-FLUSH
6	1	2⁶ x 6⁸	CAFE DOOR
7	1	6⁰ x 6⁸	PATIO DOOR
8	1	9⁰ x 7⁰	GARAGE
9	5	2⁶ x 6⁰	FLUSH
10	2	2⁰ x 6⁰	FLUSH

WINDOW SCHEDULE

SYM	QTY	SIZE	TYPE
A	1	2⁰-4⁹-2⁰x4²	D.H. P.W.
B	6	2⁸ x 3¹⁰	D.H.
C	3	2⁸ x 3²	D.H.
D	2	2⁰ x 3²	D.H.
E	3	2⁸ x 1⁹	BSMT.
F	4	1⁸ x 3⁸	ROOF WIN.

NOTES:

1) STRUCTURAL CHANGES SHOULD NOT BE MADE WITHOUT CONSULTING ARCHITECT/CON-TRACTOR.

2) WOOD FRAMING MEMBERS TO HAVE A FIBER STRESS OF 1200 PSI.

3) WOOD FRAMING MEMBERS TO BE KEPT 2" CLEAR OF CHIMNEY MASONRY.

4) CHECK LOCAL BUILDING CODE REGARDING FLOOR INSULATION.

5) 2x6 CLG. JOISTS IN SHED DORMER TO BE EXTENDED COLLAR TIES 16" ⁰⁄c

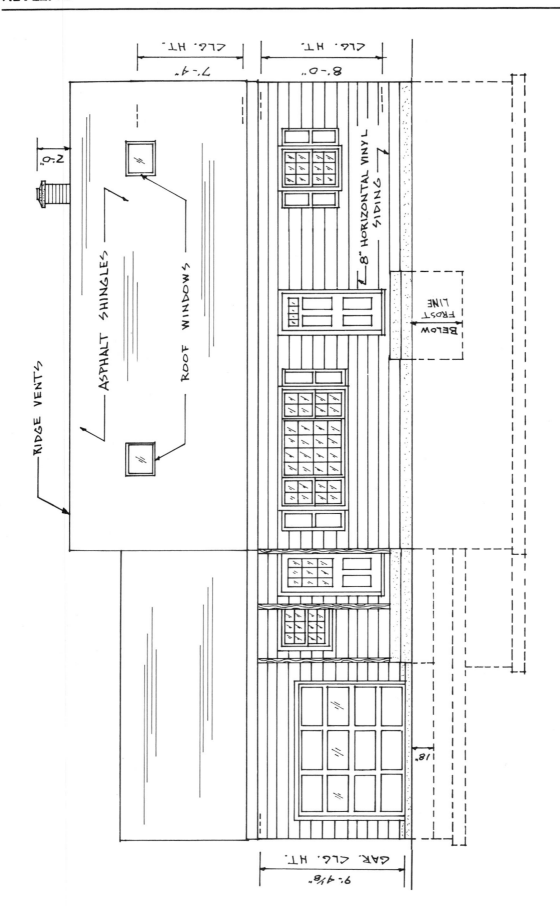

RIDGE VENTS

ASPHALT SHINGLES

ROOF WINDOWS

2'-0"

7'-4"

CLG. HT.

8'-0"

CLG. HT.

8" HORIZONTAL VINYL SIDING

BELOW FROST LINE

18"

9'-4⅛"

GAR. CLG. HT.

FRONT ELEVATION

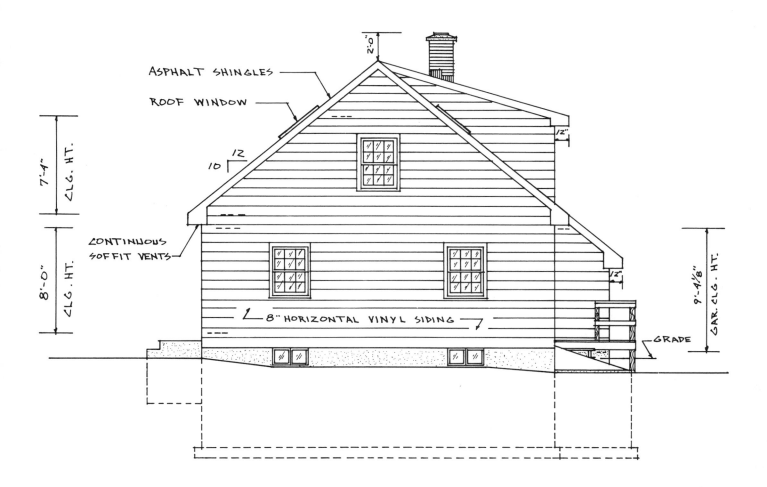

ASPHALT SHINGLES

ROOF WINDOW

7'-4" CLG. HT.

12
10

CONTINUOUS
SOFFIT VENTS

8'-0" CLG. HT.

8" HORIZONTAL VINYL SIDING

12"

12"

GRADE

9'-4 1/8" GAR. CLG. HT.

RIGHT ELEVATION

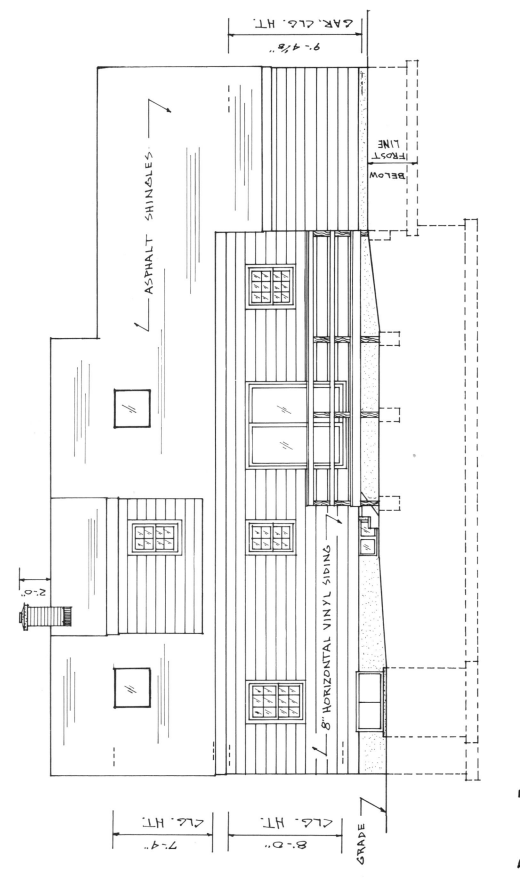

REAR ELEVATION

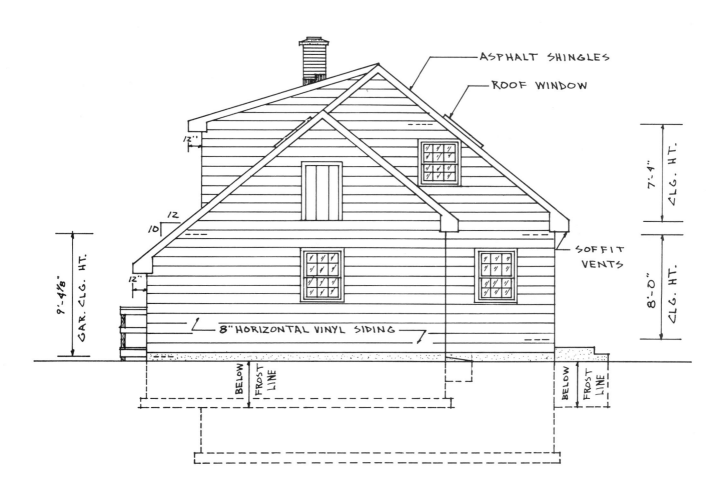

ASPHALT SHINGLES

ROOF WINDOW

7'-4" CLG. HT.

SOFFIT VENTS

8'-0" CLG. HT.

12"

12"

10 12

9'-4⅛" GAR. CLG. HT.

12"

8" HORIZONTAL VINYL SIDING

BELOW FROST LINE

BELOW FROST LINE

LEFT ELEVATION

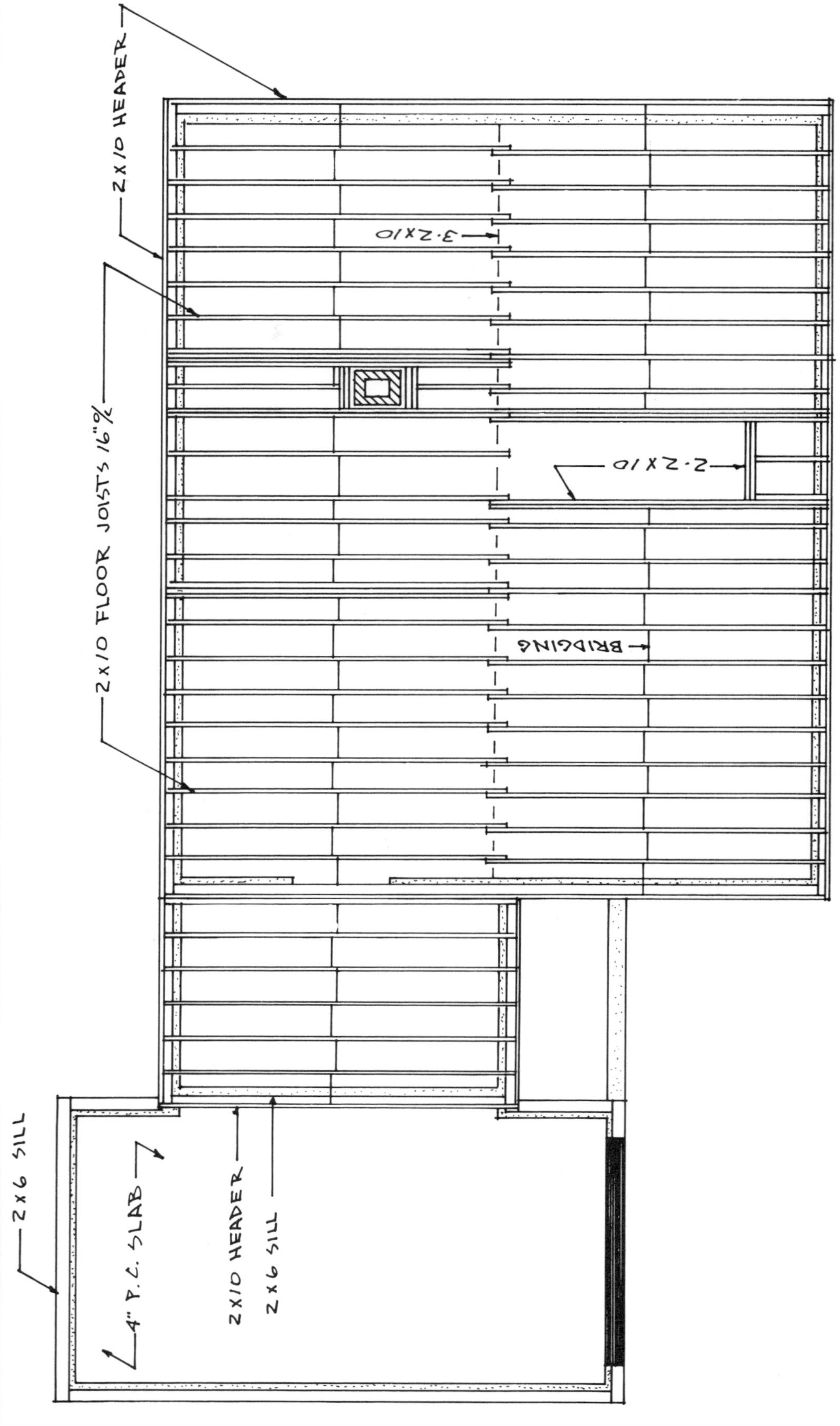

NOTES:
DOUBLE JOISTS UNDER
PARALLEL PARTITIONS.

2X10 HEADER

3·2X10

2·2 X 10

BRIDGING

2X10 FLOOR JOISTS 16"⅔

2x6 SILL

4" P.C. SLAB

2X10 HEADER

2x6 SILL

FLOOR FRAMING PLAN

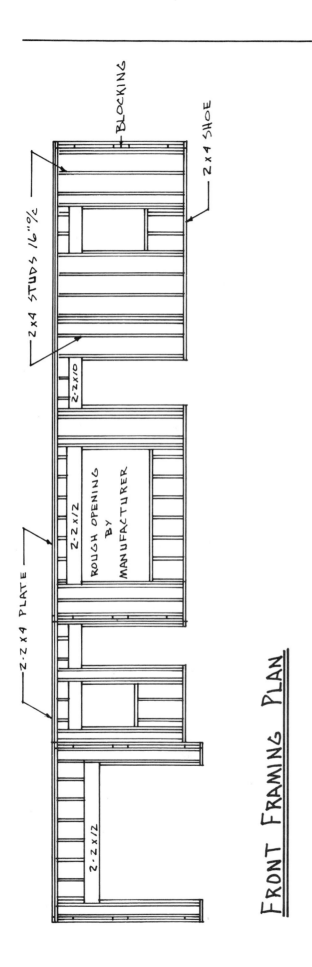

BLOCKING

2x4 SHOE

2x4 STUDS 16"%

2-2x10

2-2x4 PLATE

2-2x12

ROUGH OPENING
BY
MANUFACTURER

2-2x12

FRONT FRAMING PLAN

2-2x4 PLATE

2x4 SHOE

2-2x10

2x4 STUDS 16"%

2-2x10

REAR FRAMING PLAN

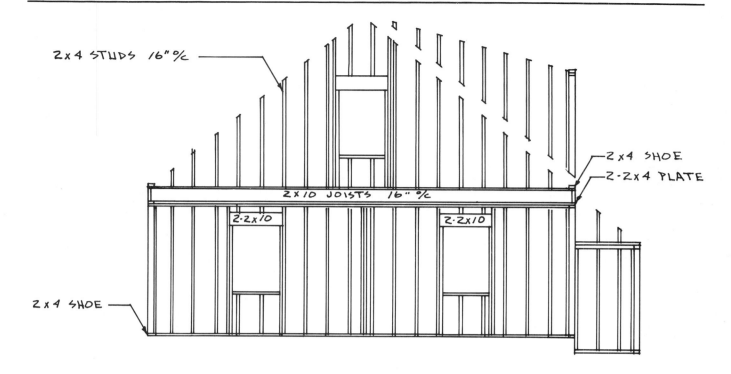

2x4 STUDS 16" %c

2x4 SHOE
2-2x4 PLATE

2x10 JOISTS 16" %c

2-2x10   2-2x10

2x4 SHOE

RIGHT FRAMING PLAN

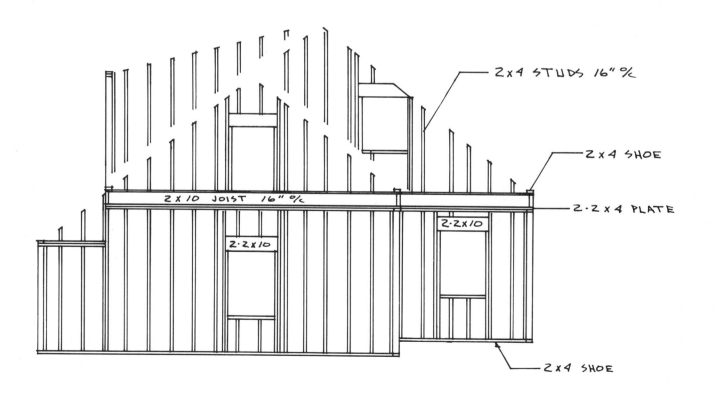

2x4 STUDS 16" %c

2x4 SHOE

2-2x4 PLATE

2x10 JOIST 16" %c

2-2x10

2-2x10

2x4 SHOE

LEFT FRAMING PLAN

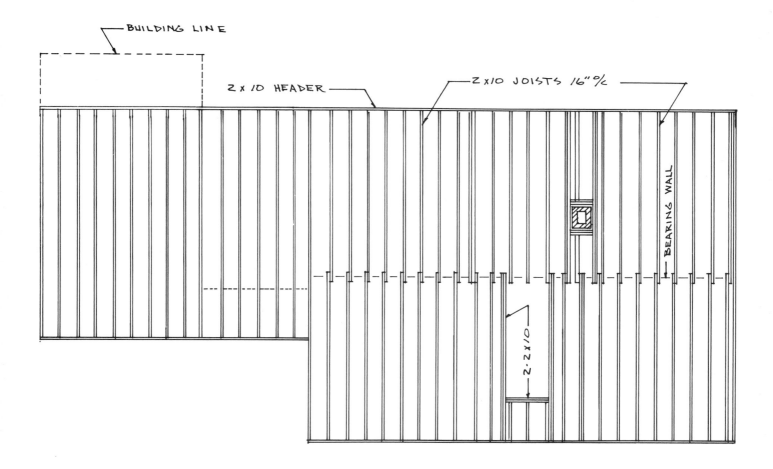

BUILDING LINE

2 x 10 HEADER

2 x 10 JOISTS 16" %

BEARING WALL

2 - 2 x 10

CEILING FRAMING PLAN

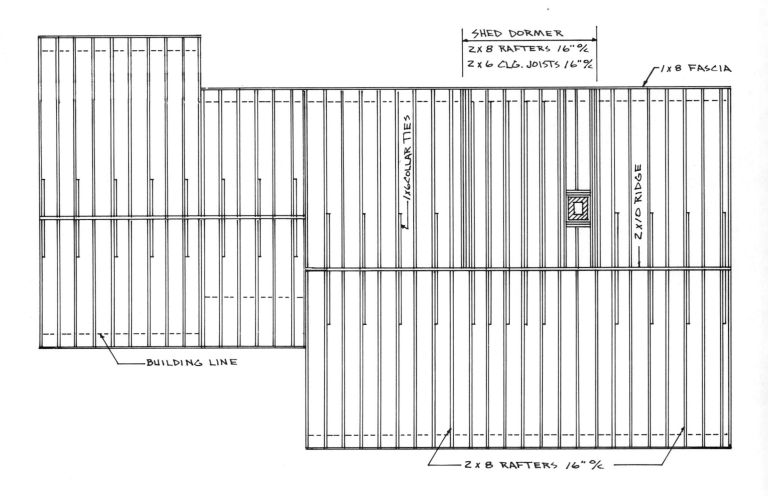

SHED DORMER
2 X 8 RAFTERS 16" %
2 X 6 CLG. JOISTS 16" %

1 X 8 FASCIA

1 X 6 COLLAR TIES

2 X 10 RIDGE

BUILDING LINE

2 X 8 RAFTERS 16" %

ROOF FRAMING PLAN

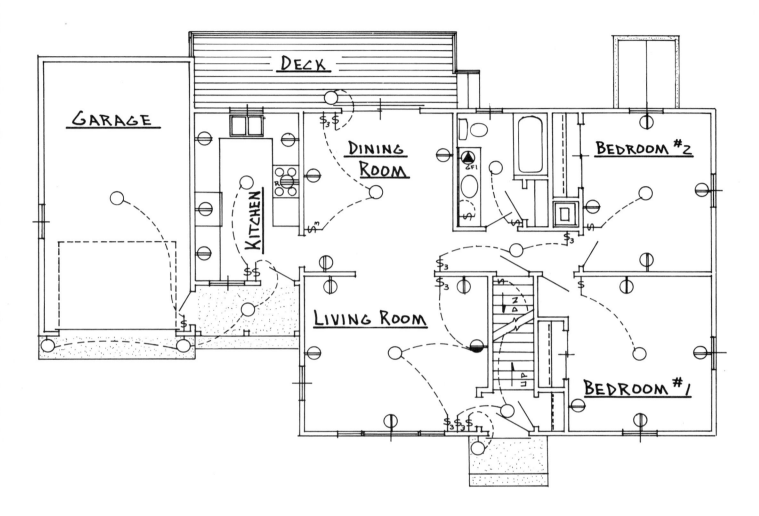

First Floor Electrical Layout

Electrical Symbols	
SYM	ITEM
$	SINGE-POLE SWITCH
$₃	THREE-WAY SWITCH
⊖	DUPLEX OUTLET
⊖R	RANGE OUTLET
⊖	SPLIT-WIRED OUTLET
▲GFI	GROUND FAULT INTERRUPTER
◯	LIGHTING OUTLET
▭	FLUORESCENT LIGHTING

NOTE:
ELECTRICAL SYMBOLS
LOCATED ON FIRST FLOOR
ELECTRICAL LAYOUT

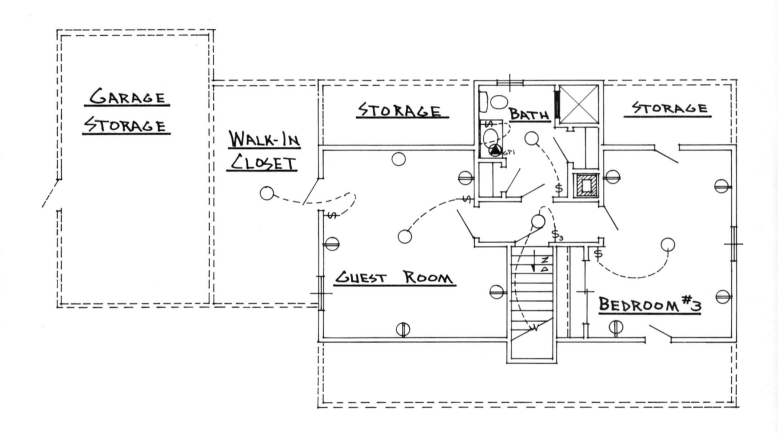

SECOND FLOOR ELECTRICAL LAYOUT

MATERIAL LIST

FLOOR SYSTEM
2 × 10 Joists----------------------58/14
2 × 10 Header------------------3/14 - 3/12 - 1/10
2 × 6 Sill--------------------------3/14 - 6/12 - 2/10
Sill Seal----------------------------180 Lineal Feet
Anchor Bolts----------------------17
1/2" × 4' × 8' Plywood-----29 Sheets
Bridging----------------------------49 Pairs
3 1/2" ⌀ Lally Columns-------3/8
3-2 × 10 Beam------------------4/16 - 2/10 - 1/12

WALL SYSTEM
2 × 4 Shoe--------------------------3/14 - 6/12 - 2/10
2-2 × 4 Plate----------------------6/14 - 12/12 - 4/10
2 × 4 Studs-------------------------44/10 - 226/8
Door Headers
   2 × 10----------------------------2/14
   2 × 12----------------------------2/10
Window Headers
   2 × 10----------------------------6/14
   2 × 12----------------------------2/10
Housewrap----------------------1713 Square Feet
3 1/2" Insulation----------------20 Rolls
Siding----------------------------1713 Square Feet

CEILING SYSTEM (Second Floor)
Fire Resistive Sheetrock-----7 Sheets
2 × 10 Joists---------------------55/14 - 30/18
2 × 10 Header------------------2/16 - 4/14 - 4/12 - 3/10
1/2" × 4' × 8' Plywood-----37 Sheets

ROOF SYSTEM
2 × 10 Ridge--------------------2/16 - 2/10
2 × 8 Rafters-------------------54/18 - 11/16 - 24/14
1 × 6 Collar Ties--------------8/6 - 8/10

1/4 × 12 Soffit--------------------------- 114 Lineal Feet
1 × 8 Fascia------------------------------ 114 Lineal Feet
1 × 8 Rake Fascia--------------------- 128 Lineal Feet
Roofing Felt---------------------------- 4 Rolls
1/2" × 4' × 8' Plywood------------- 54 Sheets
Asphalt Shingles----------------------- 53 Bundles
2 × 6 Ceiling Joists (for shed
dormer)------------------------------------- 6/16

INTERIOR
2 × 4 Studs------------------------------- 265/8
Door Headers (2 × 8)---------------- 2/12
1/2" × 4' × 8' Sheetrock---------- 141 Sheets
1 × 12 Shelving----------------------- 7/8
Closet Pole------------------------------ 3/8
Baseboard-------------------------------- 422 Lineal Feet
Ceiling Moulding----------------------- 590 Lineal Feet
Stair Stringers (2 × 12)------------- 2/14
Stair Risers------------------------------ 13
Stair Treads----------------------------- 12

BASEMENT STAIRS
Stringers (2 × 12)----------------------- 2/14
Treads (2 × 10)------------------------ 3/12
Handrails---------------------------------- 2/14

DECK
Flooring----------------------------------- 126 Square Feet
Posts (4 × 4)---------------------------- 4/6
Railings----------------------------------- 56 Lineal Feet
Cap-- 28 Lineal Feet

HAZZLE

DESIGNED & DRAWN BY E. BRYANT

Measuring 26 feet long, the Hazzle has 1,795 square feet of living space.

The entrance door with its two side-lights gives access from the covered porch to the interior airlock. This area consists of a guest closet and an L-shaped stairway leading to the second floor.

By going through the double doors you will find yourself in the formal dining room, which is accented by a bay window.

Adjoining the dining room is the family room, which has access to the living room through a 6-foot archway. A U-shaped kitchen, complete with washer and dryer, is located at the other end of the house adjacent to the dining room. A full bath is situated between the kitchen and the den.

The upper level consists of three bedrooms and a bath. In addition to his and her closets, the master bedroom has a roof window and storage space. Roof windows can also be found in bedroom #2 and the bath. Bedroom #3 has been expanded to a shed dormer.

The double 4-inch vinyl siding, the double-hung windows, and the stone fireplace, in addition to a 12:12 roof pitch, give the exterior of the structure its own distinctive style.

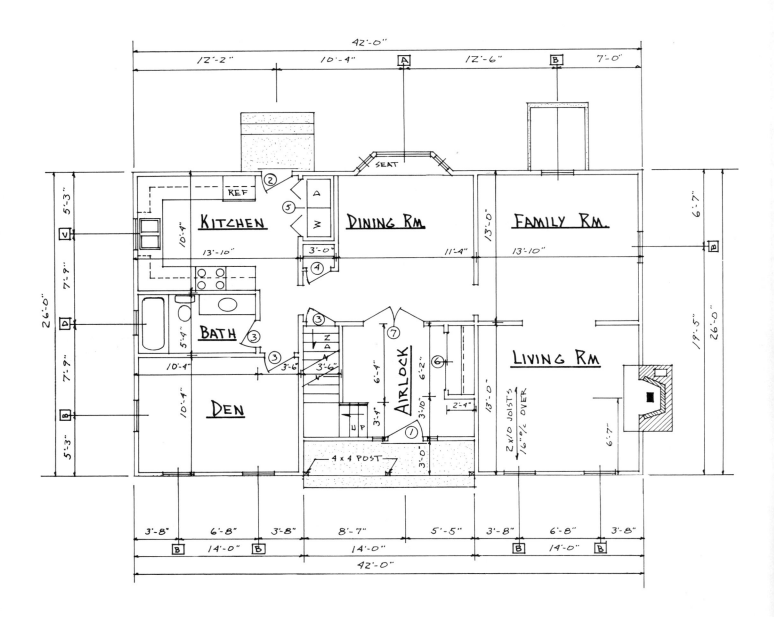

FIRST FLOOR PLAN

NOTE:
ROOF WINDOWS TO
BE LOCATED IN
MASTER BEDROOM,
BEDROOM #2 & BATH.

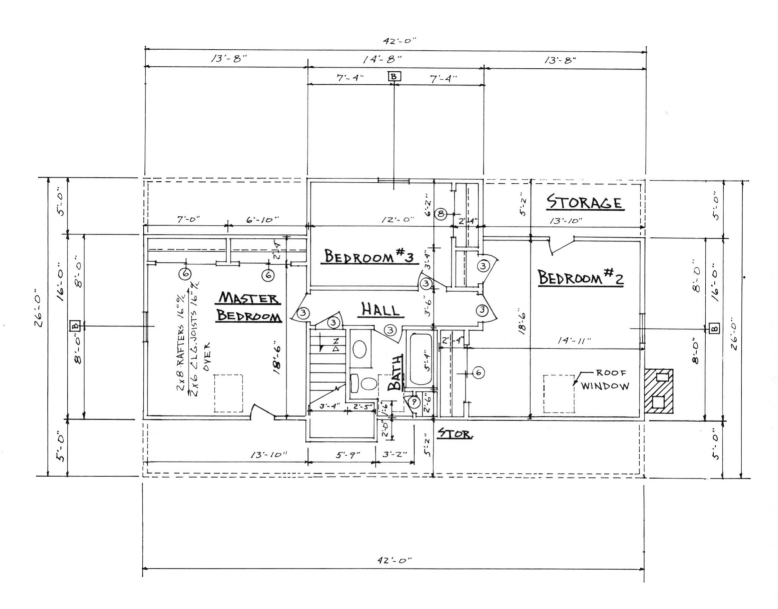

SECOND FLOOR PLAN

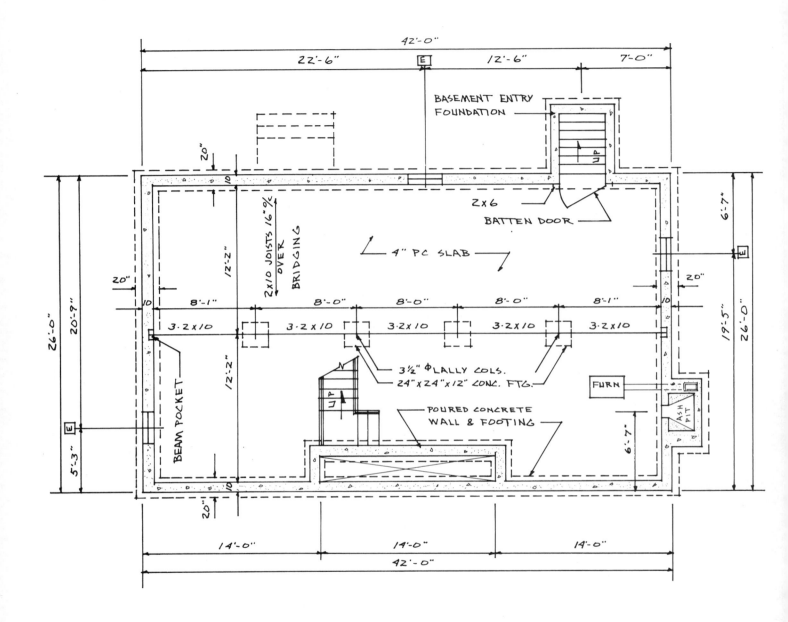

FOUNDATION PLAN

NOTES:

1) BASEMENT ENTRY FOUNDATION TO CON- FORM TO MANUFACTURER SPECIFICATIONS.

2) FIREPLACE FOOTING TO BE 12" THICK; EXTEND 6".

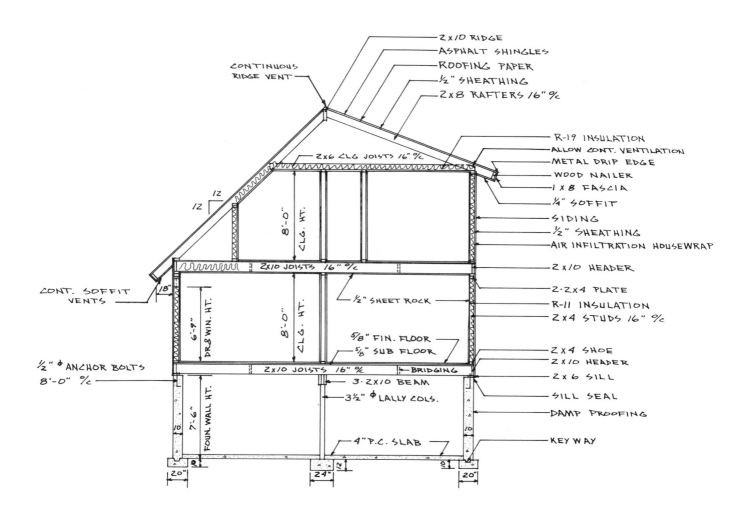

2x10 RIDGE
ASPHALT SHINGLES
ROOFING PAPER
½" SHEATHING
2x8 RAFTERS 16" ⁰⁄c

CONTINUOUS RIDGE VENT

R-19 INSULATION
ALLOW CONT. VENTILATION
METAL DRIP EDGE
WOOD NAILER
1 X 8 FASCIA
¼" SOFFIT
SIDING
½" SHEATHING
AIR INFILTRATION HOUSEWRAP

2x6 CLG JOISTS 16" ⁰⁄c

12
12

8'-0" CLG. HT.

2x10 JOISTS 16" ⁰⁄c

2 x 10 HEADER

½" SHEET ROCK

2-2x4 PLATE
R-11 INSULATION
2x4 STUDS 16" ⁰⁄c

CONT. SOFFIT VENTS

18"

6'-9" DR.& WIN. HT.

8'-0" CLG. HT.

5/8" FIN. FLOOR
5/8" SUB FLOOR

2x4 SHOE
2x10 HEADER

½" ⌀ ANCHOR BOLTS 8'-0" ⁰⁄c

2x10 JOISTS 16" ⁰⁄c

BRIDGING

2x6 SILL
SILL SEAL
DAMP PROOFING

3·2x10 BEAM
3½" ⌀ LALLY COLS.

7'-6" FOUN. WALL HT.

10

4" P.C. SLAB

10

KEY WAY

20"

24"

20"

CROSS SECTION

NOTES:

1) STRUCTURAL CHANGES SHOULD NOT BE MADE WITHOUT CONSULTING ARCHITECT/CONTRACTOR.

2) WOOD FRAMING MEMBERS TO HAVE A FIBER STRESS OF 1200 PSI.

3) CHECK LOCAL BUILDING CODES REGARDING FLOOR INSULATION.

4) WOOD FRAMING MEMBERS TO BE KEPT 2" CLEAR OF FIREPLACE MASONRY. INSULATE WITH FIBERGLASS BETWEEN WOOD & MASONRY.

5) GRADE TO BE 8" BELOW TOP OF FOUNDATION WALL.

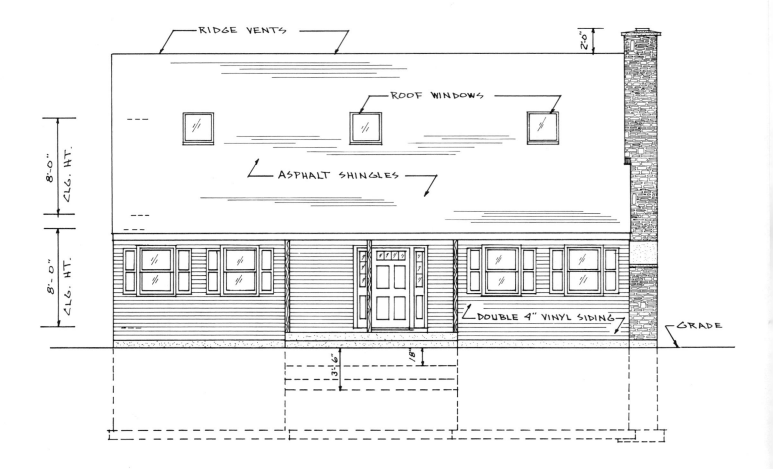

RIDGE VENTS

ROOF WINDOWS

ASPHALT SHINGLES

2'-0"

8'-0" CLG. HT.

8'-0" CLG. HT.

DOUBLE 4" VINYL SIDING

GRADE

3'-6"

18"

FRONT ELEVATION

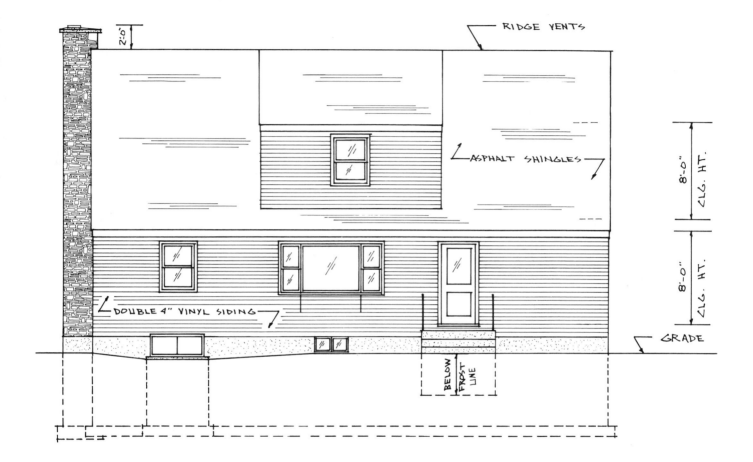

RIDGE VENTS

2'-0"

ASPHALT SHINGLES

8'-0" CLG. HT.

8'-0" CLG. HT.

DOUBLE 4" VINYL SIDING

GRADE

BELOW FROST LINE

REAR ELEVATION

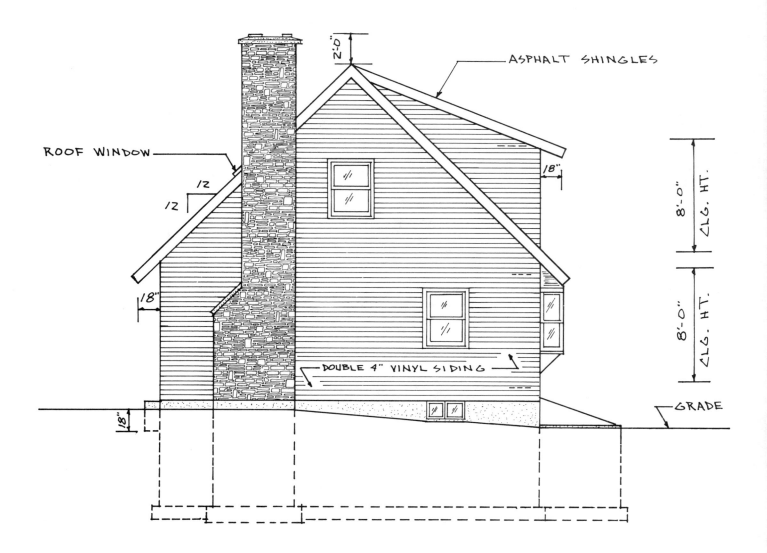

ASPHALT SHINGLES

ROOF WINDOW

2'-0"

12

12

18"

18"

8'-0" CLG. HT.

8'-0" CLG. HT.

GRADE

DOUBLE 4" VINYL SIDING

18"

RIGHT ELEVATION

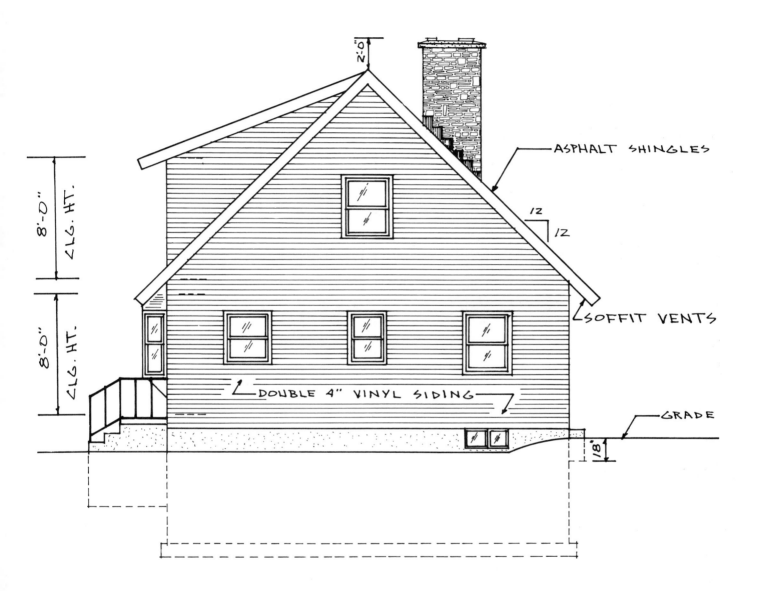

ASPHALT SHINGLES

12
12

SOFFIT VENTS

DOUBLE 4" VINYL SIDING

GRADE

8'-0" CLG. HT.

8'-0" CLG. HT.

2'-0"

18"

LEFT ELEVATION

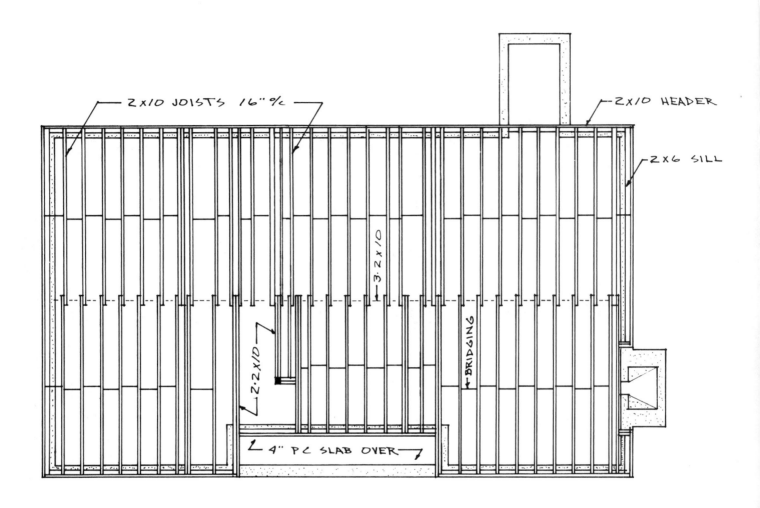

2x10 JOISTS 16" ℀

2x10 HEADER

2x6 SILL

3-2x10

2-2x10

BRIDGING

4" PC SLAB OVER

FIRST FLOOR FRAMING PLAN

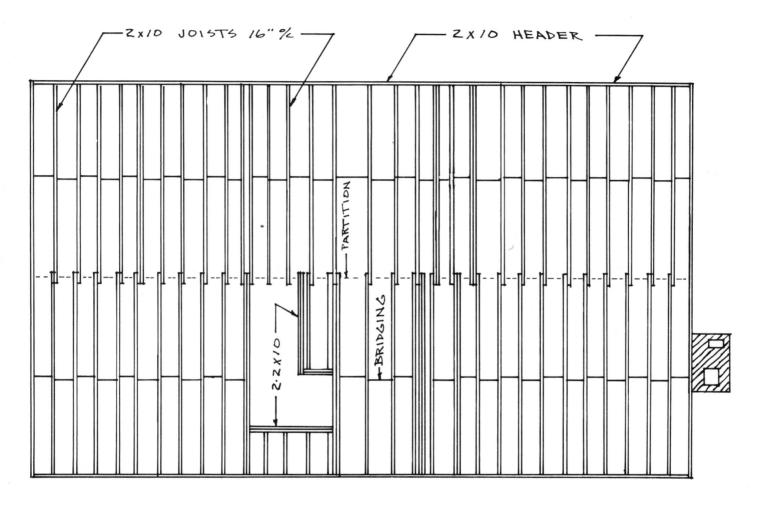

2×10 JOISTS 16"% — 2×10 HEADER

PARTITION

BRIDGING

2-2×10

SECOND FLOOR FRAMING PLAN

NOTE:
DOUBLE JOISTS UNDER
PARALLEL PARTITIONS.

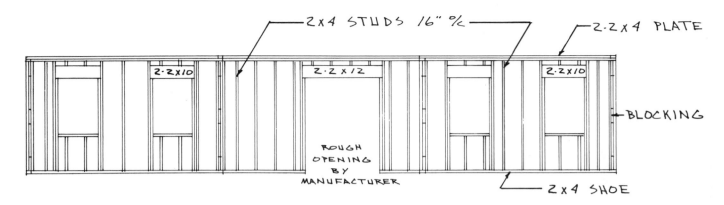

FRONT FRAMING PLAN

DOOR SCHEDULE			
SYM	QTY	SIZE	TYPE
①	1	$3^0 \times 6^8$	PANEL W/SL
②	1	$2^8 \times 6^8$	PANEL-S.C.
③	9	$2^6 \times 6^8$	FLUSH-H.C.
④	1	$2^0 \times 6^8$	FLUSH-H.C.
⑤	1	$5^0 \times 6^8$	BI-FOLD
⑥	4	$5^0 \times 6^8$	SLDG.-H.C.
⑦	1	$5^0 \times 6^8$	FRENCH DRS.
⑧	1	$4^0 \times 6^8$	SLDG.-H.C.

WINDOW SCHEDULE			
SYM	QTY	SIZE	TYPE
A	1	$8^3 \times 4^2$	45° BAY
B	10	$2^8 \times 3^{10}$	D.H.
C	1	$2^8 \times 3^2$	D.H.
D	1	$2^0 \times 3^2$	D.H.
E	3	$2^8 \times 1^4$	BSMT.

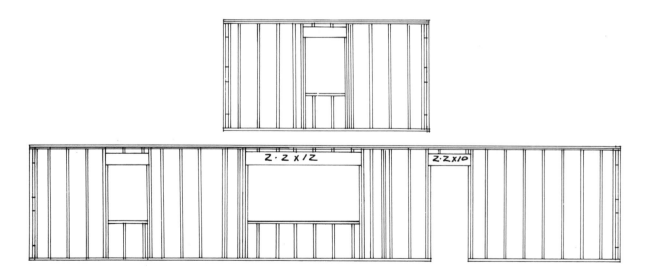

REAR FRAMING PLAN

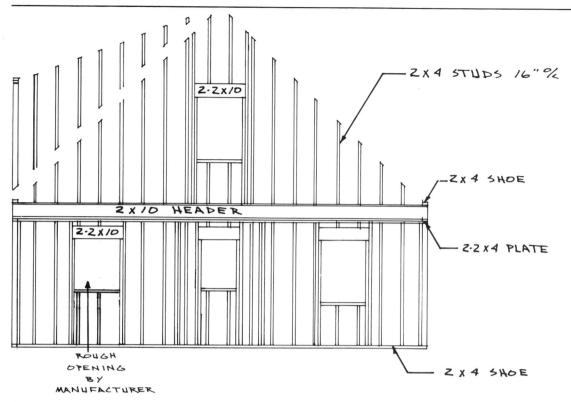

2x4 STUDS 16" %

2x4 SHOE

2x10 HEADER

2.2x10

2.2x4 PLATE

2.2x10

ROUGH
OPENING
BY
MANUFACTURER

2x4 SHOE

LEFT FRAMING PLAN

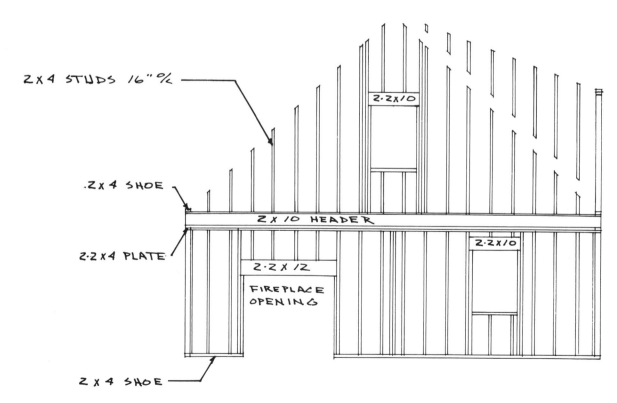

2x4 STUDS 16" %

2.2x10

2x4 SHOE

2x10 HEADER

2.2x4 PLATE

2.2x12

2.2x10

FIREPLACE
OPENING

2x4 SHOE

RIGHT FRAMING PLAN

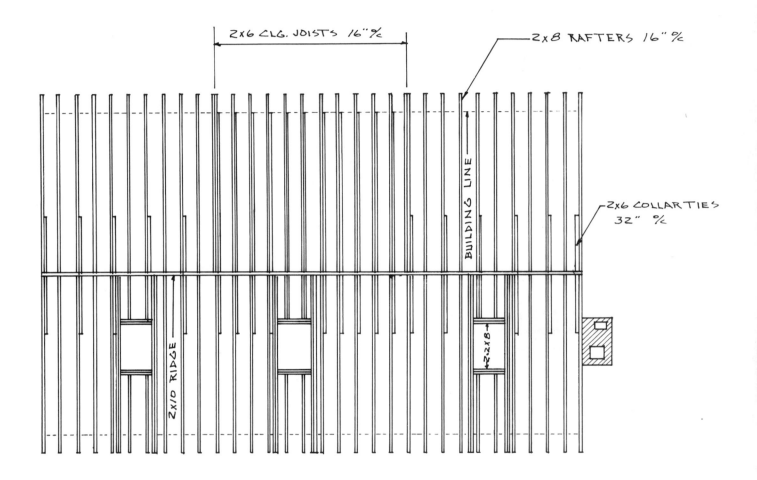

ROOF FRAMING PLAN

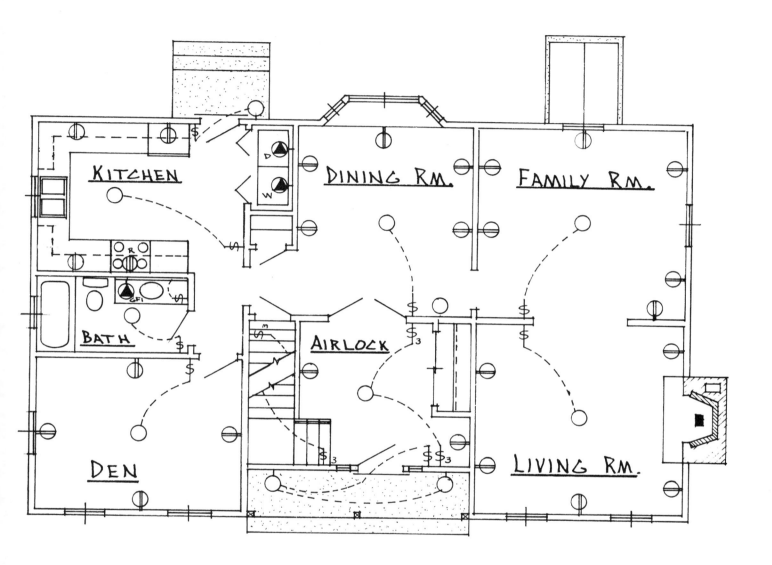

First Floor Electrical Layout

NOTE:
ELECTRICAL SYMBOLS
LOCATED ON SECOND
FLOOR ELECTRICAL
LAYOUT.

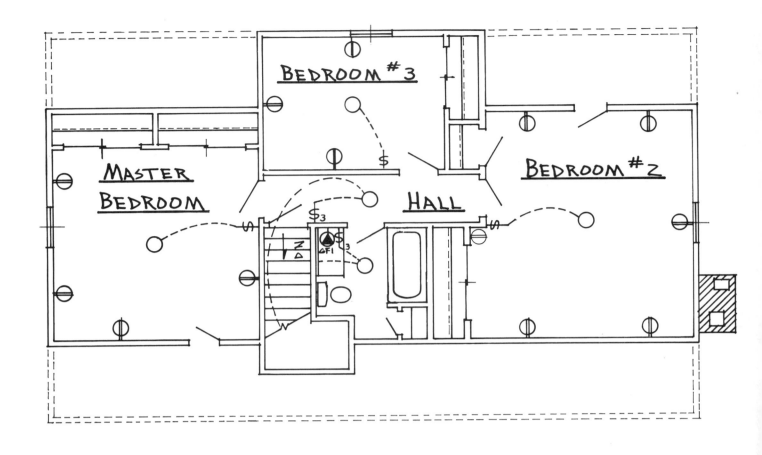

SECOND FLOOR ELECTRICAL LAYOUT

ELECTRICAL SYMBOLS	
SYM	ITEM
$	SINGLE-POLE SWITCH
$₃	THREE-WAY SWITCH
⊖	DUPLEX OUTLET
⊖ᵣ	RANGE OUTLET
◉ᴅ	DRYER OUTLET
◉ᴡ	WASHER OUTLET
◉ɢꜰɪ	GROUND FAULT INTERRUPTER
◯	LIGHTING OUTLET
▭	FLUORESCENT LIGHTING

MATERIAL LIST

FLOOR SYSTEM - First Floor
2 × 10 Joists------------------------60/14 - 10/10
2 × 10 Header----------------------8/14 - 2/12
2 × 6 Sill-------------------------------8/14 - 2/12 - 1/6
Sill Seal--------------------------------136 Lineal Feet
Anchor Bolts------------------------17
1/2" × 4' × 8' Plywood----------33 Sheets
Bridging----------------------------54 Pairs
3 1/2" ⌀ Lally Columns------------4/8
3-2 × 10 Beam-----------------------9/14

FLOOR SYSTEM - Second Floor
2 × 10 Joists-----------------------8/14 - 2/12
2 × 10 Header----------------------4/14
Bridging----------------------------55 Pairs
1/2" × 4' × 8' Plywood----------33 Sheets

CEILING SYSTEM - Second Floor
2 × 6 Ceiling Joints-----------------12/18
R-19 Insulation-----------------------26 Rolls

WALL SYSTEM
2 × 4 Shoe--------------------------8/14 - 2/12 - 1/6
2-2 × 4 Plate----------------------16/14 - 5/12
2 × 4 Studs---------------------------203/8 - 26/10
Door Headers (2 × 10)------------1/12 - 1/6
Window Headers
   2 × 10----------------------------6/12
   2 × 12----------------------------2/10
1/2" × 4' × 8' Sheathing--------56 Sheets
Air Infiltration Housewrap---------1777 Square Feet
R-11 Insulation----------------------22 Rolls

Siding--------------------------------1777 Square Feet
Fireplace Header (2 × 12)----------1/12

ROOF SYSTEM
2 × 10 Ridge--------------------------3/14
2 × 8 Rafters--------------------------60/22 - 6/10 - 6/8 - 12/16
2 × 6 Collar Ties----------------------11/10
1 × 8" Rake Fascia------------------128 Lineal Feet
Roofing Felt-----------------------------3 Rolls
1/2" × 4' × 8' Plywood------------35 Sheets
Asphalt Shingles----------------------33 Bundles
1/4" × 18 Soffit----------------------84 Lineal Feet
1" × 8" Fascia-----------------------84 Lineal Feet

BASEMENT STAIRS
2 × 12 Stringers----------------------2/14
2 × 10 Treads-------------------------3/12
Handrail--------------------------------2/14

INTERIOR
2 × 4 Studs----------------------------234/8
2-2 × 8 Door Headers-------------8/12 - 13/6
1/2" × 4' × 8' Sheetrock--------74 Sheets
1" × 12" Shelving------------------2/6 - 1/3 - 4/8
Closet Pole----------------------------2/6 - 1/3 - 3/8
Baseboard-----------------------------427 Lineal Feet
Ceiling Moulding----------------------457 Lineal Feet
Stair Stringers------------------------2/14
Stair Risers---------------------------3/12 - 1/4
Stair Treads---------------------------3/12
Railing----------------------------------1/3

Article III

Fireplance Planning

(Printed with permission of Portland Willamette Company)

When planning a new fireplace or redecorating an existing one, several things should be considered. Among them are the type, location, size, style, and outward appearance of the fireplace. Some of your decisions will be based on practicality, but most of them can be strictly a matter of personal and aesthetic preference.

TYPES OF FIREPLACES

1. The most prevalent is the durable and ever-popular masonry fireplace. They are custom built, from foundation to chimney top, of brick, stone, adobe, or concrete blocks. A variety of styles, from the traditional wall fireplaces, Swedish or corner fireplaces, to freestanding "see throughs," may be built of masonry. A good investment, they will last for the life of the house.

2. A heat-circulating fireplace is one that circulates convection-heated air, in addition to providing radiated heat from the firebox. They are a good idea for vacation homes or cottages that have no furnace, or homes where a supplementary heat source is desired.

3. Prebuilt fireplaces can be the answer to various problems which might otherwise rule out a fireplace. They are quite simple to add to existing homes. Often installed without concrete footings or a masonry chimney, they offer both installation economy and heating efficiency.

There are two types of prebuilts. One type is set into the wall and surrounded by masonry or wood paneling, with a hearth of slate, tile, or other material.

When installed, it is hard to tell that they are prebuilt fireplaces.

The second type is the freestanding metal fireplace. They are the least costly and easiest to install, yet are efficient heaters since they radiate warmth from all sides, as well as from parts of the chimney.

Simulated fireplaces, either electric or gas-fired, are often used in remodeling projects and serve many apartments and mobile homes, where wood storage and burning may be a problem. Easy to install, they're available in a variety of realistic-looking models.

CHOOSING A LOCATION

Your lifestyle is an important factor in deciding where to put your fireplace. It should be in the room or rooms where it will give the most enjoyment. So think about where you spend most of your time and what you like to do. Family hobbies and interest may suggest an ideal location. The fireplace is generally the focal point of the home.

Consider your entertaining preferences, too. Do you have small dinner parties, or usually host larger groups? Do you entertain casually, or formally?

Although the living room is the most common fireplace location, any room is a possible site—the dining room or kitchen, a library or den, even a patio, where a fireplace would add outdoor cheer and comfort on cooler evenings. A fireplace is a "must" for a family room. But, before you make your final decision, you should examine your entire floor plan and consider all of the options available to you.

Be sure to consider furniture placement and traffic

patterns. Seating and tables should be grouped to make the fireplace the center of interest. Avoid locations where room traffic must pass between fireplace and furniture.

Structural and economic considerations might also determine your fireplace location. Fireplace footings, for example, are most practical to build on outside walls. Check into your proposed chimney site. If it's too near tall trees or neighboring buildings, downdrafts can affect the flue draft.

DETERMINING SIZE

The size of your fireplace should fit the size of your room, not just visually, but from a standpoint of operating efficiency. The size of the opening, or firebox, is the key. Since fireplace heat is radiated from the brickwork that surrounds the frame, the fire should pretty well fill the firebox. This will help give you maximum heating efficiency and fuel economy.

Keep in mind, too, that the amount of heat from a fireplace will vary depending upon whether it's located in the short or long wall of the room.

So, beware of building too big a fireplace. When filled with flame, it's likely to make the room uncomfortably warm. Put a small fire in it, and it's likely to smoke, won't radiate enough heat, and won't be as visually pleasing.

DECORATIVE BALANCE

Attention should also be given to the relative importance of your fireplace to other features in the room. Do you want the fireplace to dominate? Share the limelight? Or blend into the room?

Will it set the decorative mood or style? Or complement it? What shall the mood be? Casual? Formal? Dramatic?

There are many things you can do to achieve the desired results. For example, a wall fireplace with no projections will blend into the wall. But add an extended cantilevered hearth, a rough fieldstone face, or a copper hood, and it will command attention.

Setting your fireplace into a bookshelf wall will give it importance, but not dominance. By making it part of a window wall, you can combine both view and fire into a single focal feature. You can plan your fireplace to define an area of activity, divide two rooms, or dramatize an unusual architectural feature.

Such factors will influence your choice of basic fireplace styles. Whatever style you choose, an infinite number of variations in outward appearance is possible by using different facing materials: hearths, mantels, hoods, fire screens, and accessories.

Section IV
Raised Ranches

BLU-DONDA

DESIGNED & DRAWN BY E. BRYANT

The Blu-Donda is a raised ranch that has a 1-foot cantilever in the front, thereby resulting in additional floor space on the upper level. Excluding the utility room, this house has 1,704 square feet of living space.

The upper-level floor plan consists of a living room, dining room, kitchen, bath, and two bedrooms. The lower level has a guest room, recreational room, den, bath, and utility room.

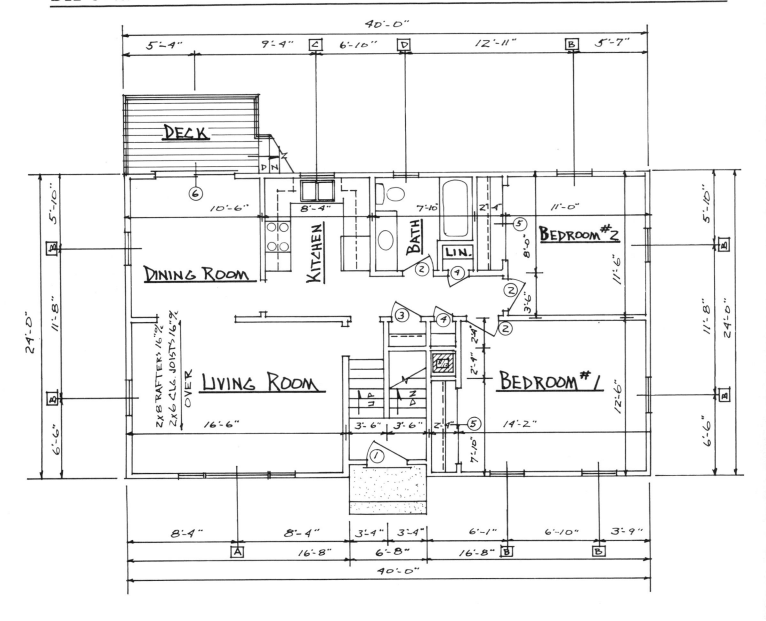

Upper Level Floor Plan

NOTES:
1) STRUCTURAL CHANGES SHOULD NOT BE MADE WITHOUT CONSULTING ARCHITECT/CONTRACTOR.

2) WOOD FRAMING MEMBERS

TO HAVE A FIBER STRESS OF 1200 PSI.

3) WOOD FRAMING TO BE KEPT 2" CLEAR OF CHIMNEY MASONRY.

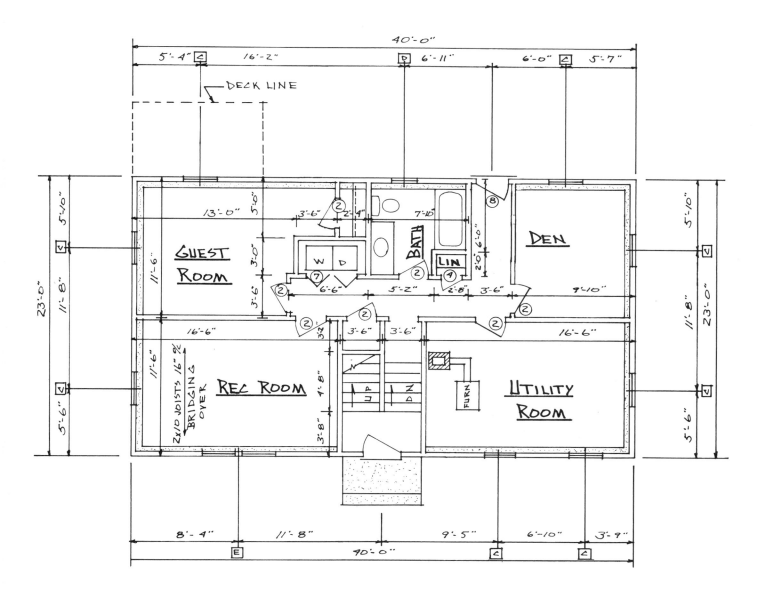

Lower Level Floor Plan

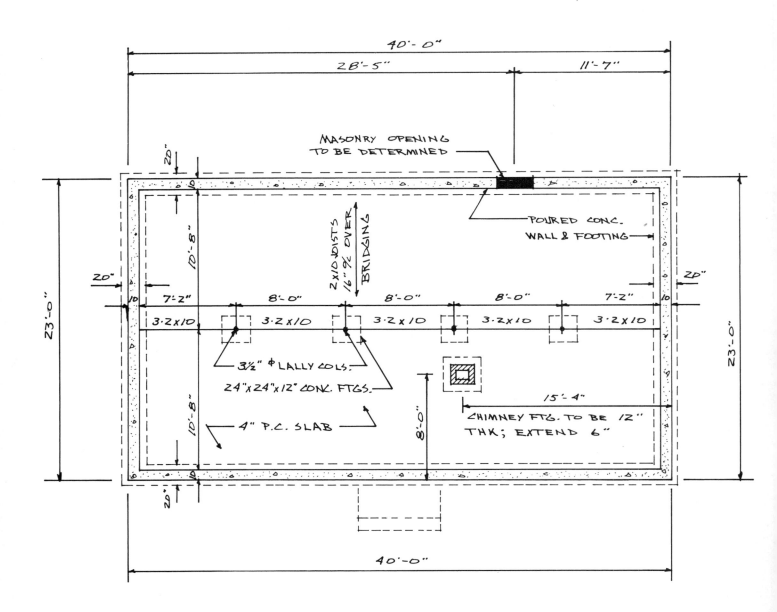

FOUNDATION PLAN

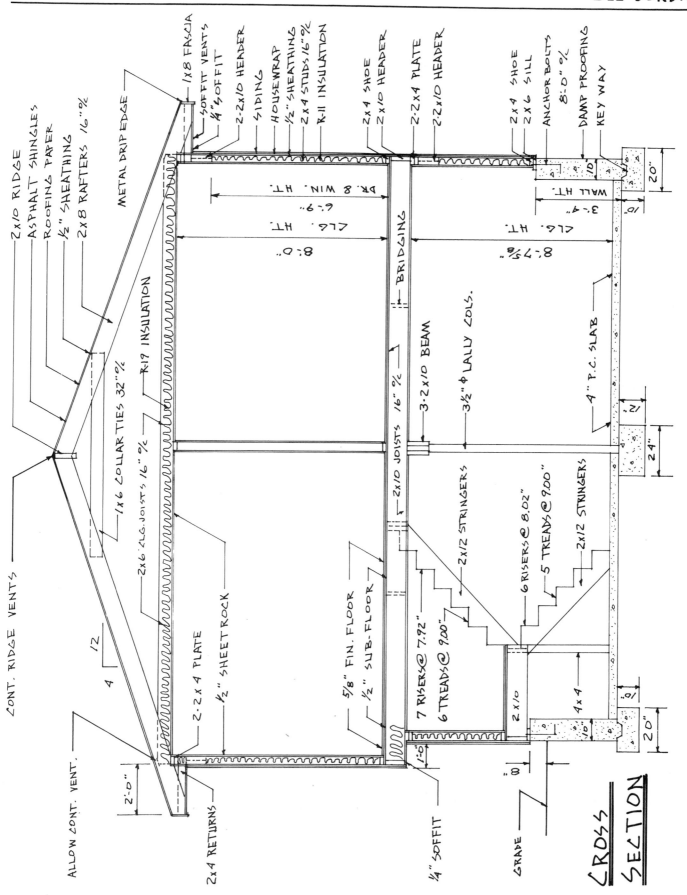

CROSS SECTION

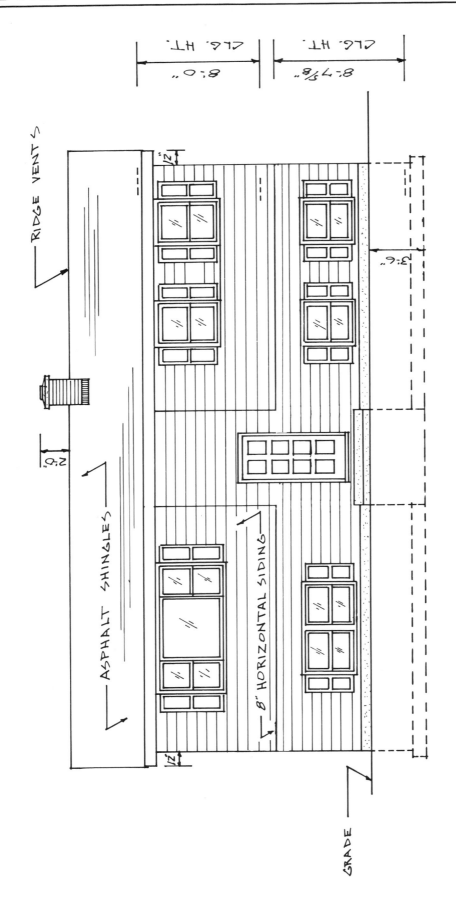

FRONT ELEVATION

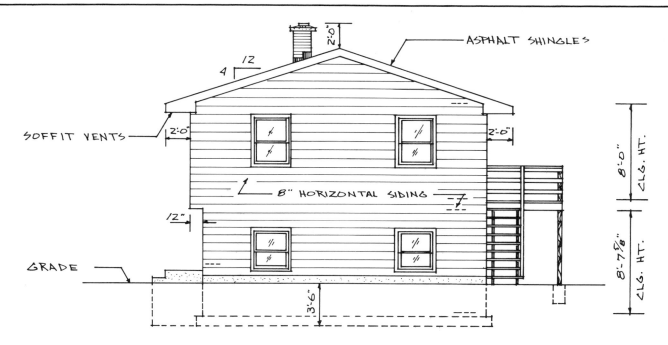

ASPHALT SHINGLES

SOFFIT VENTS

8" HORIZONTAL SIDING

GRADE

RIGHT ELEVATION

DOOR SCHEDULE

SYM	QTY	SIZE	TYPE
1	1	$3^0 \times 6^8$	PANEL-S.C.
2	10	$2^6 \times 6^8$	FLUSH-H.C.
3	1	$2^0 \times 6^8$	FLUSH-H.C.
4	3	$1^6 \times 6^8$	FLUSH-H.C.
5	2	$6^0 \times 6^8$	SLDG.-H.C.
6	1	$6^0 \times 6^8$	PATIO DR.
7	1	$5^0 \times 6^8$	BI-FOLD
8	1	$2^8 \times 6^8$	PANEL-S.C.

WINDOW SCHEDULE

SYM	QTY	SIZE	TYPE
A	1	$2^0-4^2 2^0 \times 4^2$	DH PW
B	7	$2^8 \times 3^{10}$	DH
C	9	$2^8 \times 3^2$	DH
D	2	$2^0 \times 3^2$	DH
E	1	$2^8 \times 3^2$	MULLION

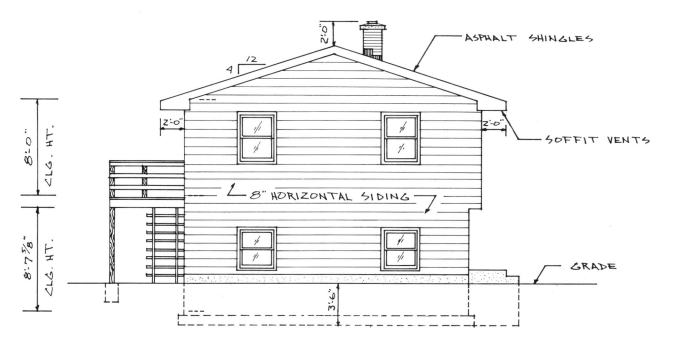

ASPHALT SHINGLES

SOFFIT VENTS

8" HORIZONTAL SIDING

GRADE

LEFT ELEVATION

NOTES:

1) HORIZONTAL AND VERTICAL STEPS TO BE POURED AT THE SAME TIME.

2) HORIZONTAL DISTANCE BETWEEN STEPS IS NOT TO BE LESS 2'-0".

3) VERTICAL STEP IS NOT TO BE HIGHER THAN THREE-QUARTERS OF THE HORIZONTAL DISTANCE.

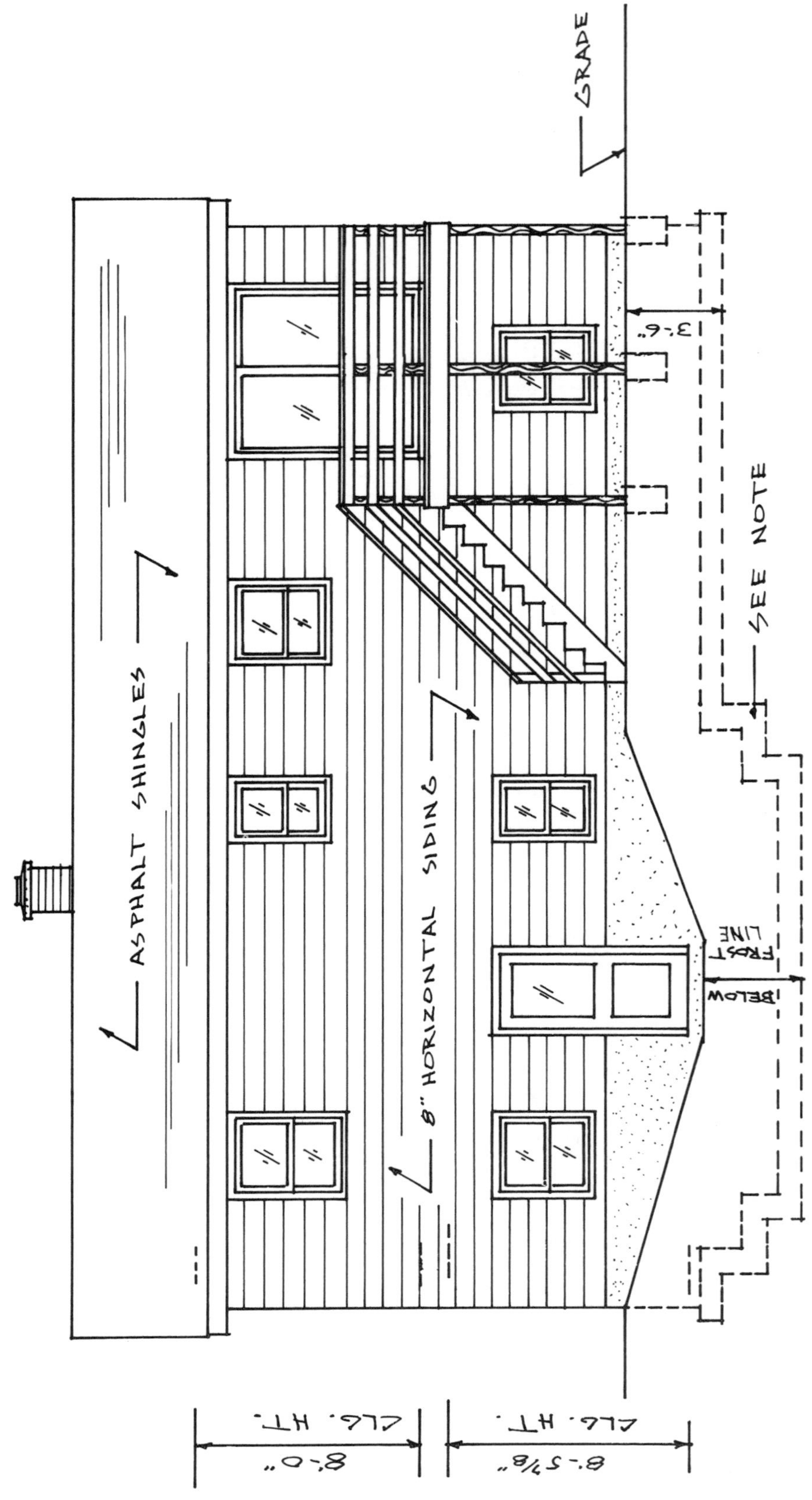

GRADE

3'-6"

SEE NOTE

FROST LINE BELOW

ASPHALT SHINGLES

8" HORIZONTAL SIDING

9'6" HT.

8'-0"

9'6" HT.

8'-5⅝"

REAR ELEVATION

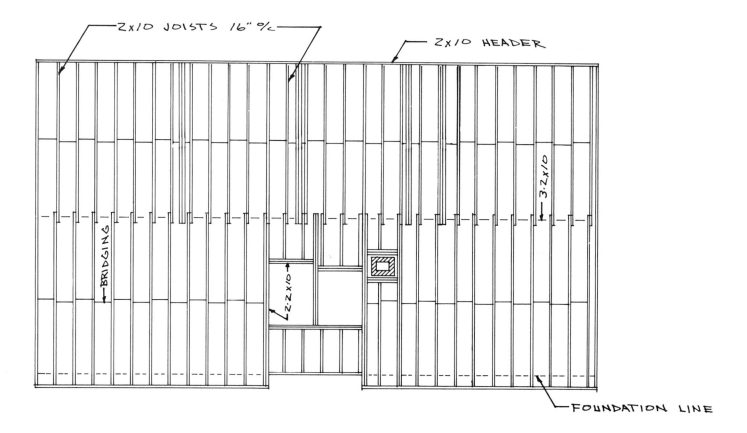

FLOOR FRAMING PLAN

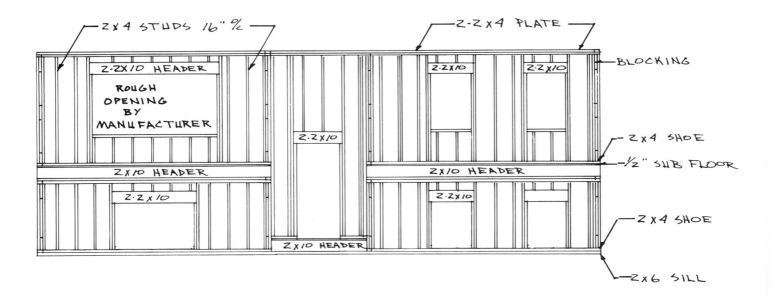

FRONT FRAMING PLAN

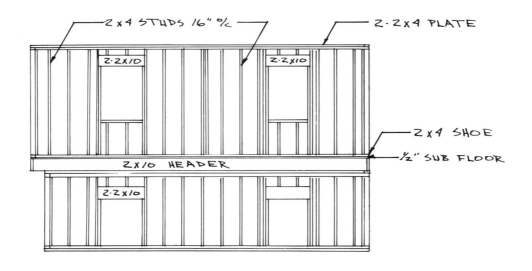

RIGHT FRAMING PLAN

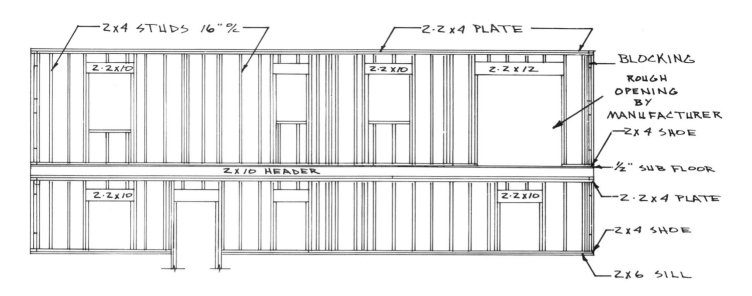

2x4 STUDS 16" %

2·2x4 PLATE

BLOCKING

ROUGH OPENING BY MANUFACTURER

2x4 SHOE

½" SUB FLOOR

2·2x4 PLATE

2x4 SHOE

2x6 SILL

2·2x10

2·2x10

2·2x12

2x10 HEADER

2·2x10

2·2x10

2·2x10

REAR FRAMING PLAN

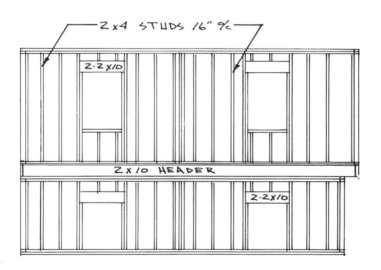

2x4 STUDS 16" %

2·2x10

2x10 HEADER

2·2x10

LEFT FRAMING PLAN

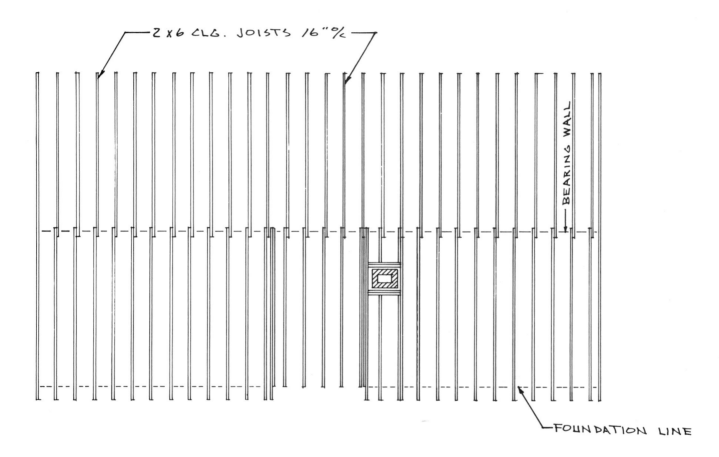

2 X 6 CLG. JOISTS 16" ⁰∕c

BEARING WALL

FOUNDATION LINE

CEILING FRAMING PLAN

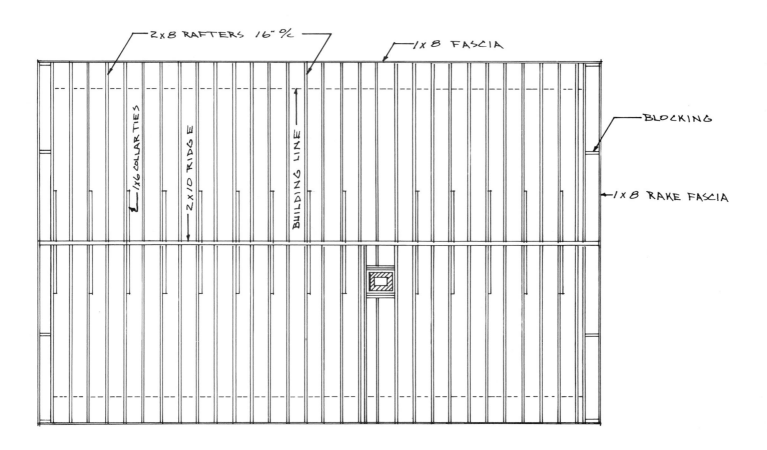

2x8 RAFTERS 16" %

1x8 FASCIA

1x6 COLLAR TIES

2x10 RIDGE

BUILDING LINE

BLOCKING

1x8 RAKE FASCIA

ROOF FRAMING PLAN

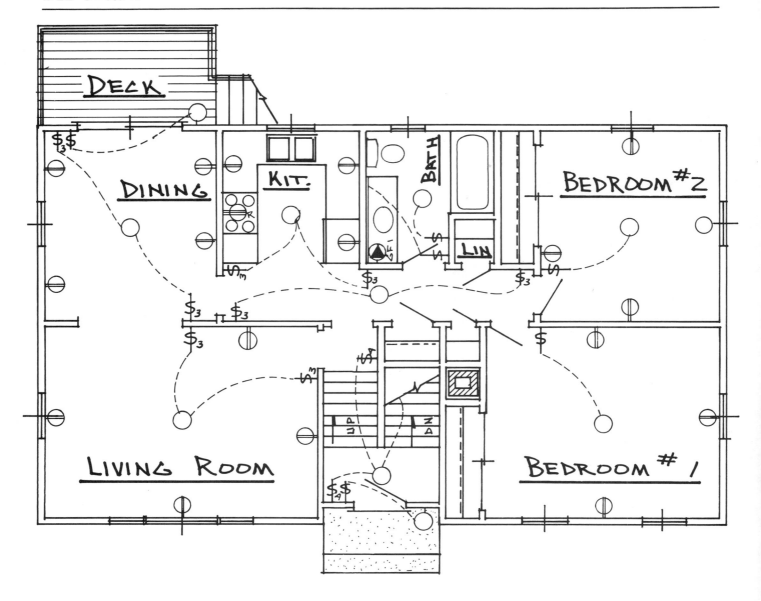

Upper Level
Electrical Layout

Electrical Symbols	
SYM	ITEM
$	SINGLE-POLE SWITCH
$₃	THREE-WAY SWITCH
$₄	FOUR-WAY SWITCH
⊖	DUPLEX OUTLET
⊖R	RANGE OUTLET
▲GFI	GROUND FAULT INTERRUPTER
◯	LIGHTING OUTLET
▭	FLUORESCENT LIGHTING
▲W	WASHER OUTLET
▲D	DRYER OUTLET

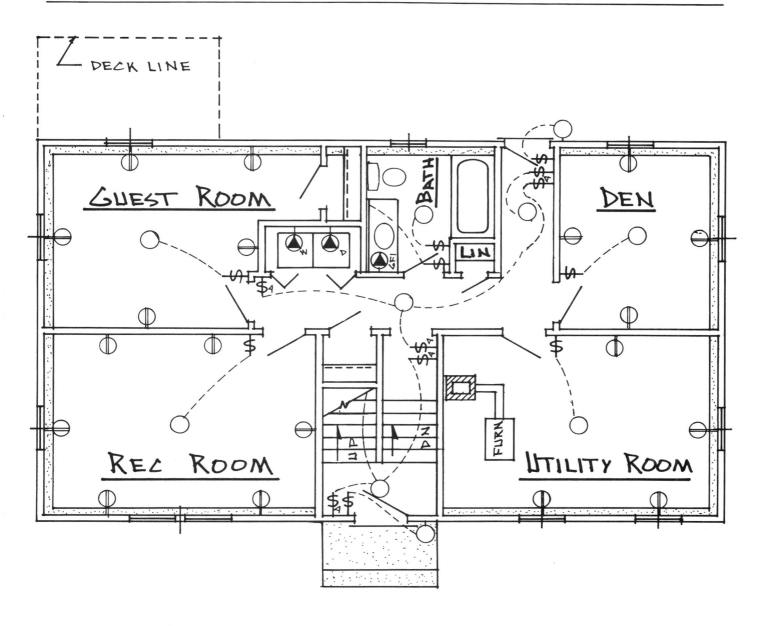

Lower Level Electrical Layout

NOTE:
ELECTRICAL SYMBOLS
LOCATED ON UPPER LEVEL
ELECTRICAL LAYOUT.

MATERIAL LIST

FLOOR SYSTEM
2 × 10 Joists-------------------------------32/14 - 41/12
2 × 10 Header-------------------------- 4/14 - 6/12
2 × 6 Sill---------------------------------- 124 Lineal Feet
Sill Seal-------------------------------------124 Lineal Feet
Anchor Bolts------------------------------ 15
1/2" × 4' × 8' Plywood------------ 29 Sheets
Bridging------------------------------------- 53 Pairs
3 1/2" ⏀ Lally Columns -------------- 4/8
3-2 × 10 Beam----------------------- 6/14 - 3/12

WALL SYSTEM
2 × 4 Shoe----------------------------------12/12 - 8/14
2-2 × 4 Plate----------------------------24/12 - 16/4
2 × 4 Studs------------------------------ 1/10 - 8/14 - 236/8
Door Headers
    2 × 10----------------------------------2/14
    2 × 12----------------------------------1/14
Window Headers (2-2 × 10)------3/10 - 2/12 - 8/14
1/2" × 4' × 8' Sheathing---------47 Sheets
R-11 3 1/2" Insulation---------------- 17 Rolls
Siding---------------------------------------1478 Square Feet
Air Infiltration Housewrap---------- 1478 Square Feet

CEILING SYSTEM
2 × 6 Ceiling Joists--------------------38/12 - 30/14
R-19 Insulation----------------------------20 Rolls

ROOF SYSTEM
2 × 10 Ridge----------------------------3/14
2 × 8 Rafters----------------------------68/16
1 × 6 Collar Ties------------------------14/8
1/4" × 24" Soffit------------------------84 Lineal Feet
1" × 8" Fascia----------------------------84 Lineal Feet
1/4" × 12" Rake Soffit-------------- 52 Lineal Feet
1" × 8" Rake Fascia----------------- 52 Lineal Feet
#15 Roofing Felt---------------------- 3 Rolls
1/2" × 4' × 8' Plywood------------- 40 Sheets
Asphalt Shingles----------------------- 4 Bundles

INTERIOR
2 × 4 Studs----------------------------- 280/8
Door Headers 2-2 × 6--------------15/6 - 3/14 - 2/12
1/2" × 4' × 8' Sheetrock----------- 166 Sheets
1" × 12" Shelving---------------------- 6/8
Closet Pole------------------------------- 3/8
Baseboard-------------------------------- 623 Lineal Feet
Ceiling Moulding----------------------- 784 Lineal Feet
2 × 12 Stair Stringers-----------------2/8 - 2/6
Stair Risers-------------------------------3/12 - 1/4
Stair Treads------------------------------3/12

DECKS
Flooring------------------------------------ 63 Square Feet
Posts-- 3/10
Railings------------------------------------- 80 Lineal Feet
Cap-- 30 Lineal Feet

TERROHN

DESIGNED & DRAWN BY E. BRYANT

The Terrohn is a raised-ranch with double 6-inch vinyl siding on the exterior. For added floor space, the upper level has a 12-inch cantilever overhang in the front of the house.

With 1,040 square feet on the upper level and 1,040 on the lower level, including the utility room, the Terrohn has a total of 2,080 square feet.

Cafe doors provide access from the centrally located kitchen to the adjacent dining room. Sliding glass patio doors separate the dining room from the outside deck, which is individually characteristic with its vertical 1- x -8-inch railing.

Bedroom #1 has its own bath complete with shower, in addition to a roomy closet and cross ventilation provided by two wall-centered double-hung windows. Bedroom #2 also has cross ventilation and a good-sized closet.

The lower level is composed of a utility room, a guest room, a den, and a family room with an adjoining powder room and access to the outside patio.

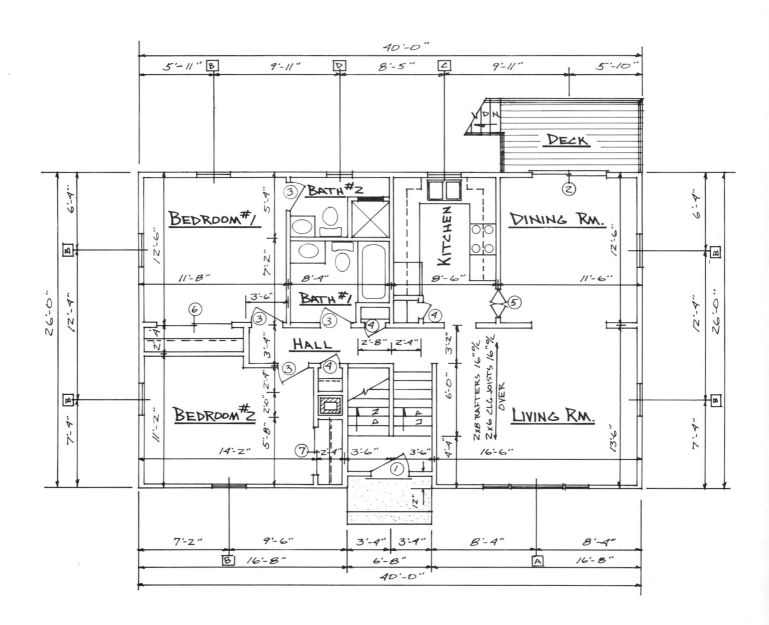

Upper Level Floor Plan

NOTE:
STRUCTURAL CHANGES
SHOULD NOT BE MADE
WITHOUT CONSULTING
ARCHITECT/CONTRACTOR.

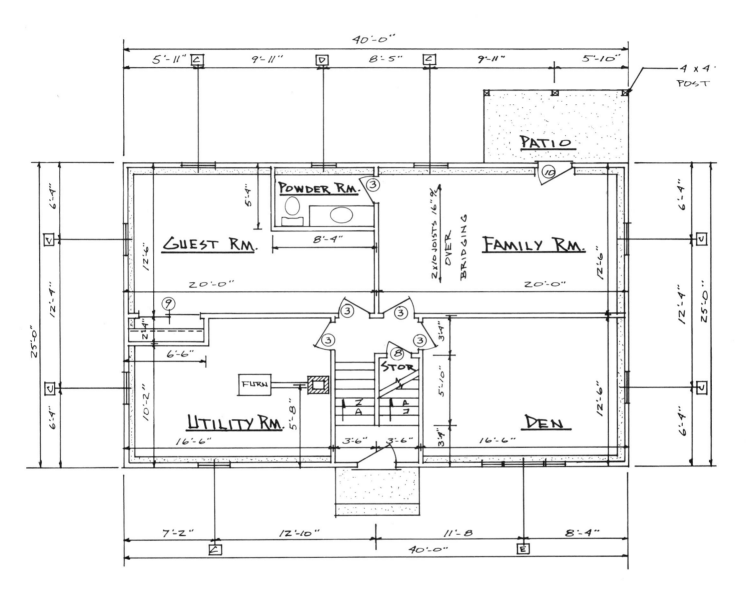

LOWER LEVEL FLOOR PLAN

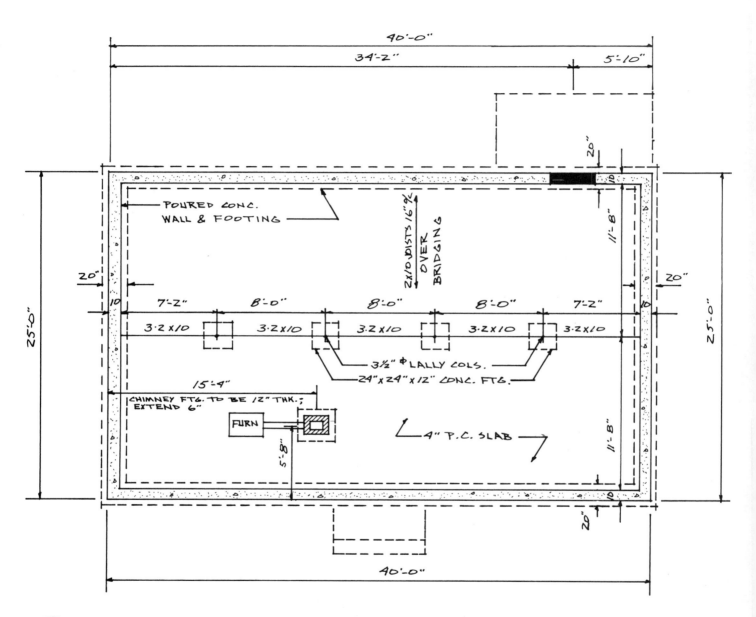

FOUNDATION PLAN

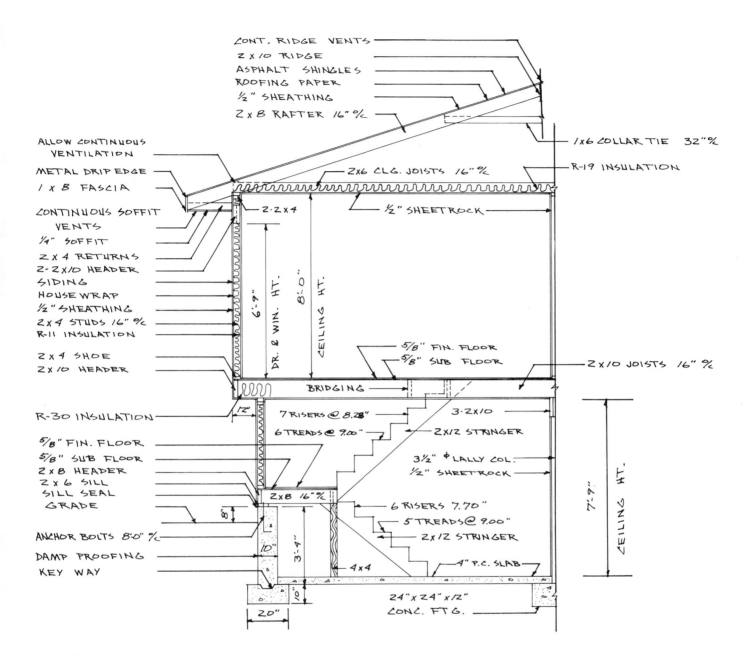

CONT. RIDGE VENTS
2 X 10 RIDGE
ASPHALT SHINGLES
ROOFING PAPER
½" SHEATHING
2 X 8 RAFTER 16" ⁰/c

1 x 6 COLLAR TIE 32" ⁰/c

R-19 INSULATION

2x6 CLG. JOISTS 16" ⁰/c

ALLOW CONTINUOUS
VENTILATION
METAL DRIP EDGE
1 x 8 FASCIA

CONTINUOUS SOFFIT
VENTS
¼" SOFFIT
2 X 4 RETURNS
2-2X10 HEADER
SIDING
HOUSE WRAP
½" SHEATHING
2 X 4 STUDS 16" ⁰/c
R-11 INSULATION

2 X 4 SHOE
2 X 10 HEADER

2·2X4

½" SHEETROCK

6'-9" DR. & WIN. HT.

8'-0" CEILING HT.

5/8" FIN. FLOOR
5/8" SUB FLOOR

2 X 10 JOISTS 16" ⁰/c

BRIDGING

R-30 INSULATION

12"

7 RISERS @ 8.28"
6 TREADS @ 9.00"

3-2X10

2X12 STRINGER

3½" ⌀ LALLY COL.
½" SHEETROCK

5/8" FIN. FLOOR
5/8" SUB FLOOR
2 X 8 HEADER
2 X 6 SILL
SILL SEAL
GRADE

2X8 16" ⁰/c

6 RISERS 7.70"
5 TREADS @ 9.00"
2X12 STRINGER

7'-9" CEILING HT.

ANCHOR BOLTS 8'0" ⁰/c
DAMP PROOFING
KEY WAY

8"

10"

3'-4"

4x4

4" P.C. SLAB

10"

20"

24"x 24"x 12"
CONC. FTG.

STAFF SECTION

NOTE:
ROUGH OPENING OF
LOWER LEVEL WINDOWS
WILL AFFECT LOWER
LEVEL CEILING HEIGHT.

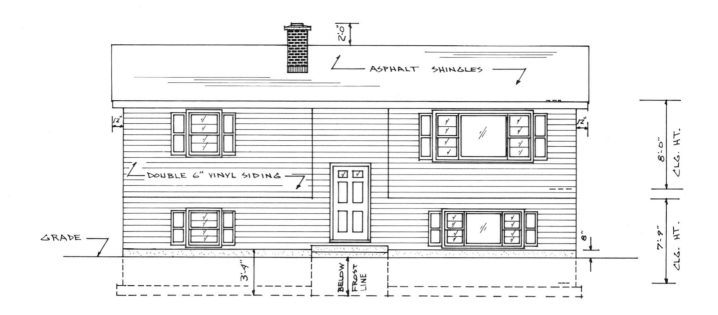

Front Elevation

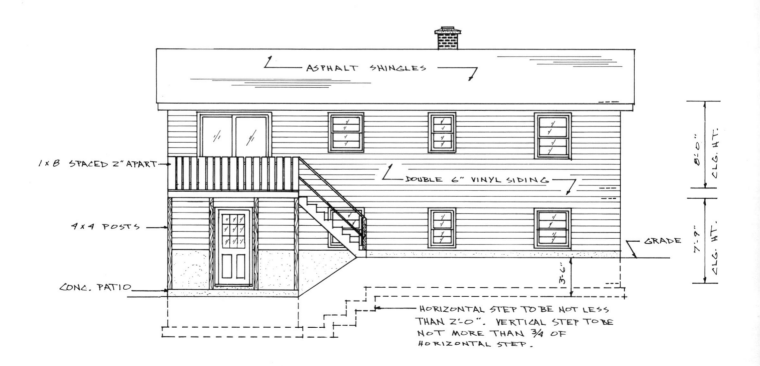

Rear Elevation

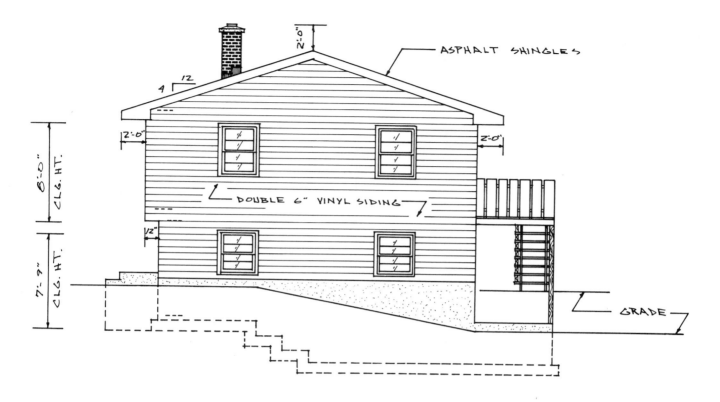

RIGHT ELEVATION

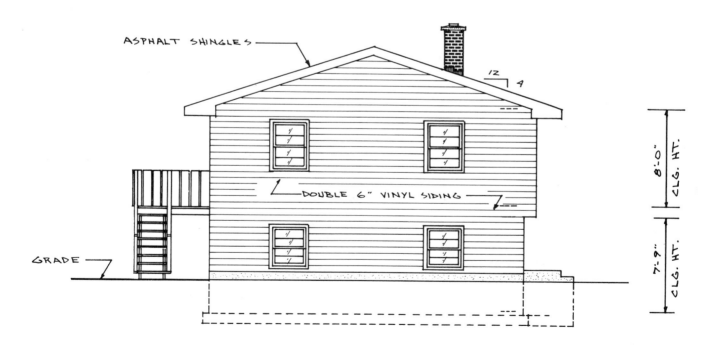

LEFT ELEVATION

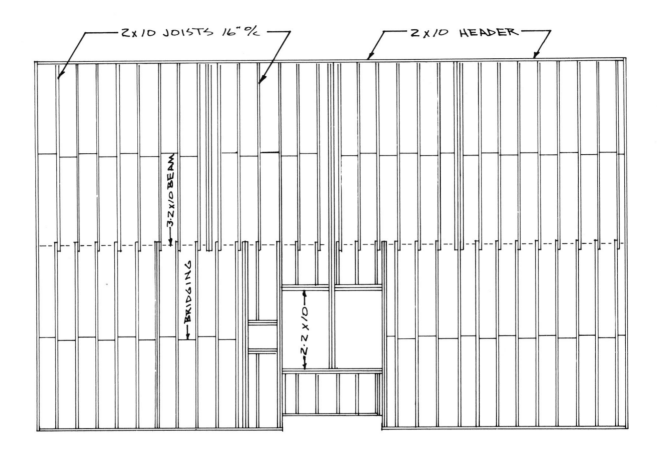

Floor Framing Plan

NOTES:

1) DOUBLE JOISTS UNDER PARALLEL PARTITIONS.

2) WOOD FRAMING MEMBERS TO HAVE A FIBER STRESS OF 1200 PSI.

3) WOOD FRAMING TO BE KEPT 2" CLEAR OF CHIMNEY MASONRY. INSULATE WITH FIBER-GLASS BETWEEN MASONRY AND WOOD.

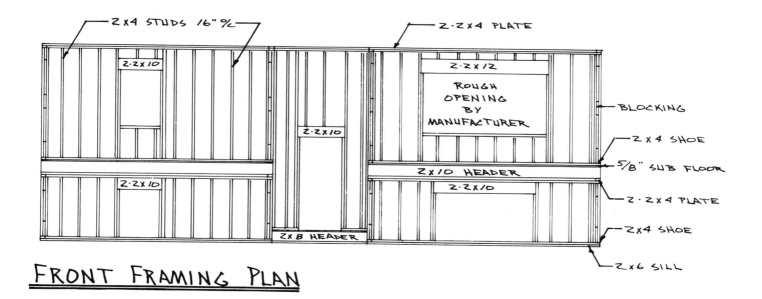

FRONT FRAMING PLAN

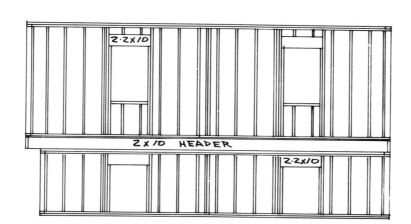

RIGHT FRAMING PLAN

DOOR SCHEDULE			
SYM	QTY	SIZE	REMARKS
①	1	$3^0 \times 6^8$	PANEL-S.C.
②	1	$6^0 \times 6^8$	PATIO DR.
③	9	$2^6 \times 6^8$	FLUSH-H.C.
④	3	$1^6 \times 6^8$	FLUSH-H.C.
⑤	1	$2^6 \times 3^8$	CAFE DR.
⑥	1	$6^0 \times 6^8$	FLUSH-H.C.
⑦	1.	$4^0 \times 6^8$	FLUSH-H.C.
⑧	1	$2^0 \times 6^8$	FLUSH-H.C.
⑨	1	$5^0 \times 6^8$	FLUSH-H.C.
⑩	1	$2^8 \times 6^8$	PANEL-S.C.

WINDOW SCHEDULE			
SYM	QTY	SIZE	REMARKS
A	1	$2^0 - 4^8 - 2^0 \times 4^2$	D.H.P.W.
B	6	$2^8 \times 3^{10}$	D.H.
C	8	$2^8 \times 3^2$	D.H.
D	2	$2^0 \times 3^2$	D.H.
E	1	$1^8 - 3^4 - 1^8 \times 3^2$	D.H.P.W.

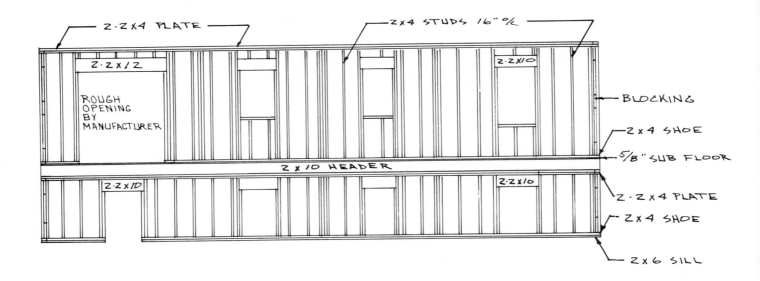

Rear Framing Plan

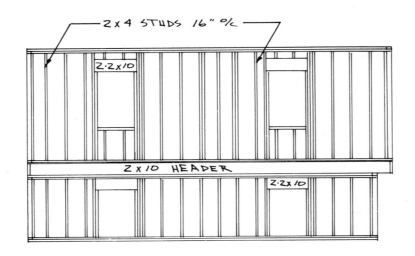

Left Framing Plan

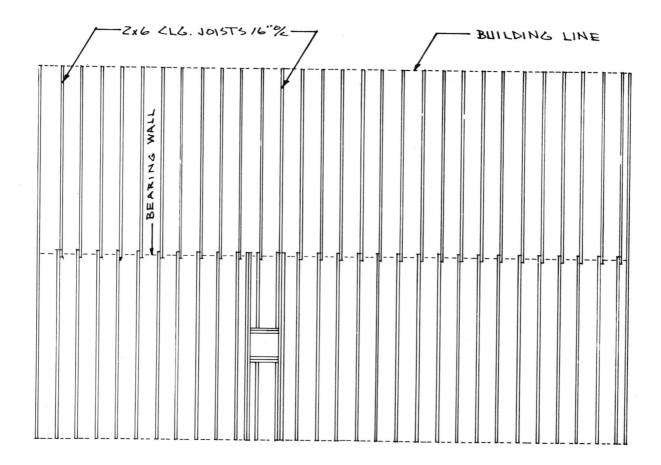

2×6 CLG. JOISTS 16"°/c

BEARING WALL

BUILDING LINE

CEILING FRAMING PLAN

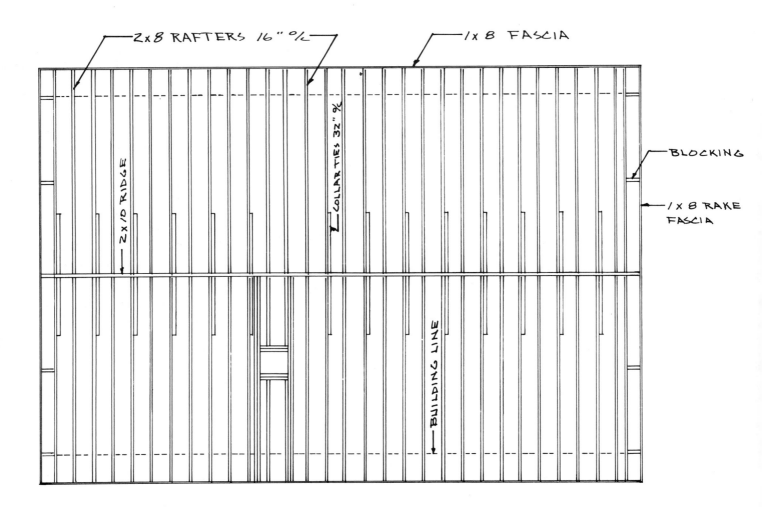

2×8 RAFTERS 16" O/C

1×8 FASCIA

COLLAR TIES 32" O/C

2×10 RIDGE

BUILDING LINE

BLOCKING

1×8 RAKE FASCIA

ROOF FRAMING PLAN

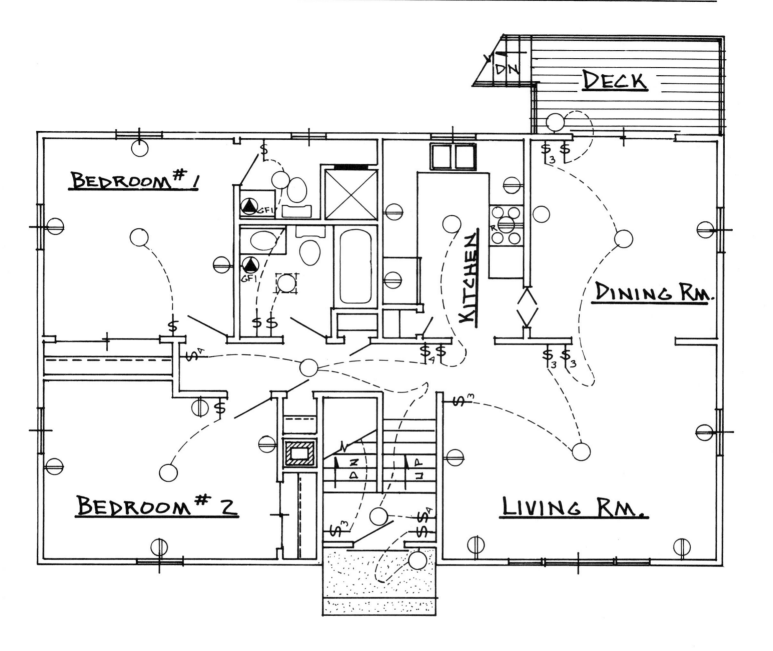

Upper Level Electrical Layout

NOTE:
ELECTRICAL SYMBOLS
LOCATED ON LOWER
LEVEL ELECTRICAL
LAYOUT.

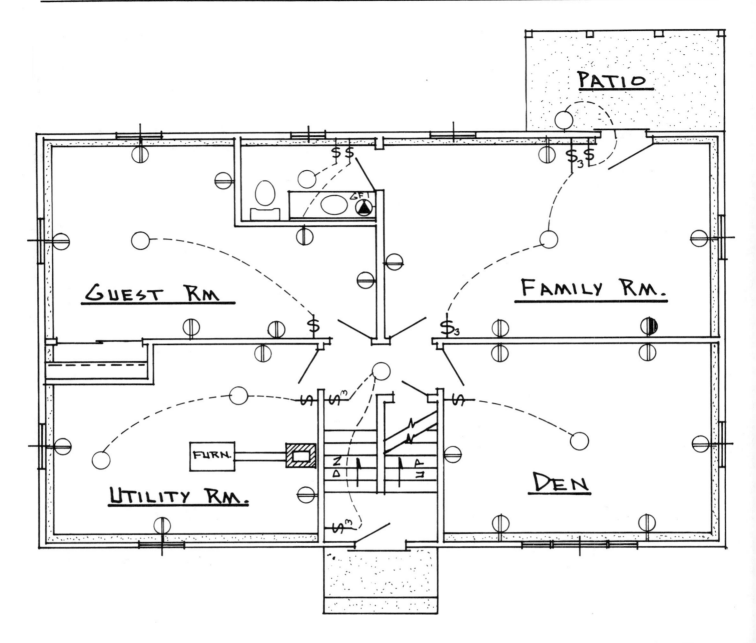

PATIO

GUEST RM

FAMILY RM.

UTILITY RM.

DEN

FURN.

LOWER LEVEL
ELECTRICAL LAYOUT

ELECTRICAL SYMBOLS	
SYM	ITEM
$	SINGLE-POLE SWITCH
$₃	THREE-WAY SWITCH
$₄	FOUR-WAY SWITCH
⊖	DUPLEX OUTLET
⊖	SPLIT-WIRED OUTLET
⊖R	RANGE OUTLET
▲GFI	GROUND FAULT INTERRUPTER
◯	LIGHT OUTLET W/MECH. VENT.
◯	LIGHTING OUTLET
▭	FLUORESCENT LIGHTING

MATERIAL LIST

FLOOR SYSTEM

2 × 10 Joists---------------------- 68/14 - (2 × 8) 2/14 - 2/8
2 × 10 Header------------------- 6/12 - 2/14 - 2/12 -
                                                       2/8 (2 × 8) 1/8
2 × 6 Sill-------------------------- 8/10 - 2/14 - 2/12
Sill Seal--------------------------- 130 Lineal Feet
Anchor Bolts--------------------- 18
1/2" × 4' × 8' Plywood--- 31 Sheets
Bridging---------------------------- 51 Pairs
3 1/2" Φ Lally Columns------ 4/8
3-2 × 10 Beam---------------- 6/14 - 3/12

WALL SYSTEM

2 × 4 Shoe----------------------- 130 Lineal Feet
2-2 × 4 Plate------------------- 260 Lineal Feet
2 × 4 Studs--------------------- 232/8
Door Headers
  (2 × 10)----------------------- 2/8
  (2 × 12)----------------------- 1/14
Window Headers
  (2 × 10)---------------------- 15/6
  (2 × 12)---------------------- 2/10A
  (2 × 10)---------------------- 2/8
1/2' × 4' × 8' Sheathing- 52 Sheets
R-11 Insulation----------------- 19 Rolls
Siding------------------------------ 1638 Square Feet
Air Infiltration Housewrap-- 1638 Square Feet

CEILING SYSTEM

2 × 6 Ceiling Joists--------- 67/14
R-19 Insulation----------------- 21 Bundles

ROOF SYSTEM

2 × 10 Ridge--------------------- 3/14
2 × 8 Rafters--------------------- 67/16
1 × 6 Collar Ties----------------- 14/10
1/4" × 24" Soffit----------------- 11/8
1" × 8" Fascia------------------- 6/14
1/4" × 12" Rake Soffit-------- 64 Lineal Feet
1" × 8" Rake Fascia----------- 64 Lineal Feet
#15 Roofing Felt------------------ 4 Rolls
1/2" × 4' × 8' Plywood------ 42 Sheets
Asphalt Shingles------------------- 42 Bundles

INTERIOR

2 × 4 Studs----------------------- 242/8
Door Headers----------------------
  (2 × 8)------------------------- 2/14 - 2/10 - 6/12 - 1/8
1/2' × 4' × 8' Sheetrock---- 154 Sheets
1" × 12" Shelving-------------- 4/8 - 2/6
Closet Pole----------------------- 2/8
Baseboard------------------------ 438 Lineal Feet
Ceiling Moulding----------------- 456 Lineal Feet
Stair Stringers (2 × 12)------ 2/8 - 2/6
Stair Risers------------------------ 13
Stair Treads---------------------- 11

DECKS

Flooring----------------------------- 66 Square Feet
4 × 4 Posts------------------------ 4/10
Railings (1 × 8)----------------- 7/12

KARLIN

DESIGNED & DRAWN BY E. BRYANT

The Karlin is a raised ranch measuring 29 × 30 feet. It features a cantilever overhang in the front, thereby allowing additional floor space on the upper level.

The washer and dryer are located in the utility room on the lower level. In addition to a den and guest room, the lower floor has a family room with access to a patio, which is covered by the upper-level deck.

The dining area on the upper level is located between the kitchen and living room. Likewise, the full bath is situated between the two bedrooms.

The exterior of the dwelling is enhanced with casement windows and 8-inch vertical siding.

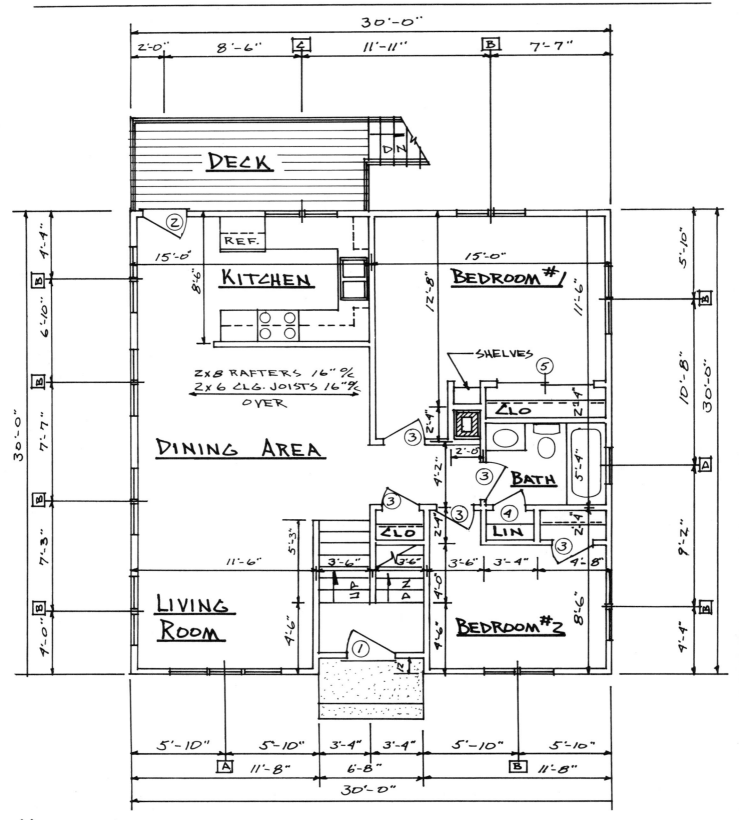

UPPER LEVEL
FLOOR PLAN

NOTES:
1) STRUCTURAL CHANGES SHOULD NOT BE MADE WITHOUT CONSULTING ARCHITECT/CONTRACTOR.

2) WOOD FRAMING TO BE KEPT 2" CLEAR OF FIREPLACE MASONRY. INSULATE WITH FIBERGLASS BETWEEN MASONRY & WOOD.

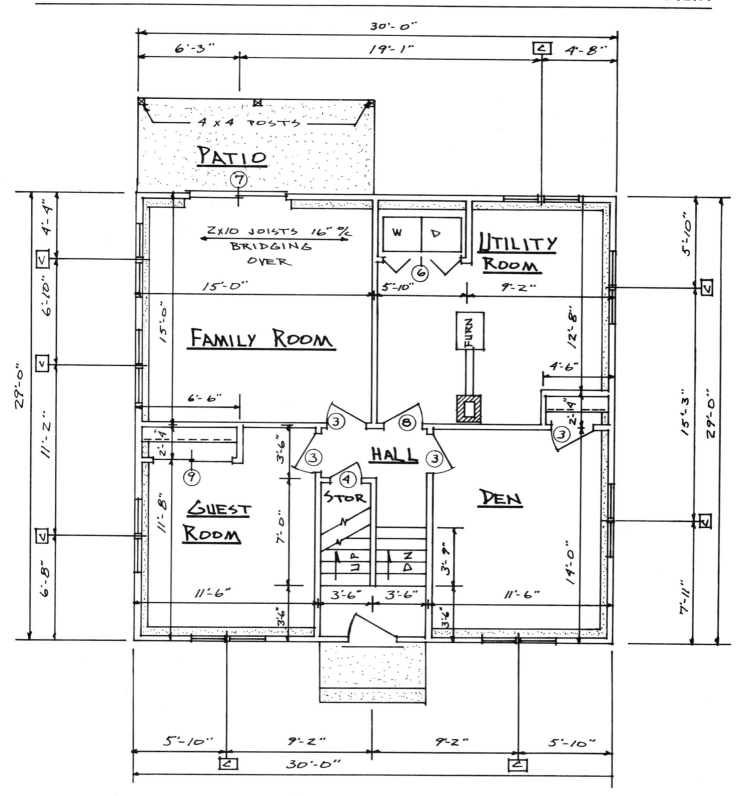

30'-0"

6'-3"   19'-1"   4'-8"

4 x 4 POSTS

PATIO
(7)

4'-4"

6'-10"

2x10 JOISTS 16" º/c
BRIDGING
OVER

15'-0"

15'-0"

W   D

(6)

UTILITY
ROOM

9'-2"

5'-10"

5'-10"

FAMILY ROOM

FURN

12'-8"

4'-6"

2'-4"

11'-2"

6'-6"

2'-4"

(3)   (8)

(3)

HALL

(3)

(3)

29'-0"

29'-0"

15'-3"

(9)

3'-6"

GUEST
ROOM

11'-8"

7'-0"

(4)

STOR

UP

DN

DEN

19'-0"

3'-9"

6'-8"

11'-6"

3'-6"   3'-6"   3'-6"

11'-6"

3'-6"

7'-11"

5'-10"   9'-2"   9'-2"   5'-10"

30'-0"

LOWER LEVEL
FLOOR PLAN

NOTE:
WOOD FRAMING MEMBERS
TO HAVE A FIBER STRESS
OF 1200 PSI.

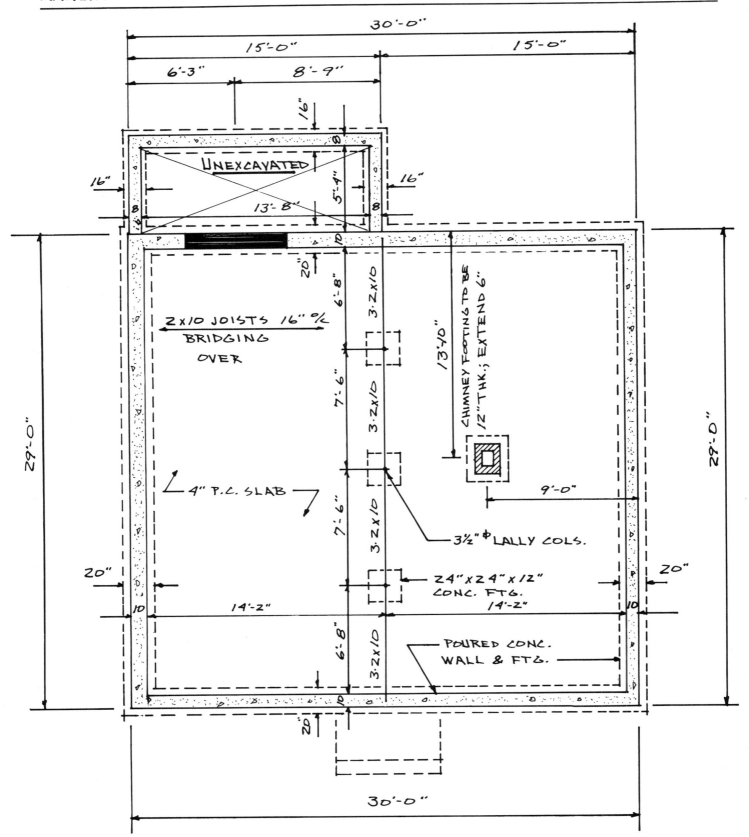

FOUNDATION PLAN

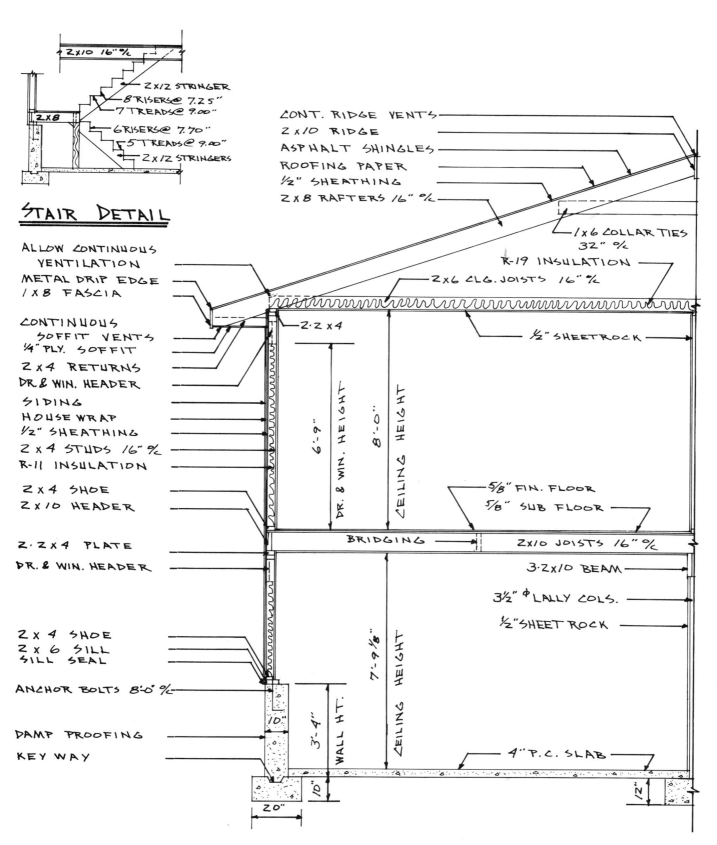

STAIR DETAIL

2x10 16" ℀

2x12 STRINGER
8 RISERS @ 7.25"
7 TREADS @ 9.00"
6 RISERS @ 7.70"
5 TREADS @ 9.00"
2x12 STRINGERS

2x8

CONT. RIDGE VENTS
2x10 RIDGE
ASPHALT SHINGLES
ROOFING PAPER
½" SHEATHING
2x8 RAFTERS 16" ℀

1x6 COLLAR TIES
32" ℀
R-19 INSULATION
2x6 CLG. JOISTS 16" ℀

ALLOW CONTINUOUS
YENTILATION
METAL DRIP EDGE
1x8 FASCIA

CONTINUOUS
SOFFIT VENTS
¼" PLY. SOFFIT
2x4 RETURNS
DR. & WIN. HEADER
SIDING
HOUSE WRAP
½" SHEATHING
2x4 STUDS 16" ℀
R-11 INSULATION

2x4 SHOE
2x10 HEADER

2·2x4 PLATE
DR. & WIN. HEADER

2x4 SHOE
2x6 SILL
SILL SEAL

ANCHOR BOLTS 8'-0" ℀

DAMP PROOFING
KEY WAY

2·2x4

½" SHEETROCK

DR. & WIN. HEIGHT 6'-9"

CEILING HEIGHT 8'-0"

5/8" FIN. FLOOR
5/8" SUB FLOOR

BRIDGING   2x10 JOISTS 16" ℀

3·2x10 BEAM

3½" Ø LALLY COLS.

½" SHEETROCK

CEILING HEIGHT 7'-9⅛"

WALL HT. 3'-4"

10"

10"

20"

4" P.C. SLAB

12"

STAFF SECTION

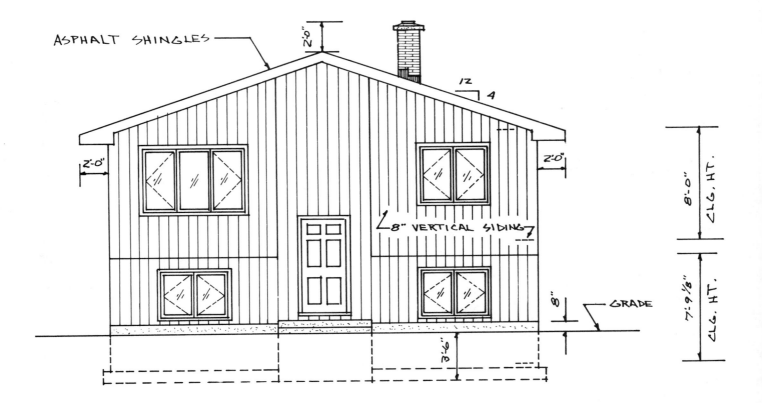

ASPHALT SHINGLES

2'-0"

12
4

8'-0" CLG. HT.

2'-0"

2'-0"

8" VERTICAL SIDING

7'-9⅛" CLG. HT.

8"

GRADE

3'-6"

FRONT ELEVATION

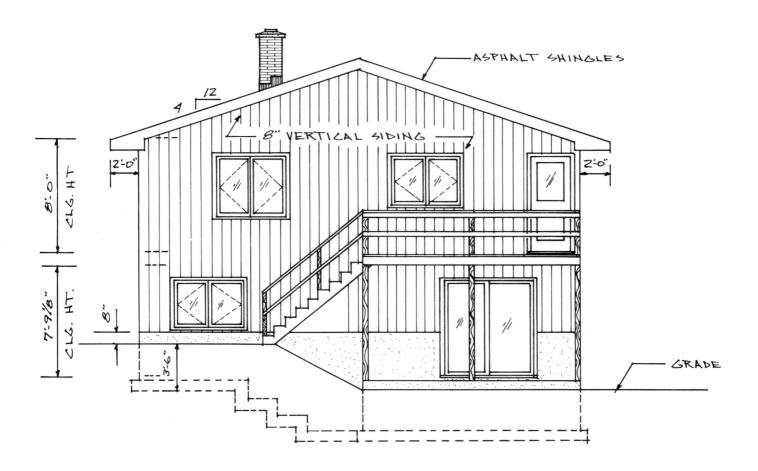

ASPHALT SHINGLES

8" VERTICAL SIDING

12
4

2'-0"

2'-0"

8'-0" CLG. HT

7'-9⅞" CLG. HT.

8"

3'-6"

GRADE

REAR ELEVATION

NOTE:
HORIZONTAL STEP TO BE NOT LESS
THAN 2'-0". VERTICAL STEP TO
BE NOT MORE THAN 3/4 OF
HORIZONTAL STEP.

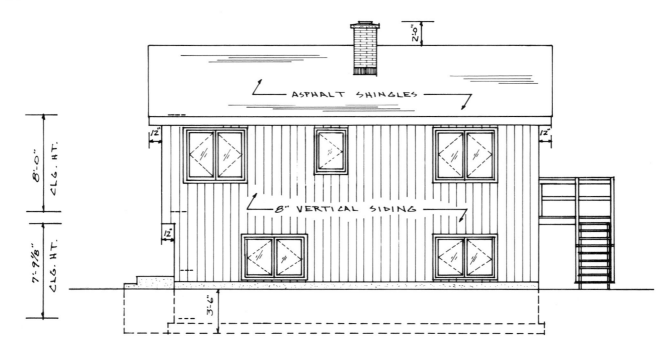

RIGHT ELEVATION

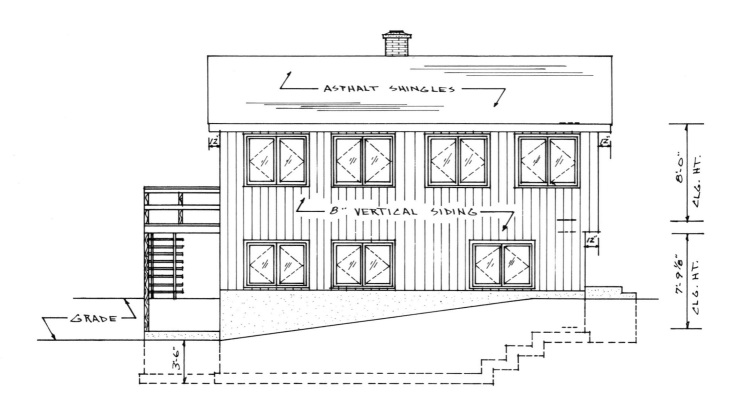

LEFT ELEVATION

NOTES:
1) WOOD FRAMING MEMBERS TO HAVE A FIBER STRESS OF 1200 PSI.

2) DOUBLE JOISTS UNDER PARALLEL PARTITIONS.

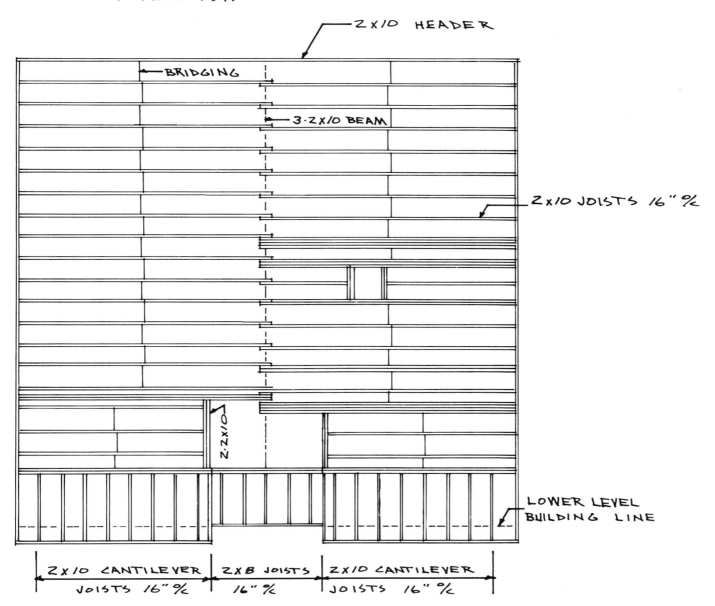

FLOOR FRAMING PLAN

WINDOW SCHEDULE

SYM	QTY	SIZE	TYPE
A	1	$7^0 \times 4^6$	CSMT.
B	8	$4^8 \times 4^0$	CSMT.
C	9	$4^8 \times 3^9$	CSMT.
D	1	$2^9 \times 3^9$	CSMT.

DOOR SCHEDULE

SYM	QTY	SIZE	TYPE
1	1	$3^0 \times 6^8$	PANEL-S.C.
2	1	2×6^8	PANEL-S.C.
3	8	$2^6 \times 6^8$	FLUSH-H.C.
4	2	$2^0 \times 6^8$	FLUSH-H.C.
5	1	$6^0 \times 6^8$	SLDG.-H.C.
6	1	$5^0 \times 6^8$	BIFOLD
7	1	$6^0 \times 6^8$	PATIO DR.
8	1	$2^6 \times 6^8$	FIREDOOR
9	1	$5^0 \times 6^8$	SLDG.-H.C.

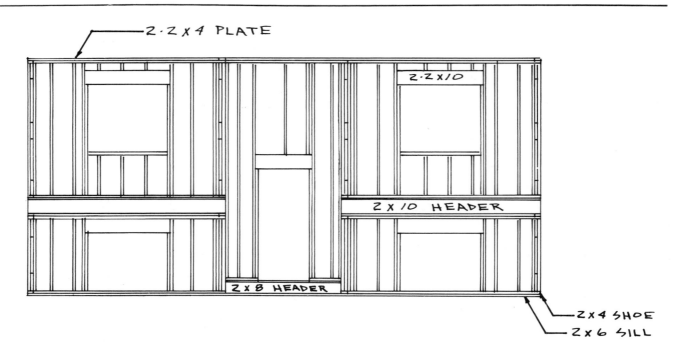

FRONT FRAMING PLAN

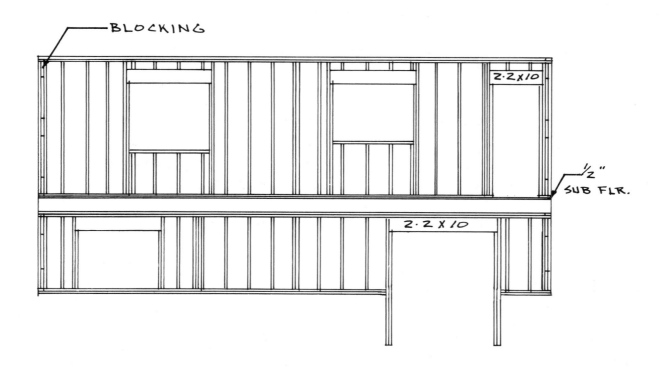

REAR FRAMING PLAN

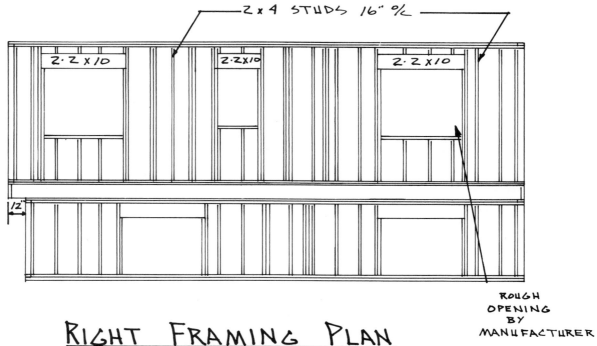

2 x 4 STUDS 16" %

2·2 X 10   2·2X10   2·2 X 10

12"

ROUGH
OPENING
BY
MANUFACTURER

RIGHT FRAMING PLAN

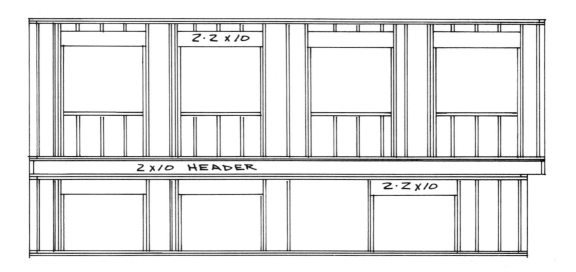

2·2 X 10

2X10 HEADER

2·2 X 10

LEFT FRAMING PLAN

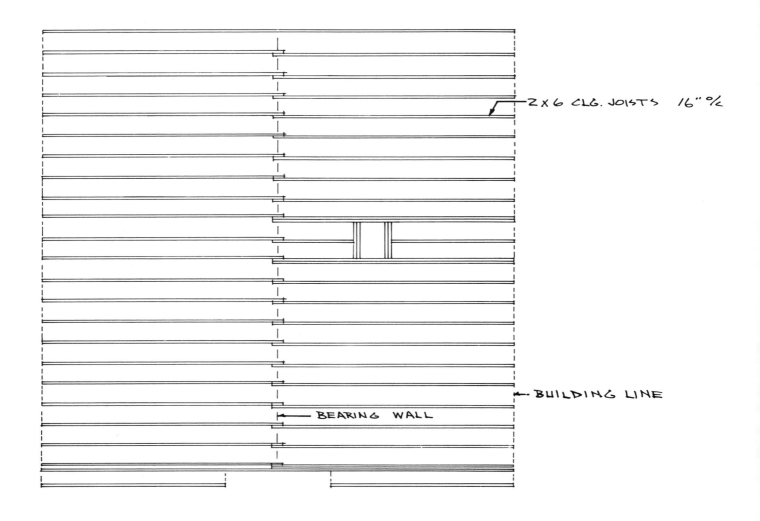

2×6 CLG. JOISTS 16" %

BUILDING LINE

BEARING WALL

CEILING FRAMING PLAN

NOTE:
WOOD FRAMING TO BE KEPT
2" CLEAR OF CHIMNEY

MASONRY. INSULATE WITH
FIBERGLASS BETWEEN
MASONRY & WOOD.

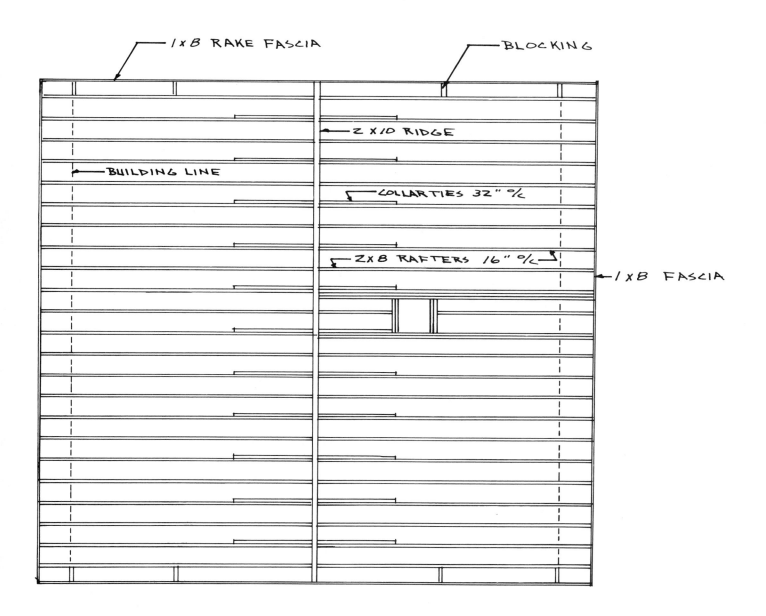

1 x 8 RAKE FASCIA

BLOCKING

2 x 10 RIDGE

BUILDING LINE

COLLAR TIES 32" O/C

2 x 8 RAFTERS 16" O/C

1 x 8 FASCIA

ROOF FRAMING PLAN

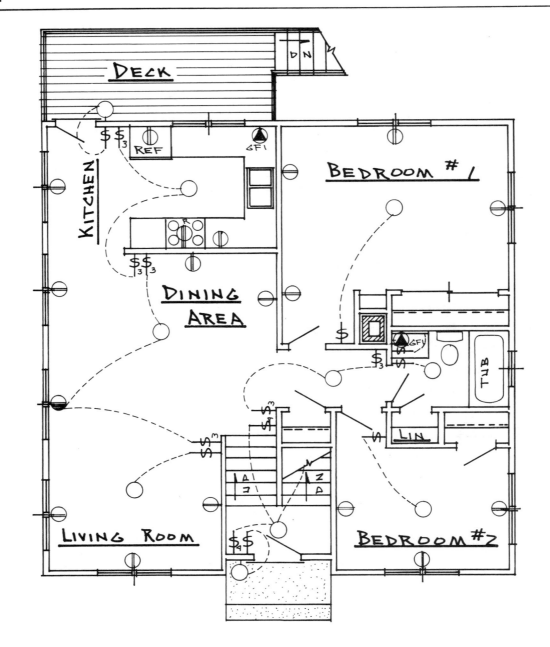

UPPER LEVEL

ELECTRICAL LAYOUT

ELECTRICAL SYMBOLS	
SYM.	ITEM
$	SINGLE-POLE SWITCH
$₃	THREE-WAY SWITCH
$₄	FOUR-WAY SWITCH
⊖	DUPLEX OUTLET
⊖	SPLIT-WIRED OUTLET
⊙GFI	GROUND FAULT INTERRUPTER
⊖R	RANGE OUTLET
⊘	LIGHTING OUTLET
▭	FLUORESCENT LIGHING
⬤W	WASHER OUTLET
⬤D	DRYER OUTLET

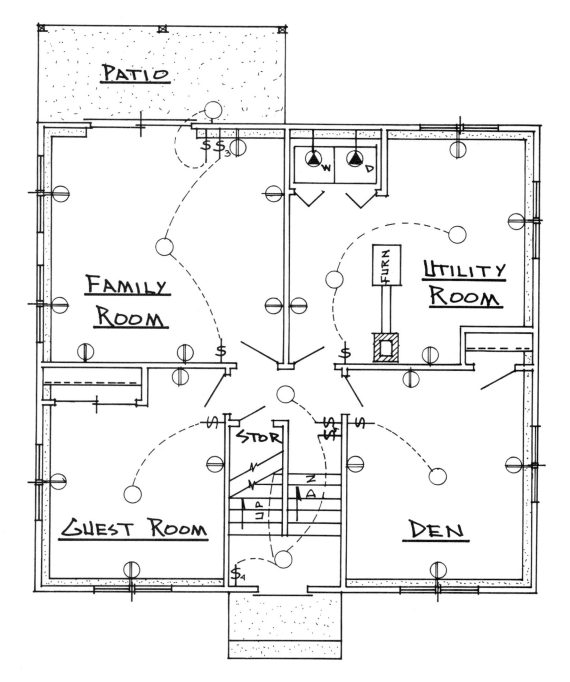

PATIO

FAMILY ROOM

UTILITY ROOM

FURN

GUEST ROOM

STOR

DEN

LOWER LEVEL

ELECTRICAL LAYOUT

NOTE:
ELECTRICAL SYMBOLS
LOCATED ON UPPER LEVEL
ELECTRICAL LAYOUT.

MATERIAL LIST

FLOOR SYSTEM
2 × 10 Joists----------------------25/16 - 9/12 - 2/8 - 23/4
2 × 10 Header------------------3/16 - 3/14 - 2/12 - 1/8
2 × 6 Sill--------------------------118 Lineal Feet
Sill Seal------------------------------118 Lineal Feet
Anchor Bolts---------------------14
1/2″ × 4′ × 8′ Plywood------19 Sheets
Bridging--------------------------35 Pairs
3 1/2″ ⌀ Lally Columns--------3/8
3-2 × 10 Beam--------------------6/10 - 1/14 - 1/16

WALL SYSTEM
2 × 4 Shoe----------------------238 Lineal Feet
2-2 × 4 Plate----------------------476 Lineal Feet
2 × 4 Studs--------------------129/8 - 80/6 - 6/14
Door Headers (2-2 × 10)------2/14
Window Headers (2-2 × 10)-18/10 - 1/6
1/2″ × 4′ × 8′ Sheathing---36 Sheets
R-11 Insulation--------------------14 Rolls
Siding------------------------------1204 Square Feet
Air Infiltration Housewrap-----3 Rolls

CEILING SYSTEM
2 × 6 Ceiling Joists------------51/16
R-19 Insulation--------------------19 Rolls

ROOF SYSTEM
2 × 10 Ridge----------------------2/16
2 × 8 Rafters----------------------49/18
1 × 6 Collar Ties----------------11/10
1/4″ × 24″ Soffit----------------8/8

1 × 8 Fascia--------------------------- 64 Lineal Feet
1/4″ × 12″ Rake Soffit----------------- 72 Lineal Feet
1 × 8″ Rake Fascia--------------------- 72 Lineal Feet
1/2″ × 4′ × 8′ Plywood--------------- 36 Sheets
Asphalt Shingles-------------------------- 4 Bundles
#15 Roofing Paper---------------------- 3 Rolls

INTERIOR
2 × 4 Studs---------------------------- 228/8
Door Headers 2-2 × 10-------------- 2/14 - 8/10 - 1/8
1/2″ × 4′ × 8′ Sheetrock------------- 130 Sheets
1 × 12 Shelving------------------------ 6/8
Closet Pole---------------------------- 3/8
Baseboard---------------------------- 409 Lineal Feet
Ceiling Moulding-------------------- 419 Lineal Feet
2 × 12 Stair Stringers----------------- 2/10
Stair Risers---------------------------- 2/12
Stair Treads--------------------------- 2/12

BASEMENT STAIRS
2 × 12 Stringers------------------------ 2/8
Risers-------------------------------- 1/12 - 1/6
Treads-------------------------------- 1/12 - 1/6

DECKS
Flooring------------------------------- 87 Square Feet
4 × 4 Posts--------------------------- 3/12 - 1/16
Railings------------------------------- 48 Lineal Feet
Cap----------------------------------- 24 Lineal Feet
2 × 12 Stringers----------------------- 2/10
2 × 10 Treads------------------------- 3/12

Article IV

Estimating

The square-footage cost of house construction is composed of the cost of materials, services, and labor needed to construct a structure. Such costs include excavation, foundation, construction of the finished house, electrical, plumbing, utility hookups, various permits, etc. However, such things as garages, porches, decks, and fireplaces are not included in the square-footage costs.

Wall height/ceiling height is also a factor in determining cost. Most houses have a standard 8-foot ceiling height. However, for energy-saving purposes, you might prefer a 7 1/2-foot ceiling height. That's all well and good, but by lowering the ceiling height, all the 8-foot Sheetrock and wallboard will have to be cut accordingly. All the 8-foot studs and sheathing will also have to be cut. The extra hours used for cutting purposes will increase labor costs.

A rectangular or square house will cost less than a six-cornered L-shaped house. More work is necessary to construct corners, thereby increasing the square footage cost.

The type of materials you use also plays an important role in determining building costs. Location of the structure to be built is also important. The costs per square foot of a house built with average building materials in the country/rural area will be less than the house constructed of better-than-average building materials in the city or metropolitan area.

As you browse through this book, you might be intrigued by one of the many floor plans it has to offer. Let's say you like the way one of the floor plans are laid out, and you're overwhelmed by the exterior of the residential structure. You are interested in building, but would like a rough estimate on how much it would cost.

To obtain such a figure, all you have to do is multiply the length by the width of the house. This gives you the square footage of the building. Multiplying the square footage by the cost per square foot of building in your area will give you an approximate cost of the house.

As an example, let's suppose that the cost per square foot for residential construction in your area is $50.00. (The cost per square foot will vary, depending on the area in which you live.) You're interested in a one-story ranch house that is 26 feet wide by 40 feet long. By multiplying 26 feet by 40 feet (width × length) we discover that the house in question has 1,040 square feet. Now, multiply the total square footage by $50.00 per square foot. The answer, $52,000, is a rough estimate of what the house would cost.

Some builders might prefer to use the cubic foot method. The cubic footage is figured by multiplying the length by the width by the height from the basement floor to the eave line. The cubic footage of the attic area is computed by multiplying the length of the structure, by the width, by the rise (from eave to top of ridge) and dividing by two. The total amount of cubic feet multiplied by the cost per cubic foot of building in your area would also give you an approximate estimate of a proposed house.

Now you have a rough estimate of the cost of your dream house. You think it falls within your budget. As you grow increasingly serious about building, you would like a more accurate estimate.

This is the time to settle down with paper and pencil and do some figuring.

A *take-off* is the process of figuring the actual cost of a structure. The object of a take-off is to compute the cost of material needed. Accompanying each set of plans in this book is a list of building materials needed to construct the basic house. The list includes the necessary building material for the structure (walls, ceilings, floors, roof, etc.). However, it does not take into account items of a more personal nature, such as kitchen appliances, kitchen cabinets, plumbing fixtures, etc.

The quantity of wood members needed to erect the basic shell are included in each set of plans. The amount of plywood needed for the subfloor for the entire structure has also been provided. The calculations for estimating the amount of finishing materials needed for each room has been left to you.

The finished floor in your house might change from room to room. Perhaps you plan to have hardwood floors in the bedroom, carpeting in the living room, and tile or sheet flooring in the kitchen.

To determine the square footage of a given room, multiply the length by the width, using the room dimensions on the floor plan. The square footage of a room will be helpful in purchasing tile flooring, because the cost of tile is figured on a square footage basis.

However, carpets and sheet flooring are usually priced by the square yard. To determine square yardage for such flooring, divide the square footage by 9 (9 square feet equals 1 square yard).

Figuring the amount of hardwood flooring needed might be more complex. Allowances for side and end matching, in addition to waste, have to be made.

The square footage of the floor area also applies to the ceiling, if it is flat.

To calculate the amount of wall area in a room to be covered with paneling, wallpaper, paint, etc., simply deduct the square footage area of the doors and windows from the square footage of the walls.

The lineal footage of doors and windows can be used to determine total trim requirements and weatherstripping.

Examine the plans of your proposed house and study the materials list. If you can obtain price catalogs from local lumber dealers, you can compute the cost of the building materials needed yourself. While doing a take-off, you should also estimate the labor involved in the construction of your residential dwelling.

Estimating the cost of your proposed house is a complex and time-consuming procedure. If you're not too thrilled about doing it yourself, you could take it to your local lumber dealer. Most likely, he will furnish you with the estimates you want, if he thinks that you will be purchasing the materials from him.

Section V

2-Story Houses

JEFFORY

DESIGNED & DRAWN BY E. BRYANT

The Jeffory is a two-story house with a gambrel roof and 1,976 square feet of living space.

The centrally located kitchen is near the rear door, thereby making it convenient for carting groceries. It is also adjacent to the dining room for ease in meal-time serving. After meals in the dining room, guests can retire to the adjacent living room for socializing around the fireplace.

Also included in the lower level are a family room, den, powder room, laundry, and foyer. The upper floor consist of four bedrooms, two baths, and ample closet space.

The exterior of the structure is accented by double-hung windows and horizontal siding.

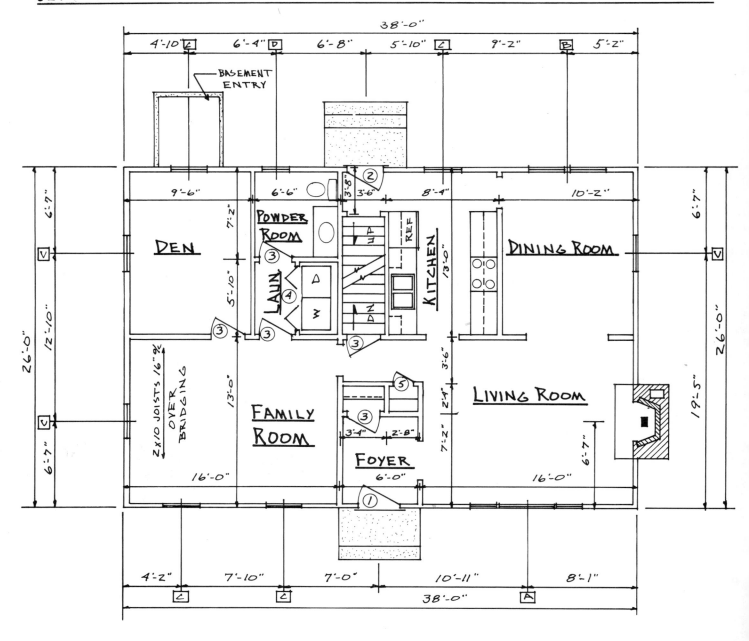

First Floor Plan

NOTES:

1) STRUCTURAL CHANGES SHOULD NOT BE MADE WITHOUT CONSULTING ARCHITECT/CONTRACTOR

2) WOOD FRAMING MEMBERS TO HAVE A FIBER STRESS OF 1200 PSI.

3) WOOD FRAMING TO BE KEPT 2" CLEAR OF FIREPLACE MASONRY. INSULATE WITH FIBERGLASS BETWEEN MASONRY AND WOOD.

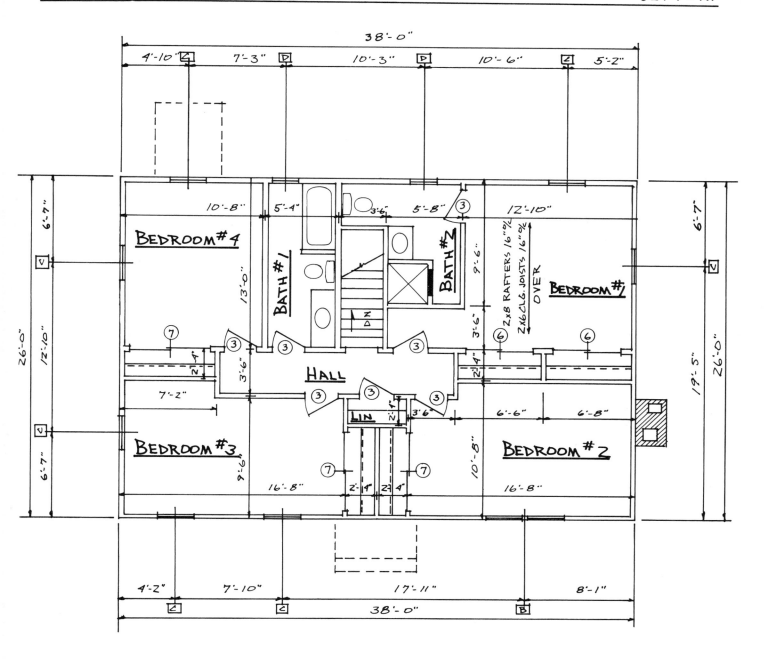

SECOND FLOOR PLAN

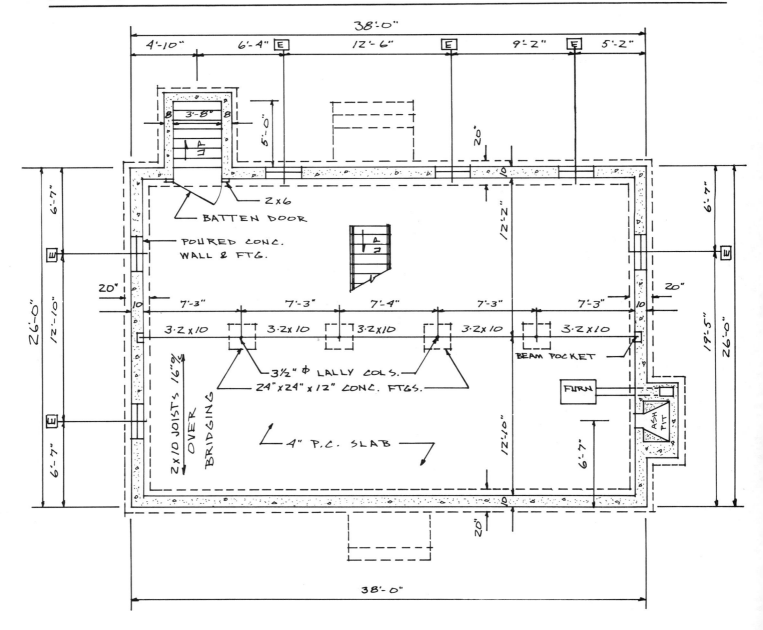

38'-0"

4'-10" | 6'-4" E | 12'-6" | E | 9'-2" | E | 5'-2"

3'-8" B

5'-0"

20'

12'-2"

2x6

BATTEN DOOR

POURED CONC.
WALL & FTG.

6'-7"

12'-10"

26'-0"

20"

7'-3" | 7'-3" | 7'-4" | 7'-3" | 7'-3"

3·2x10 | 3·2x10 | 3·2x10 | 3·2x10 | 3·2x10

3½" Φ LALLY COLS.

24"x24"x12" CONC. FTGS.

BEAM POCKET

FURN

ASH PIT

4" P.C. SLAB

2x10 JOISTS 16"o.c. OVER BRIDGING

12'-10"

6'-7"

6'-7"

19'-5"

26'-0"

20"

38'-0"

FOUNDATION PLAN

NOTES:

1) BASEMENT ENTRY
FOUNDATION TO CONFORM
TO MANUFACTURER

SPECIFICATIONS:

2) FIREPLACE FOOTING
TO BE 12"THK; EXTEND 6".

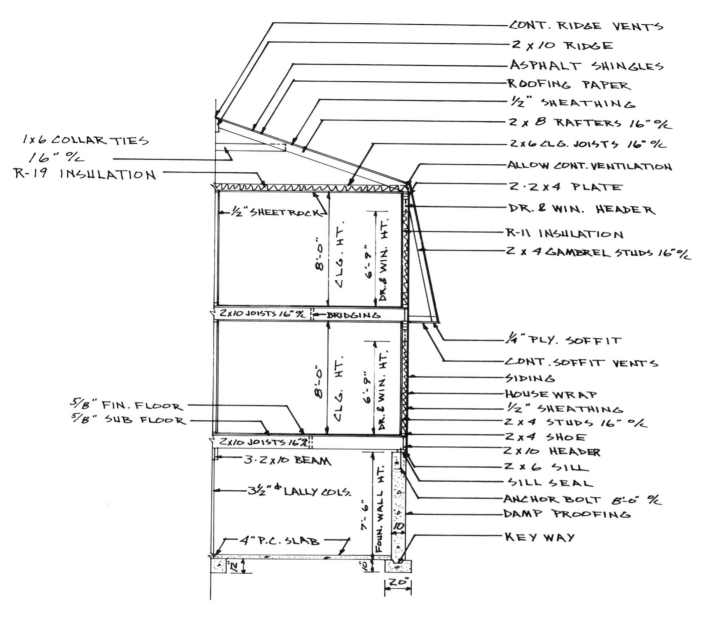

1x6 COLLAR TIES 16" O/C
R-19 INSULATION

½" SHEETROCK
8'-0" CLG. HT.
6'-9" DR. & WIN. HT.
2x10 JOISTS 16" O/C — BRIDGING
8'-0" CLG. HT.
6'-9" DR. & WIN. HT.

5/8" FIN. FLOOR
5/8" SUB FLOOR

2x10 JOISTS 16" O/C
3·2x10 BEAM
3½" ⌀ LALLY COLS.
4" P.C. SLAB
2"
FOUN. WALL HT. 7'-6"
10"
8"
20"

CONT. RIDGE VENTS
2x10 RIDGE
ASPHALT SHINGLES
ROOFING PAPER
½" SHEATHING
2x8 RAFTERS 16" O/C
2x6 CLG. JOISTS 16" O/C
ALLOW CONT. VENTILATION
2·2x4 PLATE
DR. & WIN. HEADER
R-11 INSULATION
2x4 GAMBREL STUDS 16"O/C

¼" PLY. SOFFIT
CONT. SOFFIT VENTS
SIDING
HOUSE WRAP
½" SHEATHING
2x4 STUDS 16" O/C
2x4 SHOE
2x10 HEADER
2x6 SILL
SILL SEAL
ANCHOR BOLT 8'-0" O/C
DAMP PROOFING
KEY WAY

STAFF SECTION

DOOR SCHEDULE			
SYM	QTY	SIZE	TYPE
1	1	3⁰ x 6⁸	PANEL- S.C.
2	1	2⁸ x 6⁸	PANEL- S.C.
3	12	2⁶ x 6⁸	FLUSH-H.C.
4	1	5⁰ x 6⁸	BI FOLD
5	1	1⁶ x 6⁸	FLUSH- H.C.
6	2	5⁰ x 6⁸	SLDG.- H.C.
7	3	6⁰ x 6⁸	SLDG.- H.C.

WINDOW SCHEDULE			
SYM	QTY	SIZE	TYPE
A	1	2⁰-4⁴·2⁰ x 4²	D.H. P.W.
B	2	5⁸ x 3¹⁰	DH MULL.
C	14	2⁸ x 3¹⁰	D.H.
D	3	2⁸ x 3²	D.H.
E	6	2⁸ x 1⁴	BSMT.

NOTE:
CHECK LOCAL BUILDING
CODE REGARDING
FLOOR INSULATION

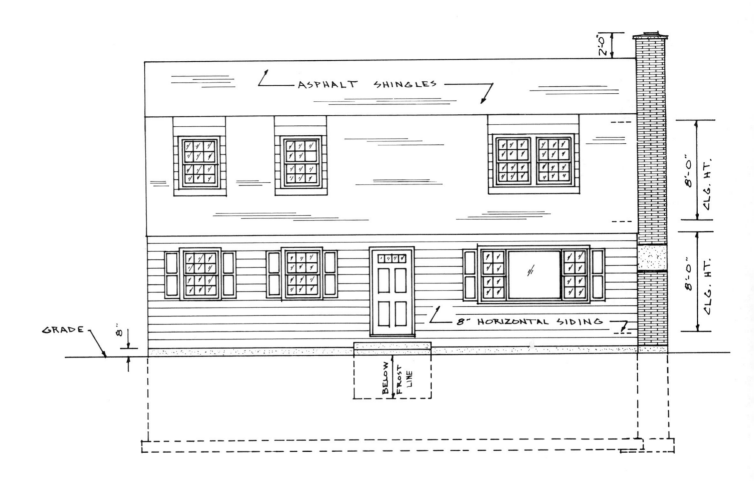

ASPHALT SHINGLES

2'-0"

8'-0" CLG. HT.

8'-0" CLG. HT.

8" HORIZONTAL SIDING

GRADE

8"

BELOW FROST LINE

FRONT ELEVATION

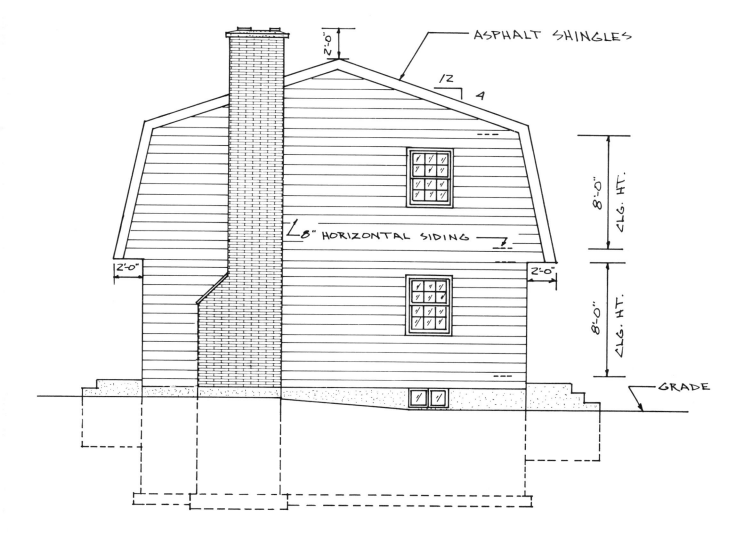

ASPHALT SHINGLES

2'-0"

12

4

8'-0" CLG. HT.

8" HORIZONTAL SIDING

2'-0"

2'-0"

8'-0" CLG. HT.

GRADE

RIGHT ELEVATION

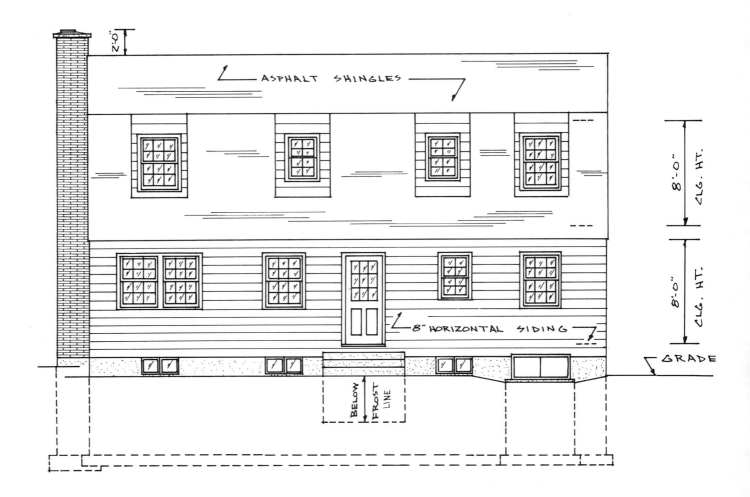

2'-0"

ASPHALT SHINGLES

8'-0" CLG. HT.

8'-0" CLG. HT.

8" HORIZONTAL SIDING

GRADE

BELOW FROST LINE

REAR ELEVATION

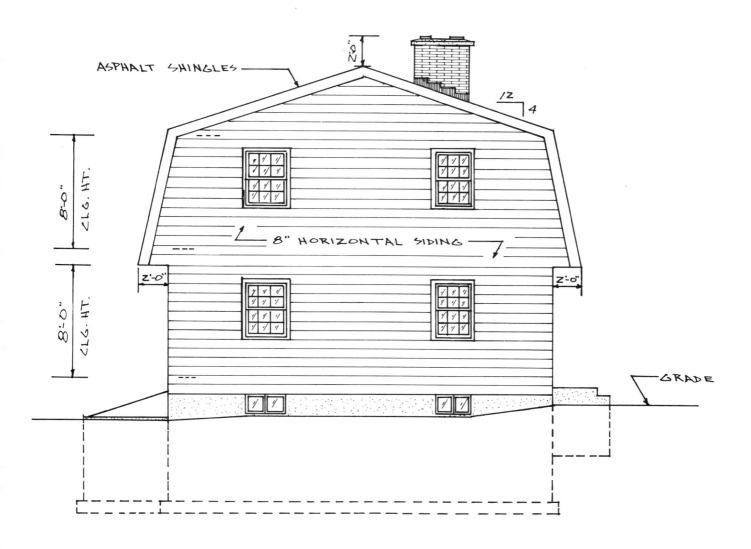

ASPHALT SHINGLES

8" HORIZONTAL SIDING

12
4

8'-0" CLG. HT.

8'-0" CLG. HT.

2'-0"

2'-0"

GRADE

LEFT ELEVATION

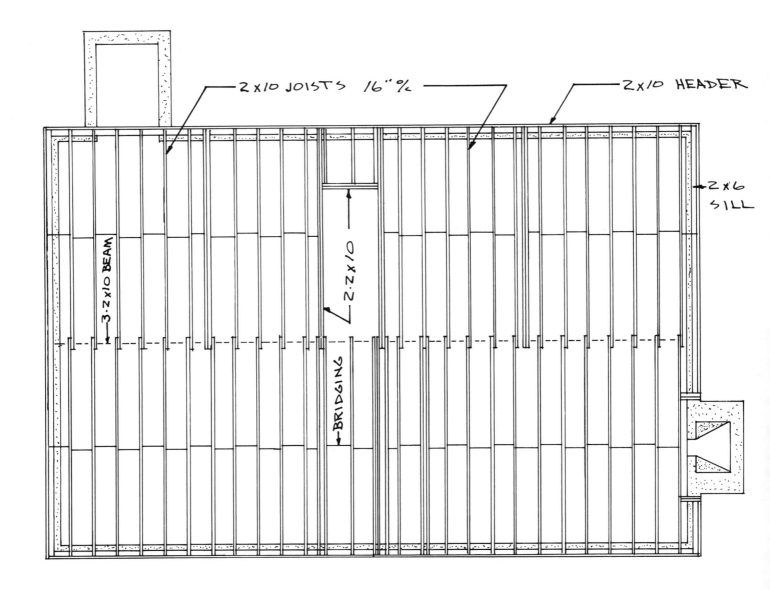

2 X 10 JOISTS 16" ℀

2 X 10 HEADER

2 X 6 SILL

3 · 2 X 10 BEAM

2 · 2 X 10

BRIDGING

FIRST FLOOR FRAMING PLAN

NOTE:
DOUBLE JOISTS UNDER
PARALLEL PARTITIONS.

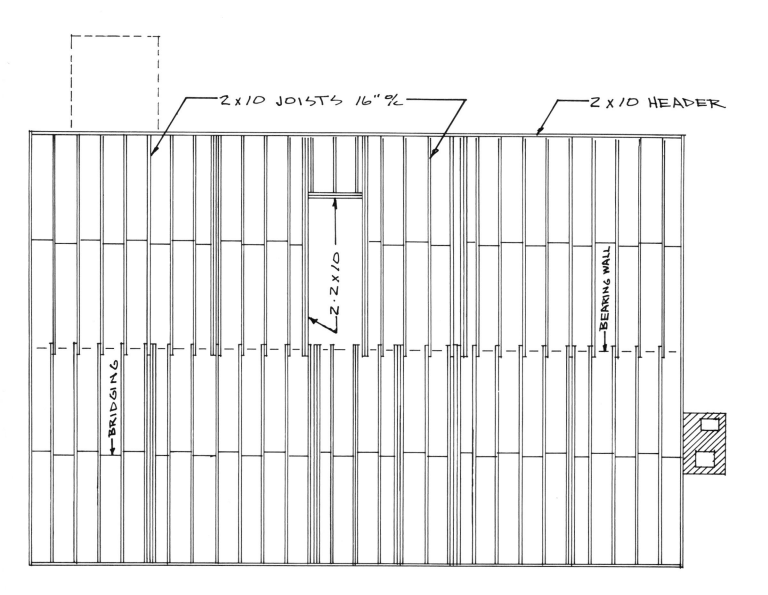

2x10 JOISTS 16" %   2x10 HEADER

2·2x10

BRIDGING

BEARING WALL

SECOND FLOOR FRAMING PLAN

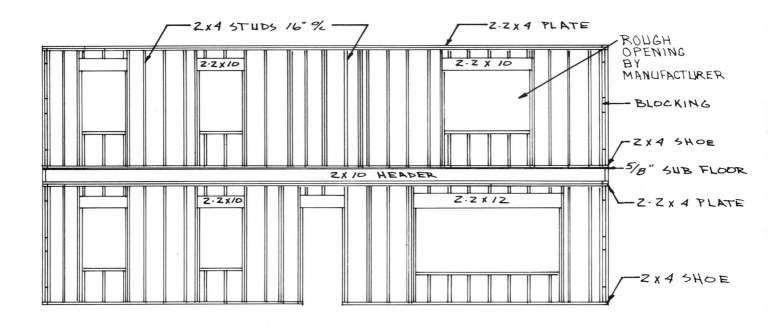

2x4 STUDS 16" %
2·2x4 PLATE
2·2x10
2·2 x 10
ROUGH OPENING BY MANUFACTURER
BLOCKING
2x4 SHOE
⁵⁄₈" SUB FLOOR
2·2 x 4 PLATE
2x10 HEADER
2·2x10
2·2 x 12
2x4 SHOE

FRONT FRAMING PLAN

2x10 HEADER
2·2x10
2·2x10
FIREPLACE
OPENING

RIGHT FRAMING PLAN

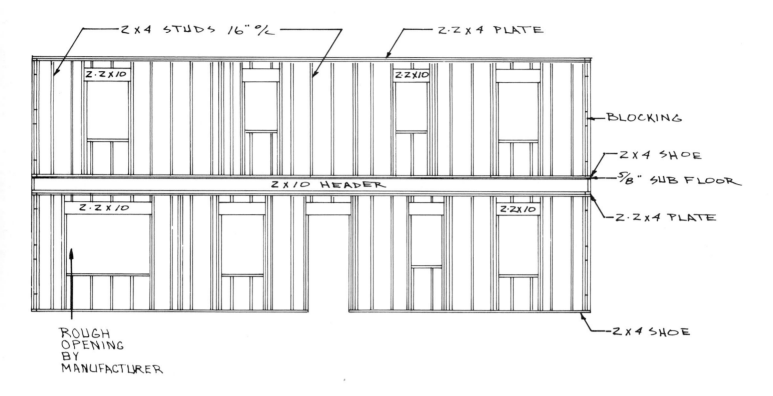

2×4 STUDS 16" °/c   2·2×4 PLATE

2·2×10   2·2×10

BLOCKING

2×4 SHOE

5/8" SUB FLOOR

2·2×4 PLATE

2×10 HEADER

2·2×10   2·2×10

2×4 SHOE

ROUGH
OPENING
BY
MANUFACTURER

REAR FRAMING PLAN

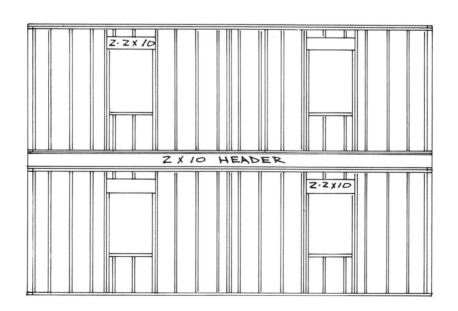

2·2×10

2×10 HEADER

2·2×10

LEFT FRAMING PLAN

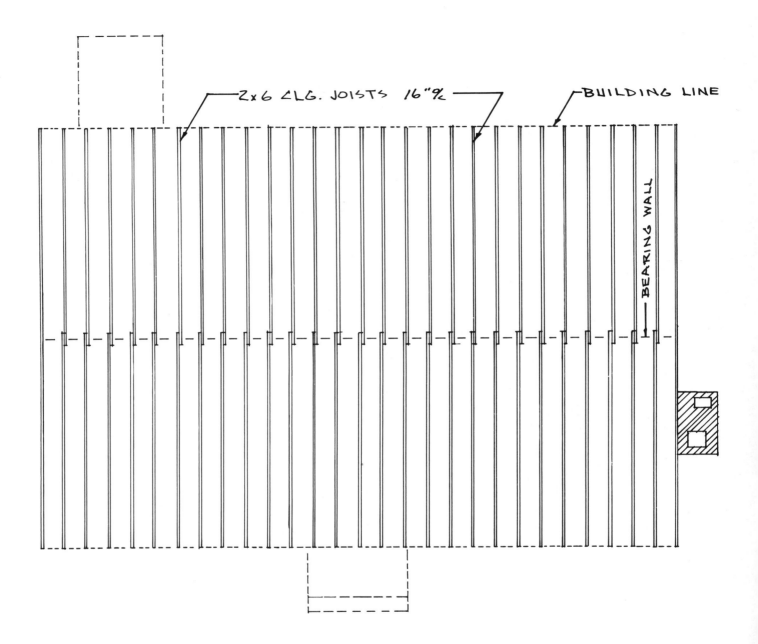

2x6 CLG. JOISTS 16" %

BUILDING LINE

BEARING WALL

CEILING FRAMING PLAN

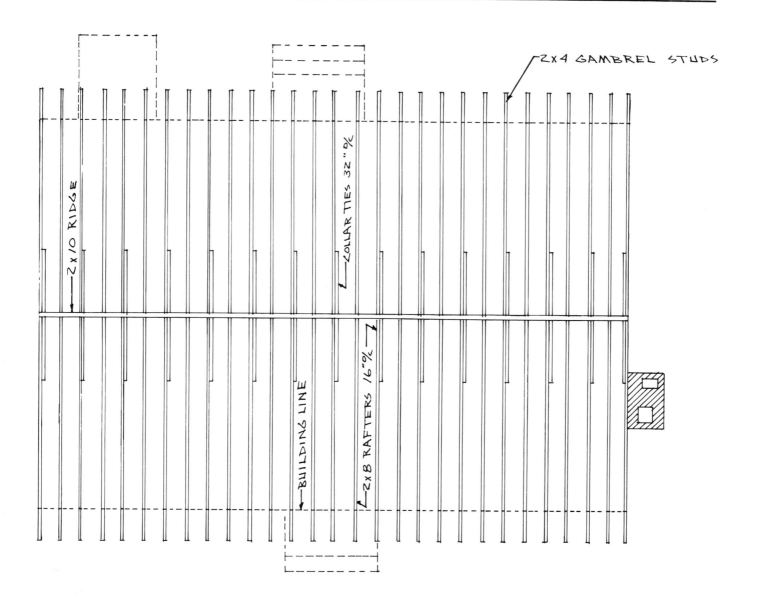

2x4 GAMBREL STUDS

2x10 RIDGE

COLLAR TIES 32" %

BUILDING LINE

2x8 RAFTERS 16" %

ROOF FRAMING PLAN

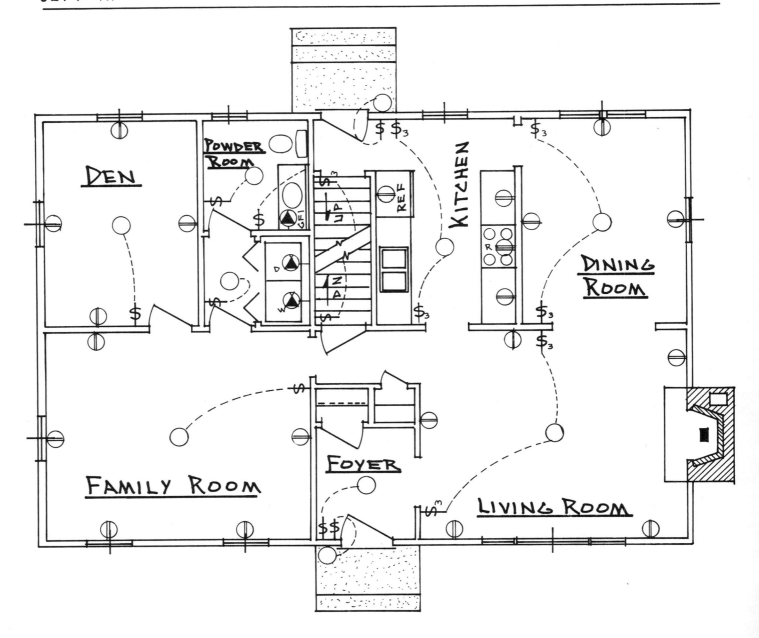

DEN

POWDER ROOM

KITCHEN

REF

DINING ROOM

R

FAMILY ROOM

FOYER

LIVING ROOM

FIRST FLOOR
ELECTRICAL LAYOUT

ELECTRICAL SYMBOLS	
SYM	ITEM
$	SINGLE-POLE SWITCH
$₃	THREE-WAY SWITCH
⊖	DUPLEX OUTLET
⊖R	RANGE OUTLET
▲GFI	GROUND FAULT INTERRUPTER
▲W	WASHER OUTLET
▲D	DRYER OUTLET
○	LIGHTING OUTLET
▭	FLUORESCENT LIGHTING

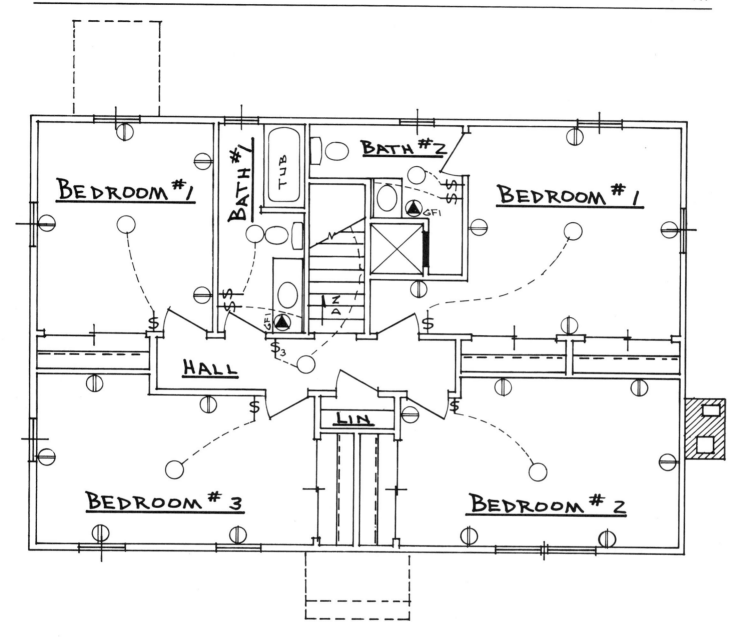

SECOND FLOOR ELECTRICAL LAYOUT

NOTE:
ELECTRICAL SYMBOLS
LOCATED ON FIRST FLOOR
ELECTRICAL LAYOUT.

MATERIAL LIST

FLOOR SYSTEM

2 × 10 Joists----------------------------------135/14
2 × 10 Header----------------------------------8/14 - 12/12
2 × 6 Sill--4/14 - 6/12
Sill Seal--128 Lineal Feet
Anchor Bolts----------------------------------16
1/2″ × 4′ × 8′ Plywood----------61 Sheets
Bridging--107 Pairs
3 1/2″ ⏀ Lally Columns------------4/8
3-2 × 10 Beam----------------------------3/14 - 6/12

WALL SYSTEM

2 × 4 Shoe----------------------------------4/14 - 6/12
2-2 × 4 Plate----------------------------------8/14 - 12/12
2 × 4 Studs----------------------------------275/8 - 1/10
Door Headers (2 × 10)------------1/14
Window Headers----------------------
    2 × 10----------------------------------8/14 - 1/8 - 2/12
    2 × 12----------------------------------2/10
1/2″ × 4′ × 8′ Sheathing--------67 Sheets
R-11 Insulation----------------------25 Rolls
Siding----------------------------------1972 Square Feet
Air Infiltration Housewrap--------2132 Square Feet
Fireplace Header (2 × 10)--------1/12

CEILING SYSTEM

2 × 6 Ceiling Joists----------------58/14
R-19 Insulation----------------------21 Rolls

ROOFING SYSTEM

2 × 10 Ridge--------------------------2/12 - 1/14
2 × 8 Rafters--------------------------58/14
1 × 6 Collar Ties--------------------15/10
1/4″ × 24″ Soffit--------------------10/8
1″ × 8″ Rake Fascia----------------92 Lineal Feet
#15 Roofing Felt----------------------5 Rolls
1/2″ × 4′ × 8′ Plywood--------------57 Sheets
Asphalt Shingles----------------------56 Bundles
2 × 4 Gambrel Studs------------------58/10

INTERIOR

2 × 4 Studs----------------------------302/8
Door Headers (2 × 10)----------------4/14 - 11/12 - 1/4
1/2″ × 4′ × 8′ Sheetrock----------186 Sheets
1″ × 12″ Shelving----------------------6/8
Closet Pole------------------------------1/14 - 1/10
Baseboard------------------------------409 Lineal Feet
Ceiling Moulding------------------------600 Lineal Feet
2 × 12 Stair Stringers------------------2/14
Stair Risers------------------------------3/12 - 1/4
Stair Treads----------------------------3/12

BASEMENT STAIRS

2 × 12 Stringers------------------------2/14
2 × 10 Treads--------------------------3/12
Handrail--------------------------------2/14

JULLIAM

DESIGNED & DRAWN BY E. BRYANT

The Julliam is a two-story residential dwelling with horizontal siding and double-hung windows. It has 1,352 square feet of living space.

The living room, with its fireplace and picture win-dow, adjoins the dining room, which is adjacent to the kitchen and has access to an attached deck.

The upper level consists of three bedrooms and a bath. A half bath is also located on the lower level.

261

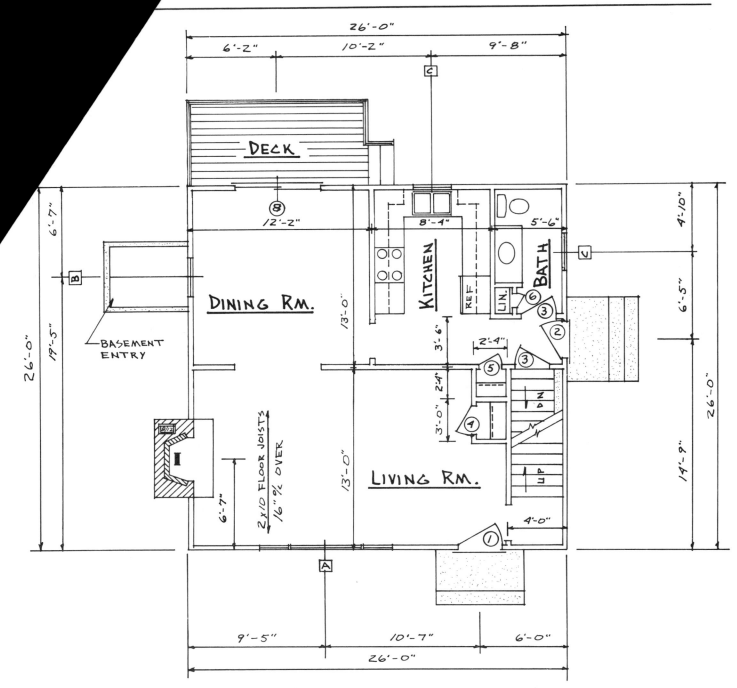

FIRST FLOOR PLAN

WINDOW SCHEDULE			
SYM.	QTY.	SIZE	TYPE
A	1	$2^0 5^{\frac{1}{2}} 2^0 \times 4^2$	P.W.
B	6	$2^8 \times 3^{10}$	D.H.
C	3	$2^8 \times 3^2$	D.H.
D	1	$2^0 \times 3^2$	D.H.
E	2	$2^8 \times 1^4$	BSMT.

DOOR SCHEDULE			
SYM.	QTY.	SIZE	TYPE
1	1	$3^0 \times 6^8$	S.C.
2	1	$2^8 \times 6^8$	S.C.
3	8	$2^6 \times 6^8$	H.C.
4	1	$2^0 \times 6^8$	H.C.
5	2	$1^6 \times 6^8$	H.C.
6	1	$1^0 \times 6^8$	H.C.
7	2	$5^0 \times 6^8$	HC. SLIDER
8	1	$6^0 \times 6^8$	GLASS SL.

NOTES:

1) WOOD FRAMING TO BE KEPT 2" CLEAR OF FIRE-PLACE MASONRY.

2) STRUCTURAL CHANGES SHOULD NOT BE MADE WITHOUT CONSULTING ARCHITECT/CONTRACTOR.

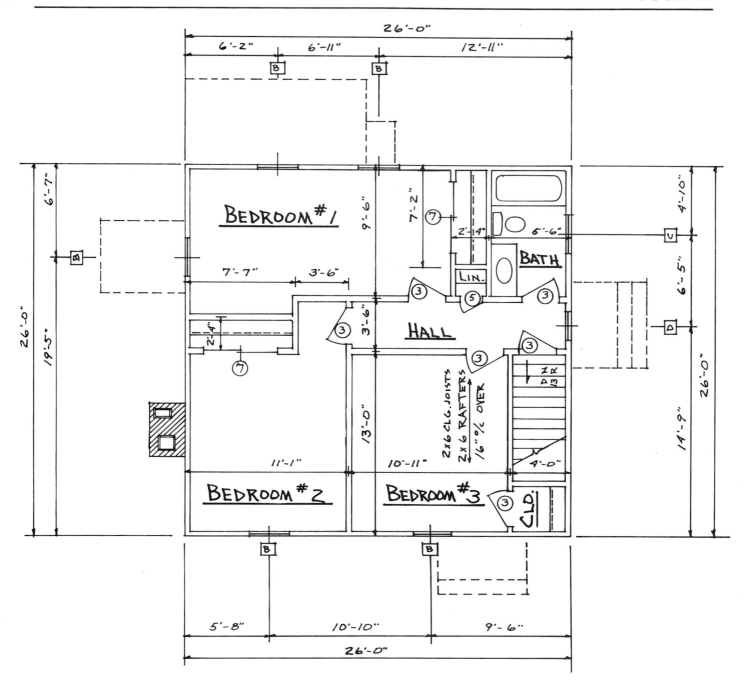

SECOND FLOOR PLAN

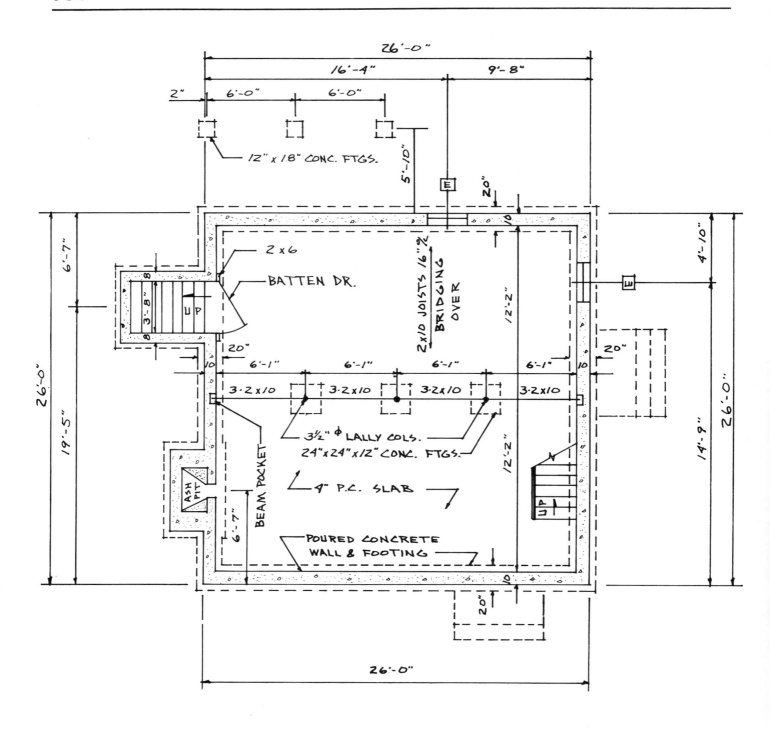

FOUNDATION PLAN

NOTE:
BASEMENT ENTRY
FOUNDATION TO CON-
FORM TO MANUFACTURER
SPECIFICATIONS.

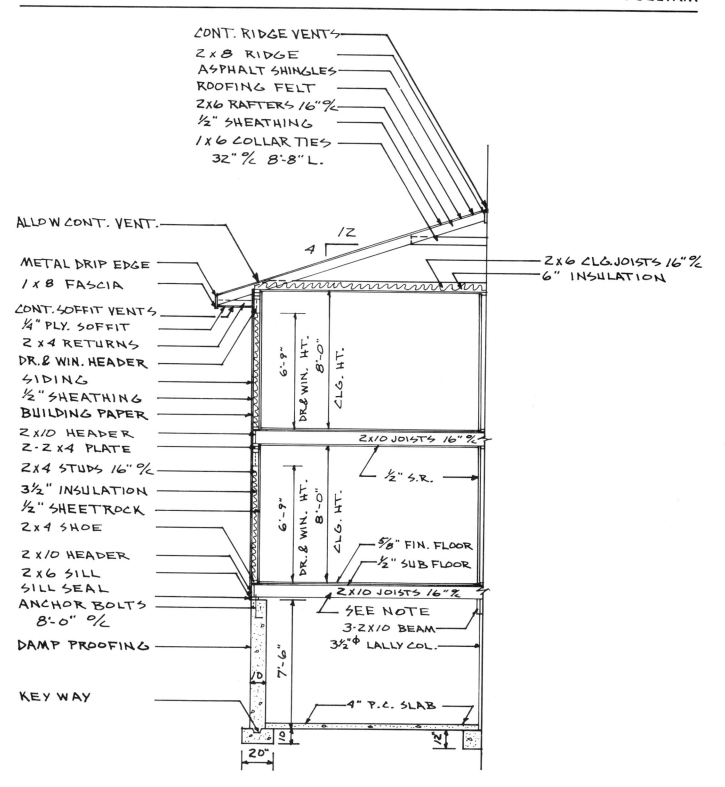

CONT. RIDGE VENTS
2 x 8 RIDGE
ASPHALT SHINGLES
ROOFING FELT
2 x 6 RAFTERS 16" %
½" SHEATHING
1 x 6 COLLAR TIES
32" % 8'-8" L.

ALLOW CONT. VENT.

METAL DRIP EDGE
1 x 8 FASCIA

CONT. SOFFIT VENTS
¼" PLY. SOFFIT
2 x 4 RETURNS
DR. & WIN. HEADER
SIDING
½" SHEATHING
BUILDING PAPER
2 x 10 HEADER
2 - 2 x 4 PLATE
2 x 4 STUDS 16" %
3½" INSULATION
½" SHEETROCK
2 x 4 SHOE

2 x 10 HEADER
2 x 6 SILL
SILL SEAL
ANCHOR BOLTS
8'-0" %

DAMP PROOFING

KEY WAY

12
4

6'-9" DR. & WIN. HT.
8'-0" CLG. HT.

6'-9" DR. & WIN. HT.
8'-0" CLG. HT.

7'-6"

10

20"

10

2 x 6 CLG. JOISTS 16" %
6" INSULATION

2 x 10 JOISTS 16" %
½" S.R.

⅝" FIN. FLOOR
½" SUB FLOOR

2 x 10 JOISTS 16" %
SEE NOTE
3 - 2 x 10 BEAM
3½" Φ LALLY COL.

4" P.C. SLAB

2"

STAFF SECTION

NOTE:
CHECK LOCAL BUILDING
CODES REGARDING
FLOOR INSULATION

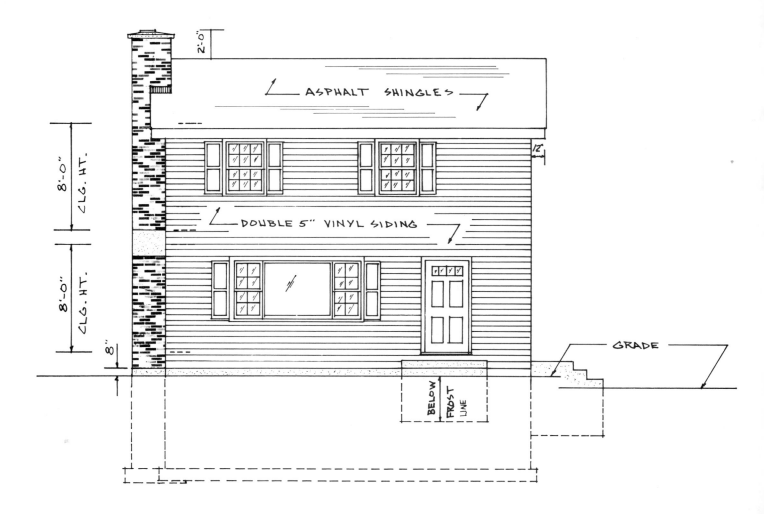

ASPHALT SHINGLES

DOUBLE 5" VINYL SIDING

2'-0"

8'-0" CLG. HT.

8'-0" CLG. HT.

8"

12"

GRADE

BELOW FROST LINE

FRONT ELEVATION

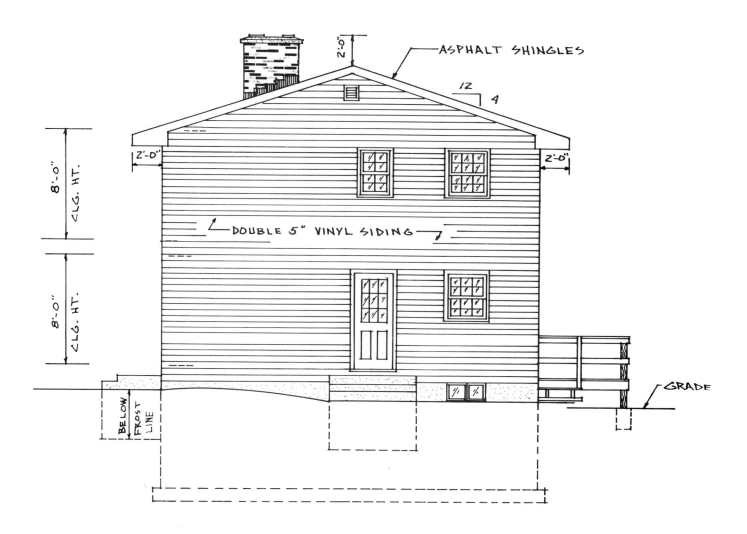

ASPHALT SHINGLES

2'-0"

12
4

2'-0"   2'-0"

8'-0" CLG. HT.

DOUBLE 5" VINYL SIDING

8'-0" CLG. HT.

GRADE

BELOW FROST LINE

RIGHT ELEVATION

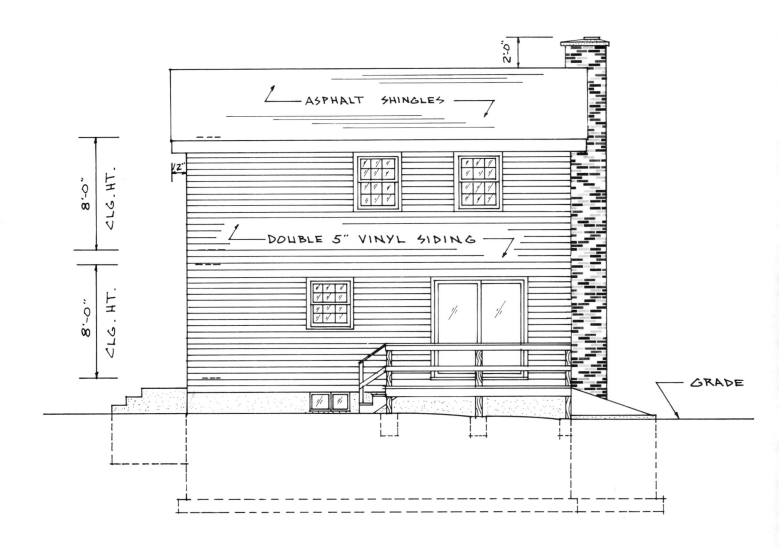

ASPHALT SHINGLES

2'-0"

8'-0" CLG. HT.

1/2"

DOUBLE 5" VINYL SIDING

8'-0" CLG. HT.

GRADE

REAR ELEVATION

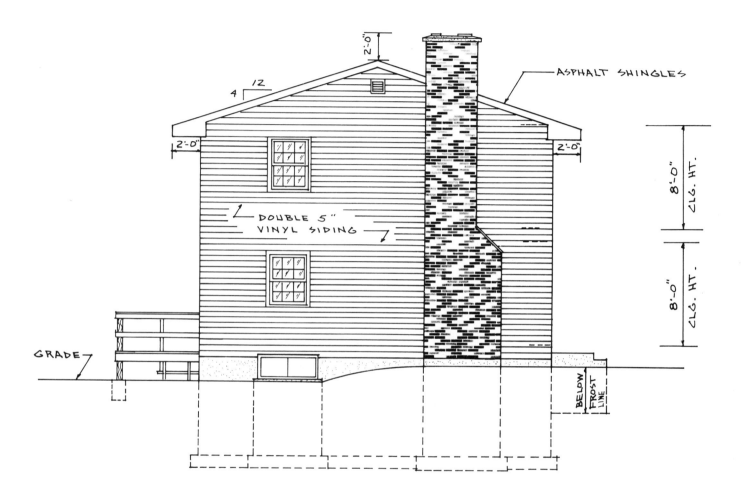

2'-0"

12
4

2'-0"

DOUBLE 5"
VINYL SIDING

ASPHALT SHINGLES

2'-0"

8'-0" CLG. HT.

8'-0" CLG. HT.

GRADE

BELOW FROST LINE

LEFT ELEVATION

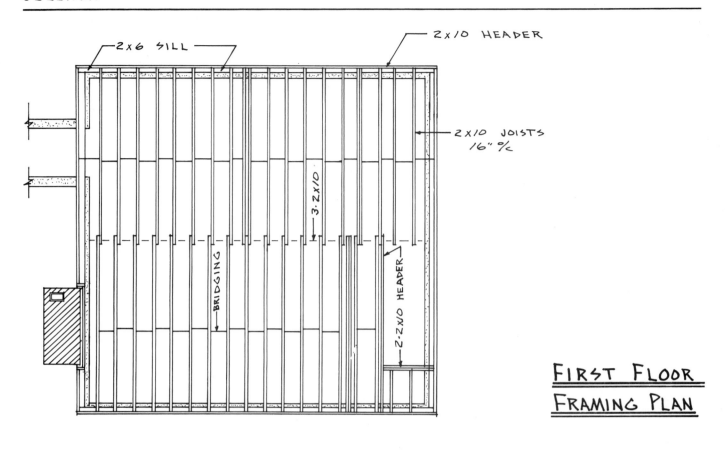

2x6 SILL

2x10 HEADER

2x10 JOISTS
16" o/c

3-2x10

BRIDGING

2-2x10 HEADER

FIRST FLOOR
FRAMING PLAN

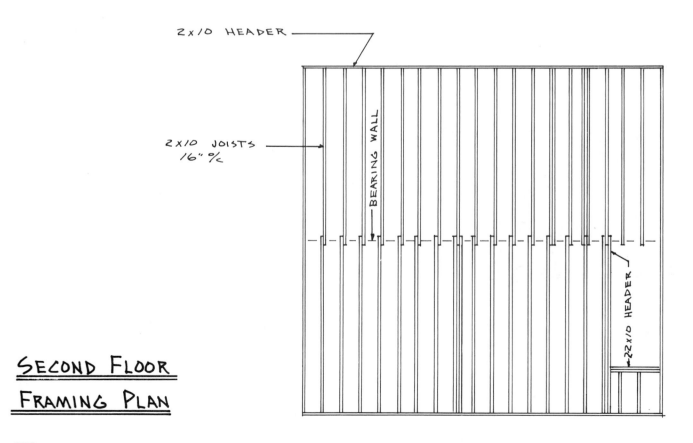

2x10 HEADER

2x10 JOISTS
16" o/c

BEARING WALL

2-2x10 HEADER

SECOND FLOOR
FRAMING PLAN

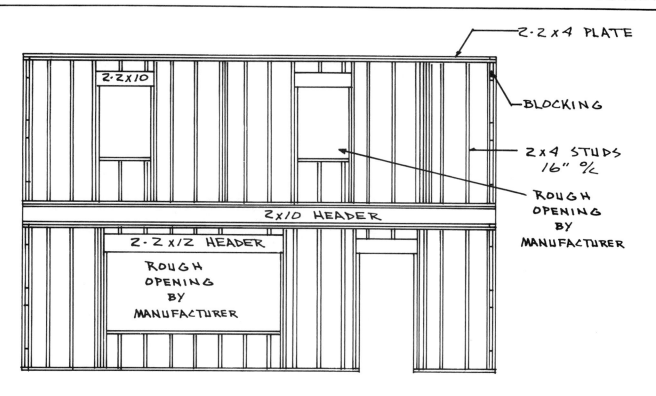

2·2x4 PLATE

BLOCKING

2x4 STUDS
16" %

ROUGH
OPENING
BY
MANUFACTURER

2·2x10

2x10 HEADER

2·2x12 HEADER

ROUGH
OPENING
BY
MANUFACTURER

FRONT FRAMING PLAN

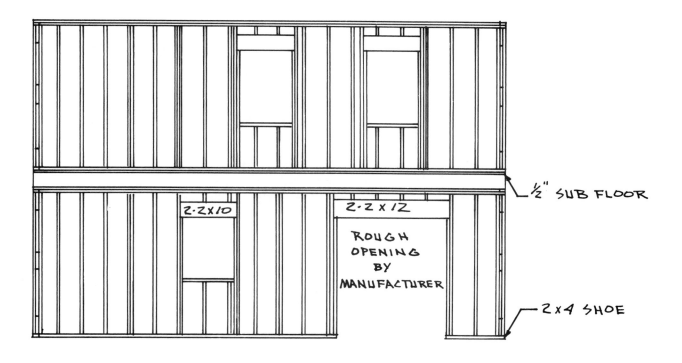

½" SUB FLOOR

2·2x10

2·2x12

ROUGH
OPENING
BY
MANUFACTURER

2x4 SHOE

REAR FRAMING PLAN

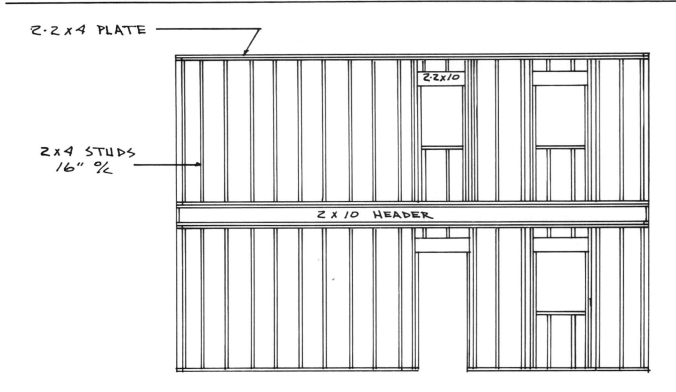

2·2x4 PLATE

2x4 STUDS
16" ⁰/c

2·2x10

2 x 10 HEADER

RIGHT FRAMING PLAN

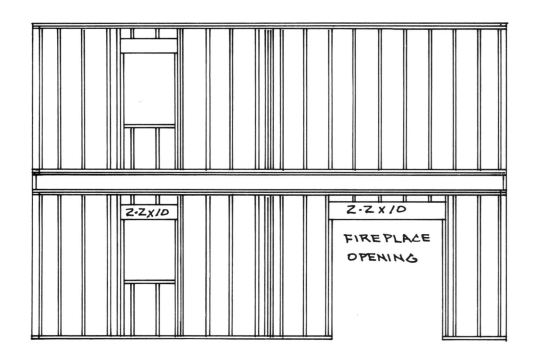

2·2x10

2·2x10

FIREPLACE
OPENING

LEFT FRAMING PLAN

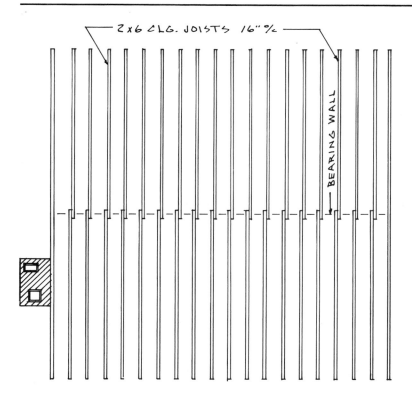

2x6 CLG. JOISTS 16" O.C.

BEARING WALL

CEILING FRAMING PLAN

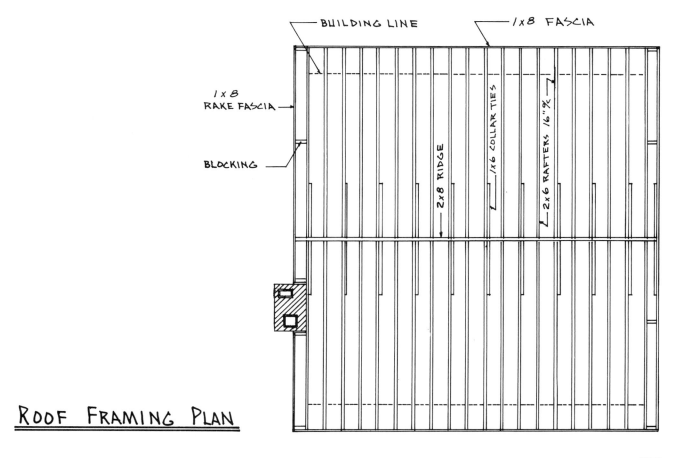

BUILDING LINE

1x8 FASCIA

1x8 RAKE FASCIA

BLOCKING

2x8 RIDGE

1x6 COLLAR TIES

2x6 RAFTERS 16" O.C.

ROOF FRAMING PLAN

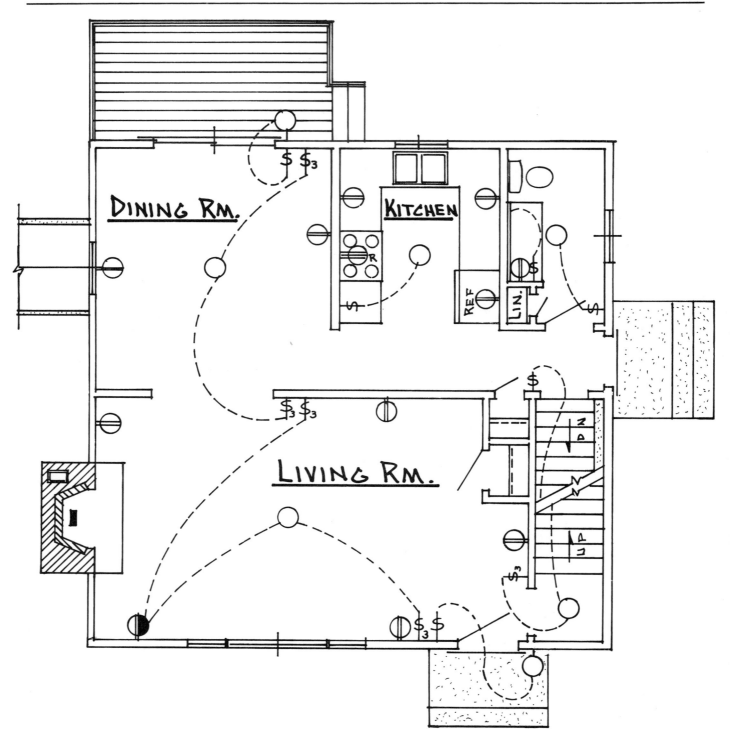

FIRST FLOOR ELECTRICAL LAYOUT

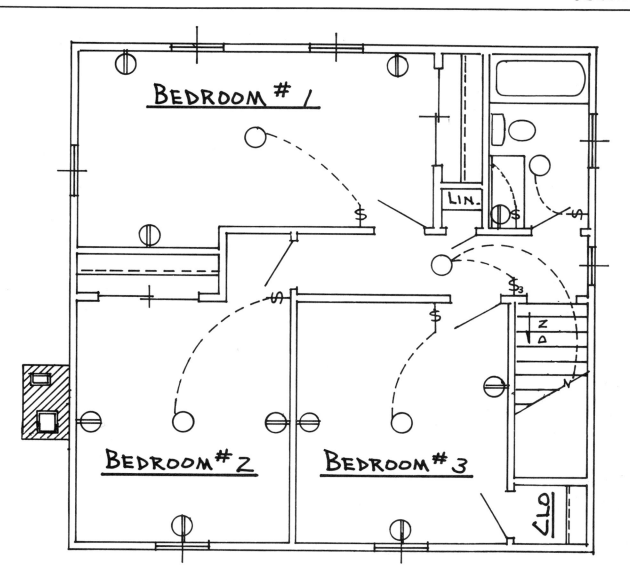

SECOND FLOOR ELECTRICAL LAYOUT

ELECTRICAL SYMBOLS	
SYM.	ITEM
$	SINGLE-POLE SWITCH
$₃	THREE-WAY SWITCH
⊖	DUPLEX CONVENIENCE OUTLET
⬤	SPLIT-WIRED OUTLET
⬤R	RANGE OUTLET
◯	LIGHTING OUTLET
▭	FLUORESCENT LIGHTING

MATERIAL LIST

FLOOR SYSTEM

2 × 10 Joists	81/14
2 × 10 Header	8/14 - 8/12
2 × 6 Sill	4/14 - 4/12
Sill Seal	104 Lineal Feet
Anchor Bolts	13
1/2" × 4' × 8' Plywood	40 Sheets
Bridging	33 Pairs
3 1/2" ⌀ Lally Columns	3/8
3-2 × 10 Beam	3/14 - 3/12

WALL SYSTEM

2 × 4 Shoe	8/14 - 8/12
2-2 × 4 Plate	16/14 - 16/12
2 × 4 Studs	210/8
Door Headers	
2 × 10	1/14
2 × 12	1/14

Window Headers (2 × 10)	5/14
1/2" × 4' × 8' Sheathing	52 Sheets
3 1/2" Insulation	19 Rolls
Siding	1660 Square Feet
Fireplace Header	(2 × 10) - 1/14
Air Infiltration Housewrap	1660 Square Feet

CEILING SYSTEM

2 × 6 Ceiling Joists	40/14
Insulation	14 Rolls

ROOF SYSTEM

2 × 8 Ridge	2/14
2 × 6 Rafters	40/16

1 × 6 Collar Ties	11/10
1/2" × 24" Soffit	7/8
1" × 8" Fascia	2/14
1/4" × 12" Soffit	8/8
1" × 8" Rake Fascia	8/8
#15 Roofing Felt	3 Rolls
1/2" × 4' × 8' Plywood	28 Sheets
Asphalt Shingles	27 Bundles

INTERIOR

2 × 4 Studs	163/8
Door Headers	
2-2 × 8	6/12
2-2 × 10	2/10
1/2" × 4' × 8' Sheetrock	70 Sheets
1" × 12" Shelving	5/8 - 1/4
Closet Pole	1/14 - 1/6
Baseboard	508 Lineal Feet
Ceiling Moulding	568 Lineal Feet
Stair Stringers (2 × 12)	2/14
Stair Risers	3/12 - 1/4
Stair Treads	3/12

BASEMENT STAIRS

Stringers (2 × 12)	2/14
2 × 10 Treads	3/12
Handrail	1/14

DECKS

Flooring (2 × 6)	75 Square Feet
Railings	48 Lineal Feet
Cap	24 Lineal Feet
4 × 4 Posts	3/6

GREGANN

DESIGNED & DRAWN BY E. BRYANT

The Gregann, a two-story residential dwelling, consists of 2,300 square feet of living space.

Located on the lower level is a foyer, airlock, den, laundry, half bath, kitchen, dining room, and living room. The kitchen, dining room, and living room have access to a wrap-around deck in the rear of the house.

The upper level consists of four bedrooms, two baths, and storage area.

The exterior is enhanced by 8-inch horizontal siding and double-hung windows.

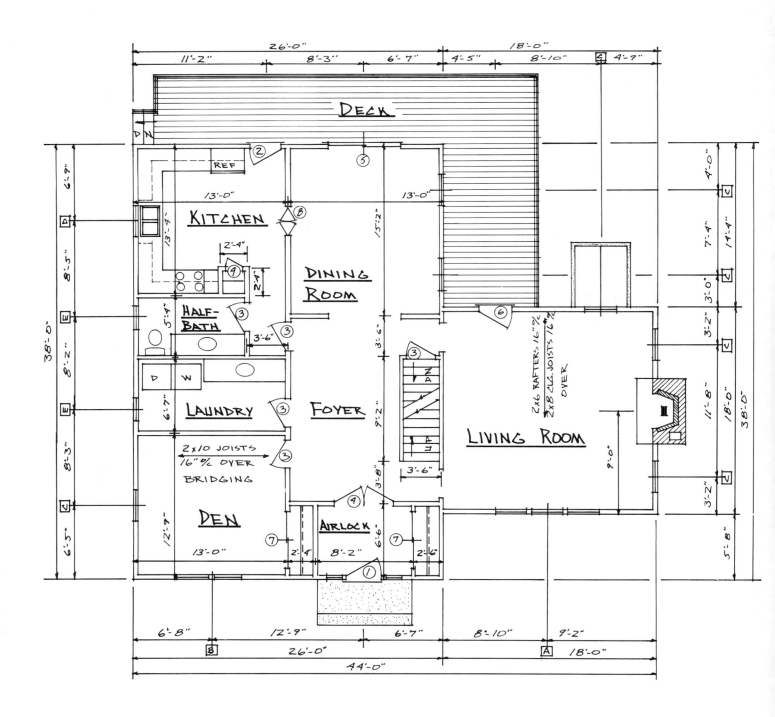

FIRST FLOOR PLAN

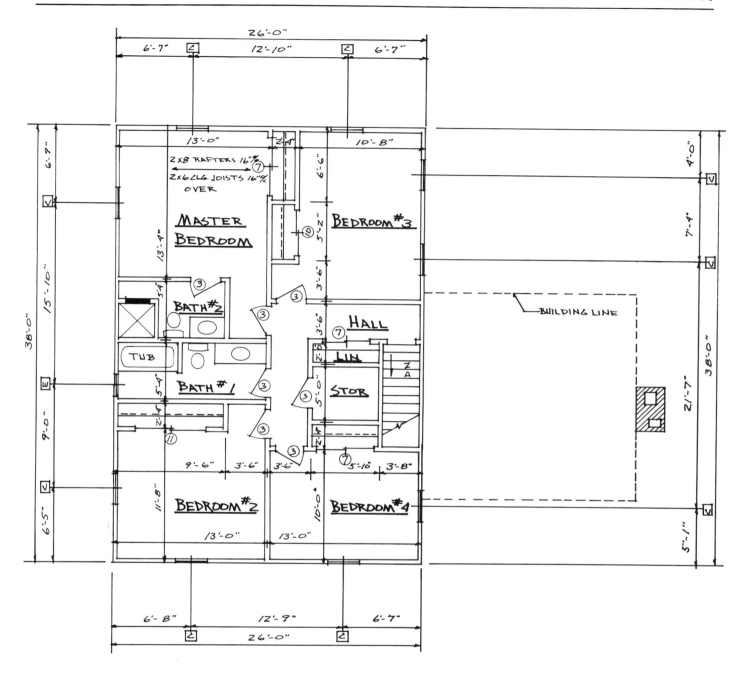

SECOND FLOOR PLAN

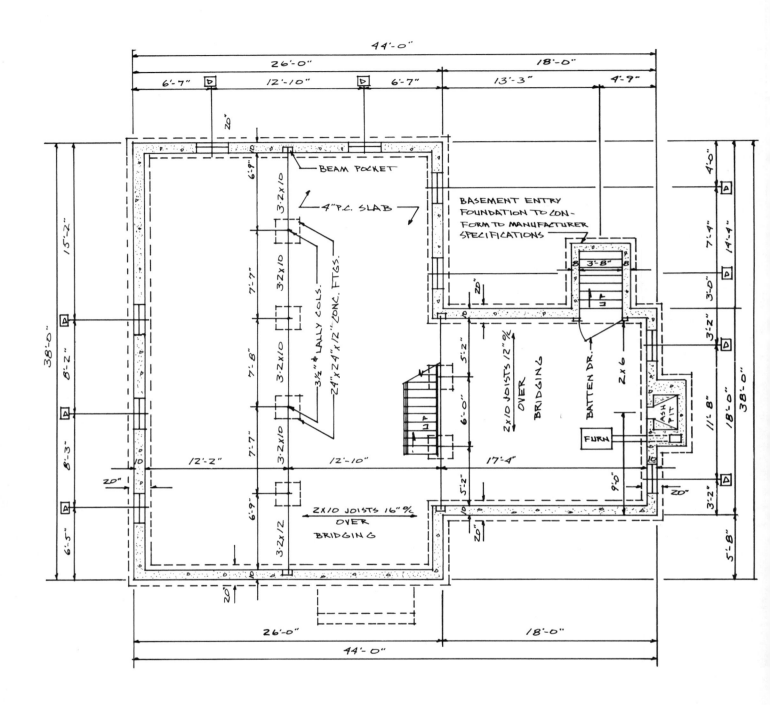

FOUNDATION PLAN

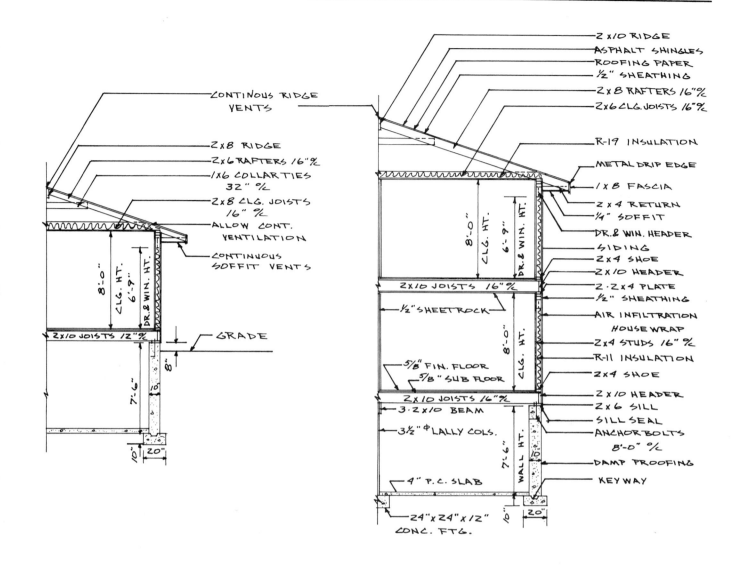

CONTINOUS RIDGE VENTS

2 X 8 RIDGE
2 X 6 RAFTERS 16" %
1 X 6 COLLAR TIES 32" %
2 X 8 CLG. JOISTS 16" %
ALLOW CONT. VENTILATION
CONTINUOUS SOFFIT VENTS

8'-0" CLG. HT.
6'-9" DR. & WIN. HT.

GRADE

2 X 10 JOISTS 12" %

8"

7'-6"

10"

10"   20"

2 X 10 RIDGE
ASPHALT SHINGLES
ROOFING PAPER
½" SHEATHING
2 X 8 RAFTERS 16" %
2 X 6 CLG. JOISTS 16" %

R-19 INSULATION
METAL DRIP EDGE
1 X 8 FASCIA
2 X 4 RETURN
¼" SOFFIT
DR. & WIN. HEADER
SIDING
2 X 4 SHOE
2 X 10 HEADER
2 · 2 X 4 PLATE
½" SHEATHING
AIR INFILTRATION HOUSE WRAP
2 X 4 STUDS 16" %
R-11 INSULATION
2 X 4 SHOE
2 X 10 HEADER
2 X 6 SILL
SILL SEAL
ANCHOR BOLTS 8'-0" %
DAMP PROOFING
KEY WAY

8'-0" CLG. HT.
6'-9" DR. & WIN. HT.

2 X 10 JOISTS 16" %
½" SHEETROCK

8'-0" CLG. HT.

5/8" FIN. FLOOR
5/8" SUB FLOOR

2 X 10 JOISTS 16" %
3 · 2 X 10 BEAM
3½" Φ LALLY COLS.

7'-6" WALL HT.

10"

4" P.C. SLAB

24" X 24" X 12" CONC. FTG.

10"   20"

LIVING ROOM SECTION

STAFF SECTION

NOTE:
CHECK LOCAL BUILDING CODES REGARDING FLOOR INSULATION.

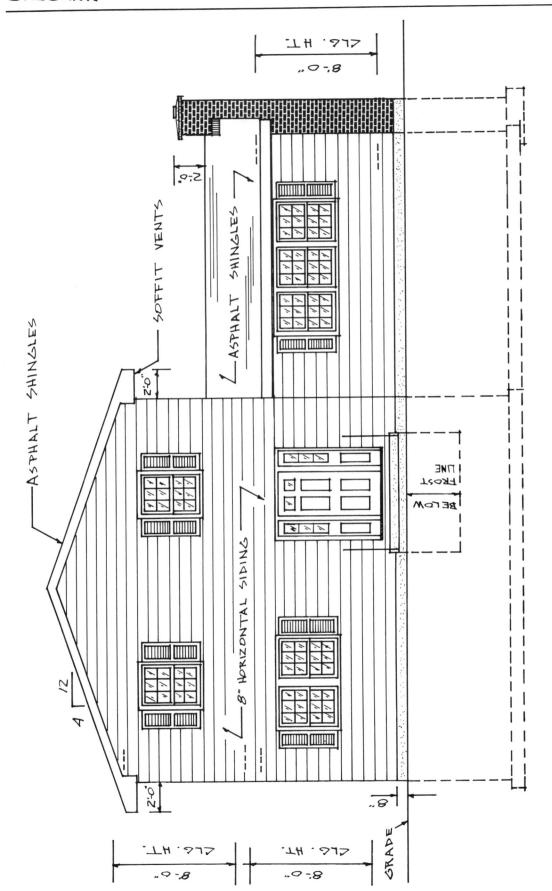

FRONT ELEVATION

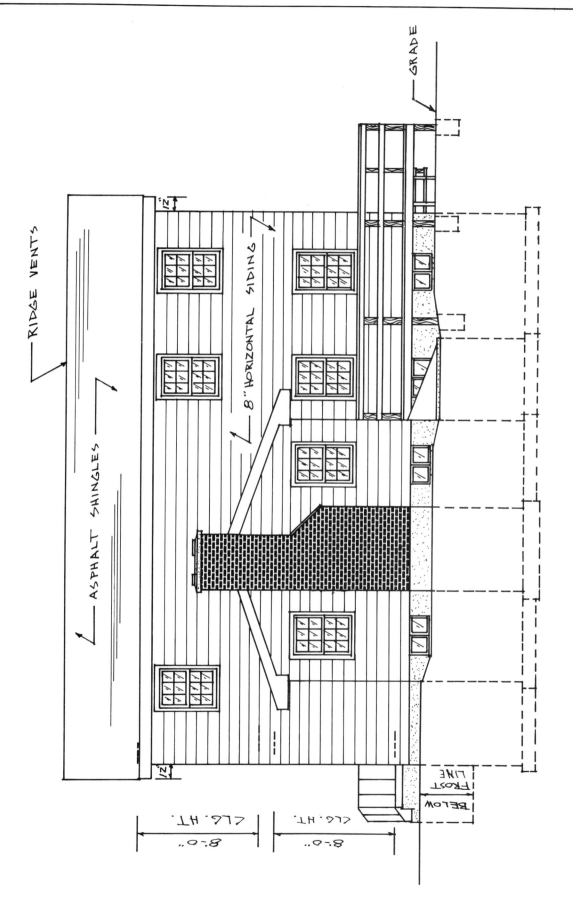

RIDGE VENTS

ASPHALT SHINGLES

8" HORIZONTAL SIDING

GRADE

FROST LINE BELOW

8'-0" 9'6" HT.

8'-0" 9'6" HT.

RIGHT ELEVATION

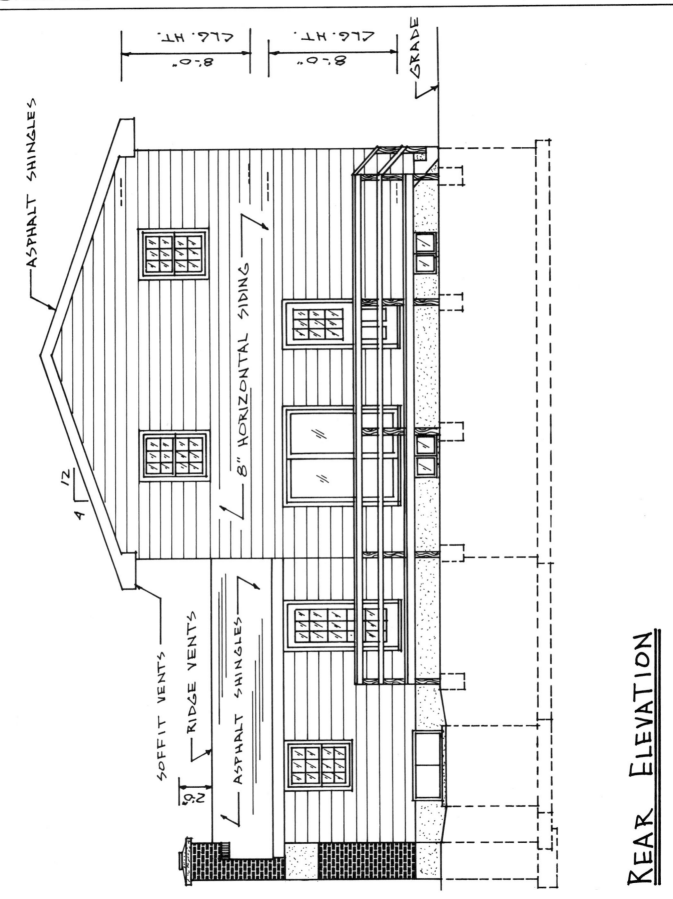

REAR ELEVATION

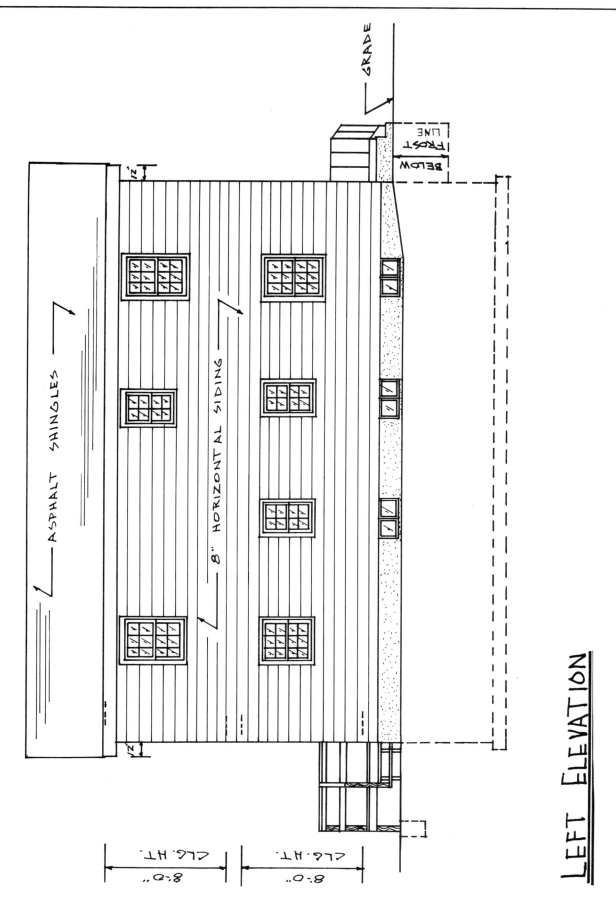

GRADE

FROST LINE BELOW

ASPHALT SHINGLES

8" HORIZONTAL SIDING

2"

2"

CLG. HT.

8'-0"

CLG. HT.

8'-0"

LEFT ELEVATION

NOTES:
1) WOOD FRAMING TO BE KEPT 2" CLEAR OF FIRE-PLACE MASONRY.

2) DOUBLE JOISTS UNDER PARALLEL PARTITIONS.

3) WOOD FRAMING MEMBERS TO HAVE A FIBER STRESS OF 1200 PSI.

4) STRUCTURAL CHANGES SHOULD NOT BE MADE WITHOUT CONSULTING ARCHITECT/CONTRACTOR.

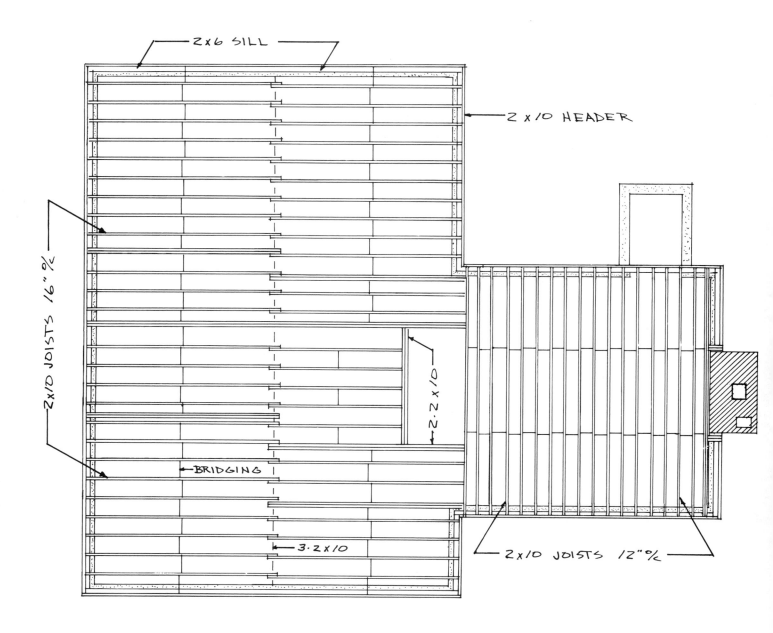

2x6 SILL

2 x 10 HEADER

2x10 JOISTS 16" %

2·2 x 10

BRIDGING

3·2 x 10

2x10 JOISTS 12" %

FIRST FLOOR FRAMING PLAN

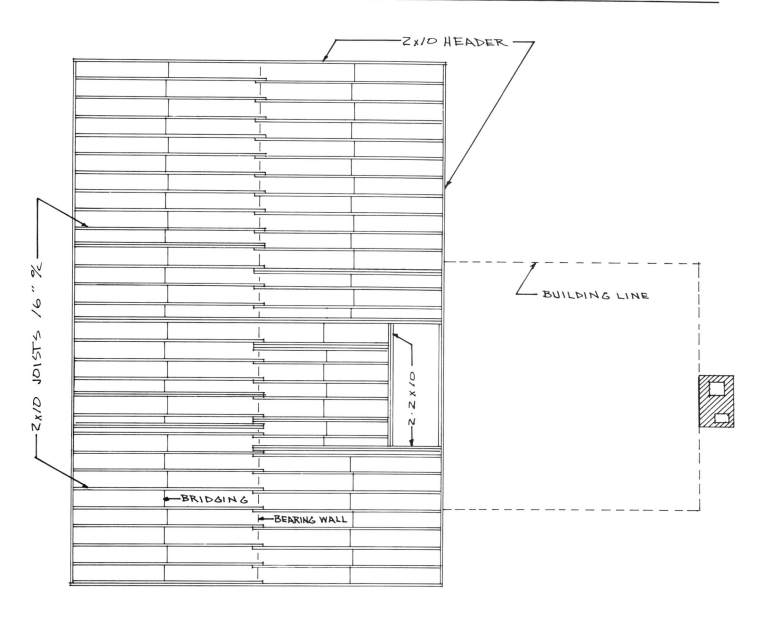

2×10 HEADER

BUILDING LINE

2×10 JOISTS 16" ⁰/C

2·2×10

BRIDGING

BEARING WALL

SECOND FLOOR FRAMING PLAN

SYM	QTY	SIZE	REMARKS
A	1	3^{10} x 8^6	TRIPLE MULL.
B	1	3^{10} x 5^8	DOUBLE MULL.
C	15	2^8 x 3^{10}	D.H.
D	1	2^8 x 3^2	D.H.
E	3	2^0 x 3^2	D.H.
D	9	2^8 x 1^4	BSMT.

WINDOW SCHEDULE

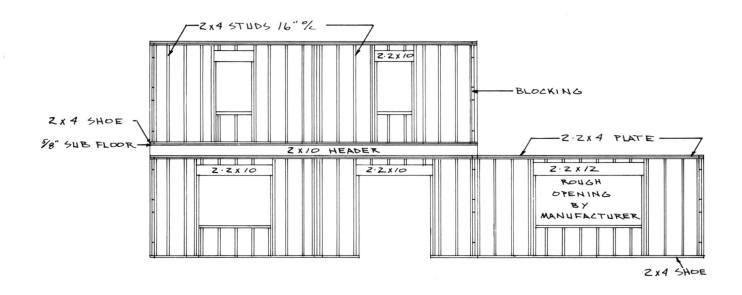

2x4 STUDS 16" ⁰⁄c

2·2x10

BLOCKING

2x4 SHOE

⁵⁄8" SUB FLOOR

2·2x4 PLATE

2x10 HEADER

2·2x10

2·2x10

2·2x12
ROUGH
OPENING
BY
MANUFACTURER

2x4 SHOE

FRONT FRAMING PLAN

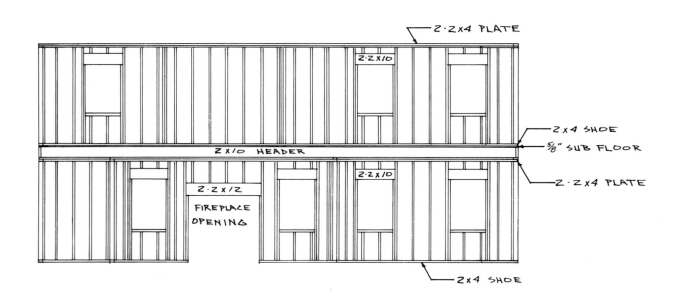

2·2x4 PLATE

2·2x10

2x4 SHOE
⁵⁄8" SUB FLOOR

2·2x4 PLATE

2x10 HEADER

2·2x10

2·2x12
FIREPLACE
OPENING

2·2x10

2x4 SHOE

RIGHT FRAMING PLAN

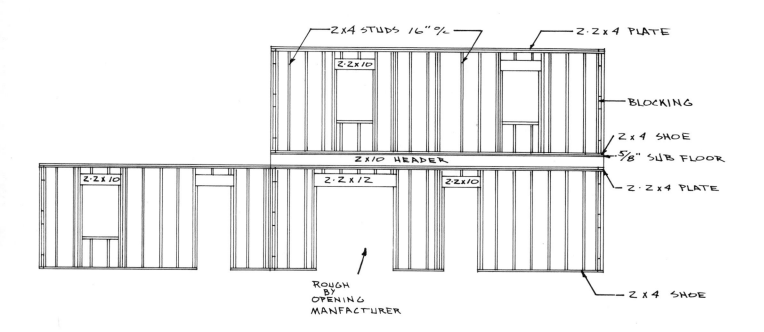

2×4 STUDS 16" ⁰/ᴄ   2·2×4 PLATE

2·2×10

BLOCKING

2×4 SHOE

·5/8" SUB FLOOR

2·2×4 PLATE

2×10 HEADER

2·2×10   2·2×12   2·2×10

2×4 SHOE

ROUGH
BY
OPENING
MANFACTURER

REAR FRAMING PLAN

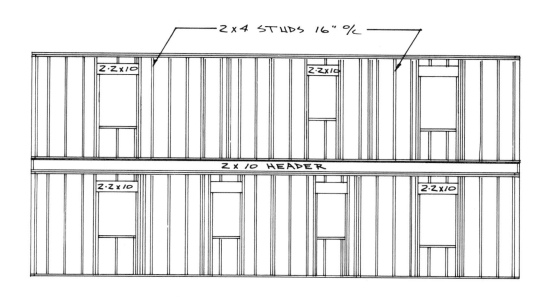

2×4 STUDS 16" ⁰/ᴄ

2·2×10   2·2×10

2×10 HEADER

2·2×10   2·2×10

LEFT FRAMING PLAN

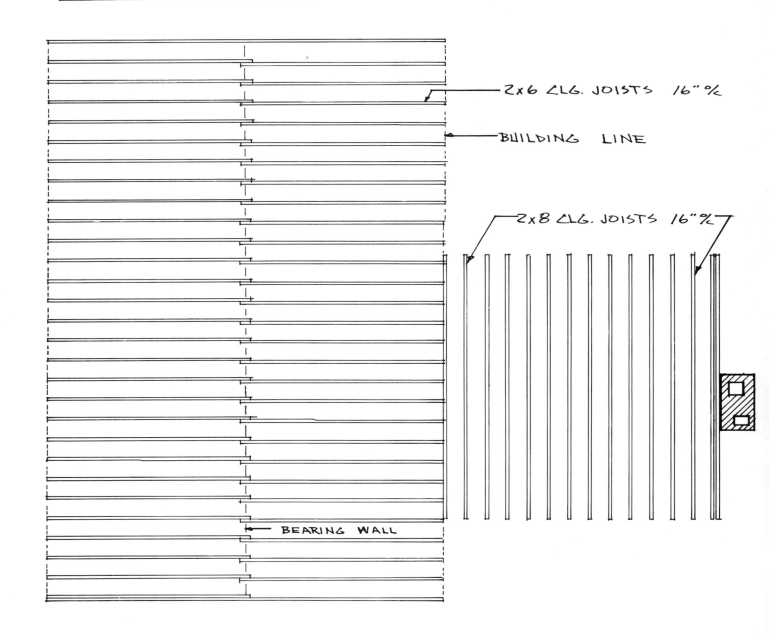

2x6 CLG. JOISTS 16" %

BUILDING LINE

2x8 CLG. JOISTS 16" %

BEARING WALL

CEILING FRAMING PLAN

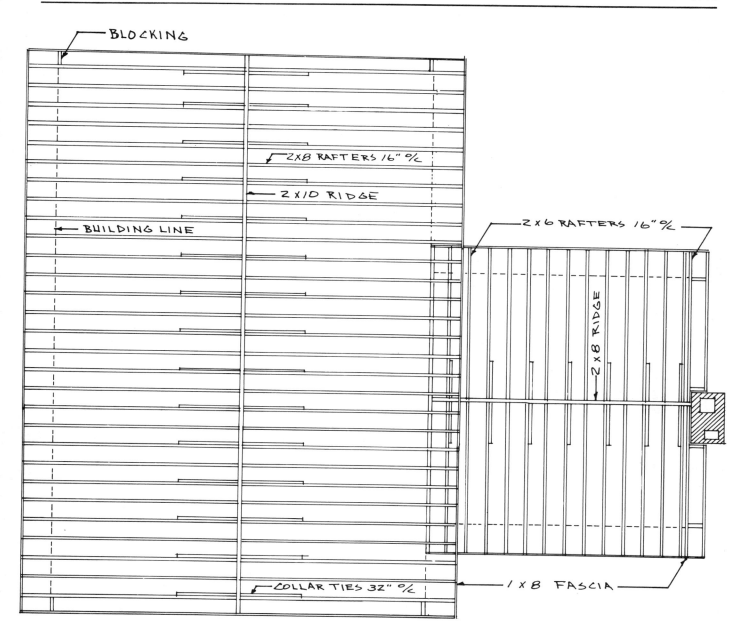

BLOCKING

2X8 RAFTERS 16" O/C

2X10 RIDGE

BUILDING LINE

2X6 RAFTERS 16" O/C

2X8 RIDGE

COLLAR TIES 32" O/C

1X8 FASCIA

ROOF FRAMING PLAN

DOOR SCHEDULE			
SYM	QTY	SIZE	REMARKS
1	1	$3^0 \times 6^8$ W/S.L.	PANEL-S.C.
2	1	$2^8 \times 6^8$	S.C.
3	12	$2^6 \times 6^8$	FLUSH-H.C.
4	1	$2 \cdot 2^6 \times 6^8$	FRENCH DRS.
5	1	$6^0 \times 6^8$	PATIO DR.
6	1	$2^8 \times 6^8$	FRENCH DR.
7	5	$5^0 \times 6^8$	SLDG-H.C.
8	1	$2^6 \times 3^8$	CAFE DRS.
9	1	$1^6 \times 6^8$	FLUSH-H.C.
10	1	$4^0 \times 6^8$	SLDG.-H.C.
11	1	$6^0 \times 6^8$	SLDG.-H.C.

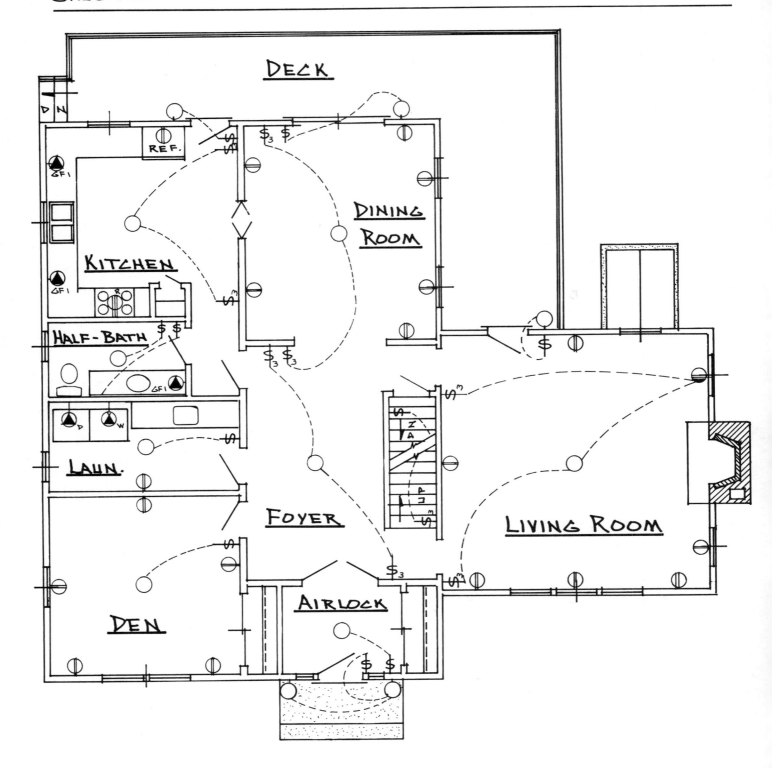

FIRST FLOOR ELECTRICAL LAYOUT

NOTE:
ELECTRICAL SYMBOLS
LOCATED ON SECOND
FLOOR ELECTRICAL LAYOUT.

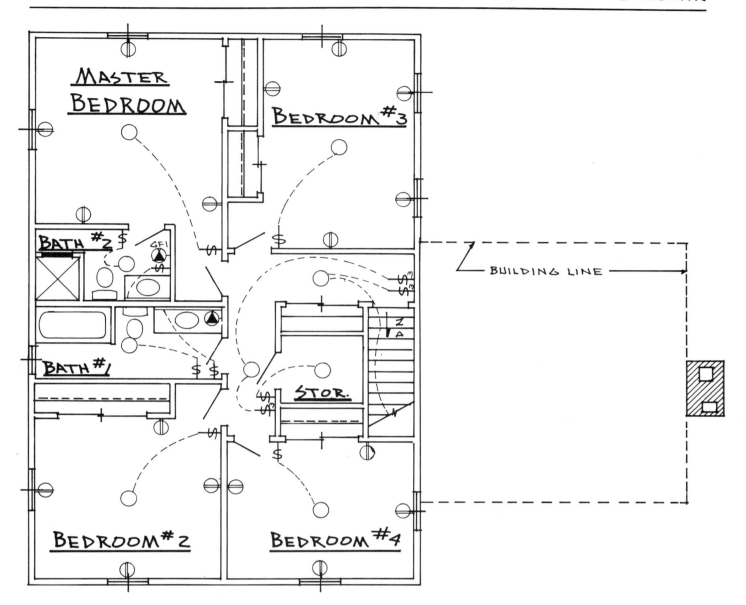

SECOND FLOOR ELECTRICAL LAYOUT

ELECTRICAL SYMBOLS	
SYM	ITEM
$	SINGLE-POLE SWITCH
$₃	THREE-WAY SWITCH
⊖	DUPLEX OUTLET
⊜	SPLIT-WIRED OUTLET
⊖R	RANGE OUTLET
▲GFI	GROUND FAULT INTERRUPTER
▲W	WASHER OUTLET
▲D	DRYER OUTLET
○	LIGHTING OUTLET
▭	FLUORESCENT LIGHTING

MATERIAL LIST

FLOOR SYSTEM

2 × 10 Joists	18/10 - 19/18 - 115/14
2 × 10 Header	2/18 - 1/16 - 7/14 - 10/12
2 × 6 Sill	2/18 - 1/16 - 3/14 - 4/12
Sill Seal	164 Lineal Feet
Anchor Bolts	22
1/2″ × 4′ × 8′ Plywood	72 Sheets
Bridging	146 Pairs
3 1/2″ ⌀ Lally Columns	6/8
3-2 × 10 Beam	4/14 - 5/12

WALL SYSTEM

2 × 4 Shoe	2/18 - 1/16 - 7/14 - 10/12
2-2 × 4 Plate	4/18 - 2/16 - 14/14 - 14/12
2 × 4 Studs	309/8
Door Headers	
2 × 12	1/14
2 × 10	2/12
Window Headers	
2 × 12	2/10
2 × 10	9/12 - 1/10 - 1/6
2 × 12 Fireplace Header	1/12
1/2″ × 4′ × 8′ Sheathing	68 Sheets
R-11 Insulation	25 Rolls
Siding	2172 Square Feet
Air Infiltration Housewrap	2172 Square Feet

CEILING SYSTEM

2 × 6 Ceiling Joists	60/14
2 × 8 Ceiling Joists	15/18
R-19 Insulation	27 Rolls

ROOF SYSTEM

2 × 10 Ridge	2/14 - 1/12
2 × 8 Rafters	58/16
1 × 6 Collar Ties	15/10 - 7/6
1/4″ × 24″ Soffit	15/8
1 × 8 Fascia	118 Lineal Feet
1/4″ × 12″ Rake Soffit	76 Lineal Feet
1 × 8 Rake Fascia	76 Lineal Feet
#15 Roofing Felt	4 Rolls
1/2″ × 4′ × 8′ Plywood	48 Sheets
Asphalt Shingles	48 Bundles
2 × 8 Ridge	2/10
2 × 6 Rafters	30/12
Metal Drip Edge	118 Lineal Feet

INTERIOR

2 × 4 Studs	287/8
2 × 10 Door Headers	11/12 - 2/10 - 1/14 - 1/4
1/2″ × 4′ × 8′ Sheetrock	113 Sheets
1″ × 12″ Shelving	5/8 - 5/6 - 1/10
Closet Pole	5/6 - 1/10
Baseboard	596 Lineal Feet
Ceiling Moulding	750 Lineal Feet
2 × 12 Stair Stringers	2/14
Stair Risers	13
Stair Treads	12

BASEMENT STAIRS

2 × 12 Stringers	2/14
2 × 10 Treads	3/12
Handrail	2/14

DECKS

Flooring	267 Square Feet
4 × 4 Posts	9/6
2 × 4 Railings	108 Lineal Feet
2 × 6 Cap	54 Lineal Feet

Article V

The Owner-Built Experience

When I was putting this book together, I thought an article about owner-built houses would be ideal.

Then I thought of Andrew (Andy) Quigley.

He recently was involved in the construction of his own house. In order to minimize the cost of house construction, he not only built the house himself; in addition, he used rough-cut lumber from his building lot.

After contacting Andy and setting up an interview with him, I decided to use his experiences as the basis for the following article.

IN THE BEGINNING

After living in a rented dwelling for over a year, Andy Quigley and his wife Denise, realized that they were paying money every month with nothing to show for it. After much careful thought and planning, they decided to build a house. They envisioned a self-designed passive-solar home with a living room, a kitchen, three bedrooms, and a bath.

They purchased a used mobile home and set it up on their lot, which they had previously purchased. It was their intention to live in the mobile home while the house was being constructed.

Andy could have hired a contractor, who would be responsible for furnishing all the materials and seeing that all work would be satisfactorily performed. The contractor would employ and supervise all subcontractors. He would order and pay for the building materials and labor, in addition to scheduling delivery of the materials and acting as a general supervisor.

Instead, Andy could have acted as his own contractor, and taken on the responsibility of obtaining sub-contractors, ordering materials, and supervising the job himself.

However, being an experienced and competent carpenter, Andy acted as his own contractor and builder. He did everything himself, including custom-building the windows. The only thing he subcontracted was the pouring of the footing and foundation walls.

BUILDING PROCEDURE

Armed with a set of building plans, Andy confidently approached the local building inspector. After looking over the plans, the inspector informed Andy that there would be no problem issuing him a building permit. But before a permit could be issued, approval had to be obtained from the planning commission.

The purpose of the planning commission is to oversee what is being built within the town limits. In the event that wetlands are on the building site, the planning commission would refer the owner to the wetlands-inlands commission, but that was not the case with Andy's lot. Everything was in order, and approval was granted from the planning commission.

The next stop was the bank, to apply for a contractor loan. However, because Andy would be using rough-cut lumber for the framing of his house, the loan officer, uneducated in the difference between rough-cut lumber and kiln-dried lumber, hesitated to approve the loan without approval of the building inspector.

So once again, Andy went back to see the building inspector, where he obtained his building permit, which enabled him to get his loan approved.

Since he was building the house in a town that

didn't have zoning, he didn't have to worry about appearing before the zoning commission. But he did have to notify the health department, which was responsible for taking perk tests.

Because he had a favorable perk test, no fill was required. By assisting the installer and doing a lot of manual labor himself, Andy saved a considerable amount of money.

HOUSE CONSTRUCTION

With the required permits, bank loan, and proper people notified, construction on the house was started.

Once the concrete was poured, Andy spent his spare time and weekends constructing the house himself. For added insulation, he used 2 × 6 studs of hemlock and red pine, instead of 2 × 4 studs. The floor joists consisted of rough-cut red oak.

The lower level floor consisted of a 4-inch poured concrete slab. Under the slab was a 6-mil polyethelene vapor barrier, which was placed over 2 inches of rigid extruded polystyrene. Beneath it all was 2 inches of smooth and compact masonry sand.

ORIENTATION

Because their house is of a passive-solar design, orientation of the structure was something to which Andy had given considerable consideration before construction began. He realized that regardless of house design or style, careful orientation of the dwelling in regard to the sun can provide warmth and comfort. In choosing his floor plan and designing his house, much thought was given to locating rooms so that the maximum gain of the sun could be realized.

Since the South wall of the house receives considerable heat from the direct rays of the sun, Andy located the living room on the Southwest side of the dwelling, on the lower level. The kitchen was placed on the Southeast corner of the building on the lower level, adjacent to the living room. By utilizing a placement, his family was able to take advantage of the morning sun in the kitchen and the afternoon and evening sun in the living room.

All the rooms on the South side of the structure make ample use of windows. One of the bedrooms located on the upper level has access to a 3-foot balcony, which extends the length of the house and also serves as an overhang. It has been calculated to receive the maximum gain of the sun.

After doing extensive research on the subject, Andy was aware that there are two things which influence the relationship between a house and the sun: altitude and azimuth. The *altitude* is the angle formed by the rays of the sun and the earth's surface. The altitude of the sun is considerably lower in the winter than the summer.

The *azimuth* is the direction from which the sun rises and sets during various seasons. It does not rise due East and set due West every day. It rises from an easterly direction and sets in a westerly direction. As the earth turns on its axis and revolves around the sun, the angle of inclination of the axis to the sun varies a little each day, causing the direction from which the sun rises and sets to vary a few degrees each day.

In the winter, when the sun is at its lowest, the sun's rays will penetrate the window area of the kitchen and living room in the Quigley home. The concrete floor slab in these rooms will absorb the rays and provide warmth long after the sun sets.

In the summer, when the sun is at its highest; the overhang/balcony provides protection against excessive heat of the sun's rays.

The Quigley family have moved in and are enjoying the comforts of their owner-built residential dwelling.

Section VI
Split-Level Home

EDNA

DESIGNED & DRAWN BY E. BRYANT

With 1,326 square feet of living space, the Edna is a split-level house with 8-inch horizontal siding on the exterior.

The living area of this residential structure consists of an airlock, with guest closet, foyer, living room, dining room, and kitchen.

The sleeping area has three bedrooms and a full bath. Bedroom #1 has its own private bath with shower.

The lower level is divided between a one-car garage and the family room, which also has a washer and dryer.

EDNA

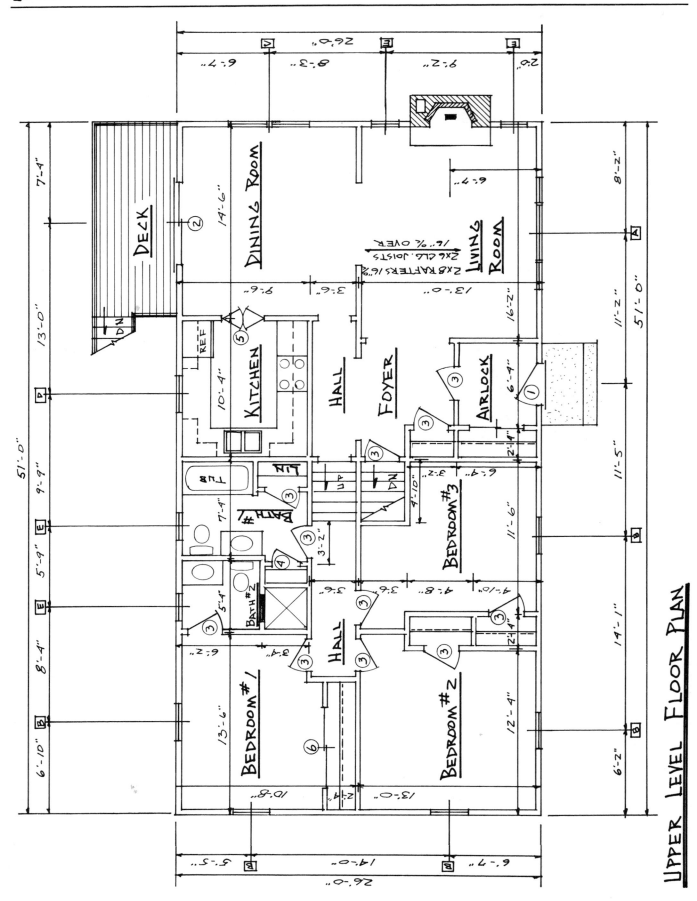

UPPER LEVEL FLOOR PLAN

300

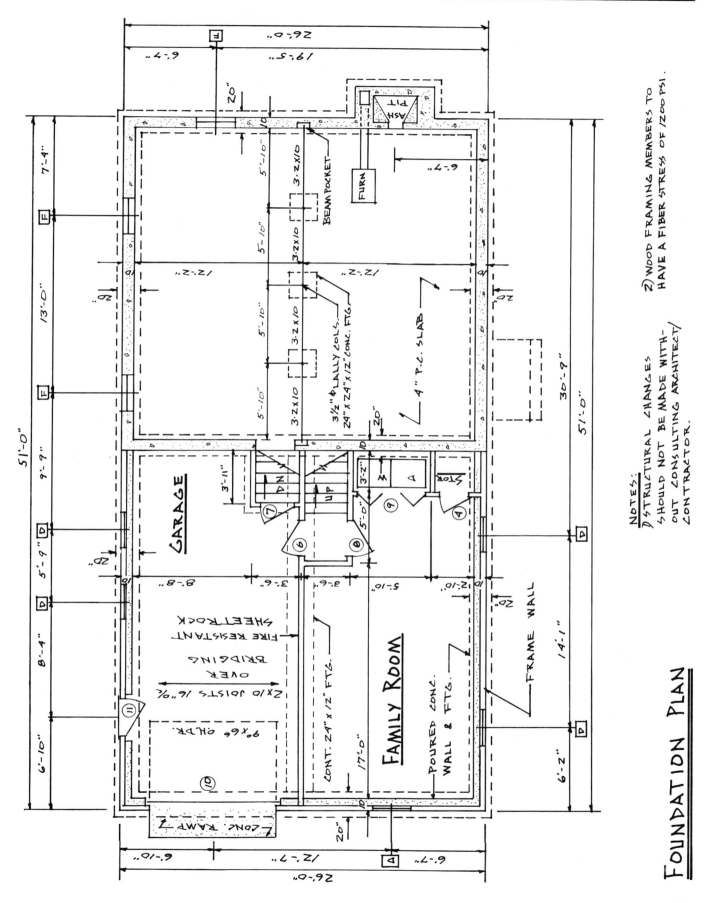

FOUNDATION PLAN

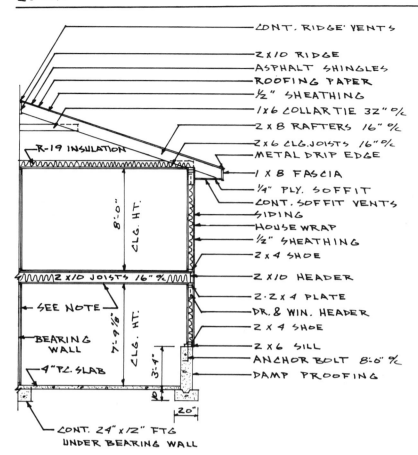

CONT. RIDGE VENTS
2 X 10 RIDGE
ASPHALT SHINGLES
ROOFING PAPER
1/2" SHEATHING
1 X 6 COLLAR TIE 32" O/C
2 X 8 RAFTERS 16" O/C
2 X 6 CLG. JOISTS 16" O/C
METAL DRIP EDGE
1 X 8 FASCIA
1/4" PLY. SOFFIT
CONT. SOFFIT VENTS
SIDING
HOUSE WRAP
1/2" SHEATHING
2 X 4 SHOE
2 X 10 HEADER
2 · 2 X 4 PLATE
DR. & WIN. HEADER
2 X 4 SHOE
2 X 6 SILL
ANCHOR BOLT 8:0" O/C
DAMP PROOFING

R-19 INSULATION
8'-0" CLG. HT.
2 X 10 JOISTS 16" O/C
SEE NOTE
7'-9½" CLG. HT.
BEARING WALL
4" P.C. SLAB
3'-4"
20"
CONT. 24" X 12" FTG
UNDER BEARING WALL

STAFF SECTION A-A

NOTES:
1) INTERIOR WALLS AND CEILING OF GARAGE TO BE COVERED WITH FIRE-RESISTANT SHEETROCK.

2) FLOOR SYSTEM ABOVE GARAGE TO HAVE R-30 INSULATION

3) CHECK LOCAL BUILDING CODES REGARDING FLOOR INSULATION.

STAFF SECTION B-B

ALLOW CONT. VENT.
2 · 2 X 4 PLATE
1/2" SHEETROCK
8'-0" CLG. HT.
5/8" FIN. FLOOR
5/8" SUB FLOOR
2 X 10 JOISTS 16" O/C
3 · 2 X 10 BEAM
3½"∅ LALLY COL.
7'-6" FOUN. WALL HT.
4" P.C. SLAB
2 X 4 RETURNS
DR. & WIN. HEADER
2 X 4 STUDS 16" O/C
R-11 INSULATION
2 X 4 SHOE
2 X 10 HEADER
SILL SEAL
KEY WAY
10"
10"
20"
24" X 24" X 12" CONC. FTG.

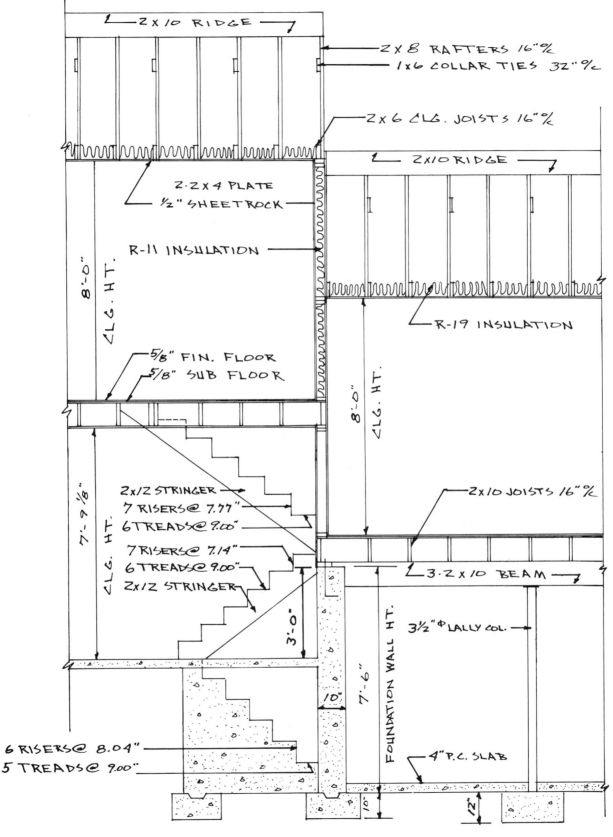

2×10 RIDGE

2×8 RAFTERS 16" %
1×6 COLLAR TIES 32" %

2×6 CLG. JOISTS 16" %

2×10 RIDGE

2·2×4 PLATE
½" SHEETROCK

R-11 INSULATION

R-19 INSULATION

8'-0" CLG. HT.

⁵⁄₈" FIN. FLOOR
⁵⁄₈" SUB FLOOR

8'-0" CLG. HT.

7'-9⅛" CLG. HT.

2×12 STRINGER
7 RISERS @ 7.77"
6 TREADS @ 9.00"

7 RISERS @ 7.14"
6 TREADS @ 9.00"
2×12 STRINGER

2×10 JOISTS 16" %

3·2×10 BEAM

3'-0"

3½" Φ LALLY COL.

10"

7'-6" FOUNDATION WALL HT.

6 RISERS @ 8.04"
5 TREADS @ 9.00"

4" P.C. SLAB

10"

12"

LONGITUDINAL SECTION STAIR DETAIL

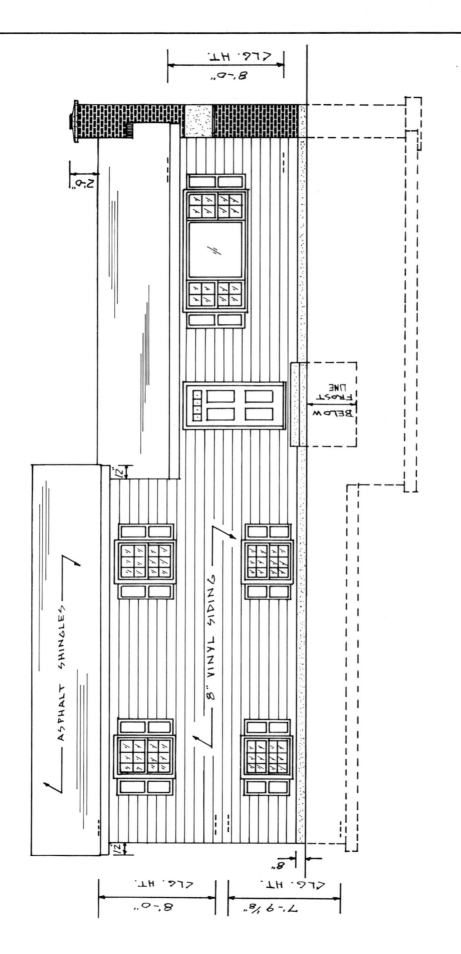

FRONT ELEVATION

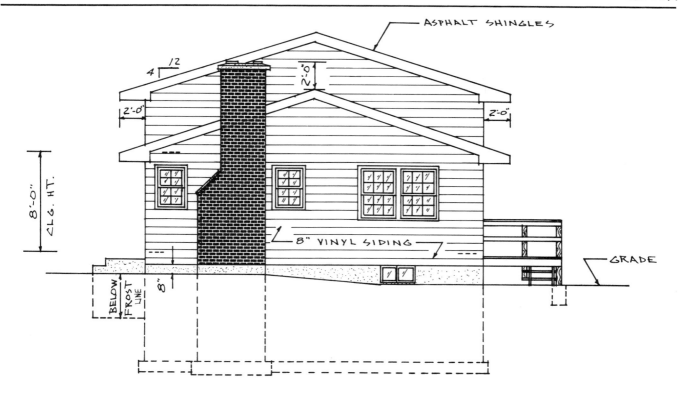

ASPHALT SHINGLES

2'-0"

2'-0"

2'-0"

4 | 12

8'-0" CLG. HT.

8" VINYL SIDING

GRADE

BELOW FROST LINE

8"

RIGHT ELEVATION

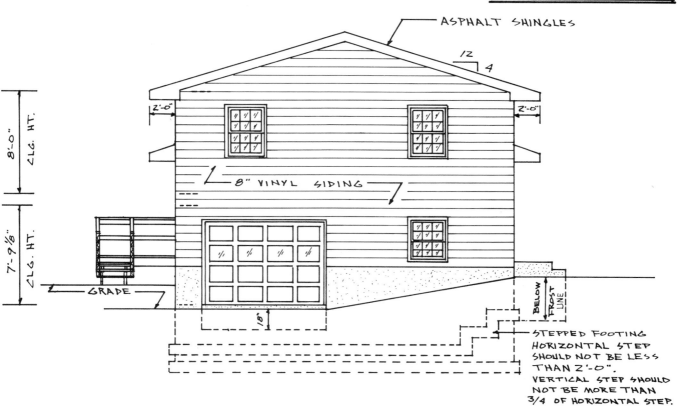

ASPHALT SHINGLES

12 | 4

2'-0"

2'-0"

8'-0" CLG. HT.

8" VINYL SIDING

7'-9⅝" CLG. HT.

GRADE

BELOW FROST LINE

18"

STEPPED FOOTING HORIZONTAL STEP SHOULD NOT BE LESS THAN 2'-0". VERTICAL STEP SHOULD NOT BE MORE THAN 3/4 OF HORIZONTAL STEP.

LEFT ELEVATION

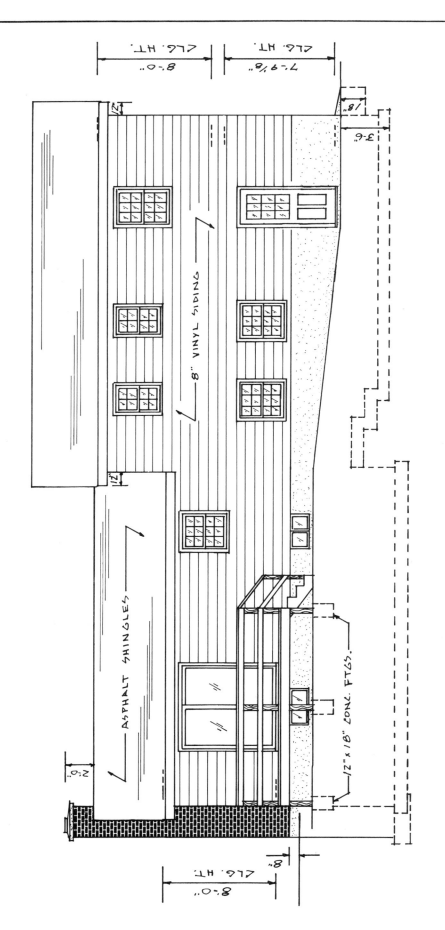

REAR ELEVATION

NOTES:
1) WOOD FRAMING TO BE KEPT 2" CLEAR OF FIREPLACE MASONRY. INSULATE WITH FIBER- GLASS BETWEEN MASONRY & WOOD.

2) DOUBLE JOISTS UNDER PARALLEL PARTITIONS.

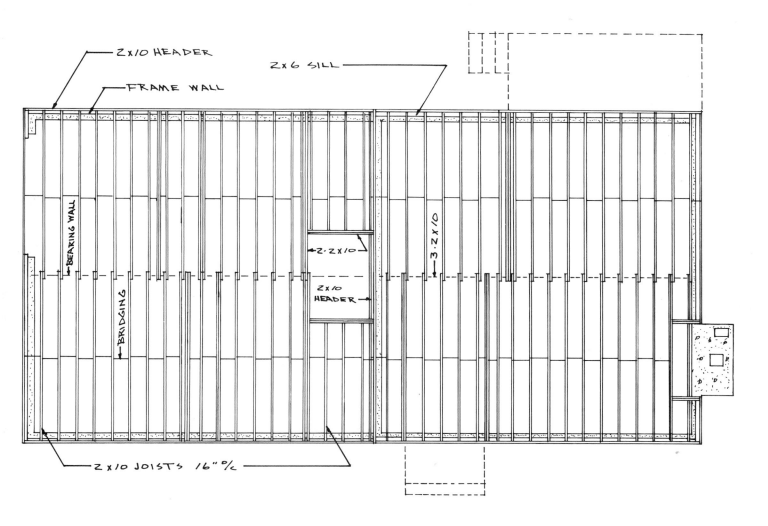

2x10 HEADER

FRAME WALL

2x6 SILL

BEARING WALL

BRIDGING

2·2x10

2x10 HEADER

3·2x10

2x10 JOISTS 16" ⁰⁄c

FLOOR FRAMING PLAN

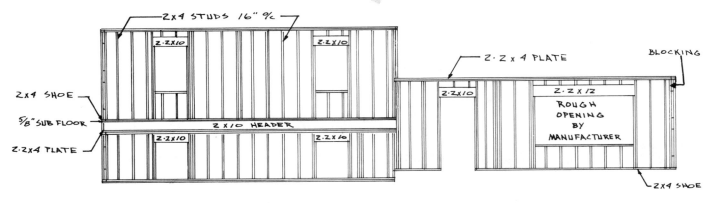

FRONT FRAMING PLAN

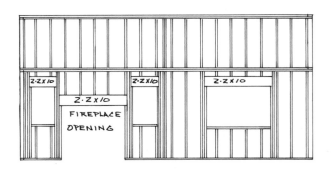

RIGHT FRAMING PLAN

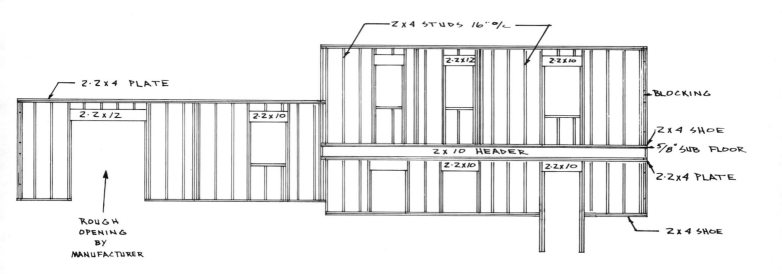

REAR FRAMING PLAN

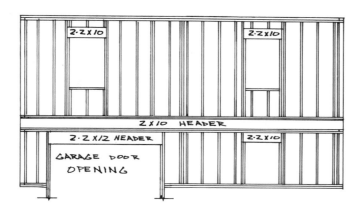

LEFT FRAMING PLAN

DOOR SCHEDULE			
SYM.	QTY.	SIZE	TYPE
①	1	3⁰ x 6⁸	PANEL - S.C.
②	1	6⁰ x 6⁸	PATIO DR.
③	10	2⁶ x 6⁸	FLUSH - H.C.
④	2	2⁰ x 6⁸	FLUSH - H.C.
⑤	1	2⁶ x 3⁸	CAFE DR.
⑥	1	2⁸ x 6⁸	FIRE DR.
⑦	1	2⁶ x 6⁸	FIRE DR.
⑧	1	2⁸ x 6⁸	FLUSH - H.C.
⑨	1	5⁰ x 6⁸	BIFOLD
⑩	1	9⁰ x 6⁶	GAR. DR.
⑪	1	2⁸ x 6⁸	PANEL - S.C.

WINDOW SCHEDULE			
SYM.	QTY.	SIZE	TYPE
A	1	2⁻4⁹-2⁰x4²	D.H.P.W.
B	5	2⁸ x 3¹⁰	D.H.
C	1	6⁻⁹ x 3¹⁰	D.H. MULL.
D	6	2⁸ x 3²	D.H.
E	4	2⁰ x 3²	D.H.
F	3	2⁸ x 1⁹	BSMT.

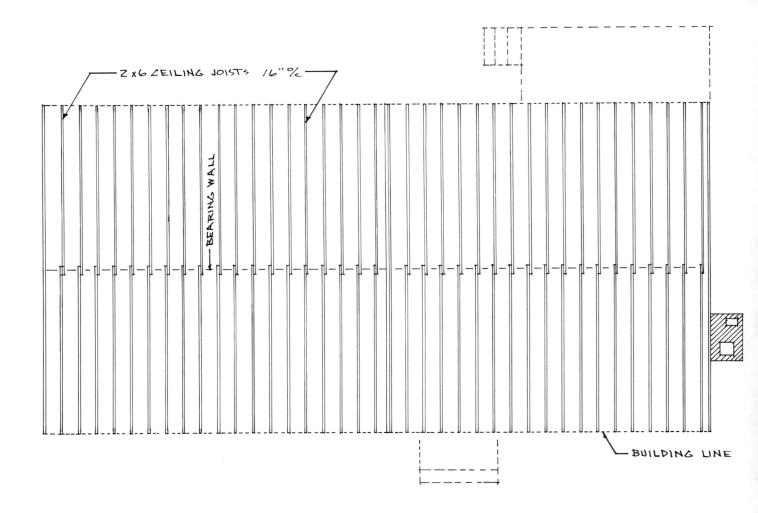

2x6 CEILING JOISTS 16" ⁰/c

BEARING WALL

BUILDING LINE

CEILING FRAMING PLAN

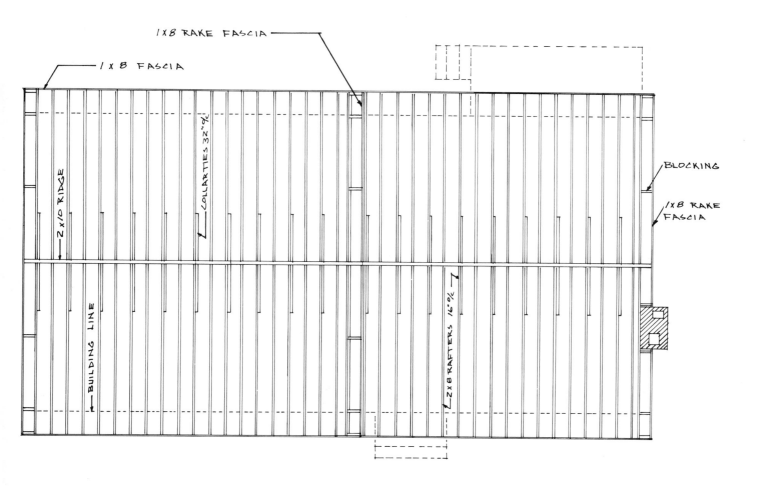

ROOF FRAMING PLAN

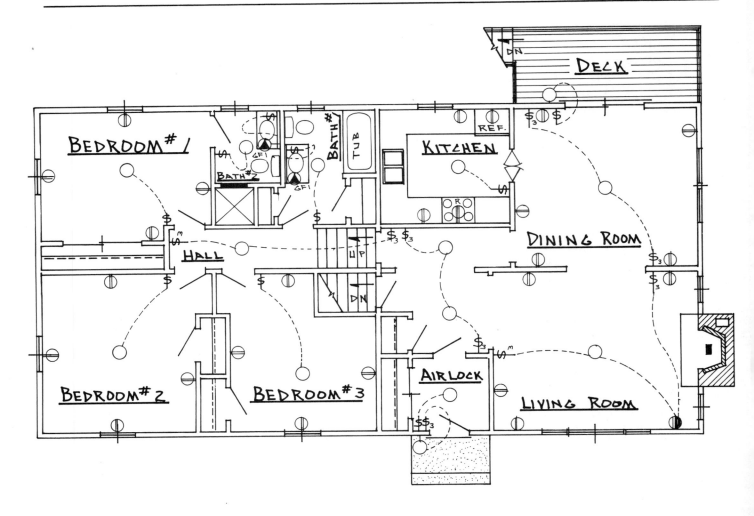

UPPER LEVEL ELECTRICAL LAYOUT

ELECTRICAL SYMBOLS	
SYM.	ITEM
$	SINGLE-POLE SWITCH
$₃	THREE-WAY SWITCH
⊖	DUPLEX OUTLET
⊖	SPLIT-WIRED OUTLET
⊖R	RANGE OUTLET
◑GFI	GROUND FAULT INTERRUPTER
◑W	WASHER OUTLET
◑D	DRYER OUTLET
◯	LIGHTING OUTLET
▭	FLUORESCENT LIGHTING

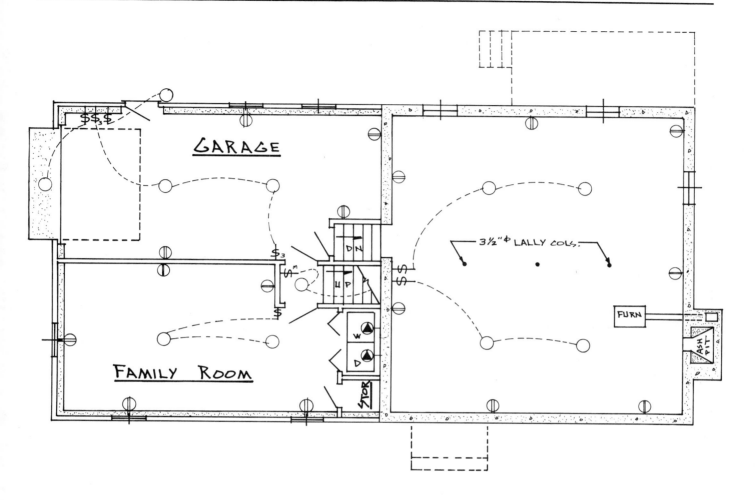

GARAGE

3½"ϕ LALLY COLS.

FURN

ASH PIT

FAMILY ROOM

LOWER LEVEL ELECTRICAL LAYOUT

<u>NOTE:</u>
ELECTRICAL SYMBOLS
LOCATED ON UPPER LEVEL
ELECTRICAL LAYOUT.

MATERIAL LIST

FLOOR SYSTEM
2 × 10 Joists----------------------6/10 - 88/8
2 × 10 Header------------------206 Lineal Feet
2 × 6 Sill--------------------------180 Lineal Feet
Sill Seal----------------------------180 Lineal Feet
Anchor Bolts----------------------23
1/2" × 4' × 8' Plywood-----42 Sheets
Bridging----------------------------76 Pairs
3 1/2" ⌀ Lally Columns--------3/8
3-2 × 10 Beam------------------3/14 - 3/12

WALL SYSTEM
2 × 4 Shoe----------------------206 Lineal Feet
2-2 × 4 Plate--------------------412 Lineal Feet
2 × 4 Studs----------------------275/8
Door Headers
  2 × 12--------------------------1/14 - 2/10 - 1/8
Window Headers
  2 × 12--------------------------2/10
  2 × 10--------------------------2/12 - 2/10 - 5/14 - 1/8
1/2" × 4' × 8' Sheathing--57 Sheets
3 1/2" Insulation----------------21 Rolls
Siding--------------------------------1792 Square Feet
Air Infiltration Housewrap---1797 Square Feet
Fireplace Header (2 × 10)--1/12

CEILING SYSTEM
2 × 6 Ceiling Joists-----------82/14
R-19 Insulation------------------28 Rolls

ROOFING SYSTEM
2 × 10 Ridge--------------------3/14 - 1/12
2 × 8 Rafters--------------------81/16

1 × 6 Collar Ties--------------------19/10
1/4" × 24" Soffit--------------------14/8
1" × 8" Fascia----------------------108 Lineal Feet
1/4" × 12" Rake Soffit----------12/8
1" × 8" Rake Fascia------------84 Lineal Feet
#15 Roofing Felt----------------------5 Rolls
1/2" × 4' × 8' Plywood----------54 Sheets
Asphalt Shingles----------------------54 Bundles
Metal Drip Edge--------------------108 Lineal Feet

INTERIOR
2 × 4 Studs---------------------------239/8
Door Headers (2 × 10)----------1/6 - 8/12 - 3/14
1/2" × 4' × 8' Sheetrock------169 Sheets
1" × 12" Shelving-----------------5/8 - 1/6 - 1/10
Closet Pole--------------------------1/10 - 1/8 - 2/6
Baseboard----------------------------358 Lineal Feet
Ceiling Moulding-------------------527 Lineal Feet
Stair Stringers-----------------------(2 × 12) 2/10
Stair Risers-------------------------7
Stair Treads-------------------------6
Fire Resistant Sheetrock--------7 Sheets

BASEMENT STAIRS
Stringers (2 × 12)------------------2/6
Risers------------------------------------7
Treads----------------------------------6

DECKS
Flooring------------------------------87 Square Feet
4 × 4 Posts--------------------------3/6
2 × 4 Railings----------------------48 Lineal Feet
2 × 6 Cap----------------------------24 Lineal Feet

Section VII

Duplex

PETAH

DESIGNED & DRAWN BY E. BRYANT

The Petah is a two-story duplex consisting of 1,888 square feet. Each unit is composed of a living room, dining room, and kitchen in addition to a half bath on the lower level. The upper level has two bedrooms and a full bath.

Separating both units is a 6-inch, 2-hour fire-rated wall, which has fire-resistant Sheetrock and sound-proofing board on both sides. This wall extends from the basement floor to the rafters.

Fire-resistant roofing materials are extended 4 feet beyond the 6-inch center wall.

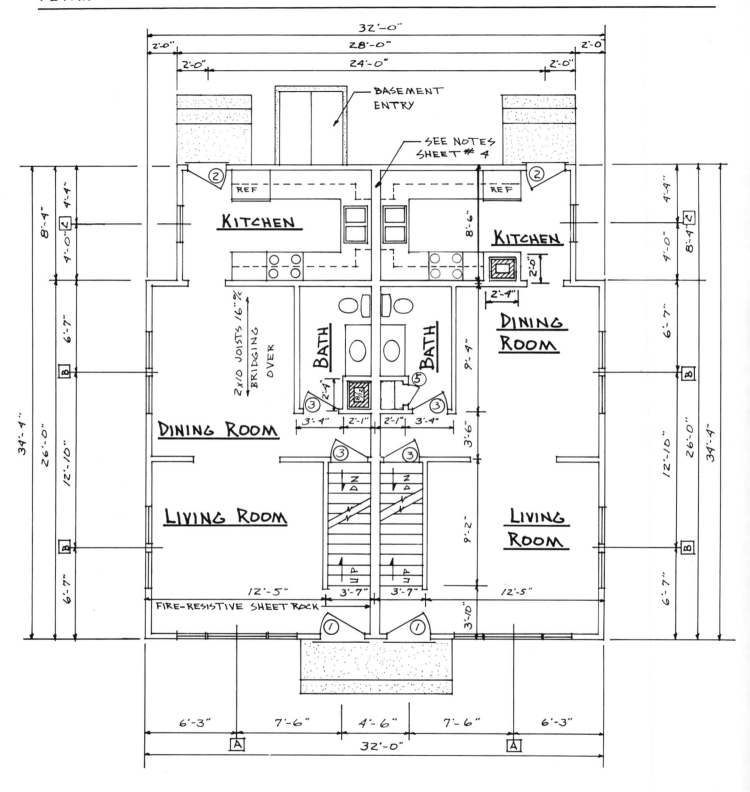

First Floor Plan

NOTES:
STRUCTURAL CHANGES SHOULD
NOT BE MADE WITHOUT
CONSULTING ARCHITECT/
CONTRACTOR.

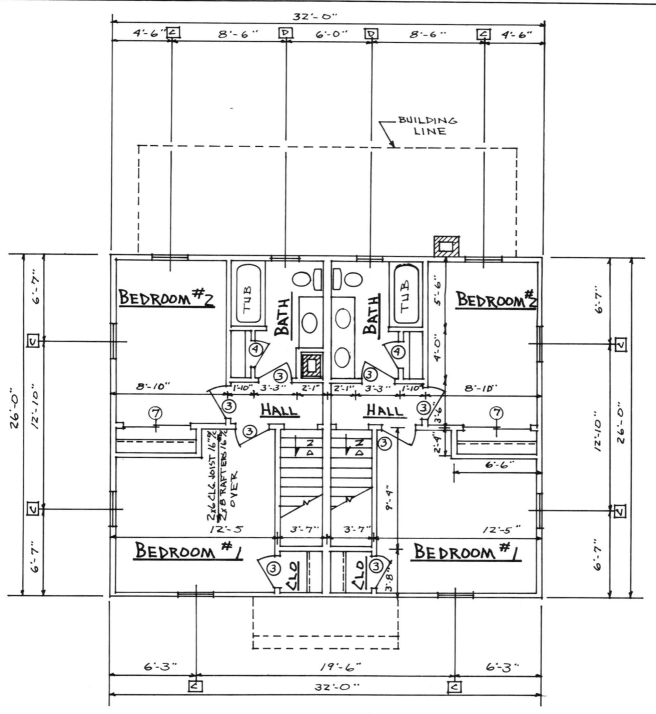

SECOND FLOOR PLAN

DOOR	SCHEDULE		
SYM	QTY	SIZE	TYPE
1	2	$3^0 \times 6^8$	PANEL-S.C.
2	2	$2^8 \times 6^8$	PANEL-S.C.
3	12	$2^6 \times 6^8$	FLUSH-H.C.
4	2	$2^0 \times 6^8$	FLUSH-H.C.
5	1	$1^6 \times 6^8$	FLUSH-H.C.
6	2	$2^6 \times 6^8$	FIRE CODE
7	2	$5^0 \times 6^8$	SLDG. H.C.

WINDOW	SCHEDULE		
SYM	QTY	SIZE	TYPE
A	2	$2^4 4^9 2^0 \times 4^2$	D.H.P.W.
B	4	$5^4 \times 3^{10}$	D.H. MULL
C	10	$2^8 \times 3^{10}$	D.H.
D	2	$2^0 \times 3^2$	D.H.
E	6	$2^8 \times 1^4$	BSMT.

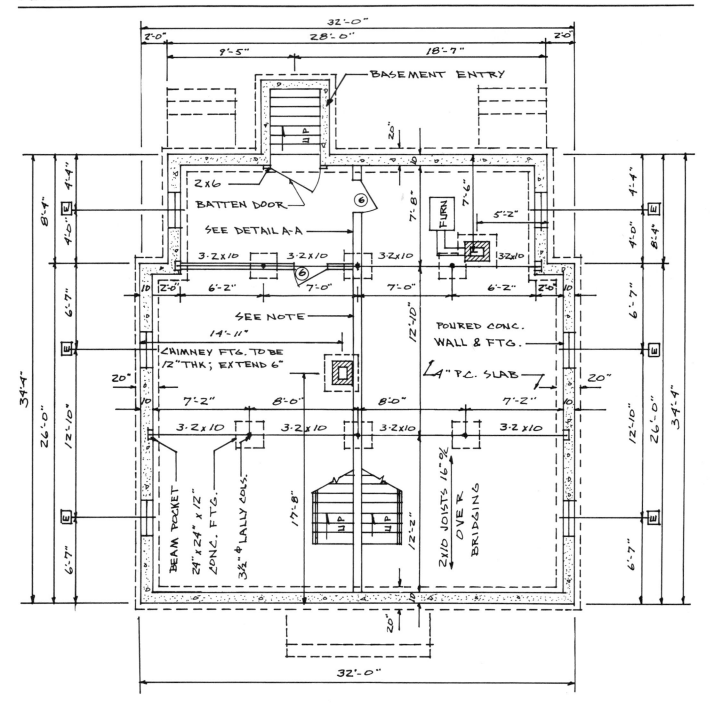

Foundation Plan

NOTES:

1) WOOD FRAMING TO BE KEPT 2" CLEAR OF CHIMNEY MASONRY.

2) BASEMENT ENTRY FOUNDATION TO CONFORM TO MANUFACTURER SPECIFICATIONS.

3) 6" CENTER WALL TO CONSIST OF 2x4 STAGGERED STUDS, WITH SOUND DEADENING BOARD AND FIRE-RESISTANT SHEETROCK ON BOTH SIDES. IT IS TO BE EXTENDED TO THE RAFTERS. SEE DETAIL A-A.

4) FIRE-RESISTANT ROOFING MATERIALS TO BE USED FOR 4'-0" BEYOND 6" CENTER WALL.

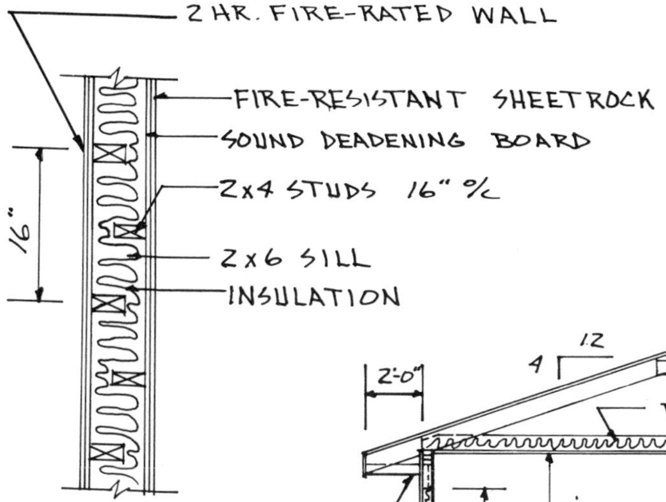

2 HR. FIRE-RATED WALL
FIRE-RESISTANT SHEETROCK
SOUND DEADENING BOARD
2x4 STUDS 16" o/c
2x6 SILL
INSULATION
16"

DETAIL A-A

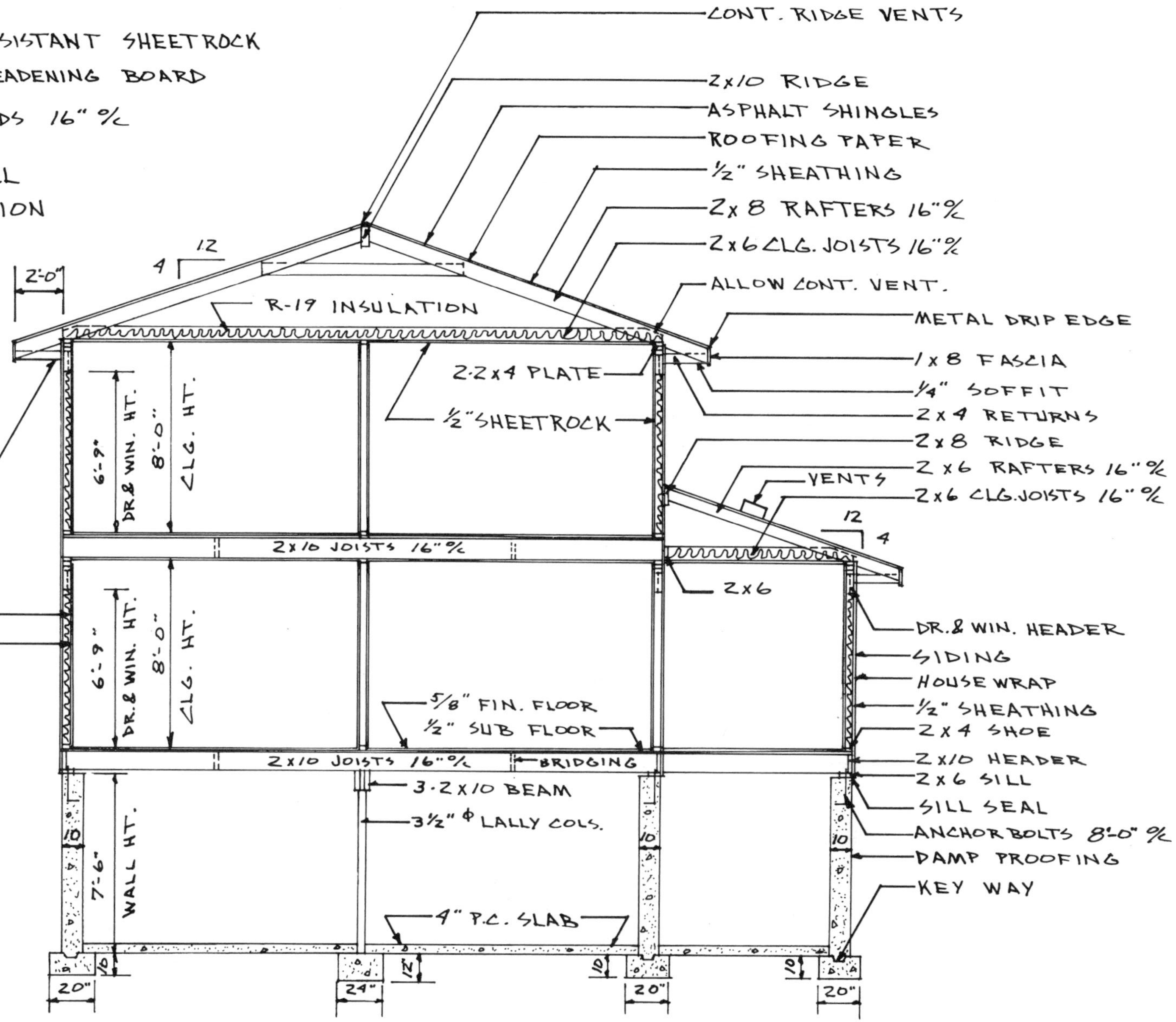

CONT. RIDGE VENTS
2x10 RIDGE
ASPHALT SHINGLES
ROOFING PAPER
½" SHEATHING
2x8 RAFTERS 16" o/c
2x6 CLG. JOISTS 16" o/c
ALLOW CONT. VENT.
METAL DRIP EDGE
1x8 FASCIA
¼" SOFFIT
2x4 RETURNS
2x8 RIDGE
2x6 RAFTERS 16" o/c
VENTS
2x6 CLG. JOISTS 16" o/c
2x6
DR. & WIN. HEADER
SIDING
HOUSE WRAP
½" SHEATHING
2x4 SHOE
2x10 HEADER
2x6 SILL
SILL SEAL
ANCHOR BOLTS 8'-0" o/c
DAMP PROOFING
KEY WAY
12
4
2'-0"
R-19 INSULATION
2·2x4 PLATE
½" SHEETROCK
CONT. SOFFIT VENTS
6'-9"
DR. & WIN. HT.
8'-0"
CLG. HT.
2x10 JOISTS 16" o/c
R-11 INSULATION
2x4 STUDS 16" o/c
5/8" FIN. FLOOR
½" SUB FLOOR
BRIDGING
3·2x10 BEAM
3½" ϕ LALLY COLS.
7'-6"
WALL HT.
10
4" P.C. SLAB
20"
24"
12

CROSS SECTION

NOTES:

1) WOOD FRAMING MEMBERS TO HAVE A FIBER STRESS OF 1200 PSI.

2) CHECK LOCAL BUILDING CODES REGARDING FLOOR INSULATION.

PETAH

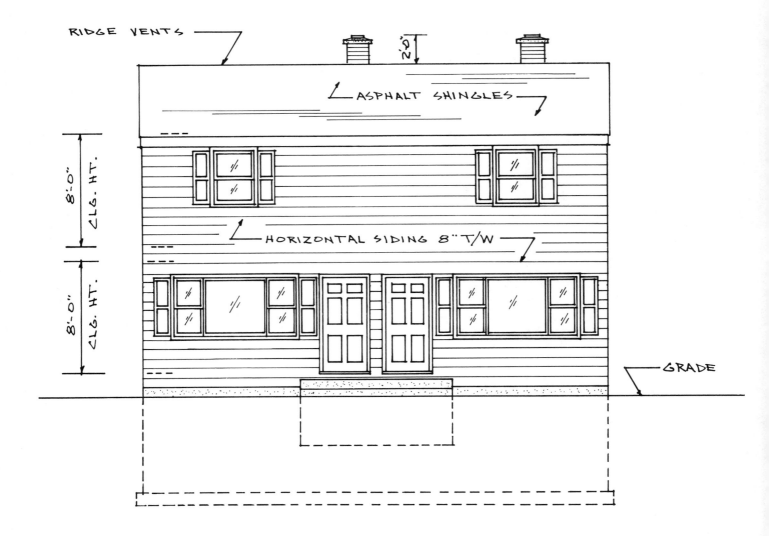

RIDGE VENTS

2'0"

ASPHALT SHINGLES

8'-0" CLG. HT.

HORIZONTAL SIDING 8" T/W

8'-0" CLG. HT.

GRADE

FRONT ELEVATION

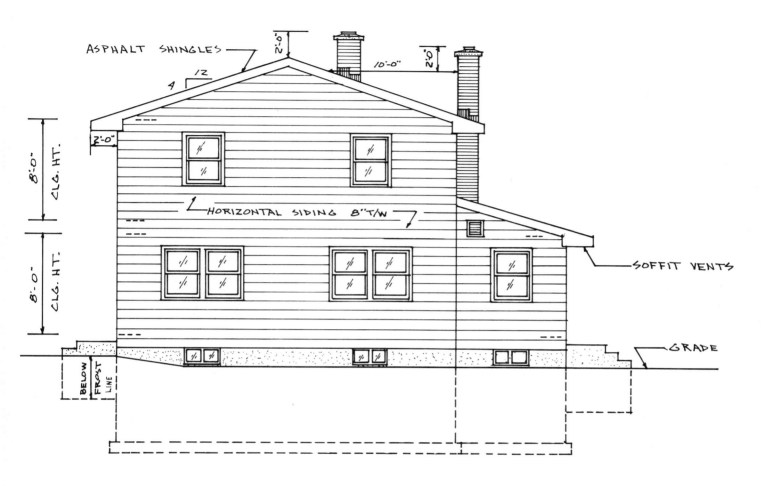

ASPHALT SHINGLES

2'-0"

10'-0"

2'-0"

12

4

8'-0" CLG. HT.

2'-0"

HORIZONTAL SIDING 8" T/W

SOFFIT VENTS

8'-0" CLG. HT.

GRADE

BELOW FROST LINE

RIGHT ELEVATION

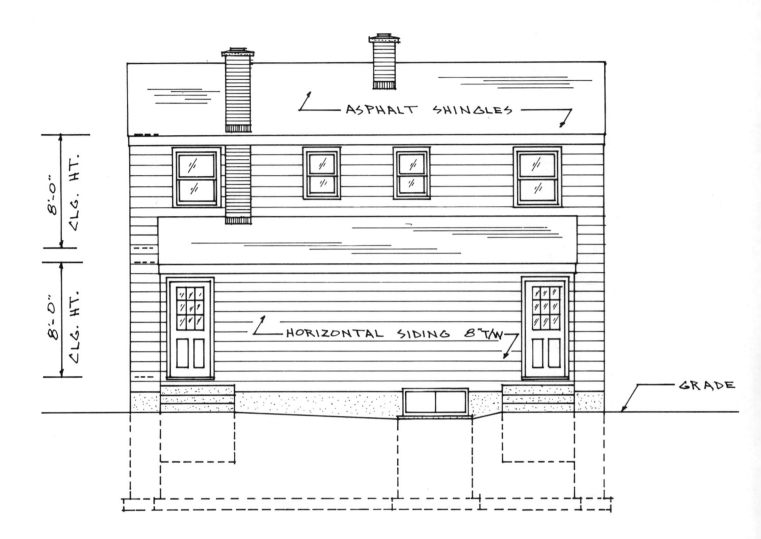

ASPHALT SHINGLES

8'-0" CLG. HT.

8'-0" CLG. HT.

HORIZONTAL SIDING 8" T/W

GRADE

REAR ELEVATION

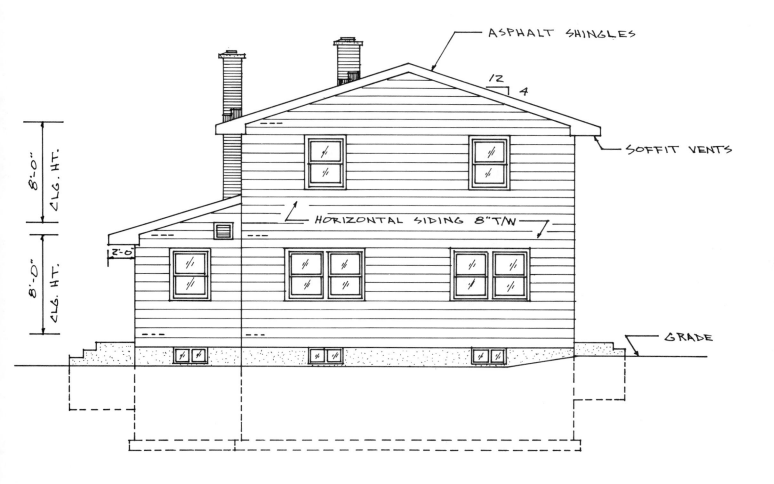

ASPHALT SHINGLES

12
4

SOFFIT VENTS

HORIZONTAL SIDING 8" T/W

8'-0" CLG. HT.

8'-0" CLG. HT.

2'-0"

GRADE

LEFT ELEVATION

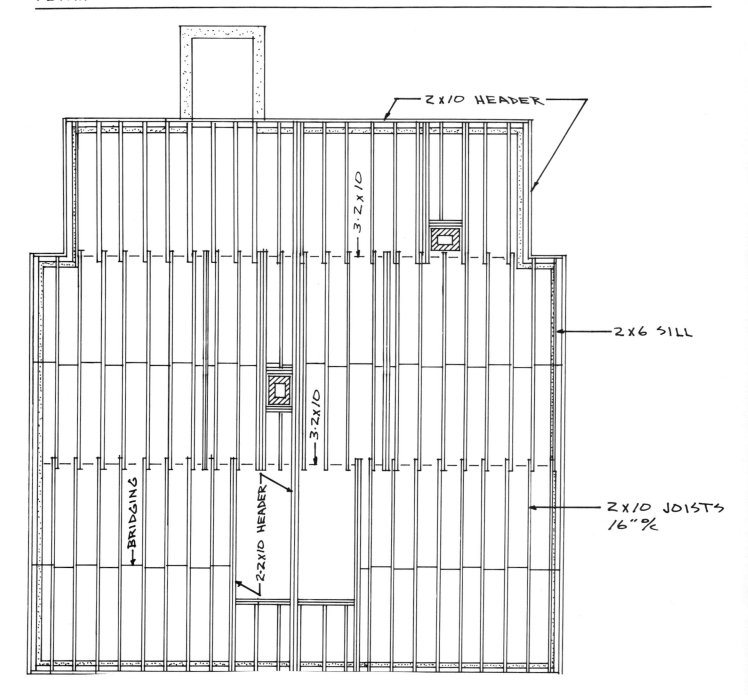

2x10 HEADER

3·2x10

2x6 SILL

2x10 JOISTS
16" ⁰⁄c

BRIDGING

3·2x10

2·2x10 HEADER

First Floor Framing Plan

NOTE:
DOUBLE JOISTS UNDER
PARALLEL PARTITIONS.

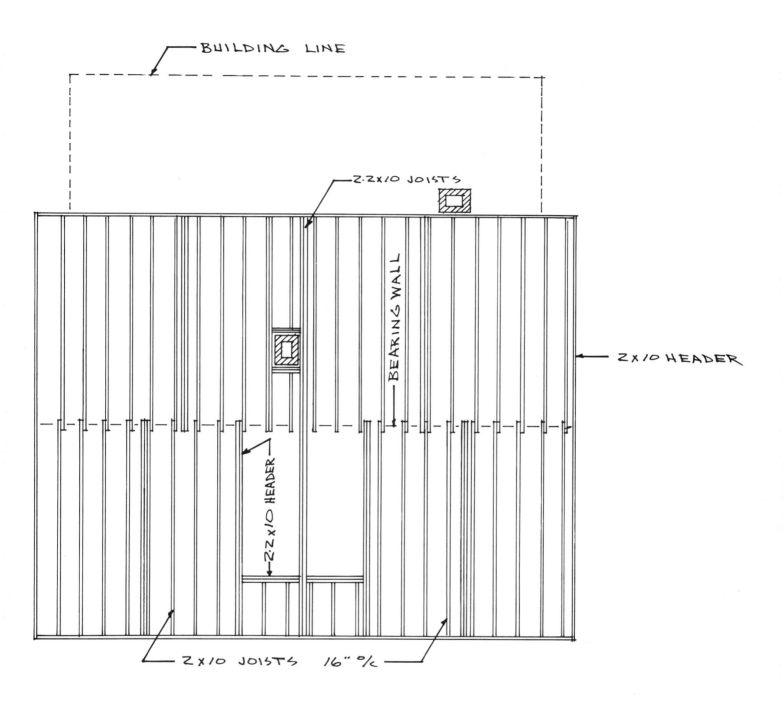

BUILDING LINE

2-2X10 JOISTS

2X10 HEADER

BEARING WALL

2-2X10 HEADER

2X10 JOISTS 16" O/C

SECOND FLOOR FRAMING PLAN

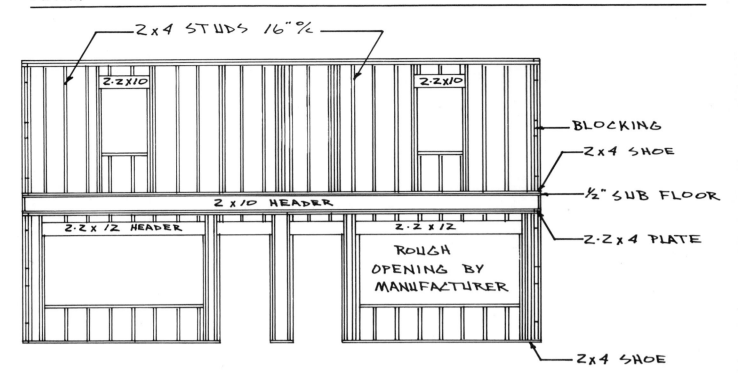

2x4 STUDS 16" %

2·2X10   2·2X10

BLOCKING

2x4 SHOE

2x10 HEADER

½" SUB FLOOR

2·2X12 HEADER   2·2X12

ROUGH OPENING BY MANUFACTURER

2·2X4 PLATE

2x4 SHOE

FRONT FRAMING PLAN

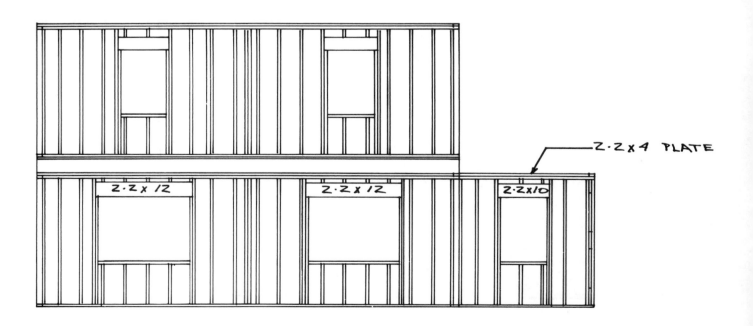

2·2X4 PLATE

2·2X12   2·2X12   2·2X10

RIGHT FRAMING PLAN

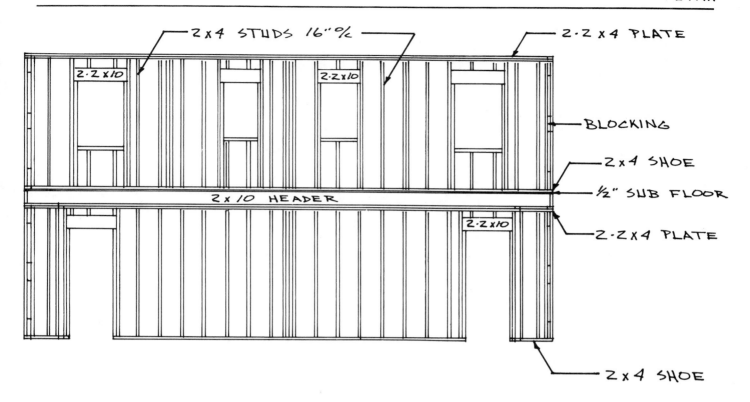

REAR FRAMING PLAN

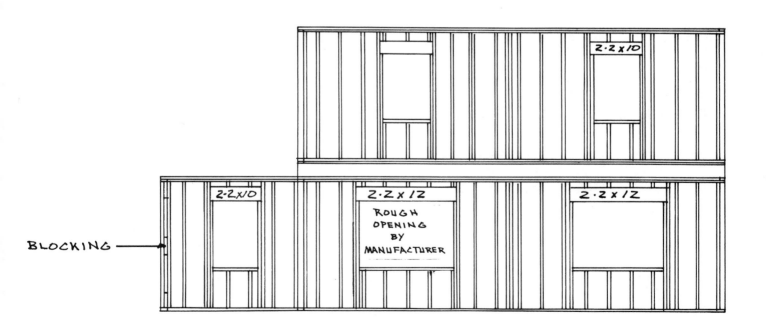

LEFT FRAMING PLAN

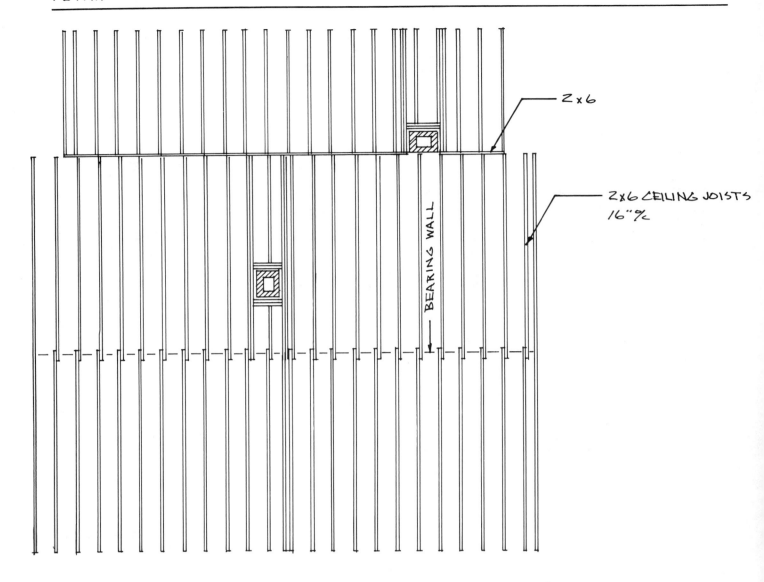

2x6

2x6 CEILING JOISTS
16" %

BEARING WALL

CEILING FRAMING PLAN

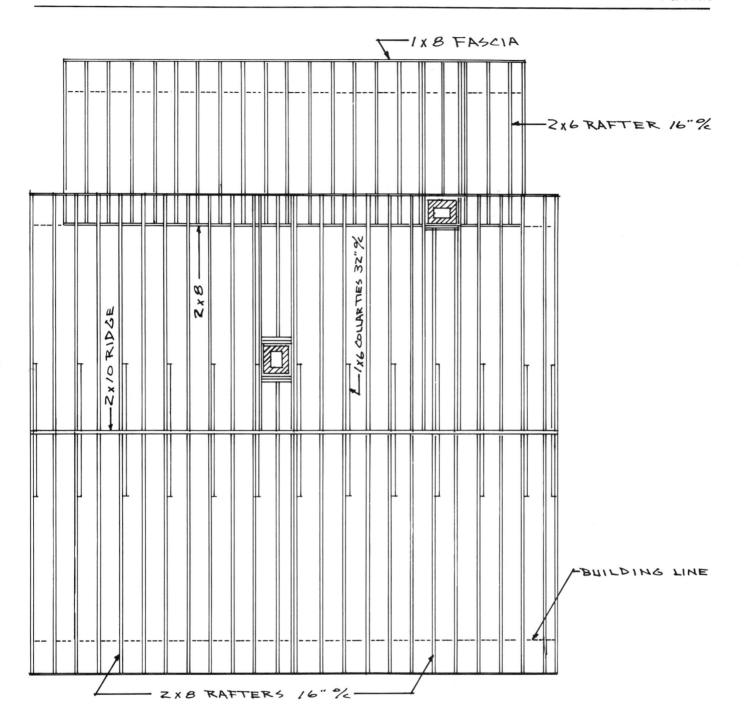

1 X 8 FASCIA

2x6 RAFTER 16" %

2x10 RIDGE

2x8

1x6 COLLAR TIES 32" %

BUILDING LINE

2x8 RAFTERS 16" %

ROOF FRAMING PLAN

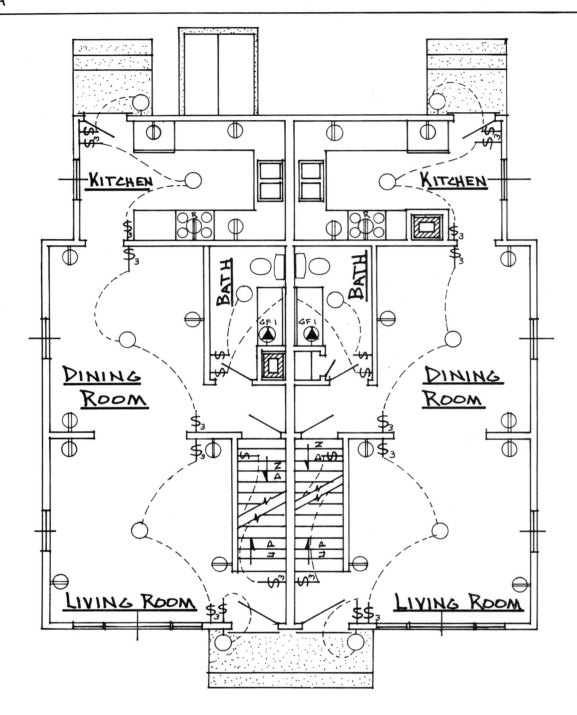

FIRST FLOOR
ELECTRICAL LAYOUT

ELECTRICAL SYMBOLS	
SYM	ITEM
$	SINGLE-POLE SWITCH
$₃	THREE-WAY SWITCH
⊖	DUPLEX OUTLET
⊖R	RANGE OUTLET
◯GFI	GROUND FAULT INTERRUPTER
◯	LIGHTING OUTLET
▭	FLUORESCENT LIGHTING

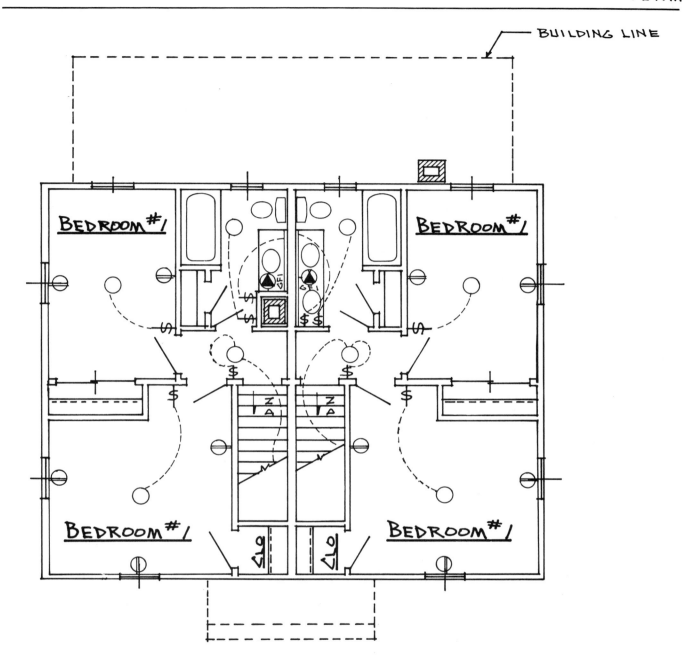

BUILDING LINE

BEDROOM #1

BEDROOM #1

BEDROOM #1

BEDROOM #1

SECOND FLOOR ELECTRICAL LAYOUT

NOTES:
ELECTRICAL SYMBOLS
FOUND ON FIRST FLOOR
ELECTRICAL LAYOUT.

MATERIAL LIST

FLOOR SYSTEM

2 × 10 Joists	26/10 - 113/14
2 × 10 Header	7/16 - 6/14 - 3/12
2 × 6 Sill	3/16 - 4/14 - 1/12
Sill Seal	133 Lineal Feet
Anchor Bolts	17
1/2" × 4' × 8' Plywood	57 Sheets
Bridging	43 Pairs
3 1/2" ⌀ Lally Columns	6/8
3-2 × 10 Beam	6/16 - 4/8 - 4/14 - 1/12

WALL SYSTEM

2 × 4 Shoe	3/16 - 4/14 - 1/12
2-2 × 4 Plate	6/16 - 8/14 - 2/12
2 × 4 Studs	269/8
1/2" × 4' × 8' Sheathing	59 Sheets
2 × 10 Door Headers	2/14
Window Headers	
2 × 12	4/12 - 4/10
2 × 10	5/14 - 1/10
3 1/2" Insulation	22 Rolls
Siding	1786 Square Feet
Air Infiltration Housewrap	1870 Square Feet

CENTER WALL

1/2" × 4' × 8' Fire-Resistant Sheetrock	47 Sheets
2 × 6 Plate	4/14 - 12/12 - 4/10
2 × 6 Shoe	2/14 - 6/12 - 2/10
2 × 4 Studs	181/8
Insulation	470 Square Feet
4' × 8' Sound Deadening Board	15 Sheets

ROOF SYSTEM

2 × 10 Ridge	2/16
2 × 8 Rafters	55/16
1 × 6 Collar Ties	13/10

1/4" × 24" Soffit	92 Lineal Feet
1 × 8 Fascia	92 Lineal Feet
1 × 8 Rake Fascia	86 Lineal Feet
#15 Roofing Felt	3 Rolls
1/2" × 4' × 8' Plywood	42 Sheets
Asphalt Shingles	41 Bundles
2 × 6 Rafters	24/12
2 × 8 Ridge/Ledger	2/14

FIRE-RESISTANT ROOFING MATERIALS

1/2" × 4' × 8' Plywood	8 Sheets
Shingles	256 Square Feet
Roofing Paper	256 Square Feet

CEILING SYSTEM

2 × 6 Ceiling Joists	56/14 - 26/8
R-19 Insulation	22 Rolls

INTERIOR

2 × 4 Studs	293/8
Door Headers (2-2 × 8)	2/14 - 2/12 - 18/6 - 1/4
1/2" × 4' × 8' Sheetrock	86 Sheets
1" × 12" Shelving	3/6 - 10/4 - 5/2
Closet Pole	2/6 - 2/3
Baseboard	396 Lineal Feet
Ceiling Moulding	450 Lineal Feet
2 × 12 Stair Stringers	2/14
Stairs Risers	3/12 - 1/4
Stairs Treads	3/12

BASEMENT STAIRS

2 × 12 Stringers	4/14
2 × 10 Treads	6/12
Handrail	2/12

Section VIII
Standard Details

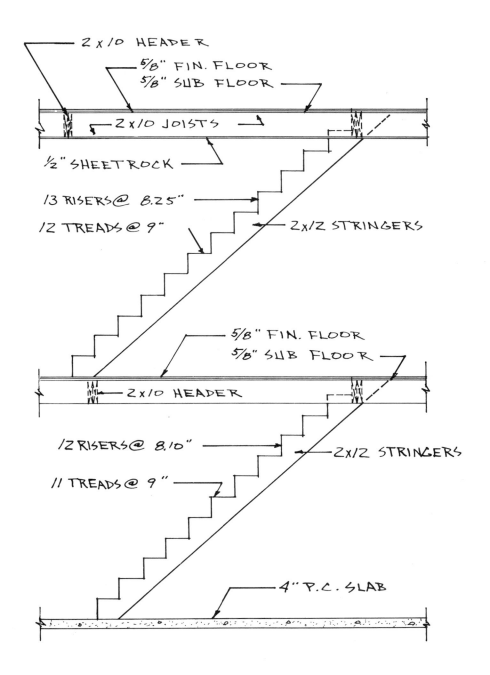

2 x 10 HEADER

5/8" FIN. FLOOR
5/8" SUB FLOOR

2 x 10 JOISTS

1/2" SHEETROCK

13 RISERS @ 8.25"

12 TREADS @ 9"

2 x 12 STRINGERS

5/8" FIN. FLOOR
5/8" SUB FLOOR

2 x 10 HEADER

12 RISERS @ 8.10"

11 TREADS @ 9"

2 x 12 STRINGERS

4" P.C. SLAB

STAIR DETAIL

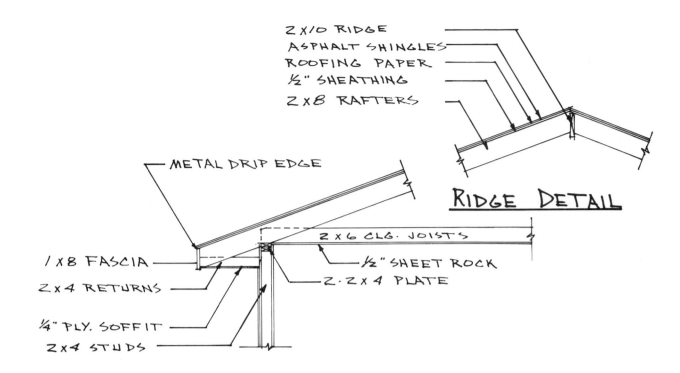

2X10 RIDGE
ASPHALT SHINGLES
ROOFING PAPER
½" SHEATHING
2X8 RAFTERS

RIDGE DETAIL

METAL DRIP EDGE

2X6 CLG. JOISTS
½" SHEET ROCK
2·2X4 PLATE

1X8 FASCIA
2X4 RETURNS
¼" PLY. SOFFIT
2X4 STUDS

SOFFIT DETAIL

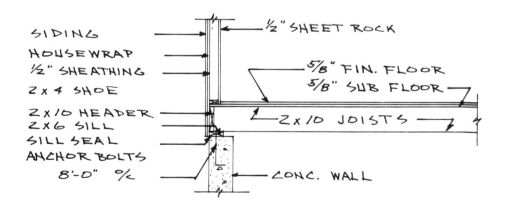

SIDING
HOUSEWRAP
½" SHEATHING
2X4 SHOE
2X10 HEADER
2X6 SILL
SILL SEAL
ANCHOR BOLTS
8'-0" ⁰∕c

½" SHEET ROCK

⅝" FIN. FLOOR
⅝" SUB FLOOR
2X10 JOISTS

CONC. WALL

FLOOR DETAIL

Other Bestsellers From TAB

☐ **THE COMPLETE BOOK OF BATHROOMS**—Ramsey and Self

Simple redecorating tricks . . . remodeling advice . . . plumbing techniques . . . it's all here. Find literally hundreds of photographs, drawings, and floorplans to help you decide exactly what kind of remodeling project you'd like to undertake; plus, step-by-step directions for accomplishing your remodeling goals. It's all designed to save you time and money on your bathroom renovations! 368 pp., 474 illus. 7″ × 10″.

Paper $15.95   **Hard $24.95**
Book No. 2708

☐ **ALL ABOUT LAMPS CONSTRUCTION, REPAIR AND RESTORATION**—Coggins

You'll find step-by-step directions for making a wall lamp or a hanging lamp from wood, novelty lamps from PVC plumbing pipe, and designer lamps from acrylic or polyester resins. Shade projects range from needlepoint and fabric models to globes, balls, and tubular forms. There are suggestions for advanced projects, using salvaged and low-cost materials, and more! 192 pp., 196 illus. 7″ × 10″.

Paper $16.95   **Hard $24.95**
Book No. 2658

☐ **101 PROJECTS, PLANS AND IDEAS FOR THE HIGH-TECH HOUSEHOLD**

If you're looking for decorative effects, you'll be impressed with the number of projects that have been included. And electronics hobbyists will be amazed at the array of projects—all of them with clear building instructions, schematics, and construction drawings. You'll also find exciting ways to use your microcomputer as a key decorative element in your high-tech atmosphere. 352 pp., 176 illus. 7″ × 10″.

Paper $16.95   **Hard $24.95**
Book No. 2642

☐ **TILE FLOORS—INSTALLING, MAINTAINING AND REPAIRING**—Ramsey

Now you can easily install resilient or traditional hard tiles on both walls and floors. Find out how to buy quality resilient floor products at reasonable cost . . . and discover the types and sizes of hard tiles available. Get step-by-step instructions for laying out the floor, selecting needed tools and adhesives, cutting tile, applying adhesives, and more 192 pp., 200 illus. 4 pages in full color. 7″ × 10″.

Paper $12.95   **Book No. 1998**

☐ **BUILDING OUTDOOR PLAYTHINGS FOR KIDS, WITH PROJECT PLANS**

Imagine the delight of your youngsters—children or grandchildren—when you build them their own special backyard play area! Best of all, discover how you can make exciting, custom-designed play equipment at a fraction of the cost of ordinary, ready-made swing sets or sandbox units! It's all here in this step-by-step guide to planning and building safe, sturdy outdoor play equipment! 240 pp., 213 illus. 7″ × 10″.

Paper $12.95   **Hard $21.95**
Book No. 1971

☐ **HARDWOOD FLOORS—INSTALLING, MAINTAINING AND REPAIRING**—Ramsey

All the guidance you need to install, restore, maintain, or repair all types of hardwood flooring at costs far below those charged by professional builders and maintenance services. From details on how to select the type of wood floors best suited to your home, to time- and money-saving ways to keep your floors in tip-top condition . . . nothing has been left out. 160 pp., 230 illus. 4 pages in full color. 7″ × 10″.

Paper $10.95   **Hard $18.95**
Book No. 1928

☐ **THE GARDENING IDEA BOOK**

Whether you have space for a full-space garden or only a pocket size back yard, this exciting collection of articles from *Farmstead Magazine* shows how you can grow all kinds of delicious, healthful fruits and vegetables. Here's expert advice and guidance that's guaranteed to make your garden more productive, easier to take care of, and less expensive! 208 pp., illustrated.

Paper $10.95   **Hard $15.95**
Book No. 2684

☐ **PLANNING AND BUILDING FENCES AND GATES**

This colorfully illustrated guide gives you all the expert, step-by-step guidelines and instructions you need to plan and build durable, cost-effective fences and gates. You will be able to design and construct just about any kind of fence you can think of—barbed wire, woven wire, cable wire, mesh wire, board fences, electric fences, gates, and much more! 192 pp., 356 illus. 8 1/2″ × 11″. 2-Color Throughout.

Paper $14.95   **Hard $22.95**
Book No. 2643

☐ **UPHOLSTERY TECHNIQUES ILLUSTRATED**—Gheen

Here's an easy-to-follow, step-by-step guide to modern upholstery techniques that covers everything from stripping off old covers and padding to restoring and installing new foundations, stuffing, cushions, and covers. All the most up-to-date pro techniques are included along with lots of time- and money-saving "tricks-of-the-trade" not usually shared by professional upholsterers. 352 pp., 549 illus. 7″ × 10″.

Paper $16.95   **Hard $27.95**
Book No. 2602

☐ **CABINETS AND VANITIES— A BUILDER'S HANDBOOK**—Godley

Here in easy-to-follow, step-by-step detail is everything you need to know to design, build, and install your own customized kitchen cabinets and bathroom vanities and cabinets for a fraction of the price charged by professional cabinetmakers or kitchen remodelers . . . and for less than a third of what you'd spend for the most cheaply made ready-made cabinets and vanities! 142 pp., 126 illus. 7″ × 10″.

Paper $12.95   **Book No. 1982**

☐ **THE COMPUTER FURNITURE PLAN AND PROJECT BOOK**—Wiley

Now, even a novice can build good looking, functional, and low-cost computer furniture that's custom-designed for your own special needs—tables, stands, desks, modular or built-in units, even a posture supporting kneeling chair! Craftsman Jack Wiley provides all the step-by-step guidance, detailed project plans, show-how illustrations, and practical customizing advice. 288 pp., 385 illus. 7″ × 10″.

Paper $15.95   **Hard $23.95**
Book No. 1949

☐ **DO-IT-YOURSELF DESIGNER WINDOWS**—Boyle

If the cost of custom-made draperies puts you in a state of shock . . . if you don't know what to do with a problem window or what type of window decor would look right in your home . . . here's all the advice and information you've been searching for. It's a complete, hands-on guide to selecting, measuring, making, and installing just about any type of window treatment imaginable. 272 pp., 414 illus. 7″ × 10″.

Paper $14.95   **Hard $21.95**
Book No. 1922

Other Bestsellers From TAB